Romantic Pasts

Edinburgh Critical Studies in Romanticism
Series Editors: Ian Duncan and Penny Fielding

Available Titles
A Feminine Enlightenment: British Women Writers and the Philosophy of Progress, 1759–1820
JoEllen DeLucia

Reinventing Liberty: Nation, Commerce and the Historical Novel from Walpole to Scott
Fiona Price

The Politics of Romanticism: The Social Contract and Literature
Zoe Beenstock

Radical Romantics: Prophets, Pirates, and the Space Beyond Nation
Talissa J. Ford

Literature and Medicine in the Nineteenth-Century Periodical Press: Blackwood's Edinburgh Magazine, *1817–1858*
Megan Coyer

Discovering the Footsteps of Time: Geological Travel Writing in Scotland, 1700–1820
Tom Furniss

The Dissolution of Character in Late Romanticism
Jonas Cope

Commemorating Peterloo: Violence, Resilience, and Claim-making during the Romantic Era
Michael Demson and Regina Hewitt

Dialectics of Improvement: Scottish Romanticism, 1786–1831
Gerard Lee McKeever

Literary Manuscript Culture in Romantic Britain
Michelle Levy

Scottish Romanticism and Collective Memory in the British Atlantic
Kenneth McNeil

Romantic Periodicals in the Twenty-First Century: Eleven Case Studies from Blackwood's Edinburgh Magazine
Nicholas Mason and Tom Mole

Godwin and the Book: Imagining Media, 1783–1836
J. Louise McCray

Thomas De Quincey: Romanticism in Translation
Brecht de Groote

Romantic Environmental Sensibility: Nature, Class and Empire
Ve-Yin Tee

Romantic Pasts: History, Fiction and Feeling in Britain, 1790–1850
Porscha Fermanis

Forthcoming Titles
Romantic Networks in Europe: Transnational Encounters, 1786–1850
Carmen Casaliggi

Romanticism and Consciousness
Richard Sha and Joel Faflak

Death, Blackwood's Edinburgh Magazine *and Authoring Romantic Scotland*
Sarah Sharp

British Romanticism and Denmark
Cian Duffy

The Lady's Magazine (1770–1832) and the Making of Literary History
Jennie Batchelor

Mary Wollstonecraft: Cosmopolitan
Laura Kirkley

Seeking Justice: Literature, Law and Equity during the Age of Revolutions
Michael Demson and Regina Hewitt

Remediating the 1820s
Jon Mee and Matthew Sangster

Visit our website at: www.edinburghuniversitypress.com/series/ECSR

Romantic Pasts

History, Fiction and Feeling in Britain, 1790–1850

Porscha Fermanis

EDINBURGH
University Press

Edinburgh University Press is one of the leading university presses in the UK. We publish academic books and journals in our selected subject areas across the humanities and social sciences, combining cutting-edge scholarship with high editorial and production values to produce academic works of lasting importance. For more information visit our website: edinburghuniversitypress.com

© Porscha Fermanis 2022, 2024

Edinburgh University Press Ltd
The Tun – Holyrood Road
12(2f) Jackson's Entry
Edinburgh EH8 8PJ

First published in hardback by Edinburgh University Press 2022

Typeset in 10.5 on 13pt Sabon LT Pro
by Cheshire Typesetting Ltd, Cuddington, Cheshire

A CIP record for this book is available from the British Library

ISBN 978 1 4744 8188 5 (hardback)
ISBN 978 1 4744 81892 (paperback)
ISBN 978 1 4744 8190 8 (webready PDF)
ISBN 978 1 4744 8191 5 (epub)

The right of Porscha Fermanis to be identified as the author of this work has been asserted in accordance with the Copyright, Designs and Patents Act 1988, and the Copyright and Related Rights Regulations 2003
(SI No. 2498).

Contents

Acknowledgements	vii
Abbreviations	ix
Introduction: Romantic Histories of Feeling	1
1. Historical Sentiment and Experience: Burke and Wollstonecraft	30
2. Historical Subjects and Ethical Character: Godwin and Carlyle	58
3. Historical Ethnogenesis and National Feeling: Scott, Moore, and Southey	86
4. Historical Style and the Man of Letters: Macaulay and Carlyle	118
5. Historical Reviewing: Specialisation and Periodical Culture	147
Epilogue: A Romantic Return?	178
Notes	190
Bibliography	255
Index	295

Acknowledgements

This book has been a long time in the making and I would like to thank several people for their contribution to it, and to my professional life more generally. First, I must thank my fellow traveller and co-editor in the field of romantic historiography, John Regan, as well as the contributors to our jointly edited collection, *Rethinking British Romantic History, 1770–1845* (Oxford University Press, 2014): Christopher Bundock, Claire Connolly, Mary-Anne Constantine, Richard Cronin, Paul Hamilton, Greg Kucich, Michael O'Neill, Rosemary Mitchell, Daniel Sanjiv Roberts, and Fiona Robertson. Their work continues to inform and inspire. I would also like to thank the attendees of a conference on romantic-era historiography funded by the Irish Research Council at University College Dublin in 2010 for their ongoing reflections and publications on this topic: in particular, Carmen Casaliggi, Jim Chandler, Gillian Dow, Javed Majeed, and Fiona Price. As this conference suggests, the support of the Irish Research Council has facilitated this book at various stages leading up to its current incarnation and for that I am profoundly grateful.

My colleagues at University College Dublin have been ever supportive and encouraging, and it is a real pleasure to work among them. A special debt of friendship and gratitude belongs to John Brannigan, Maurice Bric, Lucy Cogan, Sarah Comyn, Nick Daly, Sharae Deckard, Fionnuala Dillane, Margaret Kelleher, Michelle O'Connell, Hussein Omar, and Nerys Williams, as well as to colleagues (past and present) on my European Research Council-funded 'SouthHem' project: Lara Atkin, Sarah Comyn, Sarah Galletly, Nathan Garvey, Megan Kuster, Susan Leavy, Sarah Sharp, and Karen Wade-Wilson. Lara Atkin and Sarah Comyn, in particular, provided ongoing advice at various stages of writing (and rewriting), while Claire Connolly offered much-needed reflections on the book's introduction. At Edinburgh University Press, thanks must go to my commissioning and other editors, Michelle

Houston, Susannah Butler, and Fiona Conn, for their patience and support; to the 'Edinburgh Critical Studies in Romanticism' series editors, Ian Duncan and Penny Fielding, for their careful oversight and helpful revisions; and to my anonymous peer reviewers for their insights. Finally, I would like to thank my husband, Robert Gerwarth, for his encouragement and advice; my sister, Chloe Fermanis, for proof-reading and editing; and my two boys, Oscar and Lucian, for their love (and distraction).

* * *

Parts of Chapter 2 have appeared in Porscha Fermanis, '"A poor crotchety picture of several things": Antiquarianism, Subjectivity, and the Novel in Thomas Carlyle's *Letters and Speeches of Oliver Cromwell*', in *Rethinking British Romantic History, 1770–1845*, ed. Porscha Fermanis and John Regan (Oxford: Oxford University Press, 2014), pp. 94–120; and Porscha Fermanis, 'William Godwin's *History of the Commonwealth* and the Psychology of Individual History', *Review of English Studies*, 61 (2010), 773–800. Part of Chapter 3 has appeared in 'British Creoles: Nationhood, Identity, and Romantic Geopolitics in Robert Southey's *History of Brazil*', *Review of English Studies*, 71 (2020), 307–27. Part of Chapter 5 was first published as '"Literary dealers in the *rococo* of history:" Book Reviews and Historical Specialisation, 1820–50', *Victorian Periodicals Review*, 55.2 (2022). Copyright © 2022 The Research Society for Victorian Periodicals.

Abbreviations

C	Thomas Carlyle, *Oliver Cromwell's Letters and Speeches*
CHE	T. B. Macaulay, *Critical and Historical Essays Contributed to the Edinburgh Review*
CL	Thomas Carlyle, *The Collected Letters of Thomas and Jane Welsh Carlyle*
CME	Thomas Carlyle, *Critical and Miscellaneous Essays*
ER	*Edinburgh Review*
FR	Thomas Carlyle, *The French Revolution: A History*
HB	Robert Southey, *History of Brazil*
HC	William Godwin, *History of the Commonwealth of England*
HE	T. B. Macaulay, *The History of England*
HI	Thomas Moore, *The History of Ireland*
HMV	Mary Wollstonecraft, *A Historical and Moral View of the French Revolution*
HR	William Godwin, 'Of History and Romance'
HS	Walter Scott, *The History of Scotland*
J	Thomas Moore, *The Journal of Thomas Moore*
L	Thomas Moore, *The Letters of Thomas Moore*
LR	Adam Smith, *Lectures on Rhetoric and Belles Lettres*
PJ	William Godwin, *An Enquiry Concerning Political Justice*
R	Edmund Burke, *Reflections on the Revolution in France*
S	T. B. Macaulay, *Selections from the Edinburgh Review*
T	David Hume, *A Treatise of Human Nature*
VM	Mary Wollstonecraft, *A Vindication of the Rights of Men*
VW	Mary Wollstonecraft, *A Vindication of the Rights of Woman*

'The writers of history, as well as the readers, are sufficiently interested in the characters and events, to have a lively sentiment of blame or praise; and, at the same time, have no particular interest or concern to pervert their judgment.'

David Hume, 'Of the Study of History' (1741)

'And so evolving civilizations were able to take part in that long-drawn-out drama, the gradual suppression of emotional activity through intellectual activity.'

Lucien Febvre, 'Sensibility and History' (1941)

'How we *feel* about the past is no less important than what we *know* about it – and probably even more so.'

Frank Ankersmit, *Sublime Historical Experience* (2005)

Introduction:
Romantic Histories of Feeling

In a wry reproach to the cloistered philosopher towards the end of his four-volume *History of the Commonwealth of England* (1824–8), William Godwin argues that feeling is a more central concern for the historian than it is for the abstract thinker or political theorist. The comparative ease with which the philosopher can 'invent imaginary schemes of policy, and ... shew how mankind, if they were without passions and without prejudices, might be best united in the form of a political community' is inimical to the aims and methods of the historian, who must instead acknowledge that 'men in all ages are the creatures of passions, perpetually prompting them to defy the rein, and break loose from the dictates of sobriety and speculation'. Such passions, Godwin concludes, not only render historical actors 'very unlike the pieces on a chess-board', but also demand that the historian go beyond any general laws of human nature to account for each individual's psychological and social distinctiveness, taking into 'his estimate the materials of which they are made' and dynamically 'adapting his proceedings to their internal modifications'.[1]

Part of his ongoing—indeed lifelong—revision of the rationalist principles outlined in *An Enquiry Concerning Political Justice* (1793), Godwin's somewhat belated insistence that feelings matter and that they ought to be recorded in written history raises some of the key questions addressed by this book.[2] How could history remediate abstract philosophic ideas and general laws, and subject them to concrete experiential and evidentiary proof? When and how did historians come to understand human behaviour, and its cognitive and sensory underpinnings, as central to capturing the truth of the historical past? How, if at all, did they account for the changing norms, practices, and representations of feeling they discovered in their various studies? How did they access or recover the agency and subjectivity of historical actors and interpret the expression of feelings in historical documents and artefacts? And how did they actualise or represent historical shifts in emotional life in rhetorical and textual forms, from the inner life of individuals to the emotional economies of crowds, collectives, and institutions?

Godwin's own, evolving answers to these questions owe much to David Hume's rejection of motivational rationalism in *A Treatise of Human Nature* (1739–40), where Hume argues that reason alone does not produce moral action, and that feelings, beliefs, thoughts, and desires all work together to influence human behaviour.[3] Ironically, Hume's behaviouralist recentring of the unbounded and defiant nature of the passions leads him largely to circumscribe their relevance for historical enquiry and its written forms, favouring probabilistic approaches to historical causation over the irregularity of the passions even as he allows for the sentimental inclinations of 'feminine readers' in his influential *History of England* (1754–61).[4] Godwin, on the other hand, refuses to separate out the passions from desired structures of social organisation in his study and representation of the English past. In attempting to integrate motivating passions in a way that Hume had abjured (at least in theory) as unbefitting to the dignity of history, Godwin recognises that a study of the actual, dynamic operation of feelings—even those irrational feelings that Hume considers distasteful to modern sensibilities, such as those of religious fanatics—is essential for understanding what makes the English republican moment different from other historical times and places.

Godwin had already anticipated the historicism of this approach in his then unpublished essay 'Of History and Romance' (wr. 1797), where he argues that Hume's study of 'society as a mass' wrongly dismisses the engagement of the passions as 'a symptom of effeminacy'.[5] Promoting the speculative romance as the best way of mediating between the competing demands of necessity and contingency, Godwin rethinks the novel genre as one capable of mitigating the abstraction and determinism of 'official' history in order to 'observe the empire of motives' and 'mark the operation of the human passions'. Yet Godwin also takes seriously the idea that feelings can be studied historically, drawing on eyewitness accounts and other primary documents in his *History of the Commonwealth* to uncover both the mental lives of individual historical actors and the collective psychological changes that 'take place in the minds of generations of men'. Despite his expressed desire to be 'feeling as well as thinking', Godwin is ambivalent about the use of sentimental modes and techniques in his *History*, seeing the historian as having a special responsibility to 'the majesty of truth, and the austerity of the school in which we have entered ourselves pupils'.[6] In seeking to replace the superficial histories of 'party annalists', who 'have merely skimmed the surface' of republican history, with depth models that hope to 'analyse its contents, to assign the motives of its actors, and to trace up effects to the causes from which they sprung', Godwin introduces the paradox at the heart of romantic-era history: his *History* both objectifies feeling *and* sees it as central to a revitalised form of historical endeavour.[7]

Preliminaries

Taking its cue from Godwin's passion-oriented rethinking of the triangular dialectic between history, philosophy, and romance, this book traces the complex relationship between feeling and the making of the modern historical method in late eighteenth- and early nineteenth-century Britain. While it concedes the 'generic uncertainty of history writing' in the period, it does not see the relationship between history and the novel as an entirely open, porous, or continuously cross-fertilising circle.[8] Instead, it makes the case that feeling or, perhaps more accurately, debates about the role and status of feeling played a central role in determining both the moving boundaries between history and fiction, and how historical methods developed as the nineteenth century progressed. In so doing, it argues for an emerging distinction in the period's written history between a sentimental historicism or 'feeling history' concerned with the representation of affective states—in the way, say, of Hume's sentimental renditions of the deaths of Charles I and Mary, Queen of Scots, or Edmund Burke's theatrical depiction of the violation of Marie Antoinette—and a psychological historicism or 'history *of* feeling' concerned with the analysis of mental states or what Godwin refers to as the 'empire of motives'.

In reviving an earlier, character-driven approach to history that had itself been influential in the development of the novel, the sort of historical writing I associate with the 'empire of motives' partly reflects history's assimilation of the empirical detail and psychologising depth models of the realist novel, enabling writers to use the novel as a heuristic model for their more identifiably historical writing.[9] However, it also involves an acknowledgement that the capacity of historical agents to feel, think, and act could be a viable *object* of historical study, which was itself part of a new historicist agenda that 'recognized that societies were regulated "by the feelings, the beliefs, the ideas, the habits of heart and mind of the men who compose them"'.[10] This kind of historicism is something distinct from 'feeling history' or the understanding of feeling as a sentimental mode, instead involving the reconfiguration of psychophysiological and behavioural processes as historical phenomena. As

Lucien Febvre observes in his pioneering essay on the history of emotions, 'La sensibilité et l'histoire' (1941), this sort of history, while intimately concerned with the role of feeling in human life, actively worked to distance and displace feeling as a rhetorical register: 'it was ... quickly realized that the best way to suppress an emotion was to portray its motives or object in precise terms'.[11]

One of the larger arguments this book makes is that the ambivalence towards the expression and representation of feeling that appears in Godwin's *History of the Commonwealth* and, I suggest, in the work of other early to mid-nineteenth-century historians—such as Mary Wollstonecraft, Thomas Moore, Robert Southey, Thomas Carlyle, and Thomas Babington Macaulay—forms part of a new understanding about the role of feeling in written history: namely, the idea that feelings are historically variable and reflect changes in social, psychic, and behavioural contexts. Hume had, of course, raised the possibility that human behaviour is influenced by environment long before the 1790s. However, unlike Godwin, he does not think of subjectivity as itself a situated or historical formation that requires an 'incessant recurrence' to the 'truths of experience'; nor does he always prioritise the irregularities of feeling over the predictability of general historical laws.[12]

The group of historians I consider in this book, on the other hand, take as their starting point Hume's own pioneering views of the complexity of the human psyche and the potential unknowability of irrational, concealed, and unconscious causes of behaviour, seeking to understand mental and emotional states as historically situated.[13] Their acknowledgement that the 'regularity' theory of philosophic history is, at best, little more than 'some more or less plausible scheme' leads them to promote a different kind of history: one that dilutes the emotional functionalism of prior accounts and privileges the scrutiny of individual agents and their dynamically unpredictable actions and intentions, or what Carlyle calls the 'inward condition of Life' and the 'daily habits that regulate and support our existence'.[14]

Although the psychologism of early nineteenth-century approaches to feeling retained what we might today consider a degree of essentialism, my central premise about the gradual historicisation of feeling in romantic-era written history rests on four related arguments.[15] First, that sentimental or feeling history was *not* an uncontested way of examining even those radical disassociations in the development of historical consciousness—such as the French Revolution and the English Civil Wars—that most captured the period's historical interest, and that we should not assume that readers in the period accepted sentimental history as standard or normative. Second, that the work of the writers considered in this book demonstrates how evolving feelings and belief systems gradually began to be recognised as an important index to cultural, social, and political change over historical time. Third, that this new objectifying attitude towards feeling is both a reflection of, and underpins, the heightened awareness of the importance of empirical verification and documentary source criticism that emerged in the early nineteenth century and became the cornerstone of history's self-understanding as a discipline in the twentieth century. And fourth, that it was the representation of feeling that, to a large extent, determined both the boundaries between history and the novel, and the kind of historical writing that was subsequently endorsed as the nineteenth century progressed, resulting in debates about the role and place of feeling in written history that are still resonating in historiographical discourse today.

The territory I chart in this book is not, therefore, the familiar one of the rise (and fall) of a sentimental historicism grounded in a constructionalist capacity to resurrect the past and cultivate the feeling reader.[16] Framed primarily in relation to French historians such as Edgar Quinet and Jules Michelet, Lionel Gossman's influential view of the movement from enlightenment to romantic history argues that the techniques of the romantic historian were designed not only 'to make the reader feel that there was no barrier between him and the object' but that 'what he beheld in his mind's eye was ... the object resurrected'.[17] While Gossman's pioneering account of romantic historiography as a process of 'decipherment' and 'reconstitution' has been substantially refined in the British context in various ways over the years—not least by Mark Salber Phillips's argument that the social and the sentimental are 'two complementary kinds of knowledge' and by studies of women writers that emphasise alternative strategies of sympathetic identification and intersubjective emotional exchange—a residual sense still exists that the historians of the romantic period primarily conveyed their truths 'through a narrative medium that was geared towards sentiment and affect'.[18]

Without denying that sentimental history and the so-called 'presence paradigm' made a decisive intervention in the period's historiography, I am interested in precisely those histories that do *not* always conform to the paradigms of reconstitution, resurrection, and decipherment that have come to stand for romantic history, looking instead at written histories where feelings are suppressed, elided, neutralised, restricted, modified, displaced, rationalised, or objectified. The resistance of many of the period's historians to the kind of 'inferential colouring' used by philosophic historians such as Hume and Robertson, and later intensified in an ideological sense by Burke, problematises their characterisation as sentimental historians, and raises questions about the sort of history they understood themselves to be writing. While historians such as Wollstonecraft, Godwin, and Carlyle continue to use first-person narration, affective immersion, imaginative colouring, and other sentimental techniques, they all persistently probe their own representational strategies, introducing a reflexive dimension to their use of sentiment as a tool to move (or manipulate) the reader emotionally. They also, to a greater or lesser extent, address the inadequacies of sentimental discourse in an ethical sense, seeking to offset or supplement affective techniques by considering historical actors as social beings shaped by the wider structures of their individual and collective circumstances.[19]

By 'history', I refer in this context to those 'real', 'general', or 'official' histories that are broadly chronological, narrative, and discursive in their approach to the past. As the 'authoritative norm' that defined the genre, classical narrative history was traditionally a survey of major events, public affairs, and exemplary actions by individuals in war or statecraft—what Phillips calls 'the story of the public actions of public men'.[20] By the end of the eighteenth century, narrative history had, however, already extended its remit beyond public events, people, and transactions to include histories of manners and opinion, as well as adapting to the diversity and popularity of genres such as biography, memoir, the novel, antiquarian tracts, and travel writing. It could therefore take many forms, from the discursive presentation of constitutional, political, and religious history, to psychological portraiture and dramatic rendering, to visual description and novelistic representation.[21] While I understand the period's narrative history as encompassing all of these forms, I primarily use the term to signal its distinction from para-historical genres (such as memoir, biography, and the novel), and from conjectural and philosophic histories, or the type of history that foregrounds systematic enquiry.

In placing my emphasis on the protocols, norms, and evidentiary claims of 'real' history rather than on the novel, memoir, or biography, I am aware that I am writing against the grain of many of the best and most recent studies of the period's historiographical development, which tend to privilege the formal and conceptual innovations of para- or quasi-historical genres over those of general or official history. I am aware, too, that by focusing on official history this book may appear to prioritise so-called 'masculine' forms of political and institutional history over more 'feminised' forms or genres of historical knowledge, such as memoir, family history, travel writing, children's history, illustrated history, and the novel. It is certainly true that women writers were more likely to engage in 'multidisciplinary and generically hybrid forms', and (albeit often ironically) to disclaim or downplay the authority of their own work as contributions to historical knowledge.[22] It is also true that the professionalisation of history involved first appropriating and then abjecting the kind of social and cultural history associated with women, a point that has been borne out in several excellent studies of nineteenth-century women historians since the turn of the millennium.[23]

While this book is alert to the ways in which gender produces texts and subjects, and to the 'masculinist assumptions' of 'orthodox historiography', its aim is to offer a different account to those studies of para- and quasi-historical genres that rarely give official history more than a minor role in the period's historiographical development. Such studies tend to characterise official history as belatedly or back-footedly reacting to the new and exciting sense of history's relation to lived experience that has primarily been attributed to the rise of the novel, particularly the *Bildungsroman* and the historical novel. Alternatively, the period's official history is seen as a hiatus or transitionary stop-gap bridging two more decisive periods of historical innovation: the philosophic history of the enlightenment and the 'scientific' and professional history of the later nineteenth century.[24] While romantic historiography has since been given a second life in the work of Frank Ankersmit, Roland Barthes, Hans Kellner, and other narrativist and poststructuralist philosophers of history, it is still generally seen as part of a rehabilitation of an alternative tradition to more mainstream positivist and empirical approaches to history—one that implicitly reaches its apotheosis in the poststructuralism of the late twentieth and early twenty-first centuries.[25]

As I attempt to unravel romantic history's double status as 'alternative' and 'transitional', I trace a different but complementary story of the relationship between romantic-era historical writing and the history of modern history: one that centres on the role that feeling played in establishing historiographical boundaries and norms, and in creating new documentary and evidentiary standards in written history at the very moment when a hermeneutic understanding of history modelled on philological studies emerged in Britain. This book is not, therefore, intended to be either a survey of the historical writing of the eighteenth and nineteenth centuries or a theoretical reflection on the nature of romantic historicism. Rather, it aims to assess the role and legacies of romantic-era history in the teleologies surrounding the history of modern history-writing. In one sense, it engages in what has been called 'boundary studies' or an examination of the demarcations between and within different fields of knowledge, including questions of differentiation and specialisation. However, it is also concerned with the historical specificity of feeling, or with how feeling came to be recognised as a historical phenomenon in its own right.[26]

Without suggesting that any of the writers I consider in this book necessarily prefigure current preoccupations with the history of emotions in the ways pioneered by Febvre and others, I am concerned with how early nineteenth-century historians sought to integrate the life of feelings within the conceptual mechanisms and frameworks that they used to explain the past.[27] When, I ask, does history make room for feelings as an object of study rather than as a sentimental technique, and what place do feelings occupy in the documentation and imagination of a verifiable past? How does the representation of feeling in written history assist in establishing the boundaries between history and other types of narratives and genres, particularly the novel? How, in turn, does the novel become a means for history to make claims about its own status and value? Conversely, how are our current ways of thinking about feeling invested in the understandings of our eighteenth- and nineteenth-century predecessors? And how should we reassess our own methods and ways of understanding the historical writing of the nineteenth century—and, indeed, the history of modern history itself—in light of these prior interests in the category of what we now call the 'emotions'? The answers to these questions are important, I suggest, both for understanding the ways in which early nineteenth-century writers conceptualised and represented the past, and for how history subsequently developed as a discipline and profession.

Emotions and Affects

Historians of emotion largely agree that during the eighteenth century emotions were increasingly arranged across a spectrum, beginning with 'raw "feels" or blind sensations' without a cognitive dimension, before extending to passions (which were sometimes considered to contain some kind of limited cognitive dimension because of their intentionality), and then to affections or sentiments, which operated higher up on the cognitive scale to include, as Samuel Johnson put it, 'thought; notion; opinion'.[28] While it is true that at some stage after the mid-nineteenth century, philosophers stopped using terms such as passions, affections, and even sentiments, and began to make 'explicit the tacit epiphenomenalism of the psychological–evolutionary theory of emotions' that had first been touched on by Scottish empiricist philosophers, feeling was not yet something necessarily distinct 'from action, movement, cognition, or rationality'. Rather, it could encompass explosive, primitive, and unreflective passions alongside the type of cognitive feelings that Mary Wollstonecraft refers to in her *Vindication of the Rights of Men* (1790) as the '*rational* affections'.[29]

The feelings of this book's title are not, therefore, just the strong feelings of the passions—a 'disturbance of the mind' or 'vehemence of passion'—or even the more modulated or acculturated feelings of sentimental discourse, but rather anything that animates or motivates the mind. Feelings in this sense, as Annette Baier reminds us, need not move us very much at all, 'only enough to yield evaluations to "affect judgment"'.[30] My use of the term 'feeling' is nonetheless meant to signal its difference from competing and overlapping terms such as ideology, worldview, habitus, episteme, and *mentalité*.[31] In this respect, I draw on Raymond Williams's idea of 'structures of feeling' in *Marxism and Literature* (1977), where he argues that 'feeling' is a word chosen 'to emphasize a distinction from the more formal concepts of "world-view" or "ideology"'.[32] For Williams, it is not simply that the historian or cultural critic must go beyond a systematic study of beliefs but also that he or she must reject 'the separation of the social from the personal', and be concerned with 'meanings and values as they are actively lived and felt'. Although he rejects the term 'experience', Williams's initial distinction between feelings, on the one hand, and ideologies, on the other, is partly subsumed within a wider concept of 'being', which encompasses 'specifically affective elements of consciousness and relationships' but equally does not exclude cognitive thought or belief; as he puts it, 'not feeling against thought, but thought as felt and feeling as thought'.[33]

Brief, abstract, and embryonic as it may appear, Williams's concept of 'structures of feeling' shapes the ideas in this book in ways that meliorate more diffuse ('history of sensibilities') and more cohesive ('emotional regimes') theories of emotion.[34] First, in its emphasis on the centrality of language to the expression of human experience, and on the mutual development of language, style, forms, codes, and conventions as elements of a dynamic socio-material process. Second, in its focus on moments of subject-formation where 'immediate feeling, and then subjectivity and personality are newly generalized and assembled'. Third, in its acknowledgement of the interrelation of affects and cognitive emotions or beliefs, and its insistence that internal thoughts and feelings are socially determined. And fourth, because it concerns itself with a configuration of those emergent social and historical forces in the present that are not yet fully formed, compartmentalised, or cognised as 'history'—what Williams calls 'social experiences in *solution*'. Williams's attempt to add feeling back into the deep structure of belief systems is elastic or pliable enough to allow us to think about feeling both as actor-centred (in the form of the experiencing subject) and as part of larger socio-historical structures (such as familial, institutional, or other arrangements), which are themselves in flux or in process rather than being fixed social forms—the very dynamic, fluid, and soluble relationships between self and society that, I go on to argue, a subset of romantic-era historians were most concerned to capture or represent in their studies of the past.[35]

In focusing on written texts and/or on the illocutionary force of the written statement as speech act, I take as my starting point the idea that feelings—whether cognitive or non-cognitive, irrational or evaluative, instinctive or acculturated—can be embedded in gestures and words. In the case of written histories, feelings are sometimes expressed directly by an author or imputed to his or her actors/characters, but more often, authors embed signs in narrative descriptions that prompt readers first to recognise, then interpret and internalise them. Although I am not directly concerned with the kinds of arguments made by reader-response theorists such as Hans-Georg Gadamer, I am more interested in the idea of historical writing as a communicative process between historian and reader than in seeing such writing as indicative of real emotions (although the feelings represented can, of course, be both performative and real). I follow William Reddy in understanding feelings as neither fully performative nor fully constative, but my interest in this book primarily lies in how feelings are represented or embedded in texts rather than in how, say, Wollstonecraft felt towards Burke or how British radical writers and their conservative anti-Jacobin opponents experienced the aftermath of the French Revolution.[36]

The approach I take might therefore be considered closer to affect studies than to what is normally considered the key aim of a history of emotions: how to access, recover, and interpret the emotional life of people in past times.[37] Just as I make no claim of a sharp divide between the biological and cultural expression of emotions, I do not see affect studies and the history of emotions as fundamentally distinct.[38] This, I acknowledge, might seem contrary to some important work in affect studies, which, as Seth T. Reno has pointed out, tends to see '*affect* [as] an innate biological response, or physiological intensity, while *emotion* involves awareness of affect through memories, or narratives of accumulative experiences'.[39] My point is not to dispute this distinction but rather to see the relationship between emotions and affects as relational and intersubjective rather than oppositional. If seminal works of affect studies by Lauren Berlant, Carolyn Dinshaw, Brian Massumi, and others focus on the political and ideological implications of embodied experience and action, it is also true that affective experience can be embodied (albeit at a secondary remove) in language and text.[40] As neuroscientific research has revealed, both affects and emotions are significantly determined by unconscious and preconscious factors that go beyond the mechanisms of language, but I nonetheless question the 'presumption that the site and logic of discursive investigation must inevitably be different to the site and logic of affective investigation'.[41]

While much of the new apparatus surrounding the study of emotions grounds its analysis in historical texts—in books, documents, letters, diaries, and the like—few historians deal primarily with the representation of feelings in a rhetorical sense: that is, as a language, discourse, or style that has its own history. Reddy's concept of 'emotives' (or 'linguistic self-descriptions' that regulate the interplay between the performance and description of emotion) and Carol and Peter Stearns' idea of 'emotionology' (or the construction of emotional rules, attitudes, or standards) are helpful in elucidating the interests of this study.[42] Yet emotionology is not really concerned with how feelings are represented but rather with how they are conceptualised. Moreover, as Barbara Rosenwein has pointed out, it 'assumes that what people *think* about feelings they will eventually feel'.[43] Rosenwein's suggestion that we need to look closely at the social and cultural contexts in which the expressions of emotion are used, as well as at the specific vocabularies deployed to express 'emotion-related utterances', weighing the significance of such terms in relation to other terms as part of a larger narrative whole, best captures the primary aim of this book, which might be described as an examination of the semantics of feeling in written history.[44] Despite her emphasis on the close relationship between rhetoric and feeling, this study nonetheless differs from Rosenwein's approach in its emphasis on the historicity of the representative languages, narratives, and forms in which emotions are embedded or encoded rather than focusing primarily on the historicity of emotions themselves. In short, this book is a study of historical method and style rather than of emotional norms.

Objects and Subjects

In history's long march towards a 'proper' appreciation of documentary sources, the eighteenth and early nineteenth centuries are sometimes said to represent an 'unfortunate detour' in the methods of historical practice (philosophic abstraction followed by sentimentalism) but not in the theory of historical consciousness (historicism).[45] Theorists of historicism have long argued that eighteenth-century historical writing saw an increasing dismissal of abstract philosophical generalisation and universal grand narratives in favour of material particularities, organic forms, and a new type of individualising historical consciousness.[46] The 'long era of sensibility', the 'age of sentiment', and the 'age of feeling' are all designations meant to convey the century's gradual shift towards more feeling modes of representation that were themselves encompassed by a wider movement towards historicism. The supposedly 'scientific' forms of historical writing associated with Leopold von Ranke, B. G. Niebuhr, and others in the early to mid-nineteenth century are therefore characterised as isolated examples of modern or empirical historicist writing in a field 'otherwise largely marked by retrograde "feeling" forms of historicism', which eventually acquired the negative status of 'false, retarding presences'.[47]

Alongside this distinction between empirical and idealist forms of historicism, a second narrative argues for the gradual severing in the nineteenth century of the once close or porous relationship between history and fiction as part of a mutual tradition of *belles lettres*. This split was largely occasioned by history's 'epistemological redefinition' along the lines of the natural sciences, whereby a literary, rhetorical, or belletristic understanding of history was replaced by a greater concern for the distinction between primary and secondary sources, and by a desire to recount, as Ranke put it in a reformulation of Thucydides' earlier dictum, 'what actually happened' (*wie es eigentlich gewesen*).[48]

Essentially, as Karen O'Brien has argued, this process involved an unravelling of the alignment that had taken place between history and the novel earlier in the century, when the novel underwent a 'double transformation, at first distancing itself from historical kinds of narrative, and then approximating itself to the empirical norms and authoritative voice of history writing'.[49] This second narrative culminates with a rift in the mid to late nineteenth century between literary and scientific history, and has made for a compelling coming-of-age 'rhetoric of modernization and improvement'.[50] The consequence has been to entrench a sense of the deep division between subjective interpretation and objective empirical evidence, while also 'reinscribing in modern accounts the antagonism between Romantic inwardness and Enlightenment abstraction that is such an important part of the nineteenth-century reaction against the previous age'.[51]

The progressivism of these sorts of teleological explanations of the rise of the modern historical method has been disputed since the early 1980s in at least three significant ways: first, proponents of the 'linguistic turn' in historical studies have shown us that narrative, rhetoric, and literariness never really disappeared from historical writing and continued to haunt the discipline, even in its most positivist manifestations.[52] Second, the methodological innovations associated with archival study did not appear ready-made with Ranke in the mid-nineteenth century but rather developed slowly over the course of three centuries, as the 'genealogical axis' of medieval history and the rhetorical foundations of *ars historica* gave way to critical source reflection.[53] And third, the generic boundaries between history and literature were well established from as early as the sixteenth century, when there was a 'sharpened sensitivity' among audiences to the differences between history and fiction, and a new understanding of the fact as something divorced from ornamental or figurative language and, as William Blake noted critically, as something capable of verification by a credible source: 'he who rejects a fact because it is improbable must reject all History, and retain doubts only'.[54]

Historicism, too, has come under considerable scrutiny from feminist and poststructuralist critics over the last thirty years, both as an instrument of modernity, and as a lingering form of 'secularized theology' that harbours deterministic, presentist, and universalist claims to truth beneath its contextualist methodologies and ostensibly antifoundationalist positions.[55] A compelling critique of historicism has also been made by anticolonial and postcolonial critics such as Dipesh Chakrabarty, who defines the kind of developmental historicism that emerged in the nineteenth century as 'the idea that to understand anything it has to be seen both as a unity and in its historical development'. This stagist conceptual framework 'posit[s] historical time as a measure of the cultural distance ... that was assumed to exist between the West and the non-West', thereby legitimating universalist, comparativist, and 'internalist histories of Europe' that deny coevalness to non-European cultures and identify certain elements in the present as anachronistic.[56]

If these critiques of historicism have themselves faced ferocious criticism, they nevertheless point to the tendency to see historicism primarily as a historical methodology (contextualism, comparativism, developmentalism, and so on) rather than as a philosophical or metaphysical intervention into the way in which the individual is understood to exist in historical time and space.[57] In Friedrich Meinecke's classic explanation of the rise of historicism in Germany, the individualising viewpoint associated with historicism did not mean 'that the historical method excludes altogether any attempt to find general laws in human life' but rather that it has 'to make use of this approach and blend it with a feeling for the individual'.[58] Meinecke's admiration of Ranke (who he crucially saw as an idealist rather than as an empiricist) and his antipathy towards Hegelian monism finds its fullest expression in a *Historische Zeitschrift* essay of 1928, where he argues that 'behind all searching after causality stands, conditionally or unconditionally, the searching after values, after that which men call *Kultur* in the highest sense, i.e., breakthroughs, manifestations of the spiritual in the midst of the network of causality'.[59]

Given that Meinecke's spiritualism or vitalism is, as Jerry Szacki argues, primarily a lament on abstractionism, universalism, and any number of theories that are oriented towards the discovery of general laws, we can see historicism both as an intervention into the way human life is studied and represented, and as a corrective to the ethical deficits of philosophic abstraction and systemisation. Historicism, in other words, is 'as much an emotional category as an intellectual one', playing 'a role very similar to that of "heart" in the world of Jean-Jacques Rousseau, or of "life" in the philosophy of, say, Bergson'.[60] Jacques Bos has accordingly argued that the real innovations of eighteenth-century historicism lie not in the first part of Meinecke's famous formulation (historical method) but rather in the realm of historical ontology or the historicity of being: in particular, in the way in which the individual was understood to be an independent historical object. Capitalising on the insights of Reinhart Koselleck and others about the ways in which various entities came to have a historical force during the accelerated temporality of the *Sattelzeit* (1750–1850), Bos maintains that by the end of the eighteenth century the past was no longer seen as a source of examples for the present but was instead intimately connected with present and future stages of historical development. In this way, historical time gradually became populated with 'objects of an inherently historical nature that could be turned into objects of historical research'.[61]

The shift in historical sensibilities that occurred over the course of the eighteenth century cannot, then, just be explained by history's inclination towards a taste for sentimentalism (lively descriptions, historical evocation, proximity, affective presence, and so on), but must also take into account new attitudes to historical time itself: in particular, the shift from what has been called a 'didactic–ethical space' to a 'historical–analytic space', in which history is understood both as a series of distinct epochs and as a process of constant transformation and development.[62] The historicist suspicion towards universal, general, and natural laws evident in Godwin's *History of the Commonwealth* did not simply result in the replacement of philosophic history by sentimental history (indeed, the two had long coexisted in the work of Hume, Robertson, and others), but also meant that history was itself reconceptualised as the study of individuals and collectives as historical objects. This was an interest that history shared with a rival genre—the novel—but was also able to demarcate from fiction because of a 'dual notion of individuality', which made it possible for historians to think about the past both as 'a process shaped by intentional actions of individual people' and as 'a coherent whole structure [shaped] by the development of higher-order individualities'.[63]

Thinking about history in the early nineteenth century was also profoundly reconfigured by a new interest in the historicity of subjectivity itself. Michel Foucault's reference in 'What is Enlightenment?' (1984) to 'the historical ontology of ourselves' posits that this new area of study is essentially the history of how we 'constitute ourselves as moral agents', an idea of the subject that had already shaped the work of Scottish enlightenment thinkers but that, as Christopher Bundock notes, ironically arises most forcefully at the moment 'when society's narrative of itself becomes explicitly problematic' and when 'time loses its internal continuity' following the 'felt disorientations' of the French Revolution.[64] As Foucault argued in his 1975–6 lectures *Society Must Be Defended*, the modern idea of the subject as one situated within a historical and social location is something different to the eternal and transcendent subject of earlier philosophical discourse, and even to the empiricist idea that the subject comes into being as it takes in and transforms sensations from the outside world, pointing instead to the socio-historical embeddedness of subjectivity itself.[65]

The empiricist dissolution of the idea of a fixed human nature to one that is mutable or changes over time was accompanied by a gradual but profound shift from a causal to an actor-centred history, developed over the course of the eighteenth and nineteenth centuries in the biographical and historical writing of Wollstonecraft, Godwin, Southey, Carlyle, and others. This new acceptance of the (often unpredictable) agency of historical actors allowed for a more disaggregated view of the changing conditions of human action and of the institutional and situational environments in which these actions took place. It lent itself, in other words, to an emphasis in written history on psychological motives, decision-making processes, and subject-formation, as well as to an examination of the larger dialectic relationships between self and society, change and continuity, and agency and determinism. Individual subjectivity was therefore increasingly seen as a product not just of internal psychological processes and reactions that seemingly resisted the claims of social determinism, but also of the historical actor's continually changing relationships with other actors, and with the institutional structures that circumscribe or channel thoughts, feelings, and actions. To put it another way, subjectivity in written history was rethought as what Eric Hobsbawm has called 'political subjectivity' or the ways in which the subject negotiates 'the set of identifications which constitute the social being'.[66]

History and Novel

The working through of the relationship between self and society is, of course, the very thing that was central to the novel's claims to rival history as a means of exploring the 'deep subjectivity' of 'an endlessly developing self' within the wider social context of the self's relationship with institutional structures.[67] In *How Novels Think* (2005), Nancy Armstrong argues that the history of the novel and the history of the modern subject 'are, quite literally, one and the same'. The British novel 'provides the test case' for the formulation of a kind of subject 'that had not yet existed in writing' and was 'capable of reproducing itself ... across British culture in law, medicine, moral and political philosophy, biography, history, and other forms of writing that took the individual as their most basic unit'.[68]

There is little doubt that the *Bildungsroman* was a major experimental instrument for exploring and managing the relationship between self and society, participating in a 'struggle to individuate whenever there was a collective body, to attach psychological motives to what had been the openly political behaviour of contending groups, and to evaluate these according to a set of moral norms that exalted the domestic woman'. The novel's turn inwards to the psychologised subject endowed with an autonomous sphere of interiority was therefore a gendered, raced, and classed phenomenon, one that elevated white, male, bourgeois-individualistic categories of thought alongside the narration of 'the sex-gender systems that affective regimes underwrite'.[69] This subject-centred view of reality, with its reification of individual psychology, came to dominate both romantic modes of representation and those of classical realism, coinciding with the rise of forms of aesthetic practice that (like history itself) relied heavily on empirical density, typifying procedures, and ontological consistency.[70]

The realist novel represented a distinctive or 'special case' for philosophical empiricists, one that, as Roger Maioli has noted, was a cause of concern precisely because of its superior power to elicit belief and conform to empiricist convictions via the reproduction of 'the minutiae of real life'.[71] History had long been distinguished from poetry, tragedy, and other forms of fiction on the basis of the Aristotelian distinction between probability and possibility, but from Francis Bacon onwards history was additionally accorded a special ontological status as an empirical marker of the referential real.[72] By approximating the 'history effect', the realist novel was able to produce the experiential equivalent of historical reality (and belief) to a far greater extent than poetry, epic, romance, or tragedy. It is certainly no coincidence that a marked rise in 'anti-fiction' statements by Hume and other empiricists—and later by Jeremy Bentham, Carlyle, and Macaulay—coincided with the establishment of a 'durable novelistic practice' and a new acceptance of the nature of fictionality from the mid-eighteenth century onwards. It was at this point that, as Catherine Gallagher has noted, the word 'fiction' gains greater currency and loses its earlier meaning of deceit, dissimulation, or pretence, and when the pedagogic claims of the novel come to rest on the acceptance of fiction as a 'protected affective enclosure' and on the 'nonparticular referential status' of its characters.[73]

A second response to the ascent of the novel's cultural power involved the reconceptualisaton of fictional prose narratives as meaningful contributions to historical, philosophical, and other forms of knowledge. If Walter Scott sought to avoid the 'authenticity trap' by drawing attention to the fictional status of his novels, the point of his antiquarian attention to detail was not simply to mimic historical representation but rather to 'embody the *trope* of history' and demonstrate the capacity of the fictional text 'to do the work of history'.[74] Unlike the fiction hypothesis, these claims did not rely on a willing suspension of disbelief or on affective enclosure, but rather on two related positions: first, on a strong scepticism towards formal history and its assumed ability to represent truth in ways that were more credible than romance; and second, on claims for the epistemological seriousness of fiction as a form of evidentiary knowledge. Such claims rested on a more capacious understanding of 'truth conceived as mimetic simulation' (or *vraisemblance*)—an idea that Michael McKeon has argued cemented the status of the novel as a genre, created the category of fiction, and involved the 'novelisation' of surrounding genres, including history.[75]

Both of these positions emerged, in part, from a growing recognition that fiction's turn to philosophical realism was what Maioli has called a 'two-edged sword', enlisting in its own support an empirical, referential epistemology that was ultimately 'unreceptive to the methods of literary representation'.[76] As Frederick Burwick has pointed out, many of the period's defences of poetry were accordingly located outside of the empiricist epistemologies of Locke, Condillac, Leibniz, and Hume while also differing from older idealist accounts by rescuing aesthetic experience from the 'lower faculties of the senses and feelings'.[77] In a different vein, Hume's justification of history and philosophy as truth-directed (and value-awarding) rather than pleasure-directed (and value-deflecting) in his *Treatise* was to become the target of defences of poetry's 'higher utility' by Wordsworth, Shelley, and others, who sought to rehabilitate pleasure as the first-order source of moral improvement, without which we can have 'no general principles drawn from the contemplation of particular facts'.[78]

Hume's infamous characterisation of fictional logic as madness, deception, and 'lying' was revived by Bentham, Carlyle, and Macaulay in the 1820s and 1830s as part of an attempt to demarcate the epistemological and ontological boundaries between truth and fiction, perceived as under threat both from romantic reconstructions of the active power of the imagination and from the newly plausible fictions of the period. Reasserting, in the face of the novel's challenge, a normative hierarchy of genres in which the truth-directed function of 'true' history is superior to the pleasure-directed function of lesser genres such as poetry, epic, and the novel, Macaulay and Carlyle attempt to reoccupy the ground infiltrated by Goethe, Scott, and other novelists: 'is not ... true History', as Carlyle pithily put it in a letter to J. S. Mill in 1833, 'the only possible Epic?'[79] Accompanying this negative understanding of fiction as a form of deceit were statements of historical specialisation and self-definition, particularly the idea that historical writing is subject to various forms of ontological constraint because of its special referential relationship to an extrinsic reality. Historians had long been constrained by the requirement to invent only in accepted or customary ways—'controlled invention', as Ann Rigney has called it—but they increasingly characterised themselves as unfree in their choice of methods as well as of arguments, noting their conformity to an extrinsic superstructure of which historical documentation and other kinds of evidentiary traces were the nearest guide or approximation.[80]

Older, idealist understandings of the differences between fiction and history therefore had to confront and adapt to the combined impact of some important developments by the beginning of the nineteenth century: the sensory apparatus of empiricist psychology with its emphasis on questions of belief formation, and in particular on the different types and *qualities* of belief (and emotional experience) produced by true stories and fiction respectively; the novel's assumption of philosophical realism and its perceived threat to the privileged ontological status of history as a marker of the referential real; the increasingly documentary bent of historical theory and practice, which reified 'immediately observable, preferably archival, evidence' as capable of embodying both 'the real' and 'the truth of social situations'; and the larger representational issues surrounding what Tilottama Rajan has called 'the role of poetry versus prose as epistemic practices in an emergent modernity', which was itself part of a wider division of intellectual labour dating back to

Hobbes's idea of 'language abuses' and Locke's denotative theory of language.[81]

Armstrong's suggestion that the novel is the genre most closely aligned with the history of the modern subject is therefore one with which nineteenth-century thinkers would have both agreed and disagreed. As Godwin put it at his most provocative in 'Of History and Romance', 'true history' consists not of 'facts or dates' but rather of 'a delineation of consistent, human character, in a display of the manner in which such a character acts under successive circumstances'. Yet his 'critical-dialectical apparatus' wavers between seeing history, as opposed to the novel, as the genre best able to address the post-empiricist anxieties associated with the rise of historicism, especially the anxiety of ever being able to represent a fully embodied subject or self. Indeed, the essay is suggestive of Godwin's sense of the ways in which history—as much as the novel—could provide a discursive space in which to reconstruct the public and private identities of historical actors, as well as to test the more speculative claims of abstract philosophy and constructionalist fiction.[82] As he somewhat reluctantly concedes towards the end of the essay, history is the only area of study able to provide an image of human nature constructed on a concrete reality or naturalist ontology: 'He [the historian] does not understand the character he exhibits, but the events are taken out of his hands and determined by the system of the universe, and therefore, as far as his information extends, must be true.'[83]

Although Godwin stops short of arguing for fiction's superiority over history, and manages to both 'project and forestall' a radical, oppositional genre of 'republican romance', Jon Klancher rightly sees 'Of History and Romance' as 'the first of those romantic critical programs that promoted literary genre-reform as the means to induce greater social and ideological reform in history' itself.[84] Linked to the genre-reforming agendas of literary histories by Wordsworth, Coleridge, Hazlitt, Shelley, and others, Godwin offers a critique of enlightenment universal history that—like the similar but more gender-oriented deconstruction of enlightened masculinity in Joanna Baillie's 'Introductory Discourse' to *Plays on the Passions* (1798)—does not attempt to fuse the developments of philosophic history and the novel, but rather explores their 'potential for antagonism'. This is an exploration that, as Rajan has shown us, Godwin also undertakes in his novels, memoirs, and biographies, particularly in his representation of one of the most traumatic periods in English history: the seventeenth-century English Revolution and Civil Wars.[85] If, in novels like *Mandeville* (1817), Godwin's approach becomes something more like psychopathology, the 'psychoanalytic case history' that defines the Godwinian novel is also central to much of the historical writing produced in the early nineteenth century.[86] This kind of history focuses on the internal dynamics of the individual character, or 'case', as the best means of approximating a larger historical whole, shifting its emphasis from a sentimental historicism to a psychological and behaviouralist one.

Inside and Outside

In so far as the histories considered in this book attempt to understand the feelings, beliefs, and motivations behind individual and collective human behaviour, they are what I have called 'psychological' rather than sentimental in their approach to the past. Making this distinction is, perhaps, to risk a false dichotomy. The pre-history of psychology is, after all, deeply bound up with the histories of physiology, sensibility, sympathy, and sentimentalism, and their legacies play out in the histories of psychiatry, psychoanalysis, and neurology—all disciplines concerned with cognitive norms and abnorms.[87] Yet despite their shared origins within the discourses of moral philosophy, the distinction between sensibility/sentiment and psychology is one worth making in the context of this book's concern with the (admittedly intertwined) histories of 'feeling history' and the 'history of feeling'.

In 'La sensibilité et l'histoire', Febvre sees psychology as central to his new history of emotions. While he complains of the sort of psychological history that is 'based on old proverbs, faded literary recollections and acquired or inherited wisdom', he argues that the historian cannot understand the function of institutions, ideologies, or even ideas unless he takes up a 'psychological standpoint', which he defines as 'the concern to link up all the conditions of existence of the men of a given period with the meanings that the same men gave to their own ideas'. If Febvre's understanding of psychological history seems remarkably close to a definition of historicism itself, it is because he understands psychology not in a restricted or chauvinistic sense, but rather as a way of referring to a 'broader tradition of systematic thought about mental life'.[88]

Like Febvre, my interest is not in the pre-history of psychology or in the ways in which it emerged as a modern discipline, but rather with its epistemic cultures or how the modes of production relating to psychological knowledge emerge within written history. I am concerned, in other words, with the ways in which psycho-physiological processes are reinterpreted as historical and cultural phenomena by Wollstonecraft, Godwin, Carlyle, and other historians in the period, who attempt not just to marshal objectifying impulses so as to '*observe* the empire of motives' and '*mark* the operation of the human passions' (my emphasis), but also to represent the internal or psychic functioning of individuals and collective groups. While none of the writers I discuss ventures to psychoanalyse the dead or to produce a version of 'psychohistory' in a post-Freudian sense, many of their histories focus on the ability of individuals and collectives to act and make choices within the contexts of other factors that delimit or determine those choices. Even those histories that look at the private interactions of individual historical agents, such as Marie Antoinette or Cromwell, tend to ground their representations of individual subjectivity in wider structures of feeling and belief.

It has long been recognised that eighteenth-century empiricism provided the basic elements for the 'framework of psychologization' in which this new type of history took part: namely, 'the rejection of innate ideas, the critique of "systems" and of abstract and substantialist metaphysics, the appeal to observation and experience, and finally, the conviction that all knowledge begins in sensible impressions'.[89] For Isaiah Berlin, the major intellectual project of the enlightenment was precisely the transformation of philosophy into 'some kind of scientific psychology'. Berlin attributes the subsequent distrust towards the psychological in the historical field to late nineteenth-century positivism, arguing that:

> The invocation to historians to suppress even that minimal degree of moral or psychological evaluation which is necessarily involved in viewing human beings as creatures with purposes and motives (and not merely as causal factors in the procession of events), seems to me to rest upon a confusion of the aims and methods of the humane studies with those of natural science. It is one of the greatest and most destructive fallacies of the last hundred years.[90]

Jenny Davidson has rightly characterised the figurative or metaphorical empiricism of much eighteenth-century writing as 'a symptom of the period's persistent desire to represent . . . the facts of mental life as if they were physical realities'.[91] Yet while the symptom-language of empiricist physiology (tears, swooning, blushes, and so on) continued to play an important role in the historical writing of the period (particularly in the representation of crowds), this earlier interest in external manifestations of internal thoughts was increasingly replaced in nineteenth-century written history by a new emphasis on what the internal workings of the mind could reveal about external events and actions—an inverted emphasis on the relationship between physical sensations and internal mental processes that would later be explored more fully by those physiological psychologists who studied unconscious reflexes, such as Alexander Bain, William Carpenter, and James Sully, as well as by

Herbert Spencer's interest in behaviouralism and David Ferrier's contributions to the 'emergent discipline of neurology'.[92]

In their interest in motivation before the formal rise of scientific psychology, the historians of the late eighteenth and early nineteenth centuries were following Hume's distinction between the emotional force of ideas and impressions (or sensation and reflection) in his *Treatise*, extending his psychologising impulse from the realm of (moral/behavioural) theory to that of (historical) explanation. If Locke had prioritised the significance of the body by assigning to the senses an important role in his epistemology, Hume's idea of rational, reflective, or 'calm passions' in his *Treatise* suggests a different conceptualisation of emotion from the traditional empiricist one—a conceptualisation focused on the 'motivational rather than the affective character of emotions': 'the force of our mental actions' in the case of belief, 'no more than in any other, is not to be measur'd by the apparent agitation of the mind'. Hume thus distinguishes between the motivational quality of a passion and its phenomenal or physiological character: low-intensity feelings 'produce little emotion in the mind, and are more known by their effects than by the immediate feeling or sensation' but they are no less powerful in a motivational sense than violent ones.[93]

Daniel M. Gross has accordingly argued that Hume can 'help us do what Judith Butler urges in *The Psychic Life of Power* (1997): to think a theory of power together with a theory of the psyche'. Certainly, Hume's 'passional science' was instrumental in transforming the seventeenth-century idea of the passions as 'overtly rhetorical' into a more 'generalized psychology' that recognised that emotion is not just an externalised currency but also one potentially hardwired into the human brain via 'presentations'.[94] While Hume did not develop his 'psychological apparatus' to examine fully the kinds of non-deliberative feelings that occur outside the field of consciousness (that is, the subconscious and unconscious), the emergent idea that emotions need not always be conscious states is an important development of early to mid-nineteenth-century thinking about the human mind, and one which I argue in Chapter 2 influenced Carlyle's representations of historical character.[95]

To focus on the psychologisation of feeling in this way is to shift the emphasis away from sentimentalist explanations of historiographical innovation that centre on the importance of Smithian accounts of intersubjective or sympathetic identification in favour of accounts that foreground a different kind of behaviouralist agenda, one that encouraged an emerging interest among historians in inner experiences, motivations, and other mental processes, such as repressions, negations, and projections.[96] For Godwin and Carlyle, as much as for Hume, history is a 'science of character'. However, unlike Hume, they seek out the small details and particularities of man's nature—those very irrational, unconscious, and barely decipherable actions and motivations that Hume calls 'good for nothing' in his second *Enquiry* (1751), where his somewhat mechanistic understanding of sympathy limits the operation of sympathetic identification solely to those cases where it is possible to understand the reasons *why* agents act the way that they do.[97] For Hume, ulterior and/or irrational actions and feelings are unintelligible to even the most sympathetic of observers and are therefore unable to provide a guide to 'common experience', but it is precisely these unintelligible and sometimes even barely decipherable feelings that interest Godwin in 'Of History and Romance', where he argues for the importance of examining those 'subtle peculiarities' that lead to unintended modifications of the mind or character.[98]

Like Febvre's understanding of psychology over a century later, Godwin's approach to the historical past is not based on the associationalist psychology of Locke, Hume, Hartley, and later Sully, or indeed on the natural-scientific psychology of someone like William James, but rather on something closer to socio-psychology or what the German philosopher Wilhelm Dilthey would call 'descriptive psychology'. Whereas natural-scientific approaches to psychology sever the individual from society in favour of an emphasis on physiology, Dilthey grounds the individual psyche in the socio-historical contexts from which it originated. Arguing in his *Ideas Concerning a Descriptive and Analytic Psychology* (1894) that 'each self finds itself conditioned by an external world and reacting to it', he goes on to suggest that because this 'living unity' is 'conditioned by the milieu in which it lives and to which it in turn reacts', 'there emerges an articulated organization of its inner states', which he calls 'the structure of psychic life'.[99] Dilthey's sociological understanding of the psyche leads him to point to the lessons of history as a way of understanding the structures of human consciousness:

> We find in language, myth and religious ritual, customs, law and in the external organization of society, the products of the collective spirit in which, in Hegel's terms, human consciousness is objectivated and thus can withstand analysis. Man does not apprehend what he is by musing over himself, nor by doing psychological experiments, but rather by history.[100]

The idea that language, social structures, and customs are the external markers of the 'collective spirit', and that history is a prime location for the study of 'the genesis of the psychic nexus', is precisely the view of the historical past that I argue many romantic-era historians adopt and promote. In the chapters that follow I take up questions relating to this sociological rather than individualistic version of interiority in the work of Wollstonecraft, Godwin, Carlyle, Macaulay, and others, seeing psychological history as an attempt to mediate between the objective and subjective modes of understanding represented, on the one hand, by philosophic history, and on the other, by the novel.

Boundaries and Divisions

The final purpose of this book is to investigate what Klancher has called 'the political crisis of the Enlightenment category of literature' at the end of the eighteenth century, and hence more fully to understand the moving boundaries between history and fiction in the nineteenth century.[101] Historical studies of the relationship between history and fiction have tended to assume the porous boundaries between the two, noting the relatively late emergence of the professional historian in Britain and Ireland, and the ongoing popularity of narrative history well into the nineteenth and twentieth centuries.[102] Literary studies, on the other hand, have emphasised the competitive burden that the novel placed on history from the mid to late eighteenth century, either focusing on the self-definitions of the novel and other para-historical genres or exaggerating the extent to which general history became 'formally experimental or epistemologically radical'.[103]

The orthodoxy of these views has led some critics to suggest that the nineteenth century 'learned its history' largely from alternative sources, such as novels, poems, and paintings, rather than from official history. It is certainly true that, as O'Brien has argued, few historians before the advent of the historical novel registered the 'generic proximity of history to fiction as a threat to the epistemological validity of their work'. From the 1820s (following the publication and popularity of Scott's Waverley novels), the previously one-sided influence of history over fiction altered, calling into question any easy separation of fictional narrative and historical fact.[104] At the same time, the relationship between history and the novel was never static or one-sided; nor should the novel itself be considered a single, unchanging entity. As Emily Allen has pointed out, the novel's rise necessitated its redefinition as something culturally valuable by renegotiating its 'relationship to "pleasure" and "entertainment"', offering 'a reformed and reforming vision' of itself as a 'pedagogical force' before it turned its sights to history.[105] Yet the novelist's often highly ironic statements of factual accuracy should not be 'over-read' as a general indication of the 'epistemological adventurousness' of the period's literary culture; nor should the novel's mock defence of historical authenticity necessarily be characterised as a sign of 'productive cross-fertilisation'.[106]

In pointing to a critical over-emphasis on the threat or transgressiveness of the novel, I have no wish to deny that the novel's appropriation of history's voice and prestige produced a new language and culture of generic competitiveness from the mid-eighteenth century onwards, or that a whole family of literatures was reclassified to account for the 'cultural technology of the novel genre'.[107] Phillips has shown us the extent to which historians were under pressure to adapt and transform conventional classical narratives, and more generally to 'meet the [sentimental] demands of the period'.[108] Whether or not this resulted in a 'crisis' in historical representation, whereby 'Romantic models of literary production' produced 'an ethical and representational dilemma for historians', it certainly led to a more overt interest in genre reform and hence to debates concerning the epistemological and ontological boundaries between history and fiction. Far from conceding ground to novelists, however, historians such as Carlyle and Macaulay increasingly presented themselves as 'guardian[s]of the "real"' against those genres and fields 'perceived as indulging in "hypothesizing", "theorizing" and "speculating"'.[109]

Phillips suggests that the 'clues to the reframing of historiographical practice' in the period primarily 'lie in all the surrounding genres and disciplines': that is, in 'minor' genres rather than in the more prestigious centre.[110] Yet seeing official history as a totalising and conservative control, against which the innovations in more experimental genres can be mapped or measured, downplays the extent to which history saw itself as contributing to, as well as defending itself from, the kind of formal innovations and technologies we normally attribute to the novel. Despite the rhetoric surrounding the novel, history 'did not "collapse" into other modes of writing' but actively sought to maintain—and crucially to reinvent—its position within a hierarchy and range of historical genres that worked alongside or aslant it.[111] Focusing primarily on the rise of the novel and its affiliates also fails to take adequate account of the ongoing importance and prestige of history as a classical genre, which continued to conceptualise, brand, and market itself as something distinct from fiction, memoir, and biography.[112] As writers from Hume to Godwin found out the hard way, through negative reviews and poor sales, rivalling the novelist was not a straightforward matter and could not be accomplished simply by transferring novelistic techniques to the historical text. Like the much-maligned intermixture of fact and fiction, the place of feeling in a treatise, history, or political debate remained an uncertain one, leaving the author open to charges of vanity, egotism, and immodesty, and potentially resulting in a genre or category violation by veering into the grounds of memoir, autobiography, and other forms of ego documentation.[113] Such attacks in reviews, considered in detail in Chapter 5, are suggestive of the ways in which the historian attached a special value to the 'objective' protocols of history's narration, modifying the affective discourses of the novel in order to work within the disciplinary bounds of a genre that had always been suspicious towards sentiment, the inner life, and the expression of feeling.[114]

In questioning the claim that the relationship between history and fiction in the period is best described as porous, I have no issue with the idea that fiction played an important role in the development of historical writing and *vice versa*, or that the writing of history and fiction are interrelated activities.[115] Nor would I wish to deny the importance of considering 'the pre-disciplinary heterogeneity of history as an intellectual field', one characterised both by 'generic experimentation' and by questions about 'the viability of the hierarchies by which generic law is maintained'.[116] Indeed, my interest in the interrelationship between discursive form and historiographical function has led me to focus primarily on those writers who produced multigenre corpuses and for whom the generic evolution of the novel, history, biography, and memoir were deeply interconnected, even if their eminence in other genres has overshadowed or compromised their reputation as historians. These writers often self-consciously characterise their critical reorientation towards historical writing as either personally or professionally significant: for example, a response to the disappointments of radical and Whig–Republican public life (Godwin), a reaction to a perceived crisis in the genre of fiction (Carlyle), and a vocational and financial choice (Southey and Macaulay).

I therefore understand the writing of history and fiction as interrelated activities but not as part of a single endeavour. In suggesting that practising historians of the early to mid-nineteenth century considered historical knowledge an autonomous knowledge domain and retained to some degree a hierarchical view of genres, I see generic differentiation and historical specialisation as occurring from *within* the domain of *belles lettres* itself rather than as something imposed solely by institutional or bureaucratic professionalisation. In this respect, I follow Mary Poovey, Clifford Siskin, Michael McKeon, Robin Valenza, and others who have considered the generic differentiation between different kinds of writing in the eighteenth and nineteenth centuries. Siskin, for instance, has argued that the emergence of the romantic discipline of literature out of the broader category of *belles lettres* involved first a narrowing of its scope and then a deepening of its intellectual investments. My emphasis in this book is similarly on how history attempted to distance itself from related genres through dynamic processes of differentiation, specialisation, and (only later) institutionalisation and professionalisation.[117]

Despite my primary focus on official history, the novel remains an important touchstone for this book, not just because it is the genre best 'able to place the conventions of different literary and historical models in dialogue', but because historians in the period engage directly with written history's epistemological and ontological differences from the novel.[118] As the approach of this book attests, written history cannot be considered separately from its place within a wider literary ecology including surrounding genres and disciplines, regimes of reading and reviewing, and the more general sociology of literary forms. Yet while I consider the literary or rhetorical activity of historical writers, I also foreground the constraints placed on them by the nature of their historiographical role, and the ways in which they actively demarcate their historical work from other literary and quasi-historical forms (including their own novels, poetry, dramas, memoirs, and biographies). Many of the historians considered in this book insist on specifically historical ways of representing the self in society and develop a distinctive way of portraying the psychological complexity of feelings within the context of wider social and institutional structures.

I test this argument most explicitly in the book's first three chapters, where my interest lies in the various ways in which historians attempt either to synthesise or to sequester and differentiate written history from quasi- and para-historical genres such as the political tract, memoir, biography, and the novel. Chapters 1 and 2 examine the themes of historical sentiment, experience, and character in British representations of the French and English Revolutions, respectively, focusing on Burke and Wollstonecraft (Chapter 1) and on Godwin and Carlyle (Chapter 2). In each case, I consider how the historical subject, from the individual to the collective, is gendered, fashioned, and represented in written history. Chapter 3 turns to representations of national feeling, focusing on the increasingly racialised intersections between nationalism, antiquarianism, and ethnogenesis in the work of Scott, Moore, and Southey. In all three chapters, I demonstrate that the period's historiographical innovations emerge as much from a rehabilitation of antiquarian interests in the materiality of the past and from didactic, exemplary, and character-driven models of history—such as seventeenth-century character studies and orations—as from the 'reality effect' of the novel, or the subjectivity of the biography and memoir.

The book's final two chapters examine the ways in which generic differentiation maps on to discursive differentiation; or, in other words, the ways in which the differentiations between historical and imaginative writing take place at the level of style—a topic I consider throughout the book but deal with most explicitly in Chapter 4. The still widespread assumption that the rise of the 'man of letters' reinforced the cultural prestige of the literary domain at the expense of the specialist historian raises two questions of significance: how did early nineteenth-century authors understand their own occupational identity? And how were they received within the literary marketplace? Chapter 5 takes up similar questions concerning the identity of the 'historian' in the context of early nineteenth-century reviewing culture, focusing on those years before the onset of dedicated historical review journals. In analysing reviews of historical texts in the *Edinburgh Review* and other organs of 'higher journalism', I understand emergent changes in historical methodology as intimately connected to the praxis, marketing, and (gendered) reception of written history. Far from being irrelevant, essayists and reviewers were central to the specialisation, masculinisation, and professionalisation of historical discourse in the nineteenth century.

Following historiographical understandings of the term 'romantic', the book's period dates extend British literary periodisations to encompass Carlyle and Macaulay's written history in the mid-nineteenth century, beginning with British histories of the French Revolution written in the 1790s and ending with reflections on periodical reviewing culture in the 1840s. With the exception of Chapter 5, each chapter is structured around comparative case studies featuring either a pair or a group of authors. In part, this methodology is informed by what has been called 'persona studies' or the study of how writers manage, produce, negotiate, and self-fashion their own authorial identities within the public arena. However, I also seek to examine how these self-fashionings impact the 'unity or disunity' of the historiographical field more generally.[119] I therefore consider questions of authorial self-fashioning alongside larger themes relating to the relationship between feeling and changing historical protocols in the period, from historical experience, character, and subjectivity to more collective forms of emotional identification such as public opinion and national feeling.

As the focus on representation in many of its chapters suggests, this book emphasises the ways in which style can denote certain attitudes or feelings in written history. Notwithstanding the linguistic turn in historical studies, practising historians have proved remarkably resistant to understanding historiographical practice through the idea of style.[120] In his classic *Style in History* (1974), Peter Gay notes that style raises 'questions about the historian's central intentions and overriding interpretations, the state of his art, the essential beliefs of his culture'. Yet he also maintains that historical writing to some extent 'resists analysis in terms of "style" or figure ... Transparency to the "facts" is the historian's code of literary practice.'[121] By the mid-twentieth century, professional history had begun to stop calling attention to itself as writing, but even in its most positivist form it never managed entirely to dismiss stylistic concerns or the related issue of authorial emotions: the self-effacement of a supposedly analytical or objective approach always calls into being its own lack or suppression of passionate relation. Objectivity, in other words, did not—and does not—prevent the continued ideological uses of historical writing, and is better thought of as a rhetorical device or stylistic effect adopted by historians rather than as something inherently 'historical'.[122] I therefore use the term 'style' in this book to encompass both deliberate acts of authorial self-positioning and less intentional encodings of social relations such as various sociolects and 'national' styles, as well as the ways in which a historical text is structured and narrativised: that is, the study of discursive patterns, embodied practices, changing forms and standards, and specific vocabularies and metaphors, including the structure or logic of narrative form as a whole.[123]

Underlying this study is a great debt to Frank Ankersmit, Hayden White, Dominick LaCapra, and other proponents of the so-called 'linguistic turn' in history. This debt is too obvious and fundamental to require substantial exposition but equally it cannot be entirely ignored. Like White, I see questions of style or linguistic modes of representation as prefiguring the historical field. However, I do not always assess historical texts in tropological terms.[124] My focus in this instance is not primarily on historical poetics, patterns, tropes, or plots, but rather on what Rigney has called the 'heuristic role of fiction' and other aesthetic forms 'in the generation of discursive models that historians then adopted for their own purposes'.[125] While avoiding those linguistic accounts that endorse extreme radical constructivism, referential illusion, or rigid tropologies, this book is nonetheless premised on two assumptions inherited from the linguistic school. The first is that narrative—or, to be more precise, deep-structure narrativity—is a key characteristic of history, and that historians of all types narrativise or tell stories about the past. The second is that alterations in literary style, or the ways in which historians write, both reflect and condition important historical transitions in structures of feeling.[126]

Chapter 1

Historical Sentiment and Experience: Burke and Wollstonecraft

In *Reflections on the Revolution in France* (1790), Edmund Burke famously calls the Revolution 'the most astonishing' event 'that has hitherto happened in the world', culminating in his equally famous (non-) depiction of it as a 'monstrous tragi-comic scene' in which 'the most opposite passions necessarily succeed, and sometimes mix with each other in the mind'.[1] As Mary Wollstonecraft registers in her *Historical and Moral View of the French Revolution* (1794), Burke's mixed, fragmented, and fluctuating rhetorical strategy replicates his view of the Revolution as an 'insolent and bloody theatre' of 'continually shifting' scenes of ephemeral sensation, offering a series of impressionistic and 'glowing picture[s] of some interesting moment' that are either 'exaggerated' or dissociated from a longer, stadial history of human development.[2] To put this point differently, Wollstonecraft ties both the text's passional language and its non-coherence at the level of narrative signification with its own loss of authority, so that Burke's rapid and disjointed succession of afflicting scenes—in particular the melodramatic tableaux of the National Assembly and the attempted violation of Marie Antoinette during the October Days—are as ahistorical as any painting (or stage set) that captures only a single, discontinuous moment in time.[3]

Wollstonecraft's overriding sense that Burke's *Reflections* works via emotional effect rather than rational contiguity is the starting point for this chapter's examination of the role of feeling in the emergent historiography of the French Revolution in 1790s Britain. While *Reflections* can be understood within a variety of historical traditions from sentimentalism to stadial theory, I situate Burke's text within his understanding of changing regimes of feeling, outlining the ways in which he embeds his analysis of political rights within the practical context of contending human passions, and ties revolutionary action to unsocial feelings.[4] Burke's insight that political obedience rests 'on something more than relational calculation' was, of course, enormously important to the period's affective 'interweaving of private sentimental and public politics'.[5] However, his understanding of feeling in *Reflections* is ultimately a regulatory or disciplinary one, producing passive political subjects rather than any kind of agential political force. In representing the Revolution (and the feelings, beliefs, and judgments that underpin it) as a 'non-event' or aberrant *'lapsus naturae'*, Burke's emotional economy of primary French 'sensations' and secondary or acculturated English 'sentiments' relegates the actors of the revolutionary present to a nonexistent temporality and subjugates their lived experience to a predetermined and illusory past.[6]

Wollstonecraft's *Historical and Moral View* sets out to restore deep historical and moral causes to Burke's passional account of ephemeral revolutionary effects, redressing her earlier fear of being unable 'methodically, to unravel' those 'slavish paradoxes' in which there are 'no fixed, first principles to refute'. Understanding history as a kind of 'demonstrative science' and advocating a rationalist approach to historical knowledge, her efforts to disentangle Burke's masculinist appropriation of sentiment from the representative protocols of historical discourse are grounded, first, in a rational, cognitive, and pedagogical theory of emotion, which actively rejects the intuitionism underpinning Burke's 'gendered coding of social crisis'; second, in her revival of the 'first principles' of the civic–humanist discourse of virtue ethics and its relationship to the longer history of class antagonisms and inequalities addressed by social contract theory; and third, in her revisionist attention to the causal protocols of history's philosophic structure.[7] Even as she attempts to apply a more coherent historical logic to Burke's strategic de-rationalisation of the Revolution, Wollstonecraft's recasting of the causal determinism of stadial theory is one that allows for diverse, multitemporalising kinds of historical causation, combining a rationalist or cognitive approach to feeling with a rejection of the a-temporal abstractions of Burkean prescription. By acknowledging the existence of 'human' (or psychological) as well as socio-economic causes, she introduces into her history of the French Revolution a new, agential understanding of collective feeling that allows for the existence of an experiential, participatory, and dynamic social world.

In suggesting that Burke and Wollstonecraft's accounts of the French Revolution represent not just two opposing ideological positions but two opposing conceptions of history's epistemological foundations, my contentions in the context of this book's larger arguments are two-fold: first, that Wollstonecraft's ethical anxiety that false or specious political arguments could be concealed by seemingly natural or spontaneous feelings—a 'sentimental varnish over vice'—is one that haunts both historical interpretation and historical writing in the period; and second, that her interest in cultivating cognitive as opposed to instinctive feeling is critical to rethinking the role and place of feeling in historical discourse from the late eighteenth century onwards. Wollstonecraft rejects Burke's belief in the 'infallibility of sensibility' and his valorisation of non-cognitive feeling, but her *Historical and Moral View* nonetheless attempts to find a place in written history for a particular form of sentiment: one that—unlike Burke's instinctive, non-reasoning, and universalist sentimental discourse—is proportionate, evaluative, and linked to cognition. It is this counter-sentimental form of '*rational* affection[s]' that Wollstonecraft uses to resolve a very modern problem: the private and public impasses faced by the gendered self in a period of acute historical crisis.[8]

Public Affections and *Sensus Communis* in Burke's *Reflections*

Amid his generic fluctuations and rhetorical virtuosity, Burke astutely adopts a position of extreme sentimental naivety in *Reflections*, relying on the familiar letter format to insist that he is simply presenting 'my thoughts, just as they arise in my mind', and elsewhere defending himself from charges of vanity, insincerity, and category error by arguing that he was 'throwing out reflexions upon a political event, and not reading a lecture upon theories and principles of Government'.[9] Notwithstanding these disclaimers and his very real personal agitation over the Revolution, there is a latent sense throughout *Reflections* that Burke's intention is indeed to write 'history', albeit a polemical type of history in the rhetorical tradition of the 'controversy': one that displays little attention to 'formal method' or 'sober style', and instead emphasises the 'moral lessons' that can be drawn from 'the past errors and infirmities of mankind'.[10] In insisting that he is attending to history's moral meanings rather than to the 'shell and husk' of party factions, Burke intimates the extent to which his letter is engaged in detaching a medley of terrifying, irrational, and almost unthinkable events from a longer narrative of political and historical continuity.[11] Even as he registers the uncertainty of the Revolution as a still unfolding event as yet 'only sketched' in historical time, he positions his own act of political witnessing as a stabilising force that can delimit and foreclose historical meaning in the face of what he acknowledges to be a traumatic rupture of tradition: first, as an act of contextualisation within a genealogy of continuous, if limited, constitutional rights dating back to the 1688

Glorious Revolution; and second, as a 'prescient act of historical judgment', provocatively prefacing his notoriously eroticised passage on the persecution of Marie Antoinette with the authoritative words: 'History will record.'[12]

As an experienced orator and rhetorician, Burke understood better than most the power of harnessing emotions (and the moralising claims of history's judgment) to political causes, choosing to tie his arguments in favour of legal prescription to those positive, 'inbred sentiments, which are the faithful guardians, the active monitors of our duty', while simultaneously drawing on negative categories of emotion to express the spectre of 'deep democracy' most obviously represented by the 'horrid yells, and shrilling screams, and frantic dances' of the 'savage' crowd of revolutionary women who march on Versailles.[13] Undoubtedly a calculated rhetorical manoeuvre, Burke's identarian politics ties power to what Lauren Berlant has called the 'politics of true feeling', according to which revolutionary insurrection *feels* bad (or terrifying) and national solidarity *feels* good (or reassuring).[14] The grotesque, frenzied, and gender-divergent bodies of the revolutionary crowds play on middle-class fears surrounding the erratic behaviour and suggestibility of the mass mobilisation of the labouring classes, particularly on the demographic politics of reproduction and on the phobic idea of contagion, in order to regulate emotional responses to the Revolution.[15] Yet while Burke capitalises on the classic counter-revolutionary position that the Revolution is the pathological product of negative and irrational feelings, he also appropriates these 'gypsey predictions' for his own purposes, arguing, in the first instance, that it is impossible to consider a revolution in the 'nakedness and solitude of metaphysical abstraction'; and in the second instance, notoriously rehabilitating prejudice as a positive socio-historical force by valorising those 'untaught feelings' that condition the foundations of our 'moral sentiments' and '[render] a man's virtue his habit'.[16]

As Daniel O'Neill has pointed out, Burke's view of the Revolution is heavily immersed in Scottish enlightenment understandings of the 'science of man', both in his privileging of involuntary passions over reason and in his insistence on the value of the social passions.[17] 'History', he argues somewhat wearily mid-way through *Reflections*, 'consists, for the greater part, of the miseries brought upon the world by pride, avarice, ambition, revenge, lust, sedition, hypocrisy, ungoverned zeal, and all the train of disorderly appetites'. Burke's embattled belief that negative or malevolent passions are the primary causes and not merely the supplementary effects of historical change—'These vices are the *causes* of those storms' while '[r]eligion, morals, laws, prerogatives, privileges, rights of men' are merely 'the *pretexts*'—is suggestive of the extent to which his understanding of institutions and other political governance structures is one that is alive to their embeddedness in emotional regimes that can regulate negative or unsocial passions, even if he arguably does not see these regimes as formative of human nature itself.[18] By primarily structuring his historical subtext around the Smithian distinction between the social and unsocial passions, Burke is able to position acculturated, manly English sentiments as a counter-force to unmediated, effeminate French sensations, correlating English filiopiety with historical and precedential continuity while revolutionary feeling is unnatural or 'out of nature'.[19] French constitutional novelty and French feeling are thereby rendered ephemeral, illusory, and anachronistic within a longer stadial history of western European civilisation (and English organic continuity), such that the Revolution becomes a historical accident without deep causation, 'a kind of antihistory' occasioned by the 'falsification of man's experience in time'.[20]

Aligning the revolutionary break with a new age of cold-hearted, utilitarian, and 'wilful innovation', Burke understands the Revolution as a rupture of those long-standing western European regimes of feeling valorised by Scottish enlightenment historians such as Hume and Robertson: a view that is made explicit in his discussion of the October Days, where he argues that, from 8 October 1789 onwards, the Revolution became 'a revolution in sentiments, manners, and moral opinions' and a departure from the 'common feelings of men'.[21] Searching for historical antecedents that could explain this break from inherited chivalric codes of feeling, Burke characterises past revolutions in history as contests between natural and unnatural, selfish and unselfish, and socially constructive and socially destructive passions. The Glorious Revolution and the American Revolution are ultimately socially constructive in that they are 'a parent of settlement, and not a nursery of future revolutions', whereas the seventeenth-century English revolutionaries acted more in accordance with 'distempered passions' while still at least regenerating 'the deficient part of the old constitution' to the extent it was required. The French Revolution, on the other hand, involves both a complete suspension of sovereignty and an 'unnecessary' deviation from the 'hereditary principle of succession', resulting in a 'total' revolution of manners, feelings, customs, and laws without any obvious precedent or 'philosophic analogy'.[22]

In both its historical novelty and its 'spirit of innovation', its desire to 'begin anew', the French Revolution subverts for Burke the very standards by which past actions, events, and people can be judged, disrupting the stabilising effects of history's normative function or the way in which the past 'provides and sanctions a framework for human activity in the present' and, by extension, the future.[23] Finding prior revolutions insufficient as historical explanations for the peculiarly novel qualities of the French Revolution, Burke is forced to turn instead to classical theories of historical degeneracy and decline, representing the ideological crisis of ancient Rome as one essentially founded on selfish and other unsocial passions, such that atomised and disconnected individuals 'mark degenerated and worn out republics'.[24] Seeing an affinity between the utilitarian 'new colonies of the rights of men' in France and the military colonies Tacitus describes during Rome's decline, Burke characterises the French Revolution as the product of declining communitarianism in which 'laws are to be supported only . . . by the concern, which each individual may find in them'. This decline 'into the dust and power of individuality' equally applies to the kind of corporate identities that privatisation encourages: 'agitators in corporations', 'societies in the towns formed of directors of assignats', and 'money-jobbers, speculators, and adventurers'.[25] The French National Assembly, too, is pathologised as a private 'association' rather than a 'body politic', acting according to a 'selfish and mischievous ambition' that perverts 'all the well-placed sympathies of the human breast'. The 'gallery' thus comes to take the 'place of the house' in revolutionary France, a 'profane burlesque' of a 'sacred institution'.[26]

In predicting that the Revolution would 'dissolve [society] into an unsocial, uncivil, unconnected chaos of elementary principles', Burke represents French corporatisation as inimical to the kind of 'spontaneous' and 'inseparable' social formations that develop out of family, friendship, and habit, 'binding up the constitution of our country with our dearest domestic ties; adopting our fundamental laws into the bosom of our family affections'. As many critics have noted, the visceral ties of familial attachment become for Burke a metaphor for the 'framing of a [national] polity': 'the first principle (the germ as it were) of public affections' that lead to 'love of our county and to mankind', ultimately ensuring the unity of society in the face of class hierarchies, patriarchal laws, poverty, and other structural disparities.[27] Jason Frank has rightly pointed out that peoplehood is for Burke an affective state 'sustained through the senses'; the people are a *sensus communis* or 'community of sense' in the sense of being emotionally fused through an intergenerational and multidirectional web of 'sensuous attachments' made up of 'primary morals' and 'untaught feelings'. Through the inherence of its many parts and through the accumulated and habitual rituals of social participation, this web can produce and reproduce recognisably English structures of national feeling: 'But when we see the model held up to ourselves, we must feel as Englishmen, and feeling, we must provide as Englishmen.'[28]

As an 'avowed empiricist', it is unsurprising that Burke should base his conception of English national identity on a combination of physiological and emotional attachments.[29] Drawing on Lockean empiricism and Montesquieu's holistic view of the imbrication of political institutions and legal structures in *De l'esprit des loix* (1748), Burke sees the authority of political community as distributed not just across generations over time, but also 'horizontally' across the practices and locations of social interaction through familial and other self-regulating social networks and institutions, including the face-to-face 'subjective experiences of daily life that produce and sustain those institutions' such as heteronormative reproduction.[30] What, in his *Philosophical Enquiry* (1757), is an 'exact theory of our passions' and a 'phenomenology of the senses'—that is, universal laws grounded in the individual sensory experience of pleasure and pain, and its relationship to subject or identity formation—becomes in *Reflections* a different kind of affective theory, one in which a complex sociology of feeling links individuals, institutions, collectives, and the national body.[31] If Burke's primarily goal in his *Enquiry* is to explain 'individual subject formation understood as an effect of power', in *Reflections* his point is to show how social passions are encouraged and mediated by their institutional and socio-historical contexts.[32] The individual is 'absorbed by sociopolitical reality' to the extent that human nature itself can only be properly understood through the slow growth of institutions that survive through historical time, and that themselves originally rest on intimate or emotional foundations.[33]

As Burke's emphasis on heteropatriarchal models of inheritance and slow growth suggests, the ostensible organicism of his affective conception of peoplehood is centred in a bureaucratic or institutional form of legitimacy rather than in lived experience. Despite Burke's emphasis on a corporeal, bottom-up process of national attachment, and his accumulated networks of biologising metaphors from infection to inoculation, the end result is, as Richard Barney notes, a simulation or abstraction of both the body and the body politic.[34] Burke seemingly privileges the 'practical' and 'acquired wisdom' of generations over the 'theoretical science' of abstract philosophy and 'system', promoting a 'positive, recorded *hereditary* title' over a 'vague speculative right', as well as rejecting the 'rights of man' as an 'untested' discourse that abstracts subjects from their social relations via an equivalising system of interexchangability.[35] Yet, for all that he privileges experience over theory, morals over metaphysics, precedent over principle, and landed property over bourgeois speculative credit, Burke ultimately understands *sensus communis* as something sustained by authority and its behavioural correlative: obedience.[36] For Burke, 'the people' as a collective can never embody, authorise, or legitimate institutions. On the contrary, institutions are 'embodied . . . in persons; so as to create in us love, veneration, admiration, or attachment'. Burke's affective theory of political authority, in effect, has a circular logic, one which declines to differentiate between 'institutions of power and their social base', and sublimates the desires of individuals into the embodiments of the state by identifying the 'spirit of liberty' in the people's submission to servitude.[37]

Feelings are therefore primarily understood by Burke as social mechanisms, as differences in power and as coercive technologies of social recognition and control—ones that are ultimately conditioned by scarcity rather than excess. For all that Burke deploys the passions as a powerful rhetorical force in *Reflections*, throwing up visceral feelings of 'sensory discomfort' from agitation to involuntary nervous response, there is a 'shadow economy' of passivity in the text that attaches to the people.[38] Pride or self-love is rehabilitated as a positive feeling vested only in those who are property owners, while acquiescence, reverence, emulation, and deference are stabilising sentiments that operate across the social spectrum but most particularly work to subdue, unify, and discipline the otherwise destructive passions of the 'multitude', who are then 'called on to defer to the hierarchy that [their] own labor has produced'.[39] A 'perfect democracy' is thus, for Burke, 'the most shameless thing in the world' precisely because 'the people at large' would become the unregulated and unchecked 'standard of right and wrong'. In ascribing to the dynamics of democracy the sexualised emotion of 'shamelessness', the sentimental mode is tactically appropriated by Burke to produce political subjects who are regulated by their own 'natural' feelings and for whom a contractual consensus of feeling exists in perpetuity, restricting any kind of agential growth or self-determination.[40]

As Mike Goode has pointed out, Burkean feelings are ultimately staged in the form of 'citation', as 'an erotic attachment to the materiality of the past' and 'a sentimental communion with precedents' that allows for 'a fantasy of disembodiment whereby men project themselves out of their own historical situations'.[41] The history of 'sentimental jurisprudence' that emerges in *Reflections* is one in which the people are 'reverent political subjects' rather than existing as any kind of living, animating, or agential political force in their own right.[42] If he elsewhere dismisses emotional restraint as a response that encourages 'passivity among the victims of suffering', in the case of the French Revolution Burke deploys feeling in the service of passivity, implying that only 'the traditional order takes full account of natural feelings'.[43] It is for this reason that 'right' in *Reflections* is vested not in the people but in the representatives of inherited institutions and their written records, which are designed to encode and give permanence to such durable dispositions as reverence and obedience. For Burke, corporeal feeling is reified by and through an erotic attachment to institutions, abstracting and displacing feeling into a fetishised and virtual form of embodiment that attaches only to those individuals that act as bodily prostheses for the state. The real revolution is accordingly for Burke that 'sacrificial crisis' rhetorically enacted and embodied first by the abject, suffering aristocratic victim Marie Antoinette and then by the sublime trauma of her more actively conceived paternalistic spokesperson, Burke himself: 'Oh! what a revolution! and what an heart must I have, to contemplate without emotion that elevation and that fall!'[44]

Virtuous Passions and Affect Management in Wollstonecraft's *Vindications*

Suppressing her rising indignation at Burke's disguise of his 'sophistical arguments' in 'the questionable shape of natural feelings and common sense', Wollstonecraft succinctly identifies the problems with Burke's *Reflections* in the short advertisement to her *Vindication of the Rights of Men*: first, its reliance on the 'infallibility of sensibility' or so-called 'natural' feelings divorced from their cognitive content; and second, its grounding of virtue in the 'kind of mysterious instinct' that 'is *supposed* to reside in the soul, that instantaneously discerns truth, without the tedious labour of ratiocination'.[45] Wollstonecraft is best characterised as an ethical cognitivist rather than as a subjectivist, but her response to Burke allows for the role of 'private affections' in ethical judgment, arguing that 'the passions are necessary' (albeit insufficient) 'auxiliaries of reason'. Following Hume in rejecting motivational rationalism as the prime mover of human conduct in favour of the sacred 'feelings of the heart' that bring forth reason's 'only legitimate off-spring – virtue', Wollstonecraft sees feeling as playing a complementary rather than adversarial role when it comes to ethical decision making, understanding emotions as themselves evaluative reactions that involve and express tacit judgments.[46] Her subsequent argument that 'reflection', and not the 'blind impulse of unerring instinct', is the 'natural foundation of *rational* affections' and her understanding of virtue as a disposition learned or acquired by religious experience—'[i]f virtue be an instinct, I renounce all hope of immortality'—recognises the extent to which Burke's seemingly embedded 'public affections' are detached from their cognitive, social, and experiential contexts, as well as from the individual rights-based framework at the heart of Locke's social contract theory.[47]

Wollstonecraft thus acknowledges the social and political value of feeling, particularly in relation to what Shane Greentree has called the 'non-hierarchical' observation of 'everyday suffering'.[48] However, her cognitive understanding of emotions determines that virtue can only be *actively* acquired. Indeed, her sustained argument against instinctive feeling signals the importance of virtue as a mediating discourse in her first *Vindication*, a discourse that could replace rank, inheritance, and property as a marker of social and political value, as well as forming the basis of a more ethically grounded theory of historical development.[49] When she argues that Burke's attack on Richard Price is motivated by an 'ugly feeling' (envy of Price's rhetorical ability), Wollstonecraft signals her distaste for the kind of identity politics that attaches personal feelings to extra-individual or social formations.[50] Whereas Burke places his rhetorical emphasis in *Reflections* on ethos or the representation of virtuous character, Wollstonecraft inherits her view of virtue from Catherine Macaulay, whose writing on the Civil War Republicans in her *History of England* (1763–83) understands virtue less as a type of bourgeois identity politics and more as an ethical imperative in which public and private good are consubstantial.[51] For Macaulay, virtue is not, as Laura Mandell notes, 'a claim about the self, not an identity – it is not "privative"', but rather a 'heuristic device' 'for arriving at an objective understanding of the past' and generating a kind of 'historical realism'.[52]

For all that Wollstonecraft's *ad hominem* attacks on Burke can be understood as personal in nature, J. G. A. Pocock's view of Macaulay as a 'patriot historian', who sought 'the release of personal virtue through civic participation', is echoed in Wollstonecraft's own allegiances to a Commonwealth tradition passed on by Protestant Dissenters—one that saw the French Revolution as part of a cyclical but harmonious lineage from the Glorious Revolution of 1688, and before that the Roman Republic, rather than as anachronistic or discontinuous.[53] This tradition of civic virtue, and her involvement in circles including Joseph Johnson and Richard Price, anchors Wollstonecraft's arguments about feeling in her two *Vindications* in the idiom of what we might call 'virtuous passions' or passions centred in the practice of political justice: 'in my eyes all feelings are false and spurious, that do not rest on justice'.[54]

Historians have recently recovered the importance of Abbé Mably's classical republicanism and its emphasis on civic virtue for the intellectual origins of the French Revolution.[55] While Mably himself envisages a social elite that is much wider than the 'virtuous nobility' of classical republicanism, Wollstonecraft's argument for 'acquired' rather than 'innate' virtue is founded more in what David Bromwich has characterised as her non-utilitarian belief in 'educing good for the individual' than in either an enlarged intellectual elite or a Burkean virtual or 'imaginary whole': 'To suppose that . . . the happiness of any individual is sacrificed to promote the welfare of ten, or ten thousand, other beings – is impious.'[56] Whereas Burke places his faith in 'public affections' as a sensuous collective conjoining church, state, people, and family, Wollstonecraft's ethical individualism denies any distinction between individual transformation and social emancipation, arguing against the value of 'a supposed grand arrangement' or national body as an arbiter of virtue and morality: 'the vulgar . . . are, nine out of ten, the creatures of habit and impulse'.[57]

In rejecting Burke's idea that the social contract should function primarily as a means of inter-generational cohesion rather than as a means of discovering, defining, and reflecting moral principles, Wollstonecraft identifies Burkean feelings as technologies of statecraft and governmentality. Individual passions are harnessed by forms of emotional governance that attempt to 'culturally standardize the organization of feeling' through an appeal to the collective and unchanging values of the nation: 'In the name of the people of England, you say, "that we know *we* have made no discoveries; and we think that no discoveries are to be made in morality; nor many in the great principles of government, nor in the ideas of liberty, which were understood long before we were born".'[58] Wollstonecraft thus calls out the ideological function of Burke's *sensus communis* (and instinctive feeling more generally) in sublimating individuals to the state, and in naturalising inequitable and hierarchical power relations, self-selecting elites, and hereditary castes. Not only has Burke attempted to disguise his 'vulgar emotion of wonder' for power and rank, but his compassion extends only to misery of the abstract, fictitious, or aesthetic sort (the 'attractive Arcadia of fiction') rather than the '*inelegant* distress' of the poor, thereby reproducing the very infrastructures of social suffering that he is supposed to indict. Like Paine, who famously suggests that Burke 'pities the plumage, but forgets the dying bird', Wollstonecraft exposes the selective, limited, and exclusionary nature of Burkean emotion: the 'cynical heartlessness' behind his theatrical 'tenderness towards Monarchs' and the 'pleasing illusions' they embody.[59]

As many critics have noted, Wollstonecraft is one of the first of a long line of critics to identify the extent to which Burke's aesthetics of 'spurious, sensual beauty' offers a framework for his political and historical thinking, in particular for his disassociation of sentimental suffering from social justice.⁶⁰ Her recognition of the gendered, hierarchical assumptions at the core of both Burke's *Reflections* and his *Philosophical Enquiry* powers her reconfiguration of his version of stadial history, replacing, as Mary Spongberg notes, Burke's historical examples with examples that parody his version of historical change. Instead of seeing the Revolution as an anachronistic or untimely break with a naturally progressive set of chivalric manners and customs, Wollstonecraft instead represents the development of western civilisation as itself 'unnatural', regressive, degenerate, and inequitable: modern manners have turned man into an 'artificial monster' determined by the 'station in which he was born' and are the source of flawed systems of government that demand 'homage' to the few in ways that have 'benumbed [man's] faculties like the torpedo's touch'.⁶¹

Wollstonecraft's unmasking of the 'libertine morality' behind Burke's understanding of historical progress leads her to reproach him for his equally libertine style: in particular, for his attempt to overwhelm the reader with his 'acrobatic rhetoric', whereby '[w]ords are heaped on words, till the understanding is confused by endeavouring to disentangle the sense'.⁶² Burke had himself attempted to document a kind of revolutionary 'linguistic violence' in *Reflections*. For Wollstonecraft, however, Burke's rhetoric is a moral failing, a suite of 'slavish paradoxes' that are contingent on the linguistics of social hierarchy and power.⁶³ To write of effects without causes, of consequences without premises, and of events without order or coherence is more than abuse of language: it is to serve the interests of established power. Despite Burke's claim that '[w]e preserve the whole of our feelings still native and entire', Wollstonecraft recognises that he has 'elaborately laboured' to excite 'compassionate tears' in his audience while himself remaining unmoved, so that 'the feelings which are thus ostentatiously displayed are often the cold declamation of the head, and not the effusions of the heart'. If the whole 'vehicular' theory of Smithian moral sentiment could be said to rest in our capacity 'to move and be moved', Burke has failed to fulfil the primary criteria of sentimental discourse by neglecting to reflect a moral economy centred in sincere emotional reciprocity: 'you have often sacrificed your sincerity to enforce your favourite arguments'.⁶⁴

In suggesting that 'compassion' is the manipulative 'virtue which is to cover a multitude of vices', Wollstonecraft exposes the inherent contradictions of Burkean emotionalism, insisting that he displays all the artifice and insincerity of a sentimental novelist in the very moments in which he appears the most sincere.⁶⁵ While she is by no means the only contemporary critic to condemn Burke's emotional profiteering, Wollstonecraft is one of the few to depart from the strategy of deflecting Burke's arguments by advocating rational self-governance at the level of style, instead deliberately sacrificing a plain and polished style along the lines of Paine's vernacular prose for a warm and 'artless' sincerity modelled on Price's 'unaffected piety'.[66] Presenting her own style as one mirroring the 'reflected passion' of Burke's contradictions, Wollstonecraft nonetheless insists on the sincerity and proportionality of her words: 'I have not yet learned to twist my periods, nor in the equivocal idiom of politeness, to disguise my sentiments.' She thus characterises rational, sincere, and right-directed feelings as critical to moral reasoning: 'truly sublime is the character that acts from principle ... whose feelings give vital heat to his resolves, but never hurry him into feverish eccentricities'.[67]

If there is still a tendency today to separate Wollstonecraft's work into those texts that speak to the 'emotional heart' and those that speak to the 'political mind', it was William Godwin who first projected this division.[68] As Tilottama Rajan has argued, Godwin's editing of Wollstonecraft's work was at pains to distinguish her mature work from the 'more hastily polemical *Vindications*', as well as seeking to present her as an 'icon of sensibility' by valorising her literary over her political texts.[69] One of the many unintended effects of Godwin's characterisation of Wollstonecraft in his *Memoirs* (1798) was her subsequent devaluation for falling victim to the mania of sensibility.[70] Much of the early rehabilitation of Wollstonecraft consequently aimed to reconstruct her as a political rather than a sentimental subject. At the same time, the 'long arm' of gender dichotomy remained at work in Wollstonecraft criticism, particularly in the reproach that Wollstonecraft reproduced a 'paradigmatically liberal and male' conception of human nature and thus gave birth to a tradition of 'feminist misogyny'.[71]

The first *Vindication* certainly attempts to expose 'the social wrong of specializing a virtue to either sex', containing the germ of the issues that Wollstonecraft takes up more fully in *A Vindication of the Rights of Woman* (1792): 'I reverence the rights of men. – Sacred rights! for which I acquire a more profound respect, the more I look into my own mind.'[72] Adopting a position of 'rhetorical masculinity', Wollstonecraft deploys the 'manly' weapons of independent thought and conscience, whereas Burke is characterised as an effeminate 'pupil of impulse', a degenerate example of chivalric manhood who teasingly employs superficial emotions in the same way that women simper and pretend weakness.[73] Extending the requirement for a 'standard of virtue common to both sexes', the second *Vindication* argues more explicitly that the exclusion of women from public life, including from the new republic in revolutionary France, will retard rather than advance 'the progress of those glorious principles that give a substance to morality'. Any retention of the chilvaric system of manners will perpetuate those illusions that have historically prevented women from acting rationally.[74] In their emulation of Marie Antoinette and other exemplars of 'romance and folly', bourgeois women enable and even welcome their own oppression by men such that half 'the sex, in its present infantine state, would pine for a Lovelace'. Like their degenerate male counterparts, the domesticated women at the centre of Burke's chilvaric state are becoming 'weaker, in mind and body', and this 'acculturation' of women 'into over-developed sensibility' requires their education as new kinds of citizen–mothers and wives who act for the public good.[75]

In contemplating the productive re-education of women beyond biological reproduction and passive womanhood, Wollstonecraft roundly condemns the 'reveries of the stupid novelists who, knowing little of human nature, work up stale tales, and describe meretricious scenes, all retained in a sentimental jargon'. Yet if she here sees the sentimental novel as part of a culture of consumption that peddles in feminine weakness and suffering, elsewhere Wollstonecraft engages more seriously with the literatures of sentiment and sensibility.[76] Claudia L. Johnson and Mary Spongberg have accordingly situated Wollstonecraft within a tradition of sympathetic or sentimental historicism, seeing her later work as a revisionist rewriting of her earlier revolutionary texts. Johnson characterises Wollstonecraft's writing in the 1790s in terms of a 'revolutionary' and 'post-revolutionary' phase, understanding the former as 'championing a kind of masculinity into which women can be invited', while in the latter phase she explores new forms of female identity, revising her 'republican masculinity'. Spongberg, too, sees in Wollstonecraft's later writing a process of evolution in 'egalitarian feminism', crystallising around the figure of the 'short-lived queen' and the suffering female more generally, with whom she increasingly identifies and comes to 'evince a Burkean affectivity'.[77]

These arguments, while convincing in and of themselves, tend to hinge on a generic division between novel/travel writing and historical/political writing rather than examining the ways in which Wollstonecraft negotiates the 'double-bind' of sentimental representation: namely, that 'to the extent that women aligned themselves with sensibility rather than sense, they were complicit in their own exclusion from wider participation in the public realm'.[78] Contemplating this problematic, Mary Poovey concludes that impassioned prose is a 'theoretical trap' that Wollstonecraft must avoid in her *Vindications*: 'Instead of controlling the response of the *audience*, Wollstonecraft's rhetoric attempts to control *her own* emotions.'[79] Wollstonecraft is certainly sceptical of 'the sanguinary indices of the pulse and the blush' as an 'index of sincerity', introducing numerous passages of emotional self-suppression, particularly in her first *Vindication*: 'I pause to recollect myself; and smother the contempt I feel rising for your rhetorical flourishes and infantine sensibility'; 'I shall not attempt to follow you'; 'it would be a tedious process to shew'; 'I forbear'. Yet while Poovey reads these self-suppressions as part of a larger intention to avoid explicit confrontation with Burke, Wollstonecraft's simultaneous deferral and sublimation of feeling—the trope of restraint or virtuous control over impulse—is better seen as a strategic act of moral persuasion founded in the principles of late enlightenment rhetoric.[80]

Disgusted with the insincerity of Burke's 'clamorous grief', Wollstonecraft rejects his masculine reappropriation of sentiment in favour of reasserting arguments by Adam Smith and other Scottish enlightenment rhetoricians that the most legible and productive signs of emotion are those that 'exert that recollection and self-command which constitute the dignity of every passion'.[81] Her repression of feeling and her personal self-possession echo endorsements of silent sorrow and self-command, understanding the passions as genuine, natural signs that should nonetheless be moderated, restrained, and controlled. As Julie Ellison has pointed out, such stoicism is repeatedly invoked in 'a complex tension with masculine sentiment during the eighteenth century' and it is this tension that Wollstonecraft capitalises on here, as her manly self-possession is pitted against Burke's effeminate sentimentality.[82] At the same time, Wollstonecraft's suppressed feelings animate her text with the very emotions of contempt, indignation, and distress that she partly seeks to occlude, so that much of the rhetorical effect of her first *Vindication* arises from her strategic refusal or management of emotion.

Unlike Catherine Macaulay's more disinterested tone, Wollstonecraft's rhetorical position in this instance is closer to what Berlant has, in another context, called 'counter-sentimentalism', or the kind of sentimentalism that produces narratives that 'refus[e] to reproduce the sublimation of subaltern struggles into conventions of emotional satisfaction' but nonetheless retain a subjective vision of 'liberal empathy'. Counter-sentimentals foreground ambivalence in their struggle to resist or contain closure, 'disinheriting without disavowing' sentimentalism altogether.[83] Sentiments occupy a similarly ambivalent place in Wollstonecraft's *Vindications*, existing both as sites of negativity (in the sense that personal feelings surface either in the form of suppressions, negations and denials, or in a satirical appropriation of Burke's own voice and language) and as part of an attempt to rehabilitate cognitive or rational feeling in political discourse. As Timothy Michael has astutely pointed out, Wollstonecraft's language is warmest when 'defending the cold arguments of reason'. Wollstonecraft does not, then, entirely destroy 'the contract sentimentality makes between its texts and readers'—namely, that appropriately applied sympathy can 'lead to more virtuous, compassionate feeling and therefore to be a better self'— but she recognises that sentiments can conceal the collusion of personal and political desire. The type of feeling she considers appropriate for public discourse is therefore one characterised by sincerity and rational restraint, a restraint that provides a powerful rhetorical counter-force to the affective performativity of Burke's *Reflections*.[84]

Cause and Effect in Wollstonecraft's *Historical and Moral View*

Wollstonecraft pointedly opens her *Historical and Moral View* by arguing that it is 'necessary to guard against the erroneous inferences of sensibility' caused by 'a heart trembling to the touches of nature'. Once again advocating a rationalist account of the Revolution's 'grand theatre of political changes', she invokes the affective and physiological properties of Burke's 'theatrical idioms' only to declare them counter to her objectives as a historian.[85] Casting herself as a 'philosophic observer' who, in a canny reappropriation of Burke's own ocular and perspectival metaphors, contemplates the novel scene before her with 'the cool eye of observation', Wollstonecraft rejects as 'un-English' the French (and Burkean) taste for spectacle, 'stage tricks', and 'empty theatrical gestures'.[86] In their place, she privileges the historian's ability to abstract and generalise from particular observations. Whereas Burke prioritises instinctive or non-cognitive feeling, Wollstonecraft credits the ability to argue rationally as itself a product of historical growth and cultivation: eloquence 'gives wings to the slow foot of reason, and fire to the cold labours of investigation', 'impressing the results of thinking on minds alive only to emotion', but 'it is observable, that, in proportion as the understanding is cultivated, the mind grows attached to the exercise of investigation, and the combination of abstract ideas'.[87]

Reading Wollstonecraft's rationally cultivated historicism as a corrective to Burke's 'feeling history' allows us to see her *Historical and Moral View* as an attempt to produce a properly historical account of the French Revolution: one that can be distinguished from Burkean aestheticism, as well as, implicitly, from the more culturally 'feminine' modes of sentimental eyewitness representation exemplified by Helen Maria Williams's *Letters from France* (1790).[88] Although Wollstonecraft herself occasionally deploys the affective strategies used in different ways by Burke and Williams, she concludes that rhetorical sentimentality is a shallow technique *unless* it is accompanied by a sound 'chain of argument'. The 'object of the historian', she argues in an oblique hit at Burke, is not 'merely to fill up the sketch' but also 'to trace the hidden springs and secret mechanisms' that have 'put in motion a revolution'. Only 'the philosophical eye', 'which looks into nature and weighs the consequences of human actions', will be able to discern 'the cause, which has produced so many dreadful effects'.[89]

Wollstonecraft's insistence that the ethical task of the historian is to explicate deep historical and moral causes, rather than to outline shallow and ephemeral effects, leads her to recentre a revised philosophic methodology of causation. As Isabelle Bour has rightly argued, there are two kinds of historical causation in *A Historical and Moral View*: first, a 'socio-economic kind of causation, operating over long periods in a slow manner' (or what could be called 'deep' causation), which is largely presented in a detached, philosophic tone; and second, 'a psychological kind of causation, operating over the span of a human life' (or what could be called 'human' causation), which draws more heavily on sentimental and other literary techniques. In the first realm, Wollstonecraft condemns the false sentiment she sees as part of the degeneracy of the French character, whereas in the second realm she records spontaneous displays of sentiment on both an individual and a collective level. For Bour, 'the uneasy co-existence of these two interpretative frameworks' leads to a series of 'irreconcilable' and 'straight forward contradictions' in the text, as ultimately '[t]he grand narrative collapses into the little romance'.[90]

The apparent contradictions between a rationalist, philosophic framework and a physiological or empiricist epistemology of sensibility in Wollstonecraft's text take on a different meaning when read as deliberate responses to the same instabilities and contradictions in Burke's *Reflections*. Burke had himself sought to resolve the tension between public history and private romance by arguing that the mediating faculty of emotional response can overcome the Humean distinction between true and fictional narratives. While Wollstonecraft seeks to counteract the shallow, ahistorical nature of Burke's sensationalist account of the Revolution, her multicausal approach identifies individual and collective cases of spontaneous human emotion as practical counterexamples or demonstrative tests of those wider abstractions that Burke elucidates within his rendition of stadial history: in other words, her 'little romances' are designed to counteract the abstract and generalising principles of Burke's premodern rendition of historical development, while simultaneously enacting a redistribution of Burkean sentiment from the aristocracy to the people. The idea that these test cases cause the history's 'grand narrative' to collapse discounts Wollstonecraft's own inherent ambivalence towards progressive grand narratives. Like the Scottish enlightenment theorists, she sets stadial developmental paradigms within a history of uneven development that allows for stages of relapse and degeneracy, but she is far more sceptical of the forward trajectory of historical progress than her enlightenment predecessors.[91]

Beginning with what Fiona Price has characterised as a radical recasting of stadial history, Wollstonecraft redeploys Burke's own arguments about historical degeneracy and decline to come to radically different conclusions.[92] The opening chapters of her *Historical and Moral View* characterise the entire history of western European civilisation as one centred in unsocial and unvirtuous passions, from the 'first social systems' founded by selfish passions that wished to 'fence round their own wealth or power', to the 'civil tyranny' and cold, narrow, and unfeeling virtue of ancient Greece and Rome, to the Crusades which produced a fraudulent 'kind of bastard morality', to the seventeenth and eighteenth centuries, where 'a taste for majestic frivolity' only 'accelerated ... the refining of the senses at the expense of the heart'.[93] Burkean patriotism thus becomes, in Wollstonecraft's account, an unchanging and perpetual reiteration of unfeeling pride and self-interest (the very passions that Burke had attempted to rehabilitate in *Reflections*): the 'civil tyrants' of Greece and Rome, like the tyrants of the present day, enslave the populace while ostensibly 'loving their country ... ever showing by their conduct, that it was only a part of a narrow love of themselves'.[94]

As a historically counter-productive force, chivalric attachment produces a 'polished slavery', an 'unnatural' perversion of feeling, causing 'ignorant people' to indulge in 'reveries' and 'grow romantic, like the croisaders; or like women'. Yet unlike Burke, whose own use of degeneracy frameworks relates to the privatisation of communal or social feeling, Wollstonecraft concludes that the causes of this civilisational degeneracy are 'unjust plans of government', which abridge 'rational liberty' and 'have prevented man from rising to his just point of elevation, by the exercise of his improveable faculties'. She thus identifies in an apparently linear and progressive western European history a series of cyclical degenerations based on the 'unnatural distinction of the privileged classes': 'a state will infallibly grow old and feeble, if hereditary riches support hereditary rank'.[95] In a direct attack on the affective account of the Revolution developed by Burke, who Wollstonecraft astutely notes in her first *Vindication* would have been a 'violent revolutionist', 'had he been a Frenchman', the whole history of western European civilisation becomes a degenerative history of demagoguery based on an ongoing appeal to the romance of chivalry.[96] True progress consists of undoing Burkean chivalric fantasies and reversing 'the foibles of the multitude' via slow change, education, a free press, and transparent and representative forms of government. For Wollstonecraft, nothing normative can be taken from the English constitutional contract because the constitution is itself a document founded in inequality and must be dissolved in order to produce a more equitable arrangement. Burke's citational emphasis on precedent is thereby countered by a different 'deduction of experience': the lesson that 'every thing dear to man, can be secured only by the preservation of liberty' and 'by making government a science, instead of a craft, and civilizing the grand mass'.[97]

Wollstonecraft's distinction between the 'science' and the 'craft' of governance anticipates two other important distinctions in her history, both of which are centred in a cognitive conception of emotion and its relation to active forms of virtue ethics: 'understanding' versus 'taste' and 'manners' versus 'morals'. Arguing that 'tenderness produced merely by sympathy' is weak compared to 'the humanity of a cultivated understanding' and that it is 'morals, not feelings, which distinguish men from beasts of prey', Wollstonecraft re-establishes the distinction between cognitive and non-cognitive feeling, and passive and active virtue, raised in her first *Vindication*, and resituates it more fully within a theory of normative historical development. If the 'improvements of civil life' consist 'almost entirely in polishing the manners, and exercising the transient sympathies of the heart', then human civilisation will 'naturally fall back into barbarism'. Unlike Burke, who sees the French Revolution as a historical rupture or discontinuity in historical time, and Catherine Macaulay, who claims that 'we can gain no light from history' which 'furnishes no example' of a like revolution, Wollstonecraft understands the causes of the French Revolution as perfectly explicable within a longer history of human development detached from the active rationality of social justice.[98]

It is in her focus on the historical *explicability* of the Revolution that Wollstonecraft makes her greatest intervention into Burkean affective or sentimental historiography and its ideological resistance to novelty in human history. The Revolution and the nature of revolutionary mob violence are not anomalies or radical abnormalities but rather the residual effect of the system upheld by Burke himself, one based on the kind of 'romantic sublimity' that still holds the ignorant in thrall and causes an associative train of 'sympathetic' effects: 'a multitude long accustomed to servitude do not immediately feel their own strength; yet they soon began to tyrannize over one part of their representatives, stimulated by the other'. Although *A Historical and Moral View* ends before the regicide of the King and the imposition of the Terror, the mob violence that haunts the text is explained by a long history of servitude and repression, and by the slow violence of the *ancien régime* itself rather than by the actions of the revolutionaries or the cataclysm of the Revolution:

> The deprivation of natural, equal, civil and political rights, reduced the most cunning of the lower orders to practise fraud, and the rest to habits of stealing, audacious robberies, and murders. And why? because the rich and poor were separated into bands of tyrants and slaves, and the retaliation of slaves is always terrible.[99]

Within the long line of 'transient sympathies' that characterises western European history, present-day France is 'at that degree of false refinement, which makes every man, in his own eyes, the centre of the world' and must therefore be subjected to 'an absolute change' because its members 'have lost the cement of humanity, which kept them together'. Even Jacques Necker, with whom Wollstonecraft had corresponded and who was regarded within her circle as a symbol of Protestant emancipation, is described as 'pedantically virtuous', of an 'artificial, narrow character' manners 'stiff, and the heart cold'. Necker's coldness stands in contrast to members of the National Assembly, particularly the warmth of the Comte de Mirabeau, whose address to the Assembly is a 'master-piece'. Yet it, too, is 'written to persuade' and, like Burke's *Reflections*, relies on 'artful' 'appeals to the passions' that are out of place in the context of political justice.[100]

The revolutionaries ultimately fail to construct and embody a republic based on the rational feelings and values of civic virtue. However, Wollstonecraft's representation of French falsity is primarily centred on the figure of Marie Antoinette: from the depiction of the Queen's theatrical arrival in France, where she is received by the French populace with 'a kind of idolatrous adulation', to her financial profligacy and extravagance, to her 'preconcerted' performance as a loving mother to the Dauphin and symbolically to the whole nation. Using the very rhetorical techniques of 'striking contrast' employed by Burke, Wollstonecraft compares the Queen's 'lovely face' and 'bewitching manners' with her 'want of intelligence' and 'voluptuousness'. Here, of course, the comparison is not between elevation and fall but between reality and appearance: the Queen is a 'profound dissembler', 'a complete actress', who acts like a seductress in a sentimental novel.[101] Wollstonecraft's association of French misrule with transgressive sexuality draws on the increasingly ferocious avalanche of political pornography directed against Marie Antoinette after 1789, which was, as Spongberg notes, part of a gendered politics centred in a 'deep-rooted misogyny'.[102] Lisa Plummer Crafton has rightly argued for a more nuanced reading of Wollstonecraft's rendering of Marie Antoinette as a multivalent 'fabricated sign' that shifts from the erotic to the maternal, but the Queen remains the primary body on which Wollstonecraft's attack on Burkean conceptions of 'feeling history' is laid out.[103]

Marie Antoinette's exhibitionism suggests the extent to which the French monarchy relies on manipulating the kind of instinctive emotional attachments enshrined in Burke's *sensus communis*:

> From her fascinating smiles, indeed, was caught the careless hope, that, expanding the heart, makes the animal spirits vibrate, in every nerve, with pleasure: – yet, she smiled but to deceive; or, if she felt some touches of sympathy, it was only the unison of the moment.

The King, too, exploits theatrical displays of sensibility that reproduce false sentiments within a populace predisposed to abandon 'the serene lustre of manly firmness' and 'yield to feeling': 'their sensibility produced as mad demonstrations of joy as lately had been displayed of ferocity'.[104] Whereas Burke had represented the French revolutionaries as a rabble intent on violating the Queen, Wollstonecraft instead characterises the King and Queen as corrupting and violating influences on the people, as examples of the aristocratic 'manners' that have replaced 'morals' as the indices of inner life. They are thus symbolic of the French nation in the way that Burke suggests but *only* to the extent that they are egoists and perverted degenerates who prey on the unprincipled susceptibility of the French people to 'electrical sympathy', thereby manipulating the more sinister and coercive properties of collective feeling.[105]

Wollstonecraft draws here on the language of electricity in describing revolutionary collectives or crowds, a discourse that emerges in eyewitness accounts of the Revolution via rhetorical analogies between electrical science, collective sentiment, and the common good.[106] If she uses the term in this instance to describe the perverse manipulation of collective feeling by monarchical forces, Wollstonecraft's ethical concern with the debilitating effects of instinctive feeling also allows for a 'good' kind of electricity or spontaneous sentiment in order to represent the people purging themselves of aristocratic degeneracy. The 'central drama' of *A Historical and Moral View* may well be what Lynn Hunt has called the 'family romance', such that the King and Queen's bodies become a 'central site of political struggle between the old and the new order', but Wollstonecraft's identification of the aristocracy with 'erotic dysfunction' is also reflected back on to the people as 'macro-body': 'Every corner of the kingdom was ransacked to satiate these cormorants, who wrung the very bowels of industry, to give a new edge to sickly appetites; corrupting the morals whilst breaking the spirit of the nation.'[107] In order to produce 'a new, republican, healthy body', the people must learn to self-regulate or negotiate their own cure of those social disease associated with aristocratic contagion.[108]

Repurposing Burkean metaphors of disease, sickness, and corruption, Wollstonecraft uses the diseased physical bodies of the King and Queen to provide a point of reference for the people's shift from passive spectators in the *ancien régime* to active actors in the new republic.[109] Her 'therapeutic' history increasingly counters Burke's biomedical metaphors of bodily contagion, disease, degeneration, and paralysis with vitalist ones of awakening, immunity, and political well-being, particularly in her depictions of public rallies and street protests:

> The despotic and extravagant steps taken, to give efficiency to the *cour plèniere*, awakened the sensibility of the most torpid; and the vigilance of twenty-five millions of centinels was roused, to watch the movements of the court, and follow its corrupt ministers.[110]

Like Thomas Carlyle's later representation of the almost tragic optimism of the 'twenty-five millions' in his *French Revolution: A History* (1837), Wollstonecraft's understanding of political consensus in these moments is highly concrete, arising from 'local, specific, and radical convergences of feeling' that can 'blur individual identities and distinctions'. Whereas the Burkean revolutionary multitude is always prone to violence, savagery, and irrationality via a chaotic aggregation of individual, negative emotions, Wollstonecraft's multitude is more often united in forms of collective association that are 'triumphant', 'orderly', and rhythmically synchronous, 'marching in unison with their reflections' and advancing 'but slowly' 'with the measured step of thought, or rather sadness'.[111]

Drawn from descriptions of revolutionary festivals by Rousseau, Michelet, and others, Wollstonecraft's depiction of orderly and contemplative revolutionary crowds has three aims: first, to reconcile the collective action of the people with the principles of cognitive and virtuous feeling she outlines in her *Vindications*; second, to sever the sympathetic and emotional ties that link the people to the monarchy by redirecting them towards a more principled and orderly sensibility that animates new forms of constituent power and acts as a kind of ameliorative medicine for the national body; and third, to rethink the causal determinism of philosophic history by allowing for the prospect of radical change in the present and future.[112] Like Rousseau, Wollstonecraft's ideal revolutionary crowd is a controlled one of 'healthy stimuli management' rather than one of unruly mass violence or animal instincts, but she nonetheless represents the people as capable of experiencing, reflecting, and making choices, however premature their judgments may be.[113] As opposed to the Burkean tendency to abstract the feelings of the people, Wollstonecraft can imagine them in affective (albeit often temporary and/or volatile) relationships to the new republican state and its institutions of power, as, for example, in her description of the citizens of Grenoble acting together in 'one of those moments of enthusiasm, which ... unites all hearts', or the moment where the National Assembly vows to complete the constitution: 'The benedictions that dropped from every tongue, and sparkled in tears of joy from every eye ... produced an overflow of sensibility that kindled into a blaze of patriotism every social feeling.'[114]

In these moments of festive unison or benediction, the crowds tend to assume the instantaneous temporal category of the present, revealing the 'uneven intensities' and 'discordant rhythms' of human experiences that cannot always be subjugated to the developmental arc of stadial or progressive history.[115] More importantly, unlike Burke's passive, silent, reverent, and virtual 'multitudes', the people become both the subject and the causal agent of their own history. Through their collective exertions, they are figured as a body with an internal logic active enough to overthrow their oppressors and break away from the preordained space of Burkean inheritance and prescription. In suggesting that the people's emotional life can be pleasurable and productive rather than simply chaotic, angry, and destructive, Wollstonecraft imbues them with the germs of a future republican spirit that is simultaneously feeling and thinking.[116] Like Burke, she sees the Revolution as 'untimely' but only because it is a utopian proposition that is currently unattainable and 'improper for the degenerate society of France': 'Europe will probably be, for some years to come, in a state of anarchy; till a change of sentiments, gradually undermining the strong-holds of custom, alters the manners, without rousing the little passions of men.'[117]

In figuring the republican community primarily under the sign of the 'messianic–utopic trope', as the potentiality of 'something to come', Wollstonecraft pre-empts the view of present-day historians such as Sophie Wahnich, who argues that the French Revolution involved a radical redistribution of political power to a potentially sovereign people, 'a power transformed from unhappy and complaining bodies into a people disposing of powerful political logos'.[118] Yet Wollstonecraft also displays some ambivalence towards popular agency, seeing 'the great bulk of the people' as 'worse than savages; retaining much of the ignorance of barbarians, after ... imbibing some of the habits of degenerate refinement'. She uses gendered and racialised images of monstrosity to describe the violence against Marie Antoinette in her account of the October Days, calling the mob an 'odious' 'rabble' made up of 'vagabonds' incited by 'unnatural' feelings, although she does so primarily in order to argue that they were the dupe of the 'insidious arts' of aristocratic schemes rather than acting in a principled way as 'the effect of public spirit'. As in Burke's account, the female mob is symptomatic of an 'unnatural' type of revolutionary violence, but crucially for Wollstonecraft, the error lies in the practice and not in the precept of democratic governance: having 'neither sufficient purity of heart, nor maturity of judgment, to conduct [themselves] with moderation and prudence', the people are simply not ready to assume the mantle of sovereignty that is ultimately their right.[119]

While Wollstonecraft endorses Rousseau's conception of popular opinion or the 'general will' as the best source of political authority, her view of the revolutionary crowd echoes Aristotle's theory of class and catharsis in *Politics*, which distinguishes between the kind of cognitively based catharsis experienced by the naturally free citizens of the *polis* and that of workers or slaves, who experience 'emotional excitation, or hedonistic frenzy'.[120] Wollstonecraft's ambivalent view of the behaviour of the mob and her deferral of utopian social conditions should, however, be read in within the context of her rejection of the usurpation of education, rights, and property by the aristocratic classes. When she argues that restraint requires individuals who are leisured and educated, it is primarily to rebuke those who would limit the right of the people to access education and other resources, and naturalise a political order founded on the underdeveloped nature of their unreflective acquiescence:

> But it is a palpable errour to suppose, that men of every class are not equally susceptible of common improvement: if therefore it be the contrivance of any government, to preclude from a chance of improvement the greater part of the citizens of the state, it can be considered in no other light than as a monstrous tyranny.[121]

The domestic tragedy or 'little romance' in Burke's account thus gives way in Wollstonecraft's account to the larger social tragedy of the 'whole mass'. The people, having been enslaved for so long, act before their time and unleash the anarchy nurtured by the logic of their long oppression, an oppression that is spatialised in the text through the enclosures and 'barriers' of the architectural structures of Paris itself, which, erected 'by despotism to secure the payment of an oppressive tax', now render it a 'great prison' whose 'elegant structures' and 'magnificent porticoes' make 'anarchy more violent by concentration', 'cutting off the possibility of innocent victims escaping from the fury, or the mistake, of the moment'.[122]

It is in these very moments of chaos and anarchy that Wollstonecraft ventures to introduce her own narrative voice in direct, first-person or 'of the moment' addresses to the reader. As many critics have noted, in Book 2 of Chapter 2 there is a 'substantial shift in tone' or what Vivien Jones has characterised as something like a 'novelistic lapse'.[123] Beginning with a 'rhetorical declamation' that is similar to Burke's invocation of his memory of Marie Antoinette—'How silent is Versailles!'—the passage breaks into 'fragmented' bodily images ('foot', 'eye', 'nerves', 'heart', 'bosom', 'breath') and emotive statements. The history's philosophical style thus gives way to 'exclamatory writing to the moment', which seeks to 'record the feeling body in print' and 'display the pre-logical character of sensibility': 'I tremble, lest I should meet some unfortunate being, fleeing from the despotism of licentious freedom, hearing the snap of the *guillotine* at his heels.' Appealing to the sensibilities of her audience and haunted by this presentiment (and her own eyewitnessing) of the victims of the Terror, Wollstonecraft goes much further in harnessing anti-cognitive feeling here than she does in either of her *Vindications*, allowing for short moments of subjective emotional investment and embodied response that are nonetheless curtailed by her more analytical and philosophical objectives: such as, for example, when she concludes that the spectacle of public scenes of execution lies outside of her history and amounts to 'an insult to the reader's sensibility'.[124]

If it is important not to fixate on those moments where 'the rhetoric of the text conflicts with its argumentative surface', it is equally important not to see them merely as 'lapses' in either judgment or style. Gary Kelly has rightly argued for the deliberate 'conjunction of (feminine) novel paradigms with (masculine) history' in *A Historical and Moral View*, with Wollstonecraft attempting to reconcile both a 'gendered hierarchy in writing' and a 'sexed hierarchy of minds'.[125] In historiographical terms, the 'spectatorial dynamics' of these vivid present-tense interpolations fracture the philosophical objectivity of the text in ways that challenge the division between private reflection and historical discourse.[126] When Wollstonecraft allows herself to be a participatory actor as well as a historian and philosopher, to showcase her own proximity and acts of physical witnessing, she begins to rethink history as itself a potentially participatory and experiential rather than simply an observing discipline. Temporarily removing the distance established by her own philosophic and causal framework, one designed by Hume, Robertson, and other historians to safeguard the distinction between the 'involved' actor or participant and the 'impartial' observer or spectator, Wollstonecraft's approach enables her to layer multiple, coexisting levels of temporality—deep, human, objective, and subjective—in ways that mark out diverse and sometimes conflicting forms of historical time within a single discursive space.

From Sentiment to Experience

Using hierarchies of social and unsocial passions to sanction particular models of morally normative action, Burke's aim in *Reflections* is to immobilise historical meaning in both directions, simultaneously predicting the Revolution's future failure at the hands of internal forces within the National Assembly *and* turning the Revolution 'back towards a point of origin in "memory"' and nostalgic recollection.[127] As Zaki Nahaboo has pointed out, the centrality of prescription to Burke's stadial understanding of historical progress involves a necessary and 'constitutive forgetting of originary violence', recalling both Hume's account of how violence produces a habitual, if precarious, acquiescence in the people in his essay 'Of the Original Contract' (1748) and Ernest Renan's later idea that social forgetting is 'a crucial factor in the creation of a nation': 'it is possible', Burke writes, 'that many estates about you were originally obtained by arms ... but it is an old violence; and that which might be wrong in the beginning, is consecrated by time, and becomes lawful'.[128] Burke's premodern (and precapitalist) vision of historical progress naturalises past violences through inherited norms and the institutional forms that produce and reproduce them, resisting the pressure of radical historical change by foreclosing alternative narratives of the Revolution and defusing revolutionary struggles in the present and future.

Against Burke's methodological naturalism and his 'gendered archaic temporality of reproduction marked by repetition and immobility', Wollstonecraft's multitemporalised history shows the people challenging inherited rules of precedent, citation, and tradition. Wollstonecraft's philosophical framework provides its own, alternative idea of a normative past, one heavily influenced by the virtue ethics of classical republicanism. However, she also sketches out a regime of historicity that increasingly undermines its own causal determinism and foregrounds the extent to which any inherited norm is always open to revision. In allowing for positive examples of the people acting on their own authority, Wollstonecraft introduces the principles of novelty and contingency into her otherwise rationalist philosophic framework, foregrounding the capacity of events to disrupt a predetermined causal logic, and providing the tentative foundation from which a new agential subject could emerge.[129] Although both Burke and Wollstonecraft see collective consent as underpinning the political legitimacy of the post-1688 constitutional order, Burke's understanding of consent is primarily a negative one, resting on those habitual, affective, and voluntary attachments that ensure the absence of force as a political necessity. Any collective agential force involves the disintegration of the integrity of the national body and the chaotic aggregation of atomistic, individual, and primarily negative passions. Wollstonecraft's understanding of consent, on the other hand, rests on a participatory understanding of the large-scale solidarity and collective engagement of agential beings, who have the political capacity to act and make changes—one that in some ways preempts the current historiographical turn from structural accounts of the French Revolution to its experiential worlds.[130]

While I make no claims for Wollstonecraft's history as a 'people's history' in the sense of the recovery of the subjective experiences of ordinary historical actors, her emphasis on the historical agency of revolutionary crowds is highly sceptical of Burkean attempts to 'ensnare ordinary people in a giant web of nationhood pretending to a common interest'.[131] Both Burke and Wollstonecraft appeal to the value of experience, but whereas Burke relies on 'common' or practical experience (that is, tradition) as a means of resisting the *a priori*, metaphysical abstractions of 'first principles', Wollstonecraft rejects the reduction of experience to a form of intuitionism that distrusts the dynamic function and power of reason. Unlike Burke with his predetermined understanding of experience and his suggestion that peoplehood inheres in particular (and unchanging) forms of feeling, Wollstonecraft is interested in the potentiality of the lived experience of the Revolution's mass participants, and the extent to which their future is open, unfixed, or unbounded by the historical past. She thus understands mass association as a form of political representation rather than simply as a ritual, epiphenomenal, or physiological display. Her historiographical method is increasingly attuned to those structures of feeling that permeate ways of experiencing and being in the world, allowing for the prospective dimension of *becoming* in human history. It has long been noted that Carlyle develops precisely this type of experiential or 'human' history in his *French Revolution*, rereading Burke by replacing his 'economy of terror' with the 'economy of the event'. However, Wollstonecraft provides a model of experiential history nearly half a century before Carlyle's own representation of the Revolution as the site of a dynamic social world.[132]

Written from the vantage of 'the future perfect mode' rather than from within Burke's proleptic assumptions, Wollstonecraft's *Historical and Moral View* imagines the political possibility of a self-authorising people, even if this new democratic subjectivity remains an unrealised political reality.[133] Her view of the French Revolution rejects conservative representations of the revolutionary dynamic as essentially theatrical, spectatorial, and ahistorical by representing the people as being at the centre of a new structure of historical knowledge and meaning—as themselves potentially the proper subject of history. While Wollstonecraft remains suspicious of instinctive feeling and celebrates collective action only in its more 'healthy', 'orderly', or principled forms, her emphasis on the people's pedagogic transformation into active political consciousness involves a redistribution rather than a rejection of sentiment.[134] Even within her primarily cognitive, rationalist, and causal philosophic framework, Wollstonecraft's Revolution is a historically animating force, with the anonymous masses 'coming to life' or being lifted out of a 'world of unreflecting tradition': an idea that partly derives from her own witnessing of events in France and her extended research into eyewitness accounts of the Revolution.[135] Wollstonecraft's emerging understanding of political subjectivity as a contingent and self-correcting process thus represents historical change as emerging from within the field of experience itself. Her open and dynamic conception of experience as something severed from the lawful violences of tradition anticipates what Étienne Balibar, in his discussion of political legitimacy, has called an 'ideal universality', one that is linked to the 'notion of *insurrection*' and introduces 'the *unconditional* in the realm of politics'.[136]

Chapter 2

Historical Subjects and Ethical Character: Godwin and Carlyle

If the French Revolution was widely understood as an unfixed event belonging to the recent past and open to multiple reconfigurations, the English Revolution and Civil Wars occupied a more fully determined place in the historiography of the late eighteenth and early nineteenth centuries.[1] When Godwin began writing his *History of the Commonwealth* in January 1822, interpretations of the seventeenth-century English Republic were still dominated by Hume's eight-volume *History of England*, which was famously dismissive of religious enthusiasm and sceptical of the role of parliamentary liberty in the history of the English constitution.[2] Hume's counter-republican argument had already been ably rebutted by a series of radical and Whig rejoinders, from Catharine Macaulay's *History of England* to George Brodie's *History of the British Empire* (1822), but the history of the English Revolution remained an important means of party self-definition, not least because, as the Whig constitutional historian Henry Hallam pointed out, the seventeenth century was 'the period from which the factions of modern times trace their divergence'.[3]

Godwin himself had long rejected party histories of the English Commonwealth, arguing in 'Of History and Romance' that the ongoing differences between Whig and Tory historians paralleled earlier discrepancies between the eyewitness accounts of the republican Whitelocke and the royalist Clarendon. His subsequent distinction between the 'superficial' and the 'profound' historian condemns the former for choosing the historical perspective on the English Civil Wars that best suits his or her own prejudices, while crediting the latter with a sceptical awareness of the discontinuous and multiple possibilities of the past.[4] Correctly identifying that party prejudice had increasingly coalesced around assessments of Oliver Cromwell's life and character, Godwin saw his *History of the Commonwealth* as an evidence-based intervention into the 'accumulated slander and misconception' that characterised the existing historiography on Cromwell and the seventeenth-century republicans more generally. Moving away from Whig constitutionalism and adopting a broadly republican approach, Godwin's Cromwell is the complex and daring progenitor of 'a great and perilous [social] experiment' rather than a power-hungry usurper of English constitutional liberty or a one-dimensional hero of parliamentary democracy.[5]

Writing just over two decades later, a similarly revisionist aim marks Thomas Carlyle's *Oliver Cromwell's Letters and Speeches* (1845), where Carlyle attempts to disprove the notion that the Puritans were either 'superstitious crack-brained persons, given up to enthusiasm' or 'skillful Machiavels', as well as distinguishing his approach from those historians and biographers who do little more than amass 'a large heap of evidence and assertions', an 'Aggregate of bewildered jottings', in the haphazard and irresolute manner of the antiquarian.[6] Godwin and Carlyle were not, of course, the only historians to rethink Cromwell's life and legacies: the question of whether the Protector was good, bad, or indifferent looms large in just about every history of the seventeenth century, from Hume's *History of England* to Robert Southey's *Book of the Church* (1824).[7] Yet unlike Whig historians such as Hallam and T. B. Macaulay, who deem Cromwell a 'great general' and 'prince' but pronounce him '[i]nsignificant as a private citizen', Godwin and Carlyle both attempt to restore a sense of Cromwell as an active and emergent historical subject, who experiences years of internal conflict and external upheaval.[8]

In order to provide a dynamic sense of 'becoming Cromwell', Godwin renovates seventeenth-century historical techniques such as character sketches and orations by combining them with psychological depth models of analysis that seek to 'assign the motives' of historical actors and 'trace up effects to the causes from which they sprung'.[9] The methodology employed in the *History of the Commonwealth* is less radically experimental than the indirect, rhizomatic model of representation that marks his earlier biographies, such as his *Life of Geoffrey Chaucer* (1806) and his *Lives of Edward and John Philips, Nephews and Pupils of Milton* (1815). However, Godwin continues to value the 'involutions' of the biographical subject, situating what is essentially a biography of Cromwell within a more conventional and chronological political history.[10] Carlyle, too, is concerned more with the inner than the outer Cromwell, aiming to provide a *'glimpse into the strange seething, simmering inner-man'*. His methodology of excavating Cromwell's character from personal documents intimates his intensified consciousness of historical selfhood and his commitment to the act of fashioning a self in written history. Whereas Godwin foregrounds Cromwell's deliberative, conscious, or rational thoughts, Carlyle's purpose is to capture artless, unmediated, and unconscious moments in Cromwell's letters and speeches, a task partly prompted by his interest in involuntary psychology and German transcendental idealism, and partly by his admiration for the formal realism of eighteenth-century epistolary novelists such as Goethe, Defoe, and Richardson.[11]

In combining the *Bildung* tendencies of the epistolary novel with the ethical and didactic bent of seventeenth-century character studies, Godwin and Carlyle attempt to study the evolving identities and belief systems of individual historical actors in their wider social and historical contexts. Concerned more with motive than with affect, the goal of their character studies is not to affect the reader deeply, but rather to reveal the psychic propensities or inner constructions of the mind through techniques such as self-dramatisation, invented orations, indirect narration, and internal rhetoric.[12] These internalising techniques reflect, I suggest, a wider shift within written history from the 1820s onwards from a physiological focus on the outward or bodily manifestations of affective experience towards a behaviouralist study of the historical self as an internalised subject-in-formation.[13] The transition from externalised character studies towards the study of the subjective mind in process emanated, in part, from literary models of character that emphasised psychological depth principles alongside the more pedagogical questions attaching to sentimental education. However, the emphasis on interiority in written history also emerged from two other developments that provided new technologies for the staging of historical selves: first, theories of the instability of the self in enlightenment faculty psychology; and second, revised understandings of classical rhetoric that emphasised both narrative's power to engage the emotions and the ways in which the internal workings of the human mind could be used to represent historical character.[14] Changing understandings of rhetoric, newly psychologised accounts of identity, and the ascent of the sentimental novel should therefore be understood as interrelated developments that were repurposed in early nineteenth-century historical writing.

Internal Rhetoric, Faculty Psychology, and Historical Character

In lectures twelve to fifteen of his widely circulated 'Lectures on Rhetoric', delivered in 1763, Adam Smith outlines a method of 'indirect narration' in written history, one that focuses not on descriptions of the 'quality of an object' but rather on 'the effect it has on those who behold it'.¹⁵ Unlike the 'direct' method of narration, which describes 'the external objects that are the objects of our senses', the indirect method narrates internal reactions as displayed by historical actors or spectators, primarily via physiological markers that 'affect the body ... and distort it in different ways'.¹⁶ Drawing a distinction between the poetic techniques of the 'indirect' and 'animated' Shakespeare and those of the 'direct' and 'allegorical' Spenser, Smith argues that the indirect method is 'in most cases by far the best', particularly in relation to descriptions of 'compound invisible objects' such as historical actors or characters. By allowing the historian to reveal the 'internal causes' or 'dispositions of the mind', an indirect account of the historical past 'will be more interesting and lead us into a science no less usefull': 'the knowledge of the motives by which men act'.¹⁷

Placing character and motive at the centre of his historical theory and practice, Smith's methodology partly aligns with older theories of ethical generalisation originating in classical sources such as Livy and Plutarch, and culminating in Lord Bolingbroke's *Letters on the Study and Use of History* (1752).¹⁸ As an instructive or 'useful' discourse, history requires the historian 'first, to give an account of the prevailing temper and passions of the [historical actor] ... and afterwards to give such observations of his conduct as will open up the general principles on which he acts'. Smith thus promotes character description primarily as a means of providing governing principles for the 'induction of ethical maxims' rather than as a way of illuminating the inner, emotional, or subjective dimensions of historical actors.¹⁹ Yet Smith's method of representing internal causes and effects also anticipates an important revision of the classical rules of historical exemplarity in historiographical practice, redirecting theories of causation inwards and effectively promoting a new kind of 'psychologically oriented criticism' that focuses on the study of the human mind.²⁰

In advocating an internalised or indirect approach to historical narration, Smith was drawing on Hume's pioneering account of identity in his *Treatise of Human Nature*. In the section titled 'Of personal identity', Hume first articulates the idea that a person is 'nothing but a bundle or collection of different [sensory] perceptions'. This 'bundle thesis' of personhood rejects older metaphysical or 'substance' theories of the self as constant or stable, and instead maintains that the self is in 'perpetual flux and movement': 'Our eyes cannot turn in their sockets without varying our perceptions. Our thought is still more variable than our sight, and all our other senses and faculties contribute to this change.'²¹ If Hume prioritises a perceptive ontology over all others here, it is because it helps to resolve the problem faced by sceptical philosophers that the mind might be totally inscrutable or unknowable. By identifying the mind with its perceptions, individual subjects can be known but only, Hume argues, indirectly or via 'scrutable perceptions':

> For my part, when I enter most intimately into what I call myself, I always stumble on some particular perception or other, of heat or cold, light or shade, love or hatred, pain or pleasure. I never can catch myself without a perception, and never can observe any thing but the perception.[22]

Like Hume, Smith can be broadly characterised as an empirical sensationalist and his method of indirect narration bears a close relationship to Hume's indirect theory of the self, in which interiority depends on bodily perception (and its limitations): in both cases, it is only that which is perceptible or scrutable that can provide any form of knowledge about internal thought and hence about subjectivity. As David Reisman has pointed out, Smith's interest in scrutability helps to explain his humanist interest in *belles lettres* more generally:

> whereas the natural sciences can but describe the 'primary qualities' of an object, the arts, recognising that size and shape are but a small part of our total sensory experience, can help us to convey to others our subjective perceptions of 'secondary experiences'.[23]

The latent empiricism of Smith's 'Lectures on Rhetoric' becomes more obvious in his later distinction between facts that are 'externally observable' and consist of 'transactions that pass without us', and facts that are 'internal' or 'the thoughts, sentiments or designs of men, which pass in their minds'. External objects can be described via either the indirect or the direct method, but internal objects such as 'passions and affections', which 'are the object of none of our senses', are not perceivable directly, and can *only* be described indirectly by their perceivable effects on others.[24]

Smith's empiricist understanding of historical character is reiterated in lecture fifteen, which argues that it is generally best 'to describe the character in the same order as the different views of a character naturally present themselves to us'. In lecture eighteen Smith similarly maintains that historical narration should occur 'in the same order as that in which the events themselves happened' since 'the mind naturally conceives that the facts happened in the order they are related'.[25] While he goes on to argue that the logic of cause and effect is paramount in historical discourse, Smith nonetheless advocates for a narrative that is 'faithful to experience' and the internal ordering mechanisms of human perception.[26] In part, Smith's emphasis on sequential ordering can be reconciled with his desire to distinguish a properly narrative history from philosophic or systematic enquiry (which may or may not take a sequential form), but he also promotes 'natural chronology' as a means of replicating 'the human mind unfolding its faculties in order'. He thus characterises the historical actor as an emergent subject, who is capable of evolving or changing over time—a view also taken up by other Scottish moral philosophers such as Dugald Stewart, whose *Elements of the Philosophy of the Human Mind* (1792) likewise emphasises the importance of observing and following the 'operations of our own mind'.[27]

Along with Hume's 'bundle thesis' of personhood, Smith's indirect method of character analysis provided one of the foundations for a new study of historical selfhood that was distinct from earlier character sketches or portraits of human character.[28] Encouraged, on the one hand, by Puritan religious introspection and the idea that individual lives formed part of a divine providential narrative, and on the other, by the vogue for secret histories and memoirs that blurred the boundaries between history and fiction, character sketches were a crucial part of seventeenth-century historiography, even if these sketches were sometimes sequestered from primary historical accounts.[29]

In her study of the economy of inner meaning in the long eighteenth century, Deidre Lynch diagnoses a gradual transformation from early modern character sketches to romantic approaches to character, with the former seeing character as generic, figural, or typological (that is, as exemplar) and the latter representing character as imbued with an 'inner life with "deep" meanings' (that is, as identity). Lynch dates this new focus on identity to the Shakespeare criticism of the 1770s and 1780s, which developed the view that Shakespeare's characters inaugurated the modern individuated subject and its 'project of self-production'.[30] Carlyle himself did much to perpetuate a 'depth' view of character, maintaining in 'Goethe's Works', published in the *Foreign Quarterly Review* in 1832, that Goethe's characters, and in particular his Hamlet-like Wilhelm Meister, have 'a verisimilitude and life that separates them from all other fictions of late ages. All others, in comparison, have more or less the nature of hollow vizards, constructed from without inwards, painted *like*.'[31]

While eighteenth-century historians had already demonstrated a more persistent and regular use of the unseen or inner motivations of character than the humanist exemplarity of early modern set-pieces, their representation of internal motives tended to be represented via the 'indirect' physiological markers Smith outlines (tears, sighs, blushes, and so on). The popularity of the coming-of-age novel, and its reinvention in the historical novel, ensured that internalised conceptions of character increasingly became relevant to the representation of historical actors in written history.[32] Following Scott's Waverley novels, British readers expected both a dynamic 'sense of character ... shaped by the density of material relations' and one that allowed for an internalised sense of reality, with historians increasingly recognising the value of those techniques that 'allowed novelists to display unmediated access to other minds'.[33] This is not, of course, to suggest that exemplarity entirely disappeared as a criterion in written history. As Stefan Collini has pointed out, nineteenth-century thought is shot through with the 'survivals and mutations' of the language of civic humanism while also being increasingly imbued with a new psychologising preoccupation with the internal patterns and perceptions of the human mind.[34]

Alongside this acknowledgement of the inner life of historical actors, Mark Salber Phillips has pointed to a simultaneous awareness in the early nineteenth century of the affective power of primary documents as expressive and dramatic texts, which could effectively be arranged and edited rather than simply reworked into narrative.[35] This was, of course, a recognisable strategy in eighteenth-century epistolary fiction and accordingly brought history closer to fictional forms, especially to 'Richardson's desire to create "dramatic" narratives' through familiar letters.[36] If, as some critics have claimed, it was precisely at this time that epistolary fiction went out of fashion, historical writers in the early to mid-nineteenth century undertook new experiments in documentary editing, 'expanding the ethical possibilities' of sentimental fiction and historical biography 'in tandem with ... more traditional defense[s] of [historical] exemplarity'.[37]

Carlyle's own interest in individual memory and subjective writing was partly a reflection of the primary sources on the English Revolution he read over a twenty-year period, such as Clarendon's *History of the Rebellion* (wr. 1646–8; pub. 1720), Ludlow's *Memoirs* (pub. 1698–9), Milton's prose works, Thomas Burton's *Diary* (pub. 1828), and the Thomason Tracts and the D'Ewes manuscripts in the British Museum.[38] Godwin, too, paid special attention to eyewitness accounts when writing his *History of the Commonwealth*, poring over correspondence, memoirs, biographies, parliamentary reports, extracts from the Journal of Commons, records at the State Paper Office, the Order Books of the Council of State, and the Commonwealth Tracts held at the British Museum.[39] While both writers sometimes simply quote or incorporate this material into their accounts of the English Revolution, they also use eyewitness accounts to create character sketches and internalised first-person orations—a rhetorical technique that was widely used from antiquity to the seventeenth century but had otherwise largely been abandoned by the mid-eighteenth century. Hugh Blair notes approvingly in his *Lectures on Rhetoric and Belles Lettres* (1783), for example, that orations have been put aside by modern historians on the basis that they are unsuitable to the factual nature of historical writing by forming 'a mixture which is unnatural in History, of fiction and truth'.[40]

In reviving the classical custom of illuminating the motives of historical actors by creating fictitious speeches, Godwin and Carlyle foreground the role of subjective experience in constructing the self-in-society, using internalised speech to resolve 'ambiguous or conflicting imperatives for attitude, decision, and action'.[41] Dating back to Aristotle and Plato, the idea of self-examination or self-persuasion was a critical part of eighteenth-century moral philosophy, particularly for those thinkers who rejected Lockean associationalist principles and other empiricist theories primarily concerned with the role of the faculties in responding to external stimuli. Even those seventeenth- and early eighteenth-century thinkers who were open to empiricism, such as Francis Bacon and Lord Shaftesbury, tended to see the rhetorical self as a moral agent, who is able to debate conflicting or multiple viewpoints before coming to a committed decision. Bacon argues in his *Advancement of Learning* (1605), for instance, that internal rhetoric or self-examination provides the means by which reason 'is able to guide the proclivities of the mind' over man's natural desire to satisfy the appetites, emotions, or affections. Shaftesbury, too, advocates self-examination or internal dialogue in his *Soliloquy; or Advice to an Author* (1710) as a mechanism of conscience and as a means of encouraging reason to gain control over the passionate energies of the psyche.[42]

For both Bacon and Shaftesbury, the negotiative, dialogic, and discursive aspects of internal rhetoric are essential to any kind of functional definition of the self, as well as to the process of ethical decision making.[43] Following the interventions of empirical faculty psychology, nineteenth-century moral philosophers such Richard Whately tended to see internal rhetoric in more ambivalent terms: that is, as something separable from virtue and even conducive to the undermining of virtue. In his *Elements of Rhetoric* (1826), Whately is forced to defend the use of pathos or 'emotional appeals in public rhetoric', arguing for the need to excite '"rational and *rightly directed*" emotions' in order to establish both the propriety and desirability of a proposed action. Drawing on the ideas of the British moral sense school of philosophy, Whately's view of moral sense positions it as an innate faculty founded on (primary) emotions rather than (secondary) reasoning—one that can be either cultivated or corrupted but nonetheless provides the most significant means of arbitrating what is right and wrong.[44] Jean Nienkamp, in her study of the history of internal rhetoric, accordingly isolates a critical distinction between what she calls 'cultivated' (Bacon and Shaftesbury) and 'uncultivated' (Whately) internal rhetoric, with the former aligned with moral reasoning and the suppression of emotions, and the latter with the idea of producing rational or rightly directed emotions in order to reinforce moral precepts.[45]

Godwin, like Whately, tends to conceive of subject formation as an internal struggle between passions and reason. He therefore sees internal rhetoric as 'uncultivated' or separable from virtue. However, Godwin is more suspicious than Whately of sentimental communication, oratory, and other kinds of emotional, persuasive, or performative utterances, particularly those that attempt to assign to words a promissory function. As Angela Esterhammer has pointed out, throughout *Political Justice* 'performative utterances violate the role that Godwin assigns to language in an ideal society' by moving away from accuracy, veracity, and 'communicative truth'. Many of Godwin's novels similarly demonstrate the disastrous result of dialogues or speech acts in which words are 'not fully constative representations of reality'.[46]

Focusing on exactly these moments of internal doubt, dissolution, and self-deception, Godwin's representation of Cromwell in his *History of the Commonwealth* in many ways rests on the distinction in his *Letters of Mucius* (1785–6) between the learned and persuasive functions of rhetoric, and his juxtaposition of 'the reasonings of the wise' with the 'speeches of the eloquent'.[47] Like the 'peculiarly performative identities' of Godwin's fictional characters, Cromwell's internalised testimony demonstrates how identities can be deformed by self-persuasion and fraudulent beliefs that distort the civic–humanist tradition of republican virtue, as well as revealing the interrelationship between private or personal feeling and institutional systems.[48] Carlyle, on the other hand, sees Cromwell's letters and speeches as the most authentic way of representing his character, emphasising his hero's sincerity, especially during those candid moments of human behaviour and motivation in which unmediated and/or unconscious impulses come into play. Yet while Carlyle focuses more on the unmediated self of Cromwell's letters and speeches than he does with any overt form of self-examination or internal rhetoric, he increasingly inserts his own editorial interventions into Cromwell's own accounts of events, ventriloquising Cromwell's responses to actions and events in ways that problematise his claims to unmediated representation.

Internal Rhetoric in Godwin's *History of the Commonwealth*

If, in 'Of History and Romance', Godwin provides the 'philosophical underpinning' for a type of history that allows for acts of affective and imaginative identification, by the 1810s and 1820s he had come to associate historical writing with 'patient enquiry and sober judgement', arguing in his *History of the Commonwealth* that what 'few uncertain conjectures' the historian is allowed are 'restrained at every moment by the majesty of truth, and the austerity of the school in which we have entered ourselves pupils'.[49] Despite Godwin's ongoing rejection of a disembodied objectivity towards the past, his strict scrutiny of documentary evidence acts as a disciplining force to the historical scepticism he promotes elsewhere, resulting in a sense that the historian's activity is not primarily rhetorical or performative but rather consists of 'a fair and severe examination of evidence, and the not suffering any respect of persons, or approbation of a cause, to lead the writer to misapprehend or misrepresent the nature of facts'.[50] The 'dearest aim' of his *History* is thus 'to attend to the neglected, to remember the forgotten, and to distribute an impartial award on all that was planned and achieved during this eventful period'.[51]

Partly viewing history through the recuperative lens of memory, Godwin's desire to be 'impartial' is sometimes in tension with his quest to uncover sites of oblivion in ways that attend to the persistent and active interconnections between past, present, and future. Drawing on the lessons of his Dissenting education, as well as on Mary Wollstonecraft's emphasis on a radical Commonwealth counter-tradition of rational Protestant Dissent, Godwin focalises his *History* in terms of a diminished present and desired future, representing English history after the Restoration as 'the history of negotiations and tricks', 'revenues and debts', 'corruption and political profligacy'. Although he declines to draw explicit parallels between the English republicans and French Jacobins, arguing instead for the historical uniqueness of the English Revolution, Godwin nonetheless contrasts a sublime republican fervour and fraternalism with the sobriety of modern times, maintaining that Englishmen have become 'the sons of the fog and the mist . . . we turn speculative man and calculators: timorous prudence and low circumspection fix their stamp on all we do'.[52]

Yet even as he admits to a desire to revive republican fervour in England, Godwin's understanding of impartiality is intimately tied to questions of documentary evidence and the rejection of party bias, reflecting both his long-standing resistance to projective and partisan accounts of the English Civil Wars, and his embrace of eyewitness and other primary sources that could be used to test secondary sources for biases and inaccuracies.[53] Godwin is certainly clear about his difficulties with sources, making the process of source criticism open and transparent, and foregrounding the impossibility of ever fully reconstructing or reviving the past. He notes with respect to the governance of Ireland under Cromwell, for example, that 'much is left in obscurity'; and in relation to Cromwell's dealings with Charles I, he reveals his ongoing interest in historical contingency by maintaining that 'a very small change . . . may make the most essential change in the spirit of the tale'. Spoken words, in particular, are 'merely expressive of an intention' and can therefore 'never be weighed against a tissue and series of historical facts'.[54]

Godwin nonetheless concedes that eyewitness accounts and other primary documents serve as the most direct and immediate link to the historical events and personages of the times.[55] Even within the formally conservative confines of official history, he is more committed to the narrative possibilities offered by eyewitness accounts than he is to philosophic methods of causation, maintaining that abstract speculations have no 'place in history', and questioning the desirability of a distanced, impersonal objectivity towards the past: 'If the events of which I treat had preceded the Universal Deluge, or passed in the remotest island of the South Sea, that ought to make me sober, deliberate and just in my decisions: it ought not to make me indifferent to human rights, improvement or happiness.' Prizing impartiality *only* to the extent that it avoids ideological and polemical debate, Godwin instead wishes to be the kind of transferential or intersubjective historian who is 'feeling as well as thinking': 'I have no desire to be thought to look upon such transactions with indifference . . . If to treat good and evil as things having no essential difference, be impartiality, such impartiality I disavow.'[56]

Godwin's insistence on the importance of personal feeling and 'microscopical observations' 'gleaned' from 'indications' hints at the ongoing influence of the sympathetic and 'agent-centred historicism' he outlines in 'Of History and Romance'.[57] In that essay, his objection to philosophic history rests both on its distrust of exciting strong, 'effeminising' feelings in the reader and on its reliance on abstract categories and universal laws rather than on individual character, motives, and beliefs.[58] Arguing that readers are inherently more interested in the exploits of a daring individual than they are in those of a group of senators, Godwin revives a history of character and motive in the *History of the Commonwealth*, juxtaposing character studies in order to emphasise 'common structural features and significant sequences' within republican history, and drawing comparisons and parallels between central figures such as Cromwell, Fairfax, Lilburne, Ireton, and Vane. He compares for instance, Fairfax's innocence in council with Cromwell's superior powers of penetration, and Ireton and Vane's inflexible integrity with Cromwell's adaptability.[59] Godwin is certainly more consistently interested in individual character portraits than Hume, who becomes increasingly concerned in the final section of the last volume of his *History of England* to trace the longer progressive arc of European social, political, and economic systems. While Godwin retains a philosophic structure, dividing his content into distinct chapters on constitutional law, religion, Scottish and Irish affairs, and so forth, he nonetheless reverses Hume's concluding emphasis on metanarratives of progress by essentially appending a biography of Cromwell to the end of his chronological account of the English Revolution.

It was for this reason that the *Congregational Magazine* noted in 1825 that Godwin observes a 'much more sparing use of those gratuitous explanations, conjectures, philosophizings ... of which modern historians, after the fashion of Hume, have become so fond'. Although he is criticised by some reviewers for retaining the outlines of a philosophic structure, there is a consensus among critics that Godwin has correctly recognised the primary goal of a 'new type' of historian: that of identifying himself with the motives of the historical actors he describes, diving 'into the human heart with an almost Shakespearean power'.[60] In the second volume of the *History*, Godwin even talks of calling up historical personages from the dead, returning, even if only momentarily and with an acute sense of its impossibility, to that historiography of presence asserted more forcibly in 'Of History and Romance':

> History in some of its most essential members dies, even as generations of men pass off the stage ... If we could call up Cromwel from the dead ... how many doubts would be cleared up, how many perplexing matters would be unravelled, and what a multitude of interesting anecdotes would be revealed to the eyes of posterity!

Godwin's previously confident assertion that history is a matter of evidentiary fact is here replaced by the tentative language of 'seemings', 'inferences', and 'gropings', suggesting that there is no clear or unmediated ontological reality for the historian to access and resurrect. Yet despite his acknowledgement of history's speculative nature, Godwin continues to minimise sentimental and suasive techniques throughout his *History*, claiming that 'he has endeavoured to guard [him]self against mere declamation, and that form of language in which passion prevails to the obscuring of judgment'.[61]

Godwin's rejection of rhetorical sentimentality as a historical mode is particularly evident in the *History*'s trial scenes, where, unlike Hume's affective account of the spectators' 'unsuborned tears', the trial and execution of Charles I is rendered in the idiom of legal formality, and largely given over to an evaluation of the veracity of prior accounts.[62] Godwin's description of Cromwell's death is not particularly affecting either, concentrating instead on debunking myths relating to conversations between Cromwell and Goodwin, a divine who was at his death bed.[63] Refusing to shed a tear for either distressed monarchy or disillusioned republicans, it is only the topic of Ireland that leads Godwin to lower his mask of assumed impartiality.[64] Although relegated to the safe sanctuary of a footnote on the margins of the text, Godwin's reaction to Cromwell's treatment of the Irish people is remarkable both for its uncharacteristic deployment of affect and for its foregrounding of his own identity as a feeling subject:

> It was this picture that caused my pen to drop from my hand, at the close of the twentieth chapter of the Third Book of my work. I endeavoured to figure to myself three fourths of the territory of Ireland without an inhabitant – no soul left through its cities, its uplands, its vallies, its farm-houses, and its granges, but the English invaders, and their English families. I own the weakness of my understanding and my imagination; I could not take it in.[65]

Yet despite this being one of the few instances of authorial identification with the historical past, Godwin goes on to deny the theory of conquest popularised by Augustin Thierry and to undermine his own sentimental rendition of Irish resettlement by concluding that '[n]o transaction in history has experienced so extensive and successful a misrepresentation', and that a massacre and expulsion of all the 'native Irish' would not have been in the interests of the new settlers because of the cost of bringing labourers from England.[66]

Godwin's rationalisation of the English land settlements is part of his attempt to defend Cromwell from attacks by both Whigs and Tories. In volume three he provides an apology for the severity of Cromwell's actions while Lord Lieutenant of Ireland, arguing that, although '[t]here is scarcely a military commander on record, who was endowed with a more kindly and liberal disposition', Cromwell was forced to exhibit 'some examples of an appalling severity' while nonetheless believing that 'a certain cruelty in such a case was real humanity'. Godwin dismisses another possible motive—Cromwell's hatred of popery—with a disclaimer: 'How far he was influenced by these less manly and enlightened considerations it is perhaps impossible for us to pronounce.' Ultimately, Godwin defends Cromwell's actions at Drogheda and elsewhere in utilitarian terms: 'Nothing can be more obvious, than the horror and violent revulsion of the human heart at the contemplation of such a scene. But the true question is, as to the mode in which the greatest good shall be effected.'[67]

As David O'Shaughnessy has noted, Godwin, in effect, synthesises both sides of the argument about the British invasion of Ireland, acknowledging Irish civility to a degree but also defending Cromwell and condemning Catholic superstition, priestcraft, and violence.[68] While Cromwell's brutal, possibly even genocidal, behaviour in Ireland is a fault that Godwin cannot completely elide, his in-depth consideration of Cromwell amounts to a reassessment of the character of a historical actor who had been dismissed, even by radical and Whig historians like Catherine Macaulay, as a 'base, vain-glorious man'. Godwin represents the overthrow of Vane as an unfortunate detour in English history, but he justifies Cromwell's actions by arguing that his reign was necessarily one of experiments, during which he was 'driven from one inconsistent and undesirable mode of proceeding to another'. By volume four Cromwell is transformed from a model of hypocritical self-deception, who has made 'a dupe of himself', into an almost heroic figure struggling with the practical realities of dealing with an unenlightened and ungrateful populace.[69]

Godwin's representation of Cromwell bears a striking resemblance to his portrayal of William Pitt in his earlier *History of the Life of William Pitt* (1783).[70] A precursor of the slow progress that alters Cromwell's intentions and warps his understanding, Pitt begins by promoting parliamentary enquiry, but eventually temporises on key issues of governance and speaks in a 'dry and unanimated style'. Like Pitt, Cromwell is represented as the victim of his own uncontrollable spirit of ambition and self-deception, a conversion that is similarly depicted in the *History of the Commonwealth* through a series of internalised orations:

> This is the true key and explanation (thus reasoned Cromwel) to the unsettled and unnatural state of the people of England, from the commencement of the commonwealth, and in reality from the beginning of the civil war ... Once give them a king, and this unnatural state will be brought to an end ... I am called, by a most striking series of events, and (as Cromwel no doubt thought) by the voice of God himself, to seize the vacant throne; and by so doing I shall secure the everlasting gratitude of posterity.[71]

As the *Monthly Magazine* commented in 1829, Godwin aims to convey here a sense of a mind in process, showing the necessity under which Cromwell acted and using eyewitness sources to imagine how his leading agent might have thought, spoken, and acted.[72] In highlighting the rhetorical nature of deliberative or self-persuasive thought, Godwin is able to dramatise the conflicting interplay between reason and desire in Cromwell's psyche, using the oration technique to show how circumstances pervert Cromwell's capacity for reason, as well as imbuing cultural institutions (such as the monarchy) with the capacity to deform self-understanding and virtue in ways that highlight the socio-historical situatedness of the ethical deliberator.[73]

Repurposing a method of psychological determinism he had pioneered in *Political Justice*, Godwin's orations emphasise that historical individuals are socially conditioned beings, tracing behaviour to opinion and belief, and arguing for the importance of creating ideational environments that facilitate the development of the rational faculties. The ongoing tension in the *History* between Godwin's preoccupation with individual historical actors and his desire to illuminate the wider social structures and institutional identities that shape those individual characters is resolved, first, by linking Cromwell's motives to the larger social and political discourses of which he is part; and second, by extending the study of psychological impulses to an analysis of institutions, collectives, and political states. The *History* takes into account, for instance, the collective psychological phenomena of seventeenth-century England, such as the mind-set of various religious groups, and the fluctuating feelings and beliefs of the English public, representing the republican moment as an unresolved clash between emergent modern, enlightened forces and feudal, anarchic forces, which do not (as yet) conform to the process of rational improvement envisaged in *Political Justice*.[74]

In a series of psychological observations on the 'public mind' in volume three, Godwin showcases the conflict between the conservative forces of custom and the revolutionary activity involved in the dynamic restructuring of custom:

> Those who remained unconvinced were still a clog and an impediment to such as deemed themselves of more ripened judgment: and it was of the last importance to calculate the numbers of those who adhered to the old impressions, how tenaciously they would resist innovation, and in what degree, whether with a quicker or slower process, they were likely to be brought over by persons who desired to enlighten them.[75]

Unlike Burke and Wollstonecraft's epiphenomenal representations of revolutionary crowds, Godwin's collectives are not ritual crowds or even depictions of enthusiastic, sympathy-driven interactions, but rather representations of opposing mental states or attitudes. 'Nothing', he argues, 'can be more unlike than the different frames of public mind demanded under these two forms of government. Wherever a court exists ... the manners and habits of the court will diffuse themselves on every side.'[76] When Godwin locates political belief in unfixed or undecided collective mentalities, he not only provides a history of the public mind, but also situates those collective mental states within larger structures of belief that are closely entangled with institutional systems from monarchy to republicanism.

Tilottama Rajan has argued that Godwin's negative representation of the unenlightened 'tyranny of the majority' during the Cromwellian interregnum ultimately makes the *History of the Commonwealth* the history of collectivity interfering with an individual's relation to his own conscience.[77] Godwin's political rationalism and antipathy towards mass political action are well known, and there is indeed a strong sense throughout the *History* that the English people are not yet sufficiently enlightened to appreciate republicanism. Michael Edson has more recently reframed Godwin's antipathy to mass protest in a more positive way, arguing that it is suggestive of Godwin's interest in nonconformity, pluralism, and epistemic diversity. While Godwin is nearly always opposed to plebeian revolutions, he takes a consistently sociological approach to the collective mind. The 'multitude' in the *History*, however misguided, is a barometer for social change, suggesting both Godwin's acceptance of the importance of 'divergent opinions and ideologies', and his understanding of individual judgment as a faculty with social dimensions.[78]

Yet, like Burke, Godwin isolates a problematic discrepancy between theory and practice when it comes to revolutions: since he believes that government is founded in opinion, it naturally follows that reform can best be achieved by slowly changing people's opinions. In theory, then, it is wrong 'to impose the most unequivocal benefit upon a man, or body of men, which he or they want the inclination to accept' in the way of the imposition of Puritanism via a military dictatorship. However, in practice, no theory will fit every case, and in the case of the English Republic, Godwin appeals to the law of general advantage in arguing that its plebeian unpopularity—and the question of consent more generally—is of secondary concern to its wider social benefits.[79]

The discrepancy between theory and practice that Godwin isolates in relation to the issue of the Republic's unpopularity re-emerges in a more historiographical context at the very end of the *History*, where Godwin reflects on the practical business of writing history and raises the representational problem with which this book began: the extent to which the emotional complexity of historical actors defies the theoretical dictates of the 'philosopher in his closet'. Commenting on a letter from Warwick to the Protector three weeks after the death of his grandson, Godwin maintains that private sentiments smooth 'the rugged brow of history, and relieve[s] the harshness and severity of its delineations and reflections'. Here he tentatively reasserts the value of (private) romance over (public) history, arguing that it is in relation to personal and domestic sentiment 'that a tale of fictitious adventures so strikingly excels the reality of recorded events': in the romance 'we can look without rebuke into the inmost heart of our personages, and describe all they thought, and all they felt; while in history we can only collect a dry outline, and timidly allow ourselves in a few uncertain conjectures'.[80] Godwin thus ends the final volume of his *History of the Commonwealth* with a sense of the limitations of the kind of history he has himself pursued in its first three volumes, returning, to some degree, to the sceptical agenda and methodological self-consciousness more aggressively asserted in 'Of History and Romance'.[81]

Historical Subjectivity in Carlyle's *Cromwell*

Carlyle's first attempts to write on the seventeenth century were structured around a series of psychologically oriented 'mental portraits' or 'sketches of English character' along the lines of Friedrich Schiller's focus on national character in *A History of the Thirty Years War* (1793).[82] Carlyle began by taking notes for an unfinished 'Essay on the genius & character of Milton' and 'a kind of Essay on the Civil Wars' in March and April of 1822, but it was not until twenty years later, in 1842–3, that he returned to the idea of writing sketches of the seventeenth century.[83] Published posthumously by Alexander Carlyle as *Historical Sketches of Notable Persons and Events in the Reigns of James I and Charles I* (1898), these sketches isolate climactic scenes from the two reigns in question, as well as experimenting with different ways of revealing the character of individual historical actors, such as Charles I, Jenny Geddes, and Lord Strafford. Carlyle refers to his unfinished sketches as 'fragments' that were 'fished out . . . from much other Cromwellian rubbish'. Indeed, the very nature of the 'sketch' is suggestive of its resistance to an overarching narrative or philosophic design: even the chronological order and chapter divisions later supplied by Alexander Carlyle provide little in the way of philosophic generality or narrative structure to these self-proclaimed 'fragments' from the wreckage of the past.[84]

Carlyle's interest in the 'Biography of great men' in *On Heroes, Hero-Worship, and the Heroic in History* (1841) subsequently led him to focus his attention solely on Cromwell. However, he continued to search for a form that could adequately capture the drama and interiority towards which he strived: 'No work I ever tried gets on worse with me than this of Cromwell. I know not for my life in what way to take it up, how to get into the heart of it, what on earth to do with it.'[85] Carlyle's comments suggest that the writing of *Cromwell* was in many ways a 'personal struggle', but he was troubled not so much by the contentious nature of his material as by its resistance to dramatic and symbolic treatment.[86] As Chris Vanden Bossche has pointed out, Carlyle struggled to isolate climactic scenes that could provide a 'structural nucleus' for his work and even considered the idea of casting it in the form of an epic drama in twelve acts, as well as contemplating other fictional forms, including imaginary dialogues between Mrs Cromwell and Dr Sinnott, and an invocation to the ghost of Cromwell. Yet apart from the 'great scene' of Jenny Geddes, he was distressed to find that the history of the English Republic contained 'no *action*' and was 'not *dramatic*'.[87]

If Carlyle found Cromwell 'amorphous' as a biographical subject, it was not for lack of an immersion into his hero's life and times. In preparation for the writing of his history, he went to St Ives and Hinchinbrook, where Cromwell had grown up, and inspected the battlefields of Naseby and Dunbar.[88] The problem, as Carlyle had already recognised in his earlier 1830s essays on history and biography, was both conceptual and formal, and revolved around the methodological difficulties of narrating the interior life and motivations of ultimately unstable and unknowable subjects:

> But if one Biography, nay our own Biography, study and recapitulate it as we may, remains in so many points unintelligible to us; how much more must these million, the very facts of which, to say nothing of the purpose of them, we know not, and cannot know![89]

Desperate for a new form that could capture both the dramatic shape and the interiority he deemed essential to producing a lived experience of the past, Carlyle decided to create a sort of hybrid historical biography of Cromwell through his letters and speeches, one that could imbue a traditionally objective form of writing with a greater sense of subjective inwardness. Like Godwin, Carlyle is highly alert to the special significance of primary documents for uncovering both the biographical subject and his or her social context. Cromwell's letters and speeches are the lone beacons of 'faint authentic twilight' in the antiquarian darkness he describes, and it is only by reviving the 'spoken' and written contents of these kinds of primary, subjective, and often personal documents that he can hope to deliver a living, breathing history of the seventeenth century, in which he will 'struggle piously, passionately, to behold, if but in glimpses, the faces of our vanished Fathers'.[90]

Although he expresses his dissatisfaction with inaccurate secret histories written from an overtly subjective perspective, such as Bishop Burnet's *History of his Own Time* (1734), Carlyle repeatedly emphasises the special value of authentic acts of original perception in creating his expressive portrait of Cromwell, arguing for the inherent historical meaning of his hero's words:

> Even if false, these words, authentically spoken and written by the chief actor in the business, must be of prime moment for understanding of it. These are the words this man found suitablest to represent the Things themselves, around him, and in him, of which we seek a History.[91]

Vowing to rescue Cromwell's 'authentic utterances' from the 'foul Lethean quagmires' and 'unspeakable Historical Provinces' where they lie buried by pedants, dilettantes, and other examples of 'prurient Stupidity', Carlyle prioritises Cromwell's self-expression above all other historical accounts while simultaneously recognising the potential impartiality and inaccuracy of eyewitness testimony: even the most the credible of witnesses, like Cromwell, provides only a tantalising glimpse of something that is incomplete or partial, a 'kind of window through which a man *might* see'.[92]

As the nearest material record of Cromwell's everyday experience and inner life, Carlyle was attracted to the letters and speeches format because of the access it provided to the kind of unmediated inward feeling and spontaneous self-actualisation that he prized in eighteenth-century novels. Unlike the '[s]hip-loads of Fashionable Novels', which are an unfortunate hiatus in the novel's commitment to realism, the epistolary or diarised novels he associates with Defoe and Richardson attempt to present the immediacy of 'real' life and thus to align their work with the instructive value of history.[93] Drawing on the commonplace that letters are the most direct, sincere, and transparent form of written communication, Carlyle claims that Cromwell's letters are the 'fibre' and 'express image of the soul [they] came from', through which 'it becomes apparent that this Oliver was not a man of falsehoods, but a man of truths'.[94] At the same time, Carlyle is aware that Cromwell's letters are protean forms that invite reaction, dialogue, and other kinds of social exchange, and thus perform rather than simply represent his identity. Like those epistolary novels by Richardson and Defoe that Carlyle admired, Cromwell's letters reveal identity formation to be an ongoing, performative process rather than a fixed, determinate state.[95]

It becomes clear that Carlyle's objective is to show that Cromwell is 'groping his way through a very intricate business, which grows as he gropes' and therefore to demonstrate the dynamic nature of his character development as something produced 'in the moment'.[96] If he deliberately chooses a form that privileges Cromwell's voice and presents 'a monologic vision of Puritan culture' rather than the multiple and competing perspectives of his earlier *French Revolution*, it is because his goal is not just to emulate James Boswell's idea of the individual life as a portal to a wider social world, but also to use candid self-revelation in order show the evolution of the inner man.[97] Carlyle is particularly interested in the self-fashioning of Cromwell's character through the acts of speaking, writing, and reading.[98] Despite painting Cromwell as an 'inarticulate prophet' who prefers actions to words in *On Heroes*, Carlyle capitalises here on his hero's written and spoken words, seeing the quality and accuracy of his perceptions as a function of his moral character.[99]

In his review of 'Baillie the Covenanter' in the *Westminster Review* for 1842, Carlyle credits the importance of even fallible eyewitnesses like Baillie in reconstructing the past. But whereas Baillie's letters are 'like the hasty, breathless, confused *talk* of a man, looking face to face on that great whirl of things', Cromwell's letters exhibit a heroic, un-theatrical, and manly depth, the honesty of which is not to be doubted.[100] Carlyle's representation of Cromwell's honest speech and rude demeanour disrupts the dandified, polished elegance and decorum that characterises his depiction of the royalists, a rhetorical strategy that is also felt elsewhere in Carlyle's 'insistent opposition between the real and the sham, the hero and the quack' and '"savage depth" and polished, theatrical surfaces'. As James Eli Adams has pointed out, moral authority is located for Carlyle not in 'forms of civility' but rather in a 'charismatic subjectivity or interiority that is bodied forth in verbal and visual disruptions of social decorum'.[101]

Highlighting Cromwell's ability to transcend the 'demon of self-consciousness', Carlyle inverts the eighteenth-century association of heroism and rhetorical command with a new emphasis on the 'classless subject', presenting Cromwell's unselfconscious stylistic faults in letter-writing as the mark of his sincerity and authenticity: 'Practical Heroes ... do not speak in blank-verse; their trade does not altogether admit of that! Useless to look here for a Greek Temple with its porticoes and entablatures, and *styles*.'[102] In attempting to 'attach a normative masculinity' to a type of heroism that 'inheres less in action than in a mode of being', Carlyle embodies in Cromwell an extreme form of unselfconsciousness. As W. J. Fox insightfully noted in his 1846 lectures 'On the Study of History', the 'hypochondriasis' of Carlyle's Cromwell is 'the action of mind upon body, rather than of body upon mind ... With him, there is no breaking down within; there is a strong heart battling with the world, and with the things of the world.'[103] Cromwell's speeches, too, are, in the main, extempore rather than rehearsed, suggesting both a sincerity of purpose and intent, and an ideal congruence between his public and private character. While there is a basic formal division in the text between private letters and public speeches, Carlyle points to the interconnection between the free exchange of opinion in the public sphere and the domestic space of family life when he welcomes the 'little piece[s] of domesticity', the 'small family transaction[s]' that peep through 'great world-transactions', such as the marriage of a son or the birth of a child. Here Carlyle is responding to a significant change in biography exemplarity in the early nineteenth century, which, as Michael McKeon has argued, saw the gradual replacement of 'the illustrious by the domestic example'. Private experience is not an 'idle digression' or retreat from the social and political world but rather reveals 'some little of the genius of these distracted times'.[104]

Aware that in many of these sources Cromwell is writing (and speaking) at the crossroads of public and private expression, Carlyle not only privileges Cromwell's unconscious disclosures over his more overt actions or statements, but also directs the reader towards the margins, absences, silences, and gaps in Cromwell's correspondence: 'His words,—and still more his *silences*, and unconscious instincts, when you have spelt and lovingly deciphered these also out of his words,—will in several ways reward the study of an earnest man.'[105] Yet for all that the aesthetics of silence play an important role in Carlyle's theory of history, the role of the historian is ultimately to provide those silences with meaning, with Carlyle frequently embedding his own responses to Cromwell's silences into the text via a process that is signalled typographically by square brackets and italics. While most analyses of Carlyle's interventions dwell on the temporal montages and structural parallels that he creates as he merges his present-tense, first-person voice with events in the past, Carlyle also uses the interjections in an alternative way to hint at his hero's feelings, or to describe revealing gestures via physiognomic details that serve as outer expressions of Cromwell's inner life and character: '[*Does not his Highness look uncommonly animated?*]'; '[*His Highness elevating his brows; face assuming a look of irony, of rough banter.*]'.[106]

Notwithstanding his rejection of characters that are 'painted *like*', Carlyle's character portraits tend to draw on the visual or painterly techniques of portraiture. Not only did Carlyle value portraits as 'aids to his work as a biographer and historian', but the visual portrait could also, as Paul Barlow suggests, 'stand as a "symbol", a resistance to articulation by narrative'.[107] Carlyle thus uses the idiom of biographical portraiture and the iconographic, ekphrastic style to 'prompt reflection on the "interior" realm of symbolic meaning' rather than merely as an external sign of the 'great man' or as a heroic focal point for national memory.[108] Certainly, his pictorial style was integral to his embrace of physiognomy as part of 'a fully legibly expression of the person', drawing on works of nervous physiology such as Charles Bell's popular *Essays on the Anatomy of Expression* (1806; 1824; 1844). However, Carlyle also interweaves within his primary documents Cromwell's internalised self-interpretations of events and actions—'[*I would not be misunderstood in this*]'—rather than focusing purely on the outward or bodily manifestations of emotions.[109] These interjections provide a sense of Cromwell's mind in process, using the first-person present tense in order to heighten the psychological closeness of the moment: '[*There are many angry suspicious persons listening to me, and every word is liable to different misunderstandings in every different narrow head!*]'.[110]

As in Godwin's fictitious orations, theatrical self-display is internalised here, breaking down both the separation between involuntary physiology and thought/volition (and the 'rhetorical opposition' between the prophet and the dandy) in ways that attempt to reconcile the differences between Carlyle's own exaggerated style and the asceticism of Cromwell's plain, honest speech.[111] Carlyle thus uses the 'letters and speeches' format to draw on the 'personal *ethos*' and character-driven focus of autobiographical and eyewitness accounts of the seventeenth century, while simultaneously invoking the intimacy and emotional depth of the epistolary novel and other fictional forms that he had previously considered for his rendition of Cromwell's story.[112] Yet, perhaps *because* of its unwelcome proximity to epistolary fiction, Carlyle, like Godwin, is wary of the role of sentiment in *Cromwell*. At times, he extorts his reader to pity those executed or abandoned to their fate, but he also condemns a sentimental history that has 'wept for a misguided Charles Stuart, and blubbered, in the most copious helpless manner, near two centuries now' while being unable to release even a 'tributary sigh' for the death of the Leveller Corporals.[113]

It is certainly no coincidence that Carlyle indulges in the sentimentalist vein primarily in moments of private or domestic significance. When Cromwell's favourite daughter, Elizabeth, dies, for example, Carlyle evinces an intimacy with, and overt sympathy for, the bereaved father, which he asks the reader to share in a mutual outpouring of emotion:

> Hampton Court we can fancy once more, in those July days, a house of sorrow; pale Death knocking there, as at the door of the meanest hut. 'She had great sufferings, great exercises of spirit.' Yes:—and in the depths of the

old Centuries, we see a pale anxious Mother, anxious Husband, anxious weeping Sisters, a poor young Frances weeping anew in her weeds. 'For the last fourteen days' his Highness has been by her bedside at Hampton Court, unable to attend to any public business whatever. Be still, my Child; trust thou yet in God: in the waves of the Dark River, there too is He a God of help!—On the 6th day of August she lay dead; at rest forever. My young, my beautiful, my brave! She is taken from me; I am left bereaved of her.[114]

As John Rosenberg points out, Carlyle is scrupulous in distinguishing between supposition and fact in such passages ('we can fancy once more'), but he nonetheless identifies so fully with Cromwell that he becomes not editor but father and mourner himself: 'She is taken from me; I am left bereaved of her.'[115] Trans-temporal moments of 'arguing with the past', of juxtaposing past feelings and beliefs with contemporary ones, are common in Carlyle's writing. Here, however, he takes the idea of 'imaginary embodiment' even further, in that he takes on the role of ventriloquist himself. Not only is Carlyle committed to the kind of self-identification with his subject that is usually tolerated only in works of fiction, but he is also willing to ask the reader momentarily to suspend his or her disbelief when he 'fancies' or invents Cromwell's interior life and feelings, thereby practising 'an art that *fictionalizes*' rather than one that simply recreates.[116]

While this kind of fictionalisation is relatively rare in *Cromwell*, it is not in any real tension with Carlyle's documentary bent as he interweaves quotations from documents with his own suppositions in a way that recalls Godwin's account of the best kind of history in 'Of History and Romance' as a composition in which, into a 'scanty substratum of facts and dates', 'the writer interweaves a number of happy, ingenious and instructive inventions, blending them into one continuous and indiscernible mass'.[117] In other words, Carlyle is most 'novelistic' when he is closest to his documents; and his most evocative passages, such as Cromwell's death-scene and the battle-scenes at Naseby and Dunbar, are also the ones most firmly grounded in documentary detail.[118] If some critics see these kinds of 'fictive imaginings' as speculative and unverifiable, others argue that they are precisely what brought Carlyle 'into contact with the event he [was] interpreting'.[119] Carlyle certainly believed that a general insight into human behaviour was more important than the antiquarian compiling of information (as, for the most part, did his reviewers). However, his speculation is by no means guesswork, instead colouring his texts with what Rosemary Jann has called the 'didactic use of the imagined real' in a kind of fusion of antiquarian research and novelistic licence.[120]

Yet despite his belief that Cromwell's words are the 'express image of the soul [they] came from', Carlyle's original goal of disappearing behind his subject—of letting Cromwell 'do the talking'—is increasingly problematised by his interventions, comments, annotations, and fictions, resulting in an ongoing tension in the text between an epistemologically innocent faith in the authoritative nature of primary documents and the reconstructive work undertaken by the biographers and editors of such documents.[121] A second tension arises from the resistance of Cromwell's letters and speeches to editorial explanation: these raw documents, themselves often fragments, sometimes evince an antiquarian antagonism to connecting narratives, their faintly glowing presence simultaneously connoting absence and loss as both the building blocks of historical reconstruction and the fragmented reminders of a lost past.[122] Emphasising the processes of loss and decay that make historical reconstruction difficult and even impossible, Carlyle's famous vision of a 'shoreless chaos' of 'mouldering' documents not only intimates his fear of being permanently entombed in the netherworld of his innumerable sources, but also shows us a period of history so lost, so obscured by 'the wreck and dead ashes of some six unbelieving generations', that it reveals nothing but death and darkness.[123]

Carlyle draws repeated attention to the kinds of cultural vacancies engendered by a neglected past, as 'chaotic whirlwinds', 'dark abysses', and an 'indiscriminate blackness' seek to overwhelm him during the writing of *Cromwell*.[124] This is particularly true in relation to accounts of Cromwell's actions in Ireland. While Cromwell's letters initially shed some 'descending liquid' on the Irish War, Carlyle quickly reverts to images of blackness, representing the whole period as 'very dark and indecipherable': 'The History of it does not form itself into a picture; but remains only as a huge blot, an indiscriminate blackness.'[125] Despite his representation of the Irish as feckless, indolent, and 'unveracious', Ireland presents both a cultural and a representational problem for Carlyle. As John Morrow has noted, Carlyle, while opposed to repeal of the Union, attributes both past and present failures in Ireland to English misgovernment, reflecting a state of 'chronic atrophy' that culminates in the Famine.[126] Later, when describing his visit to Ireland during the second potato failure in 1849, Carlyle would give Ireland a wider personal and symbolic meaning, one that would come to determine not just his understanding of the nature of political authority but also his increasingly racialised hierarchies of human value: 'Ireland really *is* my problem; the breaking point of the huge suppuration which all British and all European society now is.'[127] Like Godwin, Carlyle tends to represent Irish history as singularly resistant to historical representation, as the site of lost, absent, or mysterious causes, although, as Ann Rigney has noted, Carlyle has a tendency to present as 'unrepresentable' that which is 'politically uncongenial' to him.[128]

The gaps in history engendered by the Irish War are made more explicit when Carlyle asks the reader to help himself through the 'great dark void, from February 1641 to January 1643', and appeals to the 'imaginative reader' to take on the editorial function by 'spread[ing] out' material into significance for himself.[129] Notwithstanding these rhetorical appeals to a prospective audience, Carlyle is sceptical about his readers' capacity to disengage from their own historical circumstances and to enter into Cromwell's world. Approximating 'the effect of verbal delivery', he often dramatises an audience who has been turned against him by false accounts of Cromwell, and attempts to stir in them a kind of conversion experience in the Scottish Presbyterian tradition, albeit a more Fichtean conversion based on one's own ability to construct meaning: 'I advise all modern readers not only to believe that Cromwell here means what he says; but even to try how *they*, each for himself in a new dialect could mean the like, or something better!'[130] Such 'preacher-congregation' addresses to the reader, and instructions for them to 'fancy' lost or unknowable motivations, not only rely on the dramatic effect of spoken delivery, but also demand imaginative involvement in a way that reminds readers of their 'own historical agency'.[131] Rejecting the false continuity of conventional, chronological historical narrative in favour of acknowledging slippages and absences, *Cromwell* thus oscillates between evocative presence and despairing absence, providing the reader with a sense of historical gaps that cannot always be bridged by documentary evidence, eyewitness accounts, or even historical interpretation but that *might* be supplemented by internalising and imaginative strategies borrowed from fiction.

Feeling Documents and the Historical Archive

In reviving those character-driven models of history that were integral to eyewitness accounts of the English Revolution and its aftermath, Carlyle and Godwin tend to favour seventeenth-century historiographical models such as character sketches and internal orations, combining these techniques with an approach that focuses more closely on depth models of character that partly emerged from their use of eyewitness sources and partly from the example of the novel, particularly the epistolary novel with its techniques of instantaneous description and reflection. Godwin primarily deploys internal orations to foreground the rhetorical component of decision making and the dynamic nature of the historical self. However, individual acts of self-persuasion or self-clarification are also socially conditioned so that the historical subject becomes the by-product of much larger social and institutional forces.[132] Carlyle's treatment of Cromwell similarly considers the connections between individual motivations and wider structures of feeling, demonstrating his awareness of the ways in which the self becomes constructed through the social acts of speaking, reading, and writing. It is only as Cromwell articulates his feelings in letters or speeches (that is, in 'spoken' or written forms) that we can know what he feels or believes. Yet whereas Godwin largely sees internal rhetoric as a conscious form of ethical self-deliberation, Carlyle's character sketches incorporate non-deliberative, unconscious, and artless moments, illuminating the 'pervasive, unconscious primary rhetoric' that shapes the evolving self.[133] For Carlyle, internal rhetoric is 'an epistemic as well as an ethical tool', or as Nienkamp puts it, 'a way of attainting and testing knowledge as well as a way of making moral decision and actions'.[134]

Carlyle and Godwin's willingness to invent orations and to use fictional strategies to 'fancy' the interior life of historical subjects points to what Karen O'Brien has characterised as the emergence of a 'novelized kind of history incorporating biographical elements, anecdotes, and epistolary and other fictional formats', one that attempted to reconcile the 'functional distinction between historians and novelists in relation to the representation of individual life stories'.[135] Carlyle and Godwin certainly share with novelists such as Richardson and Goethe a desire to portray the complexity of the individual life and mind, and to capture the immediacy of lived, subjective experience.[136] Carlyle's efforts over many years to find the best form with which to represent his contentious material, and the resulting sense of generic disintegration that pervades his work, point to his sense of the important, if problematic, role that novelistic techniques could play in the writing of history.

Godwin, too, reverts at the end of his *History* to a sense of the profound limitations of conventional historical writing, even as he remains cautious about the extent to which written history can entertain speculations, fictions, and outbursts of feeling or other forms of self-expression. While Godwin emulates internalising techniques that were partly formulated in the laboratory of the novel, he also seeks to distinguish his historical writing from his more speculative biographies and fiction, rarely deploying the kind of sentimental immersion or 'inferential colouring' utilised by Hume, Robertson, and other eighteenth-century historians. Carlyle, too, uses sentimental techniques only sparingly, reserving them almost exclusively for the domestic sphere or for other kinds of emotionally heightened spaces, and drawing his own representation of feelings from eyewitness and other documentary accounts.[137]

Carlyle and Godwin's recognition that the internal and non-verifiable elements of history, such as underlying motives, feelings, agency, and volition, can best be revealed through an examination of eyewitness and other primary historical documents forms part of an 'archival turn' in the 1820s: one that acknowledged that the historian must go beyond the written and even the 'spoken' words of the eyewitness account to develop 'an emotional and mental context for those words'. Since past experiences can be uncovered only in recorded documents and since those documents themselves are biased and/or incomplete, this kind of history involves both a commitment to empirical data and a hermeneutic 'process of interpreting the texts that constitute the historical record'.[138] In this sense, the 'romantic' Carlyle is in perfect conformity with the supposedly 'empirical' Ranke, who rejects *a priori* philosophical models that reduce history to an illustration of an underlying metaphysical idea and instead sets out to write his *Geschichten der romanischen und germanischen Völker von 1494 bis 1514* (1824) from contemporary sources, finding these sources to be 'even more beautiful, and in any case more interesting' than the romantic fiction of Walter Scott and others. As Anthony Grafton has noted, Ranke ironically 'won his status as the founder of a new historical school' largely on the basis of 'the rhetorical appeal of his documentation' finding that 'the more documentary, the more exact, and the more fruitful the research is, the more freely can our art unfold'.[139]

In developing depth models of character via eyewitness accounts and other 'feeling documents', romantic-era historians such as Godwin and Carlyle understood documentation and source criticism not as an 'abstraction from life' but as the very means of accessing and immersing themselves in the truths of historical experience.[140] As Ethan Kleinberg has pointed out, the rise of ontological realism in the nineteenth century increasingly privileged 'the text as the site by which we access the past', eventually resulting in what Dominic LaCapra has characterised as a professional form of 'archival fetishism'. The documentary archive thus became 'more than the repository of traces of the past which may be used in its inferential reconstruction' and instead became 'a stand-in for the past that brings the mystified experience of the thing itself'.[141] Despite their reverential attitude towards primary documents, Godwin and Carlyle tend to resist the antiquarian fetish of the archive by evincing a heightened understanding of the extent to which documentary sources are themselves incomplete, partial, provisional, and irrecoverable. While both historians privilege eyewitness accounts in their reconstruction of the past, they also understand these sources as ephemeral, subjective, and incomplete. Moreover, as Carlyle increasingly acknowledges, the limitations of documentary evidence do not require the historian to efface his own standpoint or experience in the act of hermeneutic interpretation, but instead compel him to make it more transparent, actively foregrounding individual biases and perspectives when attempting to create historical meaning from recorded phenomena.

Chapter 3

Historical Ethnogenesis and National Feeling: Scott, Moore, and Southey

Narratives about national character can be traced back to the Middle Ages but it was not until the early nineteenth century that the 'national paradigm' began to gain dominance in written history over constitutionalism, feudalism, and religious controversy. Historians such as Hume and Robertson, and after them Burke and Wollstonecraft, had already displayed a keen interest in national characteristics and characterologies, tying their understanding of national character either to classical contrariety models, or to enlightenment developmental frameworks that understood national characteristics as corresponding to more or less 'civilised' stages of human development. By the early to mid-nineteenth century, stadial investigations into the synchronic relationship between manners and nations had been extended to wider culturalist interests that legitimated the 'unique character of nations' and their 'alleged superiority over other nations'.[1] As the 'political instrumentalization of a national self-image', romantic-era nationalism provided the framework for the distillation of ethnic communities defined by the 'myth of common ancestry, shared historical memories, elements of shared culture, an association with a specific homeland, and a measure of solidarity'. The ethnicisation of class differences that had gradually stolen into earlier historical accounts was therefore increasingly overlaid by what Joep Leerssen has called 'romantic ethnogenesis', whereby debates about ethnic origins and myths provided the 'stamp of authenticity' for distinctively national histories.[2]

The long and complicated history of romantic ethnogenesis informed nineteenth-century written history in multiple and often competing ways. Adding a more overtly racialised layer to constructions of national identity, narratives of origin, inheritance, lineage, and descent were used to consolidate various popular and state nationalist agendas, from war propaganda to population and demographic discourse, gradually transforming older *ethnies* and patriotisms into modern ethnic nationalisms.[3] These narratives of (often) 'invented traditions' could also, however, be repurposed by those who sought to promote oppositional or counter-state narratives of national disinheritance, or to develop and sustain regional communities that could not always be comfortably assimilated into state Protestantism and other dominant, metropolitan perspectives of a nation's past. In their attention to alternative identarian models of collective attachment, non-metropolitan historical endeavours—from provincial to colonial histories—raised unresolved questions about the relationship between centres and peripheries in ways that could both reinforce and disrupt the 'official culture of the ruling elites'.[4]

Commissioned by Dionysius Lardner for his 133-volume *Cabinet Cyclopaedia*, Walter Scott's *History of Scotland* (1827) and Thomas Moore's *History of Ireland* (1835–46) intimate the ambivalent relationship between (provincial) subject and (British) nation. As a rational cosmopolite wedded to the ideals of progressive modernity, Scott concedes the long-lasting benefits of Scotland's union with England, but as a feeling Scot he acknowledges its costs and burdens. Moore's *History of Ireland*, too, exposes the violences inherent to British national expansion, adopting a more overt form of Irish national consciousness than the aestheticised sympathy of his *Irish Melodies* (1815–38), written after the unsuccessful Irish uprisings of 1798 and 1803. Reviving the nationalist tenor of his *Memoirs of Captain Rock* (1824), Moore represents Irish history as a catalogue of English racial prejudice and misgovernment.[5] However, in deconstructing some of Ireland's most cherished national self-mythologies, he also points to the limitations of sentimental attachment as a way of defining the political subject's relation to the nation, advocating for a civic alongside a Herderian-style cultural nationalism in the specific context of nationalism without a nation state.[6]

As the disjuncture between feeling and knowing in Scott and Moore's histories suggests, gradualist narratives of British national progress were plagued by the internal violences and dispossessions that characterised the Teutonic dispersal of the Celtic races, as well as by the anger and resentment forged by long histories of conquest and oppression, particularly in relation to the ongoing political disenfranchisement of Catholic Ireland.[7] Historians of British and other European colonies similarly grappled with the difficult legacies of imperial violence and dispossession alongside questions relating to national independence movements and the right to self-determination.[8] Robert Southey is explicit in his condemnation of the traumas of conquest, slavery, and colonialism in his three-volume *History of Brazil* (1819–27) while simultaneously representing the (almost) independent Brazil as an ideal conceptual space for the rejuvenation of British national identity following the crisis of the Napoleonic Wars.[9] As an early example of a model of national attachment tied to racial assimilation rather than to ethnic purity, Southey's *History* illuminates the ways in which histories of non-European colonial possessions buttressed a conceptual and ideological turn towards an imperial paradigm of national expansion in written history, one that played out at the same time as the rise of political, ethnic, and cultural nationalisms across early to mid-nineteenth-century Europe.

Focusing on the nexus between nation, ethnicity, and feeling in Scott, Moore, and Southey's otherwise very different histories, this chapter examines how the ethnonationalist politics of identity formation increasingly permeated representations of the national past in the early to mid-nineteenth century. In relation to Scott and Moore's histories, it considers two interrelated issues: first, methodological questions surrounding the epistemological value of antiquarianism and the ways in which folklore, oral culture, myths, and other vernacular sources could be endowed with historical legitimacy; and second, the representation in written history of those feelings of national belonging and other collective emotional phenomena that were themselves often tied to vernacular sources and cultural memory. In relation to Southey's representation of Brazil's transition from colony to (future) nation, the chapter examines the imbrication of racial assimilation and feelings of belonging in imperial narratives of national consolidation. Arising out of the uneven and unequal social orders of conquest, slavery, and racial capitalism, expansionist paradigms of nationhood were to become increasingly critical both to the construction of a uniquely British national history and to wider Saxonist narratives of 'Greater Britain', which would themselves later prove axiomatic in the settler turn to national sentiment in Britain's colonies.[10]

Ethnonationalism, Antiquarianism, and the Nation

It is by now well known that three narratives were dominant in the nineteenth-century historiography of the English nation. The first is the Teutonic narrative, which took its impetus from Tacitus's *Germania* (AD 98) and argued that the Anglo-Saxons had either conquered or displaced the ancient Romano-Celtic races, reinforcing both the idea of the Celt's racial foreignness and the so-called Celtic 'displacement' into geographic peripheries. The second is the narrative of the feudal 'Norman yoke' or the oppression of the demotic Anglo-Saxon tribes following the Norman conquest of England in the eleventh century. And the third is the Whig story of civilisatory progress achieved through England's unique tradition of liberal parliamentarianism and the supposed moral superiority of Protestantism.[11] 'Special paths' narratives are not, of course, confined to nineteenth-century England. However, as Catherine Hall has demonstrated, histories of England by James Mackintosh, T. B. Macaulay, and others tended to combine this racially exclusive Teutonic or Anglo-Saxon 'master narrative of descent' focused on qualities of English 'native genius' with an explanation of the 'emergence of an imperial people' in which the 'old enmities of race' between Saxon and Celt were amalgamated and effaced. This two-pronged history of English/British exceptionalism was used to construct internal hierarchies of national belonging and exclusion while simultaneously justifying the 'civilising' mission in the colonies.[12]

The politics of belonging was, however, racialised well before the so-called 'imperial turn' in the mid-nineteenth century. Notwithstanding the complexity and fluidity of the term 'race' in the seventeenth and eighteenth centuries, Charles W. Mills has argued that the 'social contract' of white liberal universalism was always a 'racial contract', resting on the cognitive capacities of the white, European rights-bearing subject, and resulting in the denial of personhood to those races considered lacking in the capacity for reason, authority, and sovereignty. As Onni Gust has pointed out in the more specific context of the politics of national belonging, the Scottish enlightenment 'science of man', and in particular the so-called 'four stages' theory, relied both on universalised understandings of personhood and on a raciology of mind that rested on a binary distinction between the emotional capacities of 'civilised' and 'savage' nations: only as societies advanced culturally and materially could they develop their capacities to feel and express sympathy for others via a shared set of manners, tastes, and sensibilities.[13]

Extending and deepening the anthropological racialism of stadial accounts of human progress, and their hierarchical schematics of emotion, early proponents of a more biologically driven account of racial difference, such as the Scottish antiquarian John Pinkerton, were able to construct internal as well as foreign others in ethnic terms, associating the Anglo-Saxons with 'social' emotions and dispositional qualities such as sympathy, compassion, rationality, civilisation, and progress and the Celts with 'unsocial' emotions and qualities such as anger, resentment, savagery, irrationality, backwardness, and violence. In Pinkerton's Scottish Teutonism, national foundation myths linked to a native 'Gothic constitution' were combined with racially essentialist accounts of Celtic inferiority.[14]

Notwithstanding the increasingly overt racialism of romantic-era ethnogenesis, Scottish, Irish, and Welsh nationalists drew on and reproduced ethnonationalist narratives to reclaim their own distinctive histories of Celtic otherness, looking to origin theories and the antiquarian past to provide counter-histories to narratives of hegemonic Englishness and loyalist narratives of union.[15] In Scotland, cultural nationalists strove to co-opt and instrumentalise the 'feudal' and 'backward' Highlands (and Scoto-Gaelic culture more generally) as a distinctive source of national peculiarity, rejecting or at least moderating Scottish enlightenment narratives of cultural assimilation within the Anglo-British state.[16] In Wales, Edward Jones's *Musical and Poetic Relicks of the Welsh Bards* (1784) drew on bardic traditions to evade a stadialist logic, promoting the existence of a highly developed Welsh national culture that predated the English one.[17] In Ireland, too, Catholic historians and antiquarians joined 'Gaelic Protestants' such as Charlotte Brooke and Sylvester O'Halloran to construct a 'golden age' of ancient Irish enlightenment followed by a subsequently dark history of disinheritance, resulting in a form of nationalism that replaced the monologic drive of progressivist narratives with the performative ambivalence of the 'colonial hybrid'.[18]

The model of nationalism that came to prevail in Britain after the French Revolution was accordingly one simultaneously invested in modernity and antiquarianism. As Yoon Sun Lee has argued, the centripetal model of nationhood depends on the pedagogic 'temporality of linear time' and evolutionary progress, but it is always in tension with the archaic time of antiquarian nationalism, a highly eroticised and performative form of nationalism that encapsulates what Homi K. Bhabha has called the 'double time' of the nation.[19] Julia M. Wright has usefully labelled these competing forms of nationalism 'inaugural' and 'antiquarian'. If inaugural forms of nationalism sought to 'cast off the vestiges of feudalism' and to soften regional differences through assimilationist or incorporationist narratives of British union, antiquarian nationalism tended to idealise an ideological attachment to the distant past as a way of reviving Scottish, Irish, and Welsh cultural traditions, undermining both the myth of an 'undifferentiated Celtic periphery' and the 'gradualist myth of modern British national identity' as one that had occurred organically and incrementally 'against an implicit backdrop of safe commerciality'.[20]

Partly driven by the cultural project of nation-building, the period's interrelated interest in ethnic origins and antiquarianism was therefore multifaceted, assuming 'competing inflections' across Britain and Ireland.[21] Most obviously, these competing positions made their way into rival ideological interpretations of the past, but they also resonated in the philosophy and practice of history itself. As Susan Manning has noted, the antiquarian underpinning of narratives of Saxonism and Celticism was accompanied by a 'cultural anxiety' about the 'epistemological status and purpose' of antiquarian activities more generally. Whereas in the seventeenth century antiquarianism and history had 'inhabited different and antagonistic conceptual spaces', over the course of the eighteenth century their spheres came closer together, as philosophic history increasingly involved itself in hypothetical or conjectural speculation about the 'science of man'. Antiquarianism thus occupied the boundary between two models of enlightenment historiography: the Newtonian tradition of accumulating evidence and the conjectural and philosophical model of the Scottish enlightenment.[22]

By the early nineteenth century, the discourse around antiquarianism tended to disparage its rationale of accumulating and recording the textual and material remains of provincial or regional cultures. Characteristically 'locale- and region-based', antiquarian activities were said to encourage a subjective and affective type of history based on particularities rather than on philosophic generalities.[23] Even those historians who rejected the abstraction and universalism of philosophic history, such as Carlyle, expressed a persistent and often ambivalent sense that antiquarianism was more concerned with the layered 'thickness or texture of the past' than it was with producing historical meaning.[24] The antiquarian favoured the 'hunt, search, or inquiry, into public time' and the decipherment or reconstruction of the remains of the past—including the 'pre-historical' or 'pre-literate' aspects of the past—over the construction of any form of universal or even national consensus. Antiquarianism was therefore valued primarily because of its provision of 'raw materials' or the 'equipment' of history for 'higher' forms of written history that involved disquisition and explanation.[25]

During the same period, the specialist discipline of archaeology began to emerge as a more inscription-based and 'scientific' alternative to antiquarianism, focusing on artefacts, antiquities, and other material remains rather than on a predominantly 'bookish' or text-based historiography of the nation's past.[26] Ridicule of the antiquarian's obsessive bookishness, pedantry, and provinciality nonetheless disguised antiquarianism's ongoing methodological authority in the context of written history.[27] In the first instance, philosophic historians had themselves borrowed from antiquarians an interest in the manners and customs of the past, signalling both the convergence of antiquarian research with political and national history, and a gradual shift from 'the cognitive to the anthropological value of historical knowledge'. In the second instance, the rise of historicism was deeply connected to the emergence of a *volkish* culture in which the experiences of the nation's people were considered the true source of political legitimacy, resulting in an acknowledgement of the historical value of demotic traditions, oral culture, and vernacular sources.[28]

Antiquarianism was also central to the development of the new kind of 'scientific' history associated with German historians such as Ranke and Niebuhr, whose so-called 'ballad theory' understood ethnographic sources such as oral traditions, folklore, and ballads as a distillation of the manners, sentiments, and customs of ancient societies in ways that resonate with Scott's 1824 'Essay on Romance'.[28] Notwithstanding ongoing attempts to divorce history from myth and tradition, the antiquarian appreciation for vernacular sources was not incidental or tangential to the rise of scientific history, which integrated antiquarian methods into more syncretic explanatory frameworks. Similarly, the emerging archaeological emphasis on prehistorical artefacts and other material evidence remained part of a broadly antiquarian sphere until at least the early twentieth century. Even as 'polymathic antiquarianism' gave way to the more positivist demands of archaeology and other specialist disciplines, the middle-class elites who typically forged historical narratives of the nation came to validate the idea of national belonging by providing material and documentary evidence of those popular myths and legends that best represented the 'deep history' of the nation.[29]

'Fated Nation': Scott's *History of Scotland* and Narratives of Union

Writing privately in his notebooks in 1832, Carlyle dismissed Scott's *History of Scotland* as an account of 'Palace intrigues, and butcheries and battles', wasting its time 'chronicling the amours' of the 'wanton' Mary, Queen of Scots and her 'sulky' paramour. While not entirely a Marian apologist, Scott does linger sympathetically over Mary's character and conduct for most of the second volume of his *History*, referring readers to sources that support his 'mournful tale' of her life and death. He does so, however, not to resurrect nostalgia for a lost Scottish Catholic monarchy but rather in order to demonstrate a more general pattern in Scottish history: 'the degeneration of prudence into passion'.[30] Unlike Godwin and Carlyle's psychologised character studies, Scott's historical actors tend to be exemplary or cautionary illustrations of wider philosophical truths, with Scott following Hume in characterising the 'mysterious transactions' of the passions as contrary to the historian's 'calm investigations'.[31] Yet Carlyle's caustic dismissal of Scott's popular narrative as a juvenile form of story-telling belies Scott's own attempt to distinguish it from the design of his *Tales of a Grandfather* series (1827–9). Whereas Scott had there omitted anything that would 'tire the attention of his juvenile reader' and confined himself to facts rather than 'an investigation of the principles out of which those facts arose', in the *History of Scotland* he proposes to deliver a 'set of truths' which form 'a chapter in the general history of man'.[32]

Scott's desire to place Scottish history within the historical continuum offered by narratives of western European progress is a product of his well-known intellectual affiliations with philosophic mentors at Edinburgh University, such as Baron Hume, Dugald Stewart, and Alexander Fraser Tytler.[33] Using a self-described 'analytical and chronological' approach, Scott applies stadial, comparative, and conjectural models of uneven human development when he compares the static and feudal Scotland of 1283 to modern-day Persia, seeing the history of modern Scotland as a dynamic case study of the transformative effects of exposure to the more civilised examples of France and England.[34] Like philosophic predecessors such as Robertson, who, in his influential *History of Scotland* (1759), dismisses the period from Kenneth Macalpine to the death of James V as 'the region of pure fable and conjecture', Scott disparages the early history of Scotland's 'twilight times' as both unedifying and lacking in adequate documentation, declaring that he will 'avoid the disgusting task of recording obscure and ferocious contests, fought by leaders with unpronounceable names'.[35]

While he largely evades (or at least does not foreground) antiquarian controversy, Scott's interest in questions of Scottish national distinctiveness is developed enough to downplay Saxonist narratives of ancient Britain. In a departure from an Anglocentric Whig historiography that saw the Druids as the upholders of liberty against imperial Rome, Scott deems the Scots and Picts the original 'free Britons' fighting against 'an incursive predatory course of hostilities' with an extreme and distinctive valour, and who, unlike the Anglo-Saxons, were never conquered by the Romans: 'the boast that Scotland's more remote regions were never conquered by the Romans is not a vain one'. In a second departure from Whig Anglo-Saxonism, Scott attributes the flowering of civilisation in Scotland to the arrival of the Normans rather than to the innate qualities of the Anglo-Saxons: 'The benefits received from this influx of foreigners [the Norman barons] and their influence, were doubtless a main step towards civilizing Scotland,' even if the Norman aristocrats contribute to an extended period of Scottish feudalism and thus to the ongoing 'disunion of the state'.[36]

As Colin Kidd has pointed out, Robertson's paradigmatic understanding of Scotland's feudal backwardness as the irrational and negative foil to England's normative progressiveness was 'the defining cliché of Scottish historical writing' in the nineteenth century, manifesting itself in an awareness of Scotland's lack of constitutional development, a distaste for the late medieval and early modern eras, and a 'consensual sigh of relief' for the Union. The Whig historiographical tradition was accordingly limited in Scotland: England was deemed to have a proud parliamentary history of consensus and 'unbroken evolution', whereas Scotland's past was 'an illiberal descent'.[37] At the same time, in depicting Scotland's 'barbarous' history of extended feudalism, clanship, and internal strife as part of 'the threshold of the modern world', Robertson was able to contextualise provincial Scottish history within the larger progressive narrative of western European history and thus to reconcile its relative 'backwardness' for a middle-class audience who wanted to find 'new conditions for consensus' within Scotland's polemical past.[38]

Writing a popular history for the broad and general readership of a cabinet miscellany, Scott likewise appeals to the sensibilities of a modern, cosmopolitan audience: one that is reconciled to Scotland's union with England but also cognisant of the value of Scotland's distinctive ethnic and national origins. Following Robertson's revisionist account of Scotland's aristocrats as foreign encroachers rather than defenders of ancient liberty, the first volume of the *History of Scotland* focuses on the ongoing struggles of the crown for political supremacy, depicting the gradual consolidation of national unity out of ethno-religious conflict.

In the budding context of ethnic and cultural nationalism, Scott's narrative of feudal Scotland's inherent disunion is centred on both a class struggle and an ethnographic distinction between 'the people' and 'the nobility': the 'vacillation and apostasy' of the Scoto-Norman nobility is imputed to their 'foreign race' and their consequent devotion to chivalry, which Scott deems unfavourable to local attachment. Apart from William Wallace, the Scottish nobles are not amenable 'to the [social] emotions which constitute patriotism', leading to 'loose and irregular conceptions on the subject of loyalty' and the dispersal of Scottish society into private and selfish passions. Here Scott revises the Anglocentric view of medieval Scotland and its people as little removed from barbarism via an assertion of the popular roots of Scottish liberty. In describing the faults of the Scottish nobility in terms of their lack of emotional attachment to the nation, he defines a nascent Scottish nationhood in affective as well as ethnic terms, noting the existence among the demotic Scots of 'that animated love of country which has been ever since so strong a characteristic of North Britons'.[39]

For Scott, as for Burke, affective attachment is the glue that binds individuals to national communities. While he rarely deploys the rhetorical sentimentalism of Burke's *Reflections*, reserving it primarily for brief internalisations of his own Scottish identity, Scott's explanation of Scottish history is grounded in two narratives, both of which rest on the principle of national feeling: the first is a revised version of the 'yoke' thesis, with the Scots unable 'to bear the foreign yoke' of the English; and the second is the story of the substitution of the encroaching ambition of the Scoto-Norman nobles for the more legitimate authority of the crown, which Scott understands in Burkean terms as 'a species of refuge ... from the subaltern oppression of a multitude of petty tyrants'. Ambition and its emotional correlative (resentment) are, for Scott, archaic and unsocial passions, which result in the dissolution of national feeling, and must be tempered by the development of those more civic emotions associated with the monarchy and national well-being.[40] The neo-royalist Scott thus reverses the aristocratic–popular tensions of the Norman yoke thesis, which linked popular rule to Anglo-Saxon democracy and royal prerogative to the Norman-French continental conquerors.[41]

It is not until the end of the thirteenth century that the authority of the Scottish monarchy allows for the influence of modern systems and manners.[42] Scott's representation of clanship as divisive to national feeling—'every clan formed the epitome of nation within itself'—follows Scottish enlightenment stadial models of uneven development, which saw Scotland as divided 'betwixt two separate races, one of which had attained a considerable degree of civilization, and the other remained still nearly in a state of nature'. From the reign of Robert Bruce onwards, Scotland begins the slow process of national consolidation and solidarity 'into one strong and inseparable stem' deserving 'the name of a kingdom'.[43] The Celtic Scots or Highlanders follow the Scoto-Saxons or Lowlanders by increasingly recognising the authority of the king rather than 'relapsing into the barbarous independence of their ancestors', even if, as late as the end of the sixteenth century, they are treated as 'if the settlement intended had been in India or America, and the persons who were to be dispossessed had been savage heathens'.[44]

Highland 'improvement' is therefore offered by Scott as an illustration of Scottish civility, progress, and national coherence. Equally, however, the treatment of the Highlanders is suggestive of those relapses into savagery and barbarity that take place in colonial settlements. Unlike

Robertson's depiction of the Highlanders as exemplars of social backwardness and James Mackintosh's elision of the Highland Scots in his *History of the Revolution in England in 1688* (1834), Scott represents the Highlanders as precursors to the colonial project in India and North America.[45] His attention to the Highlanders suggests that their anachronistic 'primitivism' remains a source of national distinction, the exotic essence of the Scottish nation post-Union. However, he also takes seriously the role that the Highlanders play in defining Scottish culture and identity.[46] While Highland society is deemed barbarous in a civic or stadialist sense, the *History of Scotland*'s pro-Union subtext is troubled by Scott's re-evaluation of the 'savage' Highlanders on the basis of positive attributes such as courage, independence, and love of country, as well as by his anxiety about cultural erasure, his affective attachment to Scottish cultural traditions and symbols, and his arguments against the encroaching centralisation of the British state.[47]

As Murray Pittock has demonstrated, Scott was an important influence on the mythologisation and 'emotional survivals' of Jacobitism, and on the nationalism of mid-nineteenth-century Scottish historians and collective groups, such as John Hill Burton, Patrick Fraser Tytler, and the National Association for the Vindication of Scottish Rights (NAVSR) (1852–6).[48] Arguments against English encroachment were not, however, necessarily separatist arguments for political independence. Tytler's *History of Scotland* (1828–43), the first two volumes of which Scott favourably reviewed in the *Quarterly Review* for 1829, appealed to Scottish bourgeois reading audiences by suggesting that Scotland could exist as 'North Britain', provided that British nationhood was inclusive and culturally sensitive. Similarly, the NAVSR formulated its 'unionist nationalism' within, rather than in opposition to, the framework of the British state, arguing against English encroachment on Scottish parliamentary, economic, and religious freedoms in order to maintain a distinctive public sphere that could keep alive Scottish identity, an identity that was increasingly linked to Scotland's role as England's imperial partner within the Empire.[49]

While Scott identifies those aspects of Scottish culture that are 'unassimilable to an Anglo-British template', such as the Scottish Presbyterian Kirk and the Scottish parliament, ethnic and cultural differences between England and Scotland are ultimately secondary in his *History of Scotland* to the greater developmental principles of civic order that define the history of western Europe.[50] Civilisation accordingly increases and accelerates in direct proportion to Scottish contact with the English: David's education in England at the court of Henry I, for instance, renders him 'the perfect example of a good and patriot king'; and the

English language first replaces the Scottish language in Lothian, the 'most civilized province' of Scotland.[51] In attributing the progressiveness of the Lowlands to the introduction of those Teutonic customs and laws that replace the old Celtic habits, Scott represents Scotland as a 'fated nation' predestined to assimilation with its more progressive neighbour. Drawing on Robertson's providential and civic–humanist mode, the *History* argues for the organic inevitability of union, which, in its most legitimate form, is not violently imposed by conquest or imperial administration but rather emerges incrementally from within the national body: 'The manners, the prejudices of so many mixed races, corrected or neutralized each other; and the moral blending together of nations led in time, like some chemical mixture, to fermentation and subsequent purity.' In emphasising both a racial and a moral blending, Scott supports British national consolidation through the processes of conciliation, assimilation, and absorption rather than through conquest. However, he is also able to see the history of Scotland as the story of national survival. Despite Scotland's lack of constitutional and parliamentary achievement, his *History* insists on the existence of a distinctive 'Scottish national spirit', which is 'energetically determined on resisting the English domination to the last'.[52]

While Scott champions the legitimacy of Scottish defensive warfare right up until the Union, the ongoing tensions between assimilation and resistance in his rendition of Scotland's national past are ultimately resolved within a Burkean model of prescription and established loyalty.[53] The text finds some space for the 'anachronistic potential' of groups like the Highlanders, but they are either placeholders who stage 'the fanciful interregnum between accredited historical discourses' or nostalgic markers of a lost national cultural distinctiveness that can be only gradually and partially revived:[54] 'It is in the political world as in the human frame; dislocations which have been of long standing ... cannot be brought back to their proper state without time, patience, and gentleness.' Actors like Mary of Guise and Mary Stuart, who ally themselves with the Catholic French over the English in the sixteenth century, are therefore wrong-headed in their alternative aims and alliances for a nation fated to be united with England, while dynastic intermarriages are 'the most natural model, perhaps, to effect a union between two kingdoms, which nature had joined, though untoward events had separated them'.[55]

By setting the Scottish national story of resistance and survival within the story of the British Union, Scott's pro-state national attempts to reconcile two potentially contradictory emotional affiliations: Scottish patriotism and North British loyalty. This in turn leads him to alternate between the rational universalism of philosophic history and more performative displays of authorial identification. Throughout the *History*, Scott's speaking subject oscillates between that of a cosmopolitan and worldly citizen of Britain and that of a provincial Scotsman, explicitly adopting the perspective of a Scot on various issues: 'A Scotsman may also argue that ...'. Certainly, he subjects English perspectives and sources to intense scrutiny: on the English view that the Northampton peace treaty of 1328 was 'dishonourable to England' Scott notes that 'before passing so heavy a censure on the Northampton parliament, these learned writers ought to have considered whether England possessed any right over Scotland; and, secondly, whether that which they claimed was an adequate motive for continuing an unsuccessful war'.[56]

Choosing ultimately to displace the history of Scottish resistance, Scott closes his narrative with the union between Scotland and England in 1707, describing the providential advance towards that 'happy consummation' 'which was destined to put the whole island under the government of a single monarch'. Unlike many of his historical novels, which deal with the contentious spaces of the recent past, Scott avoids the 1745 Jacobite uprising and the national trauma it occasions, just as he downplays Scottish religious controversy following the Reformation. The logic of his *History* suggests that the Jacobite uprising is just another anomaly in a broadly progressive history of Scottish improvement, reflecting the 'uneven political geography of the country' which will soon be assimilated by the forces of modernisation.[57]

Scott's narrative of national consensus is not, however, entirely without its emotional anachronisms. The accession of James II to the English throne is initially welcomed, with James tenderly taking leave of the Scottish people: 'A mixture of approbation and weeping followed this speech; and the good-natured king wept plentifully himself at taking leave of his native subjects.' Yet the Scottish crowd also display a more complex set of emotions, mourning their 'country's lost independence, in address becoming one who waits upon the funeral of a mother.' While describing this view as 'rash and prejudiced', Scott also acknowledges its truth, for the period 'closes the history of Scotland as a free and independent state'.[58] Scott thus ends his *History* with a melancholy nostalgia for an extinct Scottish national independence founded in the Stuart dynastic line, an affective position based in an elegiac remembrance that necessarily marks the 'modern' present as 'a historical and metaphysical dislocation from origins'.[59]

If the historiography of Scott's day did not subsequently issue a 'self-confident national historiography' because of a bi-partisan desire to mitigate the perceived parochialism of Scottish history, Scott nonetheless attempts to recentre Scottish history within wider narratives of British and western European progress. The significance of his *History* lies not so much in its methodological innovations, but rather in its harnessing of Scottish cultural signifiers and nationalist narratives of independence and liberty to the 'status quo of de-facto autonomy within the British state'. In arguing for the legitimacy of the British state, he characterises Scotland's national heroes as resistors of tyranny and encroachment rather than as revolutionary transgressors. The same position is endorsed by Archibald Alison, whose conservative adherence to Anglo-British constitutionalism likewise did not prevent him from emphasising 'the existence of a benevolent paternalist tradition' in pre-Union Scotland. It is perhaps unsurprising, then, that the assimilationist version of British nation-state formation promoted by Archibald, Tytler, and Scott led to the gradual withdrawal of Scottish radicals from the emotive language of national attachment and popular loyalism from the mid-nineteenth century onwards.[60]

'Memorable for disunion': Moore's *History of Ireland* and the 'Double Aspect' of Irish History

Wading through the painfully unresolved history of his birth country in 1834, Moore describes his *History of Ireland* as 'sad work', exacerbated by the pressure put on him by Longmans and the 'Dionysian Drag'.[61] The *History* was overdue almost before he began writing it, forcing Moore to work through the night and 'for the first time, in my literary life, making me feel myself a thorough *hack*'.[62] Frustrated that he was compelled to refuse 'light tasks' that he could have accomplished quickly for the same remuneration, Moore sometimes found the drudgery of researching and writing the *History* overwhelming: 'History (somebody says) means simply *His*-story, but it is also now *my* story, and a very dull story too.—'[63] In 1843, he was still working incessantly on the fourth and final volume of the 'incubus', which he finally finished in 1846, although it extended only to the mid-seventeenth century and elided any reckoning with Cromwell's conquest of Ireland.[64]

If Moore's journal entries intimate a less positive and lucrative engagement with the English book trade than he had experienced with *Irish Melodies*, his approach to historical sources was far from hack-like. Whereas Lardner had complained of Scott's 'rapid & careless manner of writing' the *History of Scotland* and 'begged that he would be so kind as to "throw in a few dates and authorities"', Moore laboriously consulted uncatalogued primary sources and approached them with the utmost scrupulousness, examining original manuscripts and folios at the British Museum, the Council Office, the State Paper Office, the Royal Institution, the Public Records Office, and the Royal Irish Academy in Dublin, as well as reading secondary sources on Irish history published from the sixteenth to the nineteenth centuries.[65] Positioning his own source-oriented research methods against the carelessness of Hume, Scott, and even the feted English Catholic historian John Lingard, Moore characterises the primary aims of his *History* as, first, to consult those original Irish papers that 'have remained so long unexplored & unarranged'; second, to move away from the 'narrow, sectarian principles' that colour work on Irish history; and third, to outline the defects of the deep-rooted 'Celtic principle of clanship', to the removal of which the 'Teutonic race have owed their better destiny'.[66]

Moore's concern that his *History* should be viewed as impartial and evidence-based extended to his dismissal of the Milesian fable involving the descendants of a fabulous Spanish king whose sons were said to have invaded Ireland around 1300 BC.[67] The 'fabulous claims to antiquity' associated with the Milesians were part of an origin myth that was, as Moore recognised, deeply 'connected in the minds of Irishmen with their great national cause'.[68] By promoting the ancient credentials and civility of Gaelic Ireland, economic failure and cultural barbarism could be represented as a product of English colonisation rather than as an inherent quality of pre-conquest Ireland. Feeling forced to deflate this cherished nationalist myth 'so consolatory to the pride of a people for ever struggling against the fatality of their position', Moore concedes the risk of associating himself with the 'habitual revilers and depreciators of Ireland', as indeed he was accused of doing by William Lynch, the author of *Feudal Dignities* (1830).[69] At the same time, the 'stern call of historical truth' obliges him to undertake a task both 'ungracious and painful' and to dispel any 'false scheme of antiquity': 'This is very far from being the popular view of the subject, but much as I like to be popular in Ireland, still *"magis amica veritas"*.'[70]

Moore was writing the *History of Ireland* within a hegemonic English patronage and book-marketing system, as well as for the broadly middle-class reading audiences courted by cabinet miscellanies like the *Cabinet Cyclopedia*. However, the result is not the libidinised version of Irishness associated with the 'Celtomania' of the British consumer classes and Moore's own *Irish Melodies*. Foregrounding instead the irreconcilable perspectives of Irish and English readers within the 'double public sphere' in which he was writing, Moore explicitly deploys the language of conquest to declare English rule little more than 'a monstrous system of outlawry and proscription'.[71] The same rulers who, in England, lay down 'the future establishment of representative government and free institutions' produce a system of provincial despotism in Ireland: the reign of King John, for instance, 'which, in the hands of the English historian presents so proud and stirring an example of successful resistance to wrong, exhibits, in our Irish records, but a melancholy picture of slavery and suffering'.[72] Similarly, James I, considered by Hume the 'legislator of Ireland' because of his reformation of Irish Brehon law and the customs of gavelkind and tanistry, encroaches on Irish legislative rights and 'popular feeling'.[73]

Moore thus casts a strongly revisionist eye over English historical accounts of Ireland, reconsidering, for example, the English characterisation of so-called Irish 'rebels'. James Fitzmaurice, who led the first of the Desmond Rebellions in 1569, is treated by Moore as a patriot and champion of the Irish cause, even if 'the page of history' written by the conqueror brands him a 'traitor'. Despite the failure of his rebellion in Munster and later defeat at Kinsale during the Nine Years War from 1593 to 1603, Moore similarly sees Hugh O'Neill of Tyrone as maintaining a successful 'rebel-reign' that justifies his so-called 'rebellions', even if there is little evidence of his character to be found in the historical record.[74] Indeed, the 'blank and valueless' nature of Irish records under English occupation is, for Moore, a painful reminder of the cultural erasure propagated by the English and the debased condition of the Gaelic Irish.[75] Arguing that the history of Ireland runs parallel to the history of its records and sources, Moore recognises that the very possibility of writing a cohesive national history is deeply connected to the existence of an archival infrastructure that can authenticate that history. Forced by archival paucities to reflect on documentary absences in the historical archive, he regrets 'how small is the portion of Ireland's history that relates to the affairs of the Irish people' who are 'only remembered to be calumniated or coerced'.[76]

The loosely defined 'patriotic sympathies' that imbue *Irish Melodies* are therefore replaced in the *History* by a more overtly nationalist contestation of English conquest, cultural erasure, and colonisation along the lines of Moore's *Memoirs of Captain Rock*. As in that text, the *History*'s claims rest not so much on the affective appeal of an aestheticised cultural particularity or on the creation of a distinctively Irish suffering subjectivity—the emotional primitivism of the 'wailing slave', as Young Ireland's Thomas Davis put it—but rather on the combined logic of civic and cultural nationalism. For Moore, as for Davis, the pathway to an 'inheritance'—that is, to a coherent Irish nation grounded in the notion of a birthright—is one formed by the revival of an inherent Irish 'civility' through rational education, improvement, and self-reliance: the struggle 'to learn as well as feel'.[77] The larger Irish enlightenment project of civic advancement that Moore draws on here was one 'pursued through social clubs, scholarly societies, and educational initiatives' such as the Royal Irish Academy (1787), as well as through the 'Gaelophilia' that imbued the circles of Protestant scholars and antiquarians who gathered around the Academy, and later the Gaelic Society of Dublin (1807), the Iberno-Celtic society (1818), the Irish Archaeological Society (1848), and the Celtic Society (1848).[78]

In prioritising authenticity, credibility, and documentary evidence over the politics of sympathy and the performance of Irish feeling, Moore's *History* avoids both the cultivated sentimentalism of *Irish Melodies* and the polemic nationalism of Young Ireland's accounts of Ireland's past in favour of a more scholarly approach concerned with the place of vernacular traditions in documentary history.[79] Oliver MacDonagh has argued that modern Irish historiography was born in the 1790s with the publication of Edward Ledwich's *Antiquities of Ireland* (1790), which took a sceptical approach to 'bardic fictions' and the value of ancient sources (even if, like Moore, Ledwich was unable to examine Irish language sources).[80] Moore's approach to bardic sources is similarly rationalist, sceptical, and probabilistic, devoted to 'stripping off those decorations and disguises in which matter of fact come frequently arrayed' in the early chronicles. While he distinguishes Ireland's native 'Bardic Historians' from classical mythic traditions, arguing that the 'Bards' and 'Seanachie' who flourished from the ninth to the eleventh centuries should be understood as the 'repositories of the ancient traditions of the country' with 'roots laid deep in traditional truth', Moore nonetheless sees the Christian annalists who succeed them as superior in both content and style: 'the very reverse of poetical'.[81]

Moore's anxiety about the credibility and epistemological value of the 'pre-historical' past, and his desire to produce verifiable documentary evidence for ancient Irish traditions and archaeological remains, is a product both of a remnant philosophical scepticism and of the wider discourse of authenticity associated with the emergence of romantic-era cultural nationalism. Although he elsewhere draws on an Ossianic heroic sensibility, Moore is scathing in the *History* about the forgeries of James Macpherson's *Fragments of Ancient Poetry* (1760–3), which appropriates the 'authentic' origin stories and genealogies of Irish antiquity and seeks 'to confound ... the historical affinities' between the two countries. While conceding that the Scots construct a spurious antiquity to find political precedents for the 'right of revolt against [English] tyranny', he roundly rejects Macpherson's deceptive blurring of the distinctions between 'scholarly recovery and poetic invention' by appealing to the authority of historical documentation.[82] The clash of stadialist and diffusionalist national historiographies that Clare O'Halloran has identified at the heart of the Hiberno-Scottish Ossianic pamphlet wars thus becomes, for Moore, primarily a question of authentication and a condemnation of the fabrication and falsification of historical sources.[83]

Steering a path between the 'over-sceptical', who believe that the bardic writers deserve no credit and that Irish history begins 'only with the dawn of the Christian faith', and the 'credulous', who invest 'fable with much of the grave and authoritative aspect of history', Moore's approach attempts to find a middle ground that explicates 'the true value of our traditionary memorials'.[84] By distinguishing the vernacular or 'traditionary history' of Ireland from 'fables' or 'myths', he valorises those 'old, popular remembrances, transmitted from age to age', as well as the 'speaking monuments of antiquity which are still scattered over her hills and plains'.[85] Despite his equivocation about the origin of the Round Towers and his dismissal of the Milesian myth, Moore supports, for instance, the more modest claims of historians such as Charles O'Connor and Sylvester O'Halloran that the Irish were literate before the introduction of Christianity.[86] He also establishes Ireland's distinctive ethnic pedigree, distinguishing the ancient Irish from the Gaulic Celts that populated Britain and claiming Ireland's ancient distinction as a place of spiritual power, 'The Sacred Island'.[87]

As Moore recognises, the 'double aspect' of Ireland's ancient sources (as history/romance and fact/fiction) reflects a wider lack of consensus about Ireland itself, which is deemed by ancient and modern commentators alike as either 'an island of savages' or one 'of saints'. On the one hand, the Keatings and the O'Hallorans exalt pre-Christian Ireland to the highest standard of early civilisation, a 'perfect golden age of glory, political wisdom, and refinement', while on the other, the Ledwiches and the Pinkertons pronounce the same period to be one 'un-reclaimed waste of ignorance and barbarism'. Declaring the latter view to be based on (and essentially replicating) ignorant and faulty classical sources, Moore nonetheless questions the extent to which ancient Ireland was 'a paragon of civilisation and refinement', arguing that 'the songs and legends of the country are, in such descriptions, confounded with her history; her fictions have been taken for realities, and her realities heightened into romance'.[88] Moore thus partially deflates the utopian idea of an enlightened 'golden age' of Irish bardic antiquity, but his ancient Ireland is not so much a negative space in the way of Scott's feudal Scotland as it is a self-consciously anomalous or anachronistic one produced by 'competing modes of political historiography', a characterisation of the Irish past that James Kelly, following Leersson, has called 'allochronic' and Patrick O'Malley sees as 'paramnesiac'.[89]

As the *Nation*'s reviewer pointed out in 1846, Moore's *History*, at times, veers unsatisfactorily between these competing historiographical accounts of the Irish past without displaying 'any fixed principles on Irish history'. Well known for his orientalising of Ireland in *Lalla Rookh* (1817), Moore follows Charles Vallancey's highly speculative philological logic in connecting pagan Ireland to ancient Greece and the Phoenicians.[90] While the aim of his 'oriental–diffusionalist' account is primarily to link ancient Ireland to the invention of writing in the ancient East, Moore adopts a fatalist paradigm when he maintains that Irish traditions replicate that 'ancient stationary system' which has kept 'the people of the East and their institutions so little changed through all time'. Proving the Irish 'worthy of their oriental descent', the history of Ireland likewise demonstrates 'long sterile interval[s]' of several hundreds of years where there is 'no event worthy of commemoration'.[91]

Moore's historical paradigm shifts from oriental stagnation to classical retrogradation when he considers the Irish descent into 'abasement and almost barbarism' under 'the yoke of the Danes' in the eighth century.[92] Now 'a mere shadow of sovereignty', Ireland's experience with the Danes is a 'dark and monotonous' precursor to the second abasement that comes with conquest by the English.[93] The Christian era provides Moore with more documentary clarity via monkish chroniclers and Roman annals, but it too is marked by a fatalistic history of internal division that is 'pregnant with the future': 'it is all of melancholy importance, as showing at how early a period Irishmen had become memorable for disunion among themselves'. The Irish are thus the perpetuators of their own future self-destruction, displaying a retrospective 'retentiveness of all belonging to the past' and 'incapacitating displays of melancholy, fatalism and nostalgia'.[94]

Like Scott, Moore characterises Ireland as a 'fated nation'. However, unlike Scotland, Ireland is 'fated to be the subject of faction'; in other words, Ireland is fated to undergo not union with England but rather *disunion*, particularly from the twelfth century onwards when the Anglo-Irish emerge as a distinct 'race'.[95] This period of history is one made 'more inhuman' than any other by the encoding of racial prejudice in law and by a widespread dispossession of the Gaelic Irish that involves the traumatic loss of land, language, and culture: 'a large proportion of the wretched people . . . were forced to fight for a spot to exist upon, even in their own land'.[96] Instead of a history of assimilation in the way of Scotland and Wales, Ireland's history from the twelfth century onwards becomes one of enduring sectarian division that progressively worsens and renders absurd any consensual rationale for the 1800 Act of Union.

Moore's fascination with the singularity of Irish history extends beyond the twelfth century to argue for the enduring influence of those 'principles of contrariety' that resist the 'ordinary rules and principles by which other countries are judged'. Even during Ireland's Christian fame, 'contrarieties of national character' ensure that the 'fruits of civilisation' habitually coexist with the 'violences of barbarism' just as the history of modern Ireland is 'adorned with high and shining names' but yet also 'convulsed'.[97] The nature of Irish history means that Ireland is not developmentally 'typical' in the way of Scotland, which, despite its uneven political geography of primitive Highlands and improving Lowlands, ultimately follows a stadialist logic. As in Scotland, Irish history is characterised by a much more extended period of feudalism than in England, as well as by a system of clanship that pays no deference to the rights of primogeniture and prevents the establishment of a properly genealogical system of inheritance. However, Ireland is ill-equipped to follow Scotland's progressive model of national consolidation.[98] In the constitutionally anachronistic space of Ireland, the temporalities of 'modern' and 'premodern' and 'barbarous' and 'civilised' persistently coexist: 'two thousand years have passed over the hovel of the Irish pauper in vain'.[99]

Moore is nonetheless careful to counteract the conflation of backwardness and cultural difference that marks the progressive modernity of stadial theory, reversing both the anti-Catholic gaze of English commentators and the negative imputations of continental European theologians by explicating Irish difference. He casts a revisionist eye, for instance, on Bernard of Clairvaux's 'gloomy picture of manners and morals of Ireland' during the tenth century, which is characterised by his disgust at the marriage of clergy and his understanding of Irish women as being 'in a state of almost universal concubinage'.[100] Moore likewise offsets accounts of the 'slavish mentality' of the Irish national character by introducing a counter-narrative of early independence and nationalist resistance against foreign encroachment and domination. However complacently and 'degenerately' the Irish later behave, the 'unconquerable spirit of the Irish people' rises during the Danish invasions, a period in which France became the fief of the Northmen, and the English twice, in the course of a few centuries, 'passed tamely under their yoke'.[101] The Romans, too, never attempted to conquer Ireland, with the Britons themselves viewing 'Ireland as a sign or example of liberty within their sight'.[102]

As Sharon Crozier-De Rosa has recently demonstrated, Moore's oscillation between negative and positive emotions of shame and pride is a tactical kind of 'moral battery' that was later widely used by Irish nationalists, from Young Ireland to Sinn Féin, to produce and sustain nationalist sentiment.[103] By arguing that centuries of English misrule have perverted the Irish capacity for civility and emotional restraint, Moore is able to represent the Irish as a naturally civil and sympathetic race, while also demonstrating how English laws have accustomed the Irish 'to be bad subjects', fomenting ungovernable passions of hatred and dissent, and leading to 'savage cruel acts' that are contrary to 'the general kindliness of the national temper'.[104] Moore's emphasis on the relationship between laws and manners is a response to a long English tradition of 'Gaelic barbarity' dating back to Edmund Spenser and the jurist John Davies, who argued that Irish law, manners, and language prevented social and economic progress, and that 'legal and cultural anglicisation would civilise the Irish'.[105] The idea that the Irish people are already innately civilised thus forms part of Moore's subtext for the Irish right to self-government, rendering the Irish national character proximate, if not superior, to the English, and implicitly distancing a civilised, normative, and potentially modern Ireland from conquered colonial peoples in India, North America, and elsewhere.

Moore's ongoing attempt to resituate Ireland within a Scottish enlightenment 'teleology of civility' finds its greatest test in the violent uprisings and religious factionalism that characterise the sixteenth century. Following the Reformation, the enmity between the native Irish and the settlers is exacerbated by the 'venom of religious schism' and by the negative social effects of colonisation and dispossession.[106] Notwithstanding the deceptive rhetoric of a 'civilising mission', the English/Scots plantation settlement of Ulster in 1572 disguises a 'marauding spirit' driven by greed, plunder, and fraud under the 'pretext of colonization', despoiling the Irish of their lands and making it inevitable that 'a people shamefully treated should resort to lawless revenge'.[107] Increasingly, Moore's history becomes one of English misgovernance rather than of Irish shame and degeneracy, reconfiguring a morbidly negative Irish self-image by representing the English (and the Anglo-Irish) as the antithesis of a progressive, civilising force. Moore justifies the uprisings in Dublin and Ulster that take place in 1641, for instance, by emphasising the Earl of Strafford's 'inhuman project of entirely extirpating the catholic Irish', while also noting 'the pliant readiness with which the Irish heart opens to kindness, whenever the rare experiment is tried of appealing to its better qualities'. Moore thus attempts to disassociate 'this dark chapter of our history' from the Irish character more generally: 'To the protestant the story, or legend, of the Irish massacre is from his childhood familiar; being, too often, the only remarkable event in our history with which he deigns to become acquainted.'[108]

In suggesting that English historical narratives have co-opted the trauma of Irish occupation and the seventeenth-century wars of religion in order to rationalise conquest and counter-insurgency, Moore rejects both the assumption of English civility and the presumed normality of English national sovereignty, cataloguing instead a long history of English anti-Catholicism and racial prejudice. He is in no doubt that this is a 'racial war' founded in conquest, settlement, and the politics of racial governance, involving not just English against Irish but the 'new Irish' or Anglo-Irish against the 'ancient or native Irish'.[109] While the Anglo-Irish are 'innoculated' with the 'national spirit' and are 'more Irish than the Irish themselves', they nonetheless inherit the 'worst qualities of the Irish' while retaining the 'tone and policy' of the English conquerors. Unlike Davis, who argued that the English invaders had succumbed to Hibernicisation and quasi-Catholic superstition, Moore qualifies the extent to which the Anglo-Irish could be said to have 'gone native', defining 'Irish' in a way that implies its close association with 'Gaelic' and 'Catholic'. Despite their anti-English and ostensibly counter-imperial stance, the 'naturalised' Anglo-Irish act as a master-caste and are thus unionist appropriators of Irish autochthony. Certainly, Moore's *History* does not put its narrative in the service of a besieged Protestant ascendency's sense of inevitable cultural, if not political, assimilation with Britain.[110]

In the final pages of the history, Moore offers a revisionist account of the Siege of Drogheda of 1641, noting the biases of historical accounts by Henry Tichbourne and other English chroniclers.[111] As in his post-Emancipation *Life and Death of Lord Edward Fitzgerald* (1831), where he argues for the Irish right to resist the 'monstrous doctrine of passive obedience', Moore presents the Drogheda uprisings as primarily concerned with freedom of religious worship, justifying the bloodshed by placing it in the context of religious and cultural intolerance, and defending the 'noble stand' by the Irish in defence of their ancient faith against narratives of 'Popish bondage'. Since Catholic Emancipation had by then become law through the Roman Catholic Relief Act of 1828, Moore is able implicitly to vindicate the seventeenth-century insurrections: the demands of the rebels include little more than the conditions which 'our glorious Grattan succeeded in wresting from the English ministry in the memorable year 1782'.[112]

Notwithstanding somewhat cryptic references to future suffering and injustice (presumably the atrocities of Cromwell's massacre in Drogheda in 1649), Moore's *History* ends not with colonial violence and suppression but by projecting itself forward to a period of emancipation and reform in the present. The *History*'s depiction of an anachronistic condition of 'disunion' that shuts Ireland out from historical development via auto-exoticising and backward-looking tropes of stagnation and decline is replaced by forward-looking tropes of tolerance and internal unity, implicitly representing English religious intolerance as a reactionary and dehumanising force in the inevitable movement towards future Irish independence. Despite the grim reality of ongoing Irish poverty and oppression—the final volume of the *History* was published in 1846, one of the worst of the Famine years—Moore ultimately attempts to counteract the fatalism of a bifurcated Ireland with a deferred utopianism that lies 'politically suspended' between a 'resurgent Catholic Ireland' and the 'potential of Ireland's cultural past'.[113] The *Nation* considered the first volume of the *History* to be an 'antiquarian essay' without any appeal for the Irish Catholic middle classes, as well complaining of Moore's fatalism and pessimism. However, as Moore's nationalist admirers and translators in Russia and eastern Europe recognised, and as Young Ireland itself eventually came to valorise in the work of George Petrie, Eugene O'Curry, and John O'Donovan, cultivating nationalist solidarity required both 'the heart of a patriot' and 'the learning and candour of the great antiquary'.[114]

British Creoles: Southey's *History of Brazil* and Racial Assimilation

In his long 1828 *Quarterly Review* essay against Catholic Emancipation, Southey dismisses the possibility of Irish independence and the repeal of the Union, noting here and in other review essays that British institutions and governance structures would eventually create those feelings of 'reverential attachment' necessary to preserve and expand the Empire. Ongoing anxiety over Irish intransigence and French imperialism even led him to promote a revised version of the much-maligned Spanish 'missionary' model, arguing that British domination in India and elsewhere could withstand the French threat only if it was based on a centralised system of mass conversions.[115] Given his lack of tolerance towards the causes of Catholic Emancipation and Irish independence, Southey's approval of the prospect of Brazilian independence in his *History of Brazil* may therefore, at first glance, seem surprising. In part, Southey's acceptance of Brazil's eventual political independence was the product of its role as an important part of Britain's 'informal' or 'economic' empire. However, the Peninsular War (1807–14) also had a profound impact on Southey's attitude towards questions of national self-determination.[116] Just as many of his epic poems can be read as 'allegorical denunciation[s] of French imperialism', the *History of Brazil* is marked by his 'imperialist ambitions' for Britain, simultaneously using Brazil as a means of condemning French, Portuguese, and Spanish imperialism and as an empty canvas or blank space on which to project his views on British national identity: 'here in Brazil', he writes on the first page of his *History*, are 'no tangles of crooked policy to unravel, no mysteries of state iniquity to elucidate, no revolutions to record, nor victories to celebrate'.[117]

In light of these nationalist aims, Southey's *History* reconfigures the well-trodden formula for writing on Brazil, which was generally characterised by stirring conquest and discovery narratives, sublime or heterotopic topographia, and a sentimentalised Edenic vision.[118] Southey had read Alexander von Humboldt's *Views of Nature* (1808) and *Ancient Inhabitants of America* (1810), but he does not follow Humboldt or other popular travel writers in recording physiological and emotional reactions to the Brazilian landscape.[119] On the contrary, the discovery of Brazil is anticlimactic, delaying territorial enclosure and thus any possibility of national unity: for over thirty years Vespucci's Brazilian settlements are virtually ignored by Portugal and 'Brazil was left open like a common'.[120]

Southey's subsequent accounts of the conquistadors and heroes of Portuguese and Spanish America likewise focus on the avarice and cruelty of figures such as Pizarro and Mendoza rather than on sublime discoveries. As in the quest for El Dorado described in his *Expedition of Orsua; and the Crimes of Aguirre* (1821), the pursuit of gold ends in death, mutiny, and the subjugation of Indigenous peoples, forming part of a submerged rhetoric of colonial trauma that haunts both texts.[121] At the same time, Southey's representation of the Amerindians diverges from more sentimental accounts by Robertson, Voltaire, Rousseau, and others. Opposing the primitivist myth of the 'noble savage' and echoing Adam Smith's belief in his *Theory of Moral Sentiments* that 'savages' were interested only in self-preservation and possessed 'little *natural* affection',[122] Southey instead follows David Hume in arguing that 'native savagery' was either the result of being 'cut off from the influence of the civilized world' or the product of social practices such as the 'morally brutalising effects' of slavery, caste systems, and polygamy.[123]

Recognising Southey's rejection of many of the rhetorical techniques associated with European encodings of the imperial frontier, the *Monthly Review* for December 1812 astutely noted the *History*'s lack of 'dazzling description' and its distance from the prevailing taste for sentimental effect in favour of a language of 'civic description'.[124]

By the late eighteenth and early nineteenth centuries, sentimentality had established itself as 'a powerful mode for representing colonial relations', establishing a clear link between aesthetics and ideology in the representation of discovery and conquest, and deploying sympathy as a way of producing and explaining racial difference.[125] While, in his 'Poems on the Slave Trade' (1797), Southey adopts the sentimentalising language common to anti-slavery writing, in the *History of Brazil* he prefers a more documentary style that focuses on the misdeeds of the European adventurers in the New World rather than on their suffering victims. In some ways, Southey's counter-sentimental approach reflects his sense of the ambiguous nature of paternalistic western interventionism in Brazil.[126] While most British writers distinguish the liberalism of British imperialism from the so-called 'black legend' of Spanish and Portuguese colonial policy in the Americas,[127] Southey represents Brazil as the site of an immoral pan-European colonial policy. Drake is a pirate who operates 'in the worst spirit of predatory warfare', and Raleigh uses fables such as El Dorado as 'baits for vulgar cupidity'. In the seventeenth and eighteenth centuries, the English imperial wars against Spain are rash and ill advised; and even in the present day, England's treatment of plantation slaves is deemed less progressive than that of the settlers in Brazil, where slavery is at least mitigated by frequent emancipations.[128]

Southey is thus explicit about the communal nature of European guilt in his anti-slavery critique, noting that '[t]here is an ineffaceable stigma upon the Europeans in their intercourse with those whom they treat as inferior races'. He even goes so far as to suggest that Amerindian cannibalism is less morally reprehensible than the 'moral and economic cannibalism' generated by European slave systems.[129] He is equally critical, however, of the anti-slavery policy of the Jesuits, who are against the slave trade because it dehumanises the Amerindians, but at the same time keep them 'always like little children in a state of pupillage', thereby hindering their political and intellectual emancipation, and enabling future acts of genocide. As a result, the Amerindians in Southey's *History* tend to be represented as either passive, child-like recipients of Jesuit sympathy, who have been rendered incapable of agency, or as 'savages' immersed in anthropophagic rituals such as witchcraft, infanticide, promiscuity, and cannibalism. As such, they lie outside of the bounds of sympathetic recognition shaped by the white liberal project of universal rights: 'I have to speak of savages so barbarous that little sympathy can be felt for any sufferings which they endured.'[130]

Reviewers tended to condemn Southey for his relative lack of anthropological interest. However, the *History* clearly attempts to shift the debate away from the ethnographic subject towards an assessment of European moral progress in Brazil, arguing that the 'principle of [moral] deterioration' is 'fatally and inseparably connected with ... institutions'.[131] Southey's view of the sociological development of Brazilian settler society loosely follows the Scottish enlightenment stadial model, with its imbrication of the capacity for feeling, material self-interest, and social progress. He notes, for example, that the selfish and hostile bands common to the early stages of society are perpetuated and even extended in settlements in the New World, which exhibit a persistent tendency towards 'savage' and unfeeling independence. Although Brazil progresses economically in the sixteenth and seventeenth centuries, murder is still rife and anti-slavery legislation is ignored.[132] Southey deems the state of society of Portuguese herdsmen even worse than the 'savage state' of the Amerindians, and the general degradation of both the Indians and the Portuguese is attributed to an over-abundance of cattle and horses, which prevents forms of social cultivation. The first European settlers are also hindered by the Brazilian climate, suffering terribly from tropical diseases, and from 'new diseases' arising from the intermixture of European, American, and African races.[133]

Southey thus represents the Portuguese settlers as exhibiting a prolonged period of unfeeling savagery, remaining in this stagnant, feudal state for some time.[134] By 1686 an increase of trade improves the settler state, largely because of regulations surrounding the ownership of diamond mines.[135] Initially licentious and consumed by a lust for wealth, the settlers or *moradores* become increasingly sturdy, hardy, and vigorous, primarily through their successful intermarriage with the virile South American natives. In São Paolo, for instance, 'the mixture of native blood' 'improved the race' and protected colonists from tropical diseases; and in the *mamelucos* (or mixed-race children) 'the European spirit of enterprize developed itself in constitutions adapted to the country'. Far from invoking negative orientalist images of the creolisation of European settlers in Brazil, Southey's mixed-race settlers undertake exploratory journeys into the colonial interior and secure for Portugal vast frontier territories in South America, as well as re-establishing the Portuguese claim to much of Brazil against the English and the Dutch in the seventeenth and eighteenth centuries.[136]

Despite his conservative reputation, Southey was not overly concerned by racial intermixture or by the republican inclinations of colonial settlements, predicting an inevitable process of independence and nation statehood for the settler colonies of Canada, Australia, and the Cape Colony.[137] Although he does not actively support colonial revolutionary violence, his *History* showcases the ways in which independence uprisings with some degree of popular legitimacy can encourage emotional attachment to the nation rather than fragmenting it.[138] Southey praises, for instance, João Fernandes Vieira, a mixed-race revolutionary who rebels against the Dutch in the sixteenth century. While he rejects Vieira's 'blind' Catholic superstition, he expresses admiration for his rebellion, in part because he sees Vieira as an abolitionist symbol but also because such uprisings represent an important step towards national self-identity.[139] Southey cannot condone nationalist uprisings in the context of Anglo-Irish Union or in the case of British India. However, he characterises Brazilian nationalism as a particular type of 'insurgent nationalism', one that echoes 'the virile heroism of its fore-fathers and empire-builders', as well the more local patriotism of Swiss, Spanish, and Portuguese national defenders during the Napoleonic Wars.[140] If he condemns the 'mob' of the 'lowest orders' associated with the insurrection of African slaves in the diamond mines of Minas Gerais, arguing that its ringleaders were foreigners or 'men of the mother country' rather than Brazilian settlers, Southey's support for the Portuguese revolutionaries against the Dutch nonetheless forms part of an underlying narrative of Brazilian national self-discovery in his *History*.

Southey also takes an interest in African *marronage* culture in Brazil—particularly the large *quilombo* of Palmares, which was a kind of organised federation of various Maroon communities of escaped slaves and their descendants. As Marcus Wood has pointed out, Southey produced 'the first extended account in English' of the inhabitants of Palmares and their leader Zumbi (Francisco Nzumbi), presenting the African-descended escapees not so much as dangerous insurgents or 'enemies of the State', but rather as relatively 'democratic' and 'highly organized' along the lines of classical republican communities.[141] While Southey accepts that the free state had to be contained in order to foster the movement towards hegemonic nationhood, he ultimately rejects 'the inhumane treatment of the defeated Palmares peoples' and 'the culture of slavery that had fomented its creation to begin with'.[142] He certainly celebrates the Palmares residents, stating that their history 'will not be perused without some feeling of respect for their character and compassion for their fate'.[143] Here the affective dimension of race that emerges in Southey's sentimental poems on the slave trade briefly reappears in his nostalgic, compassionate vision of a lost mixed-race, republican community. Certainly, the political will displayed by Zumbi and his mixed-race revolutionaries appears to elude Southey's passive and disengaged Amerindians, who manage to exploit the credulity of the Spaniards in their quest for gold but lack the ability to act as agents of their own progress, especially when exhibiting the unfeeling 'savagery' produced by their 'degraded' social conditions.

It is more likely that Southey saw Zumbi's resistance as a means of defaming Portuguese colonialism rather than as a means of explicitly invoking aspects of radical Afro-Brazilian consciousness. However, the racially mixed republican state of Palmares nonetheless reflects Southey's optimistic view of Brazilian progress and his belief that its peoples would eventually be blended into a racial democracy that would result in the abolition of slavery and reduce the threat of insurrections:[144]

> The grievances of the people may easily be remedied; the abolition of slavery will follow the abolition of the slave trade; the remaining savages will soon be civilized; and Indians, Negroes, and Portugueze, be gradually blended into one people, having for their inheritance one of the finest portions of the earth.

Like Moore, Southey casts the history of Brazil as one of promise, projecting the nation on to the future rather than defining it as the product of an (in)glorious past of exploration, conquest, and slavery. As he puts it in the final pages of the *History*, Brazil had the fairest of prospects if it continued to 'escape the curse of . . . Revolution', which, he felt, would 'bring on anarchy and civil war, and end in dividing the country into a number of petty and hostile states'.[145]

At the same time, the *History* can be described as legitimatory, in that it represents the process by which nations gain religious, racial, governmental, and affective cohesion. Southey's approval of the Brazilians' local patriotism is largely defined in terms of support for and attachment to the existing political order. The Portuguese settlers defend their territories from incursions by the Dutch and their resistance to authority is defensible in a way that is distinguishable from uprisings by 'native' populations in Ireland, India, and other British imperial settlements. Southey's support of an emergent Brazilian nationalism is also grounded in the language of emotional and moral reform: he is prepared to champion the Portuguese settlers as they become gradually more refined, liberal, and open to free trade; in other words, as they align themselves with the 'benign' domination of British colonial practices rather than Iberian ones.[146] As Southey's Brazilians progress towards independence from Portugal and develop a more cohesive national identity, they are invested with more refined moral sensibilities and peculiarly 'British' national qualities such as compassion, bravery, sturdiness, practicality, prudence, and moral probity, making their drift towards emancipation a vindication of a superior British colonial culture.[147]

Alongside this narrative of the internalisation of British cultural and dispositional standards by the Portuguese settlers, Southey's *History* outlines a form of national consolidation tied to models of ethnic and racial fusion. Just as in the second part of *Madoc*, with its intermarriages between Native Americans and Europeans, Southey represents successful models of independent nationhood as linked to discourses of acclimatisation, intermarriage, and emancipation from imperial control.[148] It was not uncommon for contemporary observers to attribute Brazil's prosperity to its liberality about mixed racial castes. Southey's friend, Henry Koster, argued in his *Travels in Brazil* (1816) that the 'degraded state of the people of colour in the British Colonies is most lamentable' and praised Brazil for its more enlightened attitude.[149] By presenting Brazil as a model for the productive cohabitation of races—an emerging *mestizo* culture—Southey detaches nationhood from racial purity while simultaneously making it heavily contingent on a merged or fused ethnicity. He thus sees racial amalgamation as part of the 'originary process of nation formation' that nearly always involves the absorption of ethnic and cultural difference through various forms of settlement and colonisation. If this is not entirely a vision of 'white European dominance', in that it accounts for non-European racial intermixtures and multiethnic societies, it nonetheless naturalises colonial race relations in Brazil by resting on an eventual homogeneity, producing a 'racial paradise' that is characterised by shared bloodlines and a set of inherited characteristics in a similar but more explicitly biological way than Scott's hegemonic vision of a 'blended' British nation.[150]

Southey thus ties racial assimilation to the consolidation of national feeling, linking Brazilian modernity, social hierarchy, and political behaviour to (displaced) forms of white European identity: harmony in Brazil depends both on racial amalgamation and on the emotional maturity of the increasingly 'benevolent' Portuguese settlers. As Ulla D. Berg and Ana Y. Ramos-Zayas have pointed out, this foundational narrative of Portuguese benevolence, and the 'whitening of race' that emerges as a direct result of white settler material privileges, underpins the construction of a new, blended 'tropical civilization in Brazil', ensuring that tolerance and 'intimacy, rather than racial violence, [would become] the dominant affective structure underscoring "racial democracy"'.[151] Southey's rejection of a vivid imperial rhetoric may seem at odds with later imperialist histories, but his strategy of managing and limiting affective responses to Brazil is itself a racialised means of organising the distribution of sensibilities, producing a myth of harmonious racial relations that was to have a long afterlife in Latin America. While he deflates heroic tales of discovery and conquest, Southey naturalises the European experience in Brazil via a latent Anglocentric subtext, simultaneously co-opting the hegemonic tendencies of Spanish/Portuguese imperialism and representing Britain as a more benign colonial power, divorced from the violence and cruelty associated with those regimes. Southey's *History* thus points to a tendency in early nineteenth-century colonial histories to obfuscate the profound inequalities behind racial assimilation in order to showcase a new expansionist or imperialist model of British national identity.[152]

National Methodologies and Methodological Nationalism

Despite its topicality and its meticulous research, many reviewers considered the size of Southey's *History* to be disproportionate to its value. The *Eclectic Review* thought that the incidents recorded 'by no means merited so accurate and minute a delineation, as Mr. Southey has thought proper to furnish', while the *Monthly Review* argued that a history of Brazil was not a subject worthy of Southey's immense labour.[153] Reservations about Brazil as a subject were accompanied by reservations about Southey's methods. Most reviewers agreed in praising Southey's 'labour in the accumulation of facts' and his 'indefatigable spirit of research', but nearly all of them found the work lacking in reflection and selectivity.[154] While recognising that Southey had selected a 'mode of writing history' which is 'confirmed in great measure by the authority of the ancients', the *Monthly Review* argued that Southey 'has gone greatly too far into particular detail for the taste of the present generation; which expects something more than a succession of objects and occurrences'. The *British Critic* similarly asserted that the historian's duty is not merely to record events chronologically, but to select, classify, compare, and evaluate them so that 'moral lessons are enforced, and the principles of human conduct deduced'.[155]

Southey's deliberate plan to avoid thematic divisions and digressions in the *History of Brazil* grew out of his research for another project: a projected twelve-volume history of Portugal. By drawing on the eyewitness accounts uncovered by his systematic study of sixteenth-century Spanish chronicles in the Royal Library in Lisbon in 1800, Southey hoped to counter the deductive, generalising principles and the 'Frenchified' style of philosophic historians such as Robertson, Hume, and Gibbon.[156] While acknowledging their inaccuracies, Southey saw in the 'counter-Reformation Catholic triumphalism' of the chronicles of Herrera, Oviedo, Gómara, and especially Torquemada, a means to redress the philosophic malaise that imbued the historical writing of his enlightenment predecessors.[157] Southey's plan for his history of Portugal was accordingly to open with the 'fabulous history' of Tubal.[158] Following Milton, who had used English foundation myths in his *History of Britain* (1671) as a way of establishing a national history, Southey intended to include a 'St Palaye chapter' on the Gothic period, suggesting that he did not mean to exclude fabulous or mythological history in the manner of philosophic historians.[159] By the 1820s and 1830s, Southey was less sure of the role of foundation myths in national history, complaining to his son-in-law, John Wood Warter, in 1831 that German classicists such as Karl Otfried Müller and B. G. Niebuhr 'consider history as fable and fable as history ... introducing into their text what ought to be thrown into notes, or appended in dissertations'. Southey eventually came to treat the myth of El Dorado and other foundational myths surrounding the Amazonian tribes as 'dangerous fictions' in the *History of Brazil*, but his resistance to philosophic abstraction remained a touchstone throughout his career as a historian.[160]

Preferring a 'quasi-encyclopedic approach' over abstract generalisation, Southey rejected philosophic history for three reasons: first, he dismissed its tendency to be over-deterministic, arguing that it carries 'the influence of general causes too far, considering men as entirely the creatures of the circumstances wherein they are placed'; second, he thought that philosophic history tended to favour party bias rather than factual complexity because of its conjectural tendency to deal in 'deductions and not in details'; and third, he saw the abstraction of philosophic history as detrimental to narratives that attempted to valorise public moralism and the unifying tendencies of the nation state.[161] Southey's extended thinking about the methodological problems of philosophic history suggests that the historical methods he favours in the *History of Brazil*—a return to the narrative style of the old chronicles, a rejection of philosophic abstraction, and a counter-sentimental history of the anti-sublime—are part of a deliberate attempt to rehabilitate a classical tradition that could bring all of the elements of a national history together into a narrative 'which proceeds according to the course of time and events, and records things as they intermingled in the multifold concerns of society'.[162]

As an early example of methodological or 'historiographical nationalism', Southey's revised classical model intimates the ways in which nineteenth-century narrative history repurposed the culturalist discourses of ethnic origins that originated in antiquarian debates in the service of a new imperial paradigm of national self-discovery: one that, despite its transnational and expansionist perspectives, naturalised the nation state as both a homogenous ethnic community and as a unit of historical study.[163] Southey's vision of history, like that of Scott, foregrounds the progressivist momentum of the nation state and its assimilative tendencies, which are figured as part of the foundational work of nation-building. Moore's *History*, on the other hand, rejects assimilationist narratives of national consolidation in order to represent Ireland as a site both of sovereign failure and of emancipatory national potential. However, it, too, reveals the extent to which the affective logic of belonging was organised via the national form and its institutions of social reproduction. All three histories demonstrate the ways in which nation states use foundation myths to underwrite identity and confer legitimacy. And all three histories, to varying degrees, accentuate questions of racial difference, from the budding racialism of early Celtic revivalism to questions of racial assimilation in the context of imperial expansion and colonisation.

Southey's emphasis on racial assimilation is thus a model of national identity formation nurtured by the modern racial thinking that emerged from both internal and external colonisation. Ethnonationalist ideologies provided the conceptual foundations for the establishment of new nation states and for the consolidation and expansion of older ones, rationalising British imperial expansion as a 'natural' offshoot of England's Anglo-Saxon past. As the 'external' or 'peripheral' locus of Southey's examination of national identity suggests, British nationalism and understandings of the rise of the modern nation state were developed via complex transnational processes rather than within territorially limited spaces. Nationalism, as Miranda Burgess has put it, was always a 'dynamically fractured' conceptual model, simultaneously arising out of 'complex, uneven network[s]' of imperial exchange, and from 'uneven development *within* the British isles'.[164]

Chapter 4

Historical Style and the Man of Letters: Macaulay and Carlyle

This chapter turns more explicitly to those questions of rhetoric and style that have infused the previous three chapters, considering both the relationship between style and the formation of historical protocols, and how style informs the reception of written history in periodical reviews. By examining the reception history of T. B. Macaulay's *History of England* (1848–59) and Thomas Carlyle's *French Revolution: A History*, it seeks first, to unpack the methodological conventions and disciplinary judgments that later critics and self-identified 'scientific' historians such as J. R. Seeley transmitted about their more 'popular', 'literary', and 'novelistic' predecessors; and second, to rehabilitate prose style as part of a technical discourse that reflects and mediates the domain of historical knowledge production. As discussed in the introduction to this book, I understand style very broadly as a 'mode of thinking *through*' or, perhaps more accurately, as a mode of 'historical thinking' rather than simply as an ornamental or mechanical device.[1] In other words, I consider 'style in its widest sense' or, as the biographer, critic, and editor of the *Fortnightly Review*, John Morley, put it in a reference to Thomas De Quincey's theory of 'organology': 'style ... in its relation to ideas and feelings, its commerce with thought, and its reaction on what one may call the temper or conscience of the intellect'.[2]

Contained within a long essay on the relationship between style and national character published in instalments in *Blackwood's Edinburgh Magazine* between 1840 and 1841, De Quincey's characterisation of style as an arbiter of the 'temper or conscience of the intellect' provides a way of understanding Macaulay's 'vividness', Carlyle's 'irregularity', and other personal idiosyncrasies as an index to larger questions about how stylistic practices reflect and participate in debates concerning national distinctiveness, historical specialisation, and the formation of disciplinary protocols. As Andrew Elfenbein has pointed out, it was the very status of Macaulay and Carlyle as celebrated stylists that concealed the encroaching 'threat of specialized prose' throughout much of the nineteenth century.³ By emphasising the exhibitionism of their literary techniques, Macaulay and Carlyle could be deemed amateurs and generalists even as they deployed what can only be described as markedly contrastive styles: Macaulay's style is uniform, polished, and to an extent Johnsonian, whereas Carlyle conspicuously aims to rupture the neoclassical style with a 'Gothic and Gaelic confection', an idiomatic mode that sought to synthesise the competing traditions of Anglo-Saxon Gothicism and Celtic or Gaelic emotionalism.⁴ Macaulay and Carlyle thus, to a degree, reproduce within the historiographical domain the division that had earlier emerged within poetry 'between the generic, all-purpose familiar prose style and the distinctive, stylistic stamp of genius', both of which had a partially Scottish lineage: the evolution of the Anglo-British generic style of expository prose can be traced back to the belletrists of the Scottish enlightenment such as Adam Smith and Hugh Blair, and before them to Joseph Addison and Richard Steele, while the prophetic mode partly emerged from discourses surrounding millenarianism, Covenanting enthusiasm, and the pulpit language of Scottish Presbyterian Calvinists, from John Knox to Edward Irving.⁵

Macaulay's embrace of Anglo-British stylistic norms and Carlyle's rupture of those norms therefore involved a strategic choice of different literary inheritances. However, these choices were also mediated by and through a critical reviewing culture that sought to repackage learned knowledge of all kinds into a digestible form for a broad but culturally ambitious audience. As experienced contributors to the *Edinburgh Review* and other journals, Macaulay and Carlyle, like De Quincey himself, were part of an evolving culture of generalisation, developing their interest in the practice and philosophy of history in tandem with their review essays. At the same time, they encouraged specialisation and the reconfiguration of generic hierarchies through various forms of critical gatekeeping and the assumption of historical authority and expertise.⁶

Disavowing the 'rude [and] superficial character of [a] newspaper style' that encourages the 'trick of short-hand' (or uncritical) reading, De Quincey, for instance, maintains that periodical essays should renounce annotative practices in favour of exploiting novelty and paradox, whereas 'the higher forms of history and philosophy ... ought not to be idiomatic' or 'journalistic'. If De Quincey ultimately understands the effect of periodical prose as a corruption of the natural idioms of English speech, distinguishing between 'organic' and 'mechanical' styles, his separation of 'higher' and 'lower' forms of knowledge is nonetheless a direct response to the stylistic norms inculcated by market professionalism.⁷

Carlyle's early journalism was written in a relatively conventional Johnsonian mode up until the late 1820s, when the style of his review essays became less distinguishable from the queer, hortatory style of his non-journalistic writing. Macaulay, on the other hand, followed De Quincey in arguing that 'high and grave works' like history and moral philosophy are best written without ornamentation, while periodical writing should be 'florid' and 'striking' if it is to impress the easily distracted middle-class reader.[8] Yet despite Macaulay's ostensible separation of his historical writing from his periodical authorship—a separation that he insisted must be maintained at the level of content as well as style—the anecdotal nature of his *History of England* loosened, whether deliberately or inadvertently, the rules of dignity and propriety promoted by eighteenth-century belletrists such as Smith and Blair.[9]

Even as Macaulay self-consciously sought to sequester his journalistic essays and biographical sketches from the epic style and content of his written histories, the stylistic innovations associated with review essays opened up official history to 'the more visceral language of journalism', as well as to more idiomatic and anecdotal styles than those sanctioned by the decorous prose of neoclassical history. If, at first glance, then, Macaulay and Carlyle seem a counter-intuitive pairing in a personal, stylistic, and ideological sense, they were increasingly united in their disruption of 'the dignity of history' in the service of a more 'striking' type of history: one that was both indebted to and distinguished itself from the styles, techniques, and practices emanating from review essays and periodical culture more generally. As a direct result, they were also increasingly united from the 1870s onwards by critical responses to their work as 'literary', 'essayistic', and 'unscientific', and thus by their exclusion from the emerging field of academic history.[10]

Macaulay's Inductive History and the Novelistic Style

Reflecting on the most 'universally popular' author of his generation in his 'Essay on Macaulay' (1876), John Morley ascribes Macaulay's global renown to his instinctive appeal to the sensibility of the Anglophone middle classes: 'he was in exact accord with the common average sentiment of his day on every subject on which he spoke'.[11] As much a 'middling' man as the immense reading audiences he craved, Macaulay's writing is saturated with 'the external and the superficial', 'action and movement', and the 'five senses' so that '*good* [in Macaulay's work] means good to eat, good to wear, material commodity'.[12] Morley's association of Macaulay's popularity with the concrete materialism, commercialism, and other values and belief systems of the rising middle classes invests in the emerging ideological gap between elite and popular culture that late Victorian criticism did so much to solidify, closely tying popular writing to the spread of mass literacy and the rise of the common reader, while simultaneously attempting to close that gap by recommending Macaulay's essays as 'an incomparable manual and vade-mecum for a busy uneducated man'.[13]

Himself a generalist who strove to arbitrate the domain of middle-class reading audiences, Morley's ambivalence towards Macaulay's popularity reflects a tension in nineteenth-century literary culture between what John Guillory has called 'clarity' and 'technicity'.[14] While the 'Essay on Macaulay' was not part of Morley's thirty-nine volume 'English Men of Letters' series, published by Alexander Macmillan between 1878 and 1892, it too was ideologically driven, seeking to distribute the fruits of an elite literary culture across a broader and less specialised 'middle-brow' readership.[15] Morley may have seen Macaulay as 'prosaic' compared to the 'higher genius' of Carlyle and John Stuart Mill, but his own career was, to a large extent, modelled on Macaulay's inclination towards critical essays and biographical sketches, as well as replicating the kind of accessible prose style that could act a model for readers from England to Australia.[16] Reservations about Macaulay's philosophic shallowness could therefore be appeased by Morley's desire to institutionalise an ideally transparent and 'universally valid' style that could overcome national, religious, class, and other particularities, and instantiate the Victorian man of letters as a public intellectual.[17]

Morley is less certain, however, that the *content* of Macaulay's work could straddle the divide between general and specialist readerships. Acknowledging Macaulay's encyclopaedic knowledge about Britain's past but severing it from the analytical bent of learned or expert discourse ('the spirit of analysis is not in him'), the 'Essay on Macaulay' anticipates three now long-standing assumptions about written history in the early to mid-nineteenth century: first, that it was amateur or unprofessional, designed to appeal to the 'busy uneducated man' rather than to scholars, and resonating more in the realm of middle-class polite letters than in the field of expert knowledge; second, that it capitalised on the porous boundaries between history and fiction to garner celebrity and financial gain in a largely unregulated marketplace increasingly dominated by the novel and the 'sacerdotal phenomenon' of the man of letters; and third, that it was literary or novelistic in style, more concerned with picturesque description than with causation or argument, and making no attempt to advance a philosophy of history or endorse 'a standard of disciplinary rigor'.[18]

Macaulay's own very different understanding of his 'novelistic' preference for continuous narrative emerged both from his reflections on the historiographical impact of Walter Scott's Waverley novels (and the whole discourse surrounding popular print culture and vernacular sources more generally), and from his evolving ideas on the relationship between historical writing and inductive logic. In an 1828 *Edinburgh Review* article on Henry Hallam's *Constitutional History of England* (1827), for instance, Macaulay identifies the close connection between Hallam's 'serious' content and his austere style, which is 'not florid or impassioned, but high, grave, and sober', 'such as would become a state paper' or 'a judgement delivered by a great magistrate'. Divorcing written history from advocacy and polemic, Hallam's juridical style leads Macaulay to judge the *Constitutional History* 'the most impartial book that we ever have read', an impartiality achieved through an 'absolute mastery' over 'party spirit', which Macaulay predicts will be 'offensive to many of [Hallam's] readers'. Although the more commercially oriented Macaulay sees Hallam's stylistic restraint as likely to detract from the book's popularity and sales figures, he nonetheless looks beyond its sober style to recognise a methodology that would prove critical to the development of his own historical practice: the idea that empirical details can provide quasi-scientific grounds for forming inductive conclusions.[19]

Increasingly sceptical of the value of philosophic generalisation, Macaulay saw the data-driven quality of Hallam's *Constitutional History* as a model for the history of those kinds of social and political phenomena, such as constitutions and the common law, which could be understood through the gradual and organic assimilation of factual details. A rationalist and legalist, Hallam describes his own methodology in similarly empirical terms in an 1813 letter to Lord Webb Seymour, where he argues that 'the labour of collecting facts of itself places the mind in a state adverse to the formation of general results or original theories'.[20] In one of the few revisionary accounts of Hallam's work, Michael Bentley rightly characterises Hallam as one of the English pioneers of a new type of 'systematic analysis' of the past that separated political philosophy from historical enquiry.[21] If Macaulay's famous review essay ultimately immersed Hallam in the 'Whig environment of the day' and concealed the depth of his historiographical innovation, Macaulay nonetheless presciently recognises that Hallam has departed from the *a priori*, conjectural methodology of the *philosophes* and introduced a more pragmatic methodology that treats European legal codes 'as a series of overlapping case-studies': a methodology capable of 'teach[ing] us not only the general rule, but the mode of applying it to solve particular cases'.[22]

As this reference to Hallam's case-based or analogical method suggests, Macaulay had begun to refine and filter his understanding of historical method through his critique of Benthamite utilitarianism and what he saw as James Mill's prescriptive attempt to promote a 'science of history and politics' via the application of fixed laws of human progress. Originally drawn from Aristotle's *Organon* and developed by Francis Bacon's *Novum Organum* (1620), the inductive approach in classical logic relies on similarities between particular instances to form general principles. Having studied logic, Bentham himself promoted inductive reasoning as a means of 'providing knowledge in the application of the principle of utility'.[23] In Macaulay's view, however, Bentham's acolytes had placed the principle of utility before the method of empirical observation. In his 1829 *Edinburgh Review* polemic on Mill's 'Essay on Government' (1820), written just after his review of Hallam's *History*, Macaulay dismisses Mill's 'ahistorical' approach to the 'Science of Politics' in favour of an alternative approach that works by

> observing the present state of the world,—by assiduously studying the history of past ages,—by shifting the evidence of facts . . . by perpetually bringing the theory which we have constructed to the test of new facts,—by correcting, or altogether abandoning it, as these new facts prove it to be partially or fundamentally unsound.[24]

Reiterating his approval of the 'inductive methodology' in an 1835 review of James Mackintosh's *History of the Revolution of 1688*, Macaulay argues that historical works should demonstrate the organic development of 'the state of political science and political morality in former ages'. In contrast to the 'short synthetical arguments' of his political theory, Macaulay maintains that Mill's *History of British India* (1817) provides detailed empirical explanations of the slow growth and development of Indian culture, representing a marked improvement on the speculative fallacies of philosophic historians such as Hume and Gibbon, whose chief fault is their emphasis on 'deducing general principles from facts' and 'distorting facts to suit general principles'. While Macaulay acknowledges Hume's scepticism towards the reliability of historical data, he ultimately declares him little more than an 'accomplished advocate', whose 'insidious candour' rests on a giant superstructure of sophistry: history, in Hume's hands, has become a 'political science'.[25]

Macaulay's reflections on the processual nature of the inductive methodology are suggestive of the extent to which constitutional history had become the site of important historiographical innovation in the early to mid-nineteenth century. Before E. A. Freeman and others consolidated the 'historiographical norm of the Common Law tradition', historians such as Hallam and Francis Palgrave examined the relationship between social development and legal institutions, combining an empirical analysis of statistical data with an understanding of historical progress as a sequential process. Buttressed by the methodical deployment of archival material to which he had unprecedented access, Palgrave's *Rise and Progress of the English Commonwealth* (1832) and *History of Normandy and England* (1851–61) sought to draw wider conclusions about English history from case studies of the development of its legal principles.[26] Although Macaulay followed Palgrave in favouring a vivid style and a more continuous narrative over a thematic approach, he approved of the case-study methodology initiated by Hallam, seeing the gradual and evolving testing of historical particulars as an improvement on the speculative 'vagueness which is the common fault of political philosophy'.[27]

Macaulay's preference for continuous narrative and for a sequential presentation of primary data was not, then, based solely on his desire to sell books to middle-class readers. At the same time, he understood his own endeavours as operating on a more 'human' scale of history than that of Hallam or even Palgrave. The history of experience and everyday life, he argues in his review of Mackintosh's *History of the Revolution*, could be comprehended only via an immersion in the mental and emotional worlds of ordinary historical actors: 'we ought to place ourselves in their situation'.[28] As Mackintosh, a keen reader of novels, put it in his 1821 review of the first volume of Sismondi's *History of France* (1821–44), the modern historian must borrow 'directly from the first sources', allowing them to 'kindle his imagination' and crucially 'to *antiquate* his feelings, so as to become for a moment the contemporary of those ages of which he is the historian'.[29]

On one level, this immersive 'presence paradigm' involves a recognition of the power of novelists like Walter Scott to rival works of history.[30] As Macaulay concedes in his famous *Edinburgh Review* essay on Henry Neele's *The Romance of History* (1828), the process of fusing events, whether imaginary or real, into a comprehensive whole is not a 'mere mechanical imitation of realty' but rather an imaginative process involving 'skilful selection and disposition': 'No picture then, and no history can present us with the whole truth: but those are the best pictures and the best histories which exhibit such parts of the truth as most nearly produce the effect of the whole.'[31] Appreciating that Scott's achievement involved a 'shift from a strategy of metonymic reduction (whole to part) to one of synechdochic integration (part to whole)', Macaulay suggests that it is precisely because history can reclaim 'those fragments of truth which many historians have scornfully thrown behind them' or considered 'beneath their dignity' that they can upset Scott's division of labour between depicting 'what [our ancestors] were' (fiction) and 'what they did' (history).[32]

In diagnosing 'the loss of literary innocence after Scott', Macaulay imagines an alternative kind of narrative that has 'descended below the dignity of history', one that E. P. Thompson would later call 'history from below' or the 'under-current': that is, a vernacular history drawn from popular print culture, folklore, ephemeral pamphlets, broadsheets, and other sources that antiquarian publishing societies like Scott's Bannatyne Club had done so much to promote and endorse.[33] 'Rich with colouring from romance, ballad, and chronicle', Macaulay's methodology of aggregating 'a thousand slight touches' and 'innumerable particulars' recognises that historical truth depends more on those minute, almost circumstantial, details that are typically associated with the 'reality effect' of the novel than it does on argumentation, or what Roland Barthes has called 'predictive statements'.[34] Most importantly, Macaulay's historical theory and practice draws attention to two different types of particularity in the writing of history: the particularity of the fact versus the particularity of the circumstantial detail, combining a novelistic theory of reality effect with a sense of history's distinctive ability to combine 'precious particles' of abstract meaning with facts 'in such a manner that the separation is a task of the utmost difficulty'.[35]

Macaulay thus accepts the value and power of circumstantial detail for the production of reality effect in written history. However, in valorising the role of original historical sources in relating 'the real life of the nation', he concludes that historians are free to invent only in limited, controlled, or customary ways:

> A perfect historian must possess an imagination sufficiently powerful to make his narrative affecting and picturesque. Yet he must control it so absolutely as to content himself with the materials which he finds, and to refrain from supplying deficiencies by additions of his own.[36]

In a further qualifying turn, Macaulay goes on to concede that predictive statements perform a critical and distinctive function in written history. In 'deductive' fiction, he concludes, 'the principles are given to find the facts: in history, the facts are given to find the principles; and the writer who does not explain the phenomena as well as state them, performs only one half of his office'. Indeed, '[f]acts are the mere dross of history'; '[i]t is from the abstract truth which interpenetrates them, and lies latent among them, like gold in the ore, that the mass derives its whole value'.[37]

Notwithstanding these qualifications, Macaulay's *History of England* demonstrates an ongoing resistance to abstractive or deductive principles in written history, resulting in a five-volume work that eludes a clear formal, thematic, or systematic framework, and instead allows historical knowledge to emerge, as he puts it, 'not from any single work, but from thousands of forgotten tracts, sermons, and satires; in fact, from a whole literature which is mouldering in old libraries'.[38] It is by now well established that the assimilation of these popular sources to notions of progress and continuity was the 'central synthetic task' of Macaulay's *History*, the point of which, as Borislav Knezevic has noted, is to tell the 'story of national progress, as slow and gradual as the inductive method' itself. Catherine Hall, too, has analysed the 'insular and assimilationist vision' of the *History*, relating its nationalist 'island story' more directly to Macaulay's 'Scottish Orientalism' and imperial careering, and arguing that its 'master narrative of [national] descent' is defined by 'systematic exclusions' and 'strategies of distantiation and disavowal', particularly in relation to the 'inassimilable' nature of Ireland and the 'ghostly presence' of Britain's imperial dominions.[39]

Macaulay's contemporaries agreed that the success of his *History of England* was primarily the result of the way in which 'doubts were dispelled – the chaos reduced to order'. As Francis Jeffrey saw it, Macaulay had written a brilliant response to Burke's evocation of the anarchy caused (and never entirely dispelled) by the French Revolution by returning everything to its rightful place.[40] Other commentators concurred, if somewhat more critically. J. S. Mill noted in 1849 that Macaulay's parochialism had 'ministered to English conceit' while remaining entrenched in 'the deep sleep of a decided opinion'. In his 1856 essay on Macaulay, Walter Bagehot complained of the formulaic glibness of Macaulay's narrative style and of his lack of 'passionate self-questionings': 'It is too omniscient. Everything is too plain. All is clear; nothing is doubtful ... there is a want of graduation in it.' This, Bagehot argues, in an acknowledgement of the critical relationship between historical style and content, is 'hardly the style for history', which, as a 'vestige of vestiges', should reproduce 'a heap of confusion' and uncertainties. Harriet Martineau, on the other hand, declared Macaulay stylistically brilliant but radically inaccurate in his 'habit of thought' and ultimately 'cold and barren as regards the highest part of human nature' in her obituary in the *Daily News* in 1859. Morley put it equally harshly in his 'Essay', arguing that Macaulay's 'unanalytical turn of mind kept him free of any temptation to think of love of country as a prejudice, or a passion for freedom as an illusion'.[41]

In characterising Macaulay's work as concerned primarily with the description of tastes, textures, smells, and other sensory phenomena, Morley positions Macaulay not only as unanalytical and unscientific, but also as the naive obverse of 'spiritual' historians such as Carlyle, who are at least concerned with interiority, psychology, and motive. Morley concedes that Macaulay regularly describes the thoughts and feelings of ordinary historical actors through internalised character portraits, such as when he provides a 'common view' of the unhomely Irish threat to hearth and home from inside the seventeenth-century mind.[42] Yet despite Macaulay's ability to reconstruct racialised character sketches, most reviewers conclude that he is not attracted to the interiority of psychological depth models of characterisation or to the 'passionate eras of our history'. The same 'defect', as Bagehot puts it, applies to Macaulay's treatment of the religious passion of the English Civil Wars, where the 'interior zeal' of the Commonwealth men does not suit his propensity to write from the perspective of 'an enjoying English gentleman', and ironically, given the faith of Macaulay's Scottish father, betrays his 'utter want of sympathy with the Puritan disposition'.[43]

As the so-called 'scientific method' gained greater traction in written history, later critics turned their attention to Macaulay's excessive colour and picturesque description, his exaggeration and declamatory emphasis, and what Charles Firth, following Macaulay's own indictment of Tacitus, called his tendency to 'stimulate till stimulants lose their force'. Writing in 1938, Firth considered Macaulay to be 'an orator addressing a great mixed audience' rather than a historian in any serious sense: 'The Style of Macaulay's History is the style of his speeches ... the orator is always appearing behind the historian.'[44] For other critics, the problem with Macaulay's style lay in its novelistic tendencies, which, Morley believed, operated at the expense of analytical or theoretical properties. While Morley recognises Macaulay's drive towards realism when he notes the latter's ability to 'tell a tale directly and in straightforward order', he also complains of the *History*'s unnecessary anecdotal detail.[45] For Morley and other late nineteenth-century critics, Macaulay fails to rise above the kind of organic synthesis that subordinates historical change to instinct and natural law, thereby promoting a base historical materialism described by the philosopher and biologist Herbert Spence and the Irish historian William Lecky as a methodology resembling 'low organisations, being a perpetual repetition of similar parts'—a charge that Herman Merivale and J. R. Seeley also laid at Carlyle's door when they complained that the latter was 'perpetually reiterating' the same point.[46]

Historians and literary critics today tend to agree that the lack of thematic organisation in Macaulay's *History of England* is driven by a 'hyperproduction of narrative'.[47] As George Levine pointed out years ago, the overriding form of the *History* is 'narrative, rather than thematic', resting its authority not on explicit statement but on 'the implicit value-laden contrast between past and present'. This often involves establishing interlocking networks of historical parallels, such as allusions to the Reform Acts, Catholic Emancipation, and the Crimean War as analogues to seventeenth-century problems; for example, when describing the scene at the Battle of Boyne, Macaulay moves between how it looked in 1640 and 1848, foreshadowing later events in a technique that Levine calls his 'double vision'.[48] For all his attempts to distance his review essays from his historical writing, this technique largely grew out of Macaulay's periodical essays, which combined historical commentary with contemporary comparisons, particularly when engaging with the constitutional parallels between the Glorious Revolution of 1688 and the historical legitimacy of proposed changes to franchise and parliamentary procedure during the turbulent decades leading up to the 1828–32 Reform Acts:

> We stand in a situation similar to that in which our ancestors stood under the reign of James the First. It will soon again be necessary to reform that we may preserve, to save the fundamental parts of the Constitution by alterations in the subordinate parts.[49]

In his desire to reproduce 'a true picture of the life of [our] ancestors', Macaulay is self-avowedly indebted to Scott. However, at root both his style and his methodology are more beholden to his periodical writing and to the generative effects of the kinds of documents published by the printing societies and book clubs that Scott was instrumental in pioneering: that is, archival, archaeological, and epigraphic forms of textual and material evidence, especially those sources that encapsulated folk, oral, and domestic traditions. As Rohan Maitzen has noted, Macaulay's emphasis on 'indirect agency' or 'effects stemming from diffuse causes rather than decisive acts' is a model of historical explanation compatible not just with Scott's novels but also with the para-historical genres that official history supposedly disavowed: biography, memoir, secret history, and the history of domesticity and the private life, many of which were written by women.[50] The most obvious example of Macaulay's ability to write history 'from below' is, of course, his famous treatment of quotidian life in Chapter 3 of the *History of England*, 'The State of England in 1685', which James Moncreiff recognises in the *Edinburgh Review* as an 'endeavour to lead history into a deeper and wider channel' as it relates to 'the domestic and every-day life of those times'. Pre-empting later claims by Peter Gay, John Clive, and others that this chapter is 'a pioneering piece of social history' rather than a study of 'manners' in the Scottish enlightenment sense, Archibald Alison argues for the depth of Macaulay's 'manly' originality in 'The State of England' in a review essay for *Blackwood's*, even as he compares other parts of the *History*, in equally gendered terms, to Mrs Trollope's drawing-room 'burlesques'.[51]

Despite the near universal contemporary appreciation of Chapter 3 of the *History*, Macaulay's attempt to produce an ethnography of the nation state (and to build historical knowledge from the ground up rather than from the top down) was dismissed by later Victorian critics as 'popular' history and attributed either to his non-expert idiom or to the influence of the novel. These dismissals may have arisen, in part, from an instinctive sense that the hybrid genres of women's history were the true progenitors of Macaulay's social history. However, they also rested on the grounds of superficiality, a journalistic style, and a lack of systematic arrangement. Morley saw anecdotal 'variousness' as the key to the popular appeal of Macaulay's *History*, which demonstrated the 'art of being ... various' not only in the sense of having a very wide and accurate knowledge of the past, but also in the sense of providing a 'stream of apt illustrations', a 'rapid eye for contrasts and analogies', and a 'process of complete assimilation and spontaneous fusion'. Alison, in the *Edinburgh Review*, more directly relates Macaulay's variousness to his journalism, noting the rapidity of his ideas, his short sentences, his art of abbreviation, and his ability to provide 'as condensed and brilliant a picture as it is possible to present', even if those pictures 'come tumbling out, often without much order or arrangement'.[52]

Yet while Macaulay's journalistic style involves an 'assemblage of various idioms', moving from subject to subject and appearing almost random in the way it amasses details, his *History* progresses via an assimilative series of micro-histories, representing each part 'as an analogue for the world in miniature'.[53] This is a characteristic noted by the ever attentive Bagehot, who describes Macaulay's style as one that captures unity-in-change by providing complete worlds that gradually secede each other: the narrative keeps 'continually and insensibly before the mind of the reader some one object, character, or image, whose variations are the events of the story, whose unity is the unity of it'.[54] As Bagehot recognises, Macaulay's shifting 'diorama of political picture' is a product of his rejection of a preconceived 'metaphysical ... [or] an intellectual conception of the time and character before him' in favour of a history of actions and responsive reactions.[55] This is not, of course, to suggest that Macaulay's inductive methodology is free from ideological biases, or tropological and other super-structural devices, but rather that Macaulay and his most astute critics understood the inductive, case-based methodology to be as much a *historical* approach as a literary one.

It is equally true, however, that Macaulay's *History* relies heavily on the neoclassical 'dictional devices' of Addison, Pope, and Gibbon, as well as on an 'epic structure', including a trip to the 'underworld' that is seventeenth-century Ireland, 'a chaos of bogs, thickets, and precipices, ... where half-naked savages, who could not speak a word of English, made themselves burrows in the mud'.[56] As this representation of the 'savagery' of the Gaelic Irish suggests, there is much in Macaulay's *History* that subordinates inductions from empirical data to ethnonationalism and the triumphalist narratives of Whig progressivism. Unlike Carlyle's more radical embrace of conjecture and contingency, the first few chapters of Macaulay's *History* situate the temporal instability of the past within a progressive framework towards independent English nationhood and the racial assimilation of 'three branches of the great Teutonic family with each other, and with the aboriginal Briton', just as his view of the 'nobility' of the English language of 'Milton and Burke' echoes stadialist claims that 'in rude societies the progress of government resembles the progress of language and of versification'.[57]

The relationship between language and civilisational development is a recurring trope in Macaulay's *History*, as well as an ongoing preoccupation in his review essays, where the racialisation of cultural difference often hinges either on language variances or on the pronunciation, refinement, and purification of language, particularly in relation to his othering of the Irish as racial 'foreigners': 'No man of English blood then regarded the aboriginal Irish as his countrymen ... They had an aspect of their own, a mother tongue of their own. When they talked English their pronunciation was ludicrous; and their phraseology was grotesque.'[58] Like Mackintosh, Macaulay has a view of race and the civilising force of language that is deeply entangled with Saxonist identifications: the Anglo-Saxons are the progenitors of the English nation, 'whose language we speak, in whose homes we dwell, and in whose establishments and institutions we justly glory'.[59] Comparing the Catholic Irish to the Protestant Scots, Macaulay notes that the Scots were 'of the same blood with the population of England, and spoke a tongue which did not differ from the purest English', whereas the Irish were 'Celtic, and still kept the Celtic speech and manners'.[60] The differences between the 'industrious' and 'civilised' Anglo-Saxons and 'savage' or 'wild' Celts are thus heavily entangled with questions of linguistic difference and purification.[61]

Following Augustin Thierry's ethno-characterological view of the historical past, the treatment of the so-called 'Celtic peripheries' in Macaulay's *History* marks the end of a phase in British public opinion in which Irish political and institutional grievances were viewed sympathetically. John Pinkerton's earlier anti-Celtic racialism had been kept alive by writing that denigrated the Irish character, even in works by authors committed to Catholic Emancipation such as those by John MacCulloch. However, Macaulay's understanding of the Irish people as a 'tribe' rather than a 'nation', as fixed 'metaphysical historical subjects', helped to harden ideas about the Irish character, as well as encouraging the natural right of the English to rule over 'uncivilised' populations at home and abroad: a view increasingly enshrined in the biological essentialism of later histories such as Charles Kingsley's *The Roman and the Teuton* (1860) and J. R. Green's popular *A Short History of the English People* (1874).[62] Macaulay's emphasis on national unity, his narrative organicism, and his picturesque style must therefore be understood within the context of the 'aggressive ideology of Anglo-Saxonism' that his *History* constructs, as well as in relation to his Anglicist views on vernacular language education in India and his stadial view of the 'poverty' of Hindu culture, language, and learning—a view nurtured by his own experiences in India, the instrumental rationalism of Mill's *British India*, and later by the momentous impact of the Indian Uprising of 1857.[63]

At the same time, Macaulay's Anglocentric Whig progressivism is counterbalanced by his application of an inductive methodology and by his behaviouralist concession that when history is considered 'in small separate portions' rather than as general movement towards progressive modernity it is more properly 'a history of actions and reactions', a history tied to the 'motion of the public mind'. Since the 'history of the national mind' or the 'heart and brain of the people' is also the 'history of the nation' it is necessary to look at the 'recoil' that follows 'every advance from a great general ebb'.[64] Thinking about the influence of the inductive methodology on the style and structure of the *History of England* thus allows us to view Macaulay's work on its own terms: that is, as something other than a rambling narrative in the novelistic mode and more as a distinct type of historical writing nurtured by a constant refinement of historical particulars.[65] While Macaulay intended the *History of England* to be competitive as 'a literary work in the literary marketplace', he did not understand his own popular and accessible style as a barrier to historical specialisation, representing his inductive methodology as a serious and empirically grounded intervention into the abstractions of philosophic generalisation.[66] If Morley and other later nineteenth-century critics concluded that Macaulay was a 'literary' historian who 'contributed no philosophic ideas to the speculative stock' and an amateur who declined to evaluate or address the work of specialists, Macaulay represents his own methodology as an innovation that could dilute the abstractive influence of philosophy on history. As he noted in his *Journals* in 1849, '[t]here is merit, no doubt, in Hume, Robertson, Voltaire, and Gibbon. Yet it is not the thing. I have a conception of history more just, I am confident, than theirs.'[67]

'Gothic and Gaelic': Carlyle's 'National' Style

In 1851 Carlyle claimed that Macaulay's work was 'the sublime of the commonplace', lacking any kind of 'superior merit' save 'neatness of expression'.[68] Carlyle's backhanded compliment attributes Macaulay's market-savvy success to the neat and mechanical prose style nurtured by Johnson and the Scottish belletrists. In maintaining that his own works 'were not, nor ever will be popular', Carlyle downplays his market awareness, pragmatism, and desire for an audience in favour of emphasising the singularity of his irregular style, already known by 1858 as 'Carlylese': 'I have no known public, am *alone* under the Heavens, speaking into friendly or unfriendly Space.'[69] Unlike Macaulay, then, whose writing confirms for the reader the general order of the history of the English nation, Carlyle represents his works as palimpsests that block any transparent access to the past, curtailing authorial prescriptiveness by demanding of his reader a self-conscious effort towards decipherment, interpretation, and 'productive struggle'.[70]

With his customary attention to linguistic purification, Macaulay, in turn, maintained that Carlyle wrote unintelligible 'gibberish' rather than 'good English', noting, in a reference to 'Characteristics' in 1832, that 'he might as well write in Irving's unknown tongue at once'.[71] Macaulay's reference to Carlyle's erstwhile friend, the Calvinist preacher Edward Irving—known for his charismatic style and his invention of a millenarian language of tongues—foregrounds the Scottish influences on Carlyle's style. William Wordsworth's comments to Ralph Waldo Emerson that Carlyle is 'a pest of the English tongue' and that 'no Scotchman ... can write English' is suggestive of the extent to which other contemporaries saw the excesses of Carlylese as emanating from the Scottish, as much as the Germanic, character of his writing.[72] Wordsworth's ridicule is, to some degree, a function of his own chauvinistic Anglocentrism, which disparaged equally the Scottish Carlyle and the American Emerson. However, he nonetheless cannily identifies that Carlyle's style foregrounds what is most foreign or hybrid about the English language—a technique that Wordsworth sometimes deploys himself when invoking that most performative of all Scottish texts, Macpherson's *Poems of Ossian*, but more often tends to sublimate in his deliberate attempts to purify his language of regional dialects.[73]

The syntactical, typographical, and linguistic eccentricities of Carlyle's style have long been attributed to a combination of his reading of German philosophers and the Saint-Simonians, as well as his immersion within the 'biblical present' of the Puritan sermon tradition.[74] More recently, Joanna Malecka has considered the exorcism of Carlyle's Calvinism following the post-Arnoldian secularisation of culture, and the still ongoing division between critical accounts that favour his representation of 'a dark Calvinist past' and those that favour his evocation of 'the modern spirit of Britain'.[75] By the time Carlyle came to write for the *Edinburgh Review* in the 1830s, 'Puritan old style Whiggism' had been well and truly side-lined in favour of a national style of linguistic propriety enshrined in the language and forms of the Scottish enlightenment.[76] In transforming classical rhetoric into a written form better suited to modern civil society, Blair, Smith, and other Scottish belletrists had a pedagogic goal: namely, to assist 'upwardly mobile, ambitious young Scots to master the language of power and influence' encapsulated in the best English style of Addison, Johnson, and Pope.[77]

Carlyle's own suggestion in *Two Reminiscences* (1881) that his style was originally forged in his Ecclefechan home, and then by Irving and his Annandale family, before being mediated by the Elizabethans, Milton, Cromwell, and the German Romantics, must therefore be considered alongside another, self-reflexive narrative in his correspondence: the idea that he had self-consciously to *unlearn* or divest himself of a formerly Johnsonian prose style nurtured in the Scottish enlightenment milieu of the University of Edinburgh.[78] Carlyle's correspondence suggests that his linguistic style was a deliberately disruptive rejection of inherited styles and forms that had become inadequate, describing the demise of the whole 'structure of our Johnsonian English' as a 'revolution there as visible as anywhere else!' In a letter to his friend John Sterling, Carlyle implicitly relates this stylistic revolution and the need to '*make* words' to questions of national distinctiveness, rejecting the 'Purism of Style' found in 'English Books' (or what he calls 'mere dictionary style') in the face of the invasion of 'whole ragged battalions of Scott's-Novel Scotch, with Irish, German, French and even Newspaper Cockney'.[79]

Carlyle's rejection of those decorous but outmoded Anglo-British linguistic standards enshrined by the Scottish belletrists is a response to almost a century of prescriptivism involving the purification and standardisation of literary English, which, as Robert Crawford, Janet Sorensen, and others have noted, worked alongside the development of a national print language to encourage the development of a communitarian sense of Hanoverian Britishness. The concern with linguistic propriety was particularly intense in eighteenth-century Scotland following the 1707 Act of Union, when Scots language and culture was increasingly discouraged in favour of standard English.[80] The cultural demise of Scots entailed associating 'good' English (that is, English shorn of novelty, dialects, vernacularisms, and foreign words) with bourgeois hegemony and 'bad' English with a 'rejection of traditional English liberty and customs'.[81] As a series of articles 'On the Styles of Hume, Gibbon, and Robertson' in the *Gentleman's Magazine* for January, February, and April 1832 put it, Hume's diction is 'select' and 'what is always to be commended in a Scotch author, *free* from Scottishisms'.[82]

Carlyle's privileging of his own distinctive literary style is characterised by critics such as William Makepeace Thackeray as a deliberate affront 'to admirers of Addisonian English, to those who love history as it gracefully runs in Hume, or struts pompously in Gibbon'.[83] Yet Carlyle had himself once admired the style of Hume, Blair, and Gibbon while a student at the University of Edinburgh.[84] In an early letter to a friend in 1815, Carlyle approves of Hume's 'essayistic' style, although he questions the view of national character formation in what was probably Hume's notoriously racialised essay, 'Of National Characters' (1748):

> I am highly indebted to you for Hume. I like his *Essays* better than anything I have read these many days ... But many of his opinions are not to be adopted. How odd does it look, for instance, to refer *all* the modifications of 'national character' to the influence of moral causes. Might it not be asserted with some plausibility, that, even those which he denominates moral causes, originate from physical circumstances?[85]

If Gibbon's 'winged sarcasms' formed a liberating 'epoch in the history of [his] mind', Carlyle increasingly rejects not just Hume's 'prosaic' literary style, but also his philosophical scepticism, contrasting the probabilistic English and Scottish schools of Locke and Hume with the transcendentalism of Kant and his followers in his 'State of German Literature' (1827).[86] By the time he wrote his essays on history and biography in the 1830s, Carlyle had come to see Hume as an exemplar of a universalist cultural discourse 'shorn of its distinctive Scottishness'. As Yoon Sun Lee has noted, Carlyle's 'Essay on Burns' (1854) is a depiction of eighteenth-century Scotland's 'cultural evisceration', in which Carlyle recognised that in the work of Scotland's most feted enlightenment figures 'there was nothing truly Scottish, nothing indigenous ... Scotland, so full of writers, had no Scottish culture'. Noting that Carlyle rejects this kind of cosmopolitanism in favour of the 'remarkable increase of nationality' that has taken place in nineteenth-century literature, Lee uncovers the irony of Carlyle's argument: what is most British about Burns is his Scottish nationalism.[87]

The idea that opposing standard or purified English could provide a means of resisting or at least interrogating dominant cultural hegemonies is clearly attractive to Carlyle, who often represents himself as off-centre in terms of social status and temperament: 'On the whole I am too much in the state the Scotch Pedlar thought the Londoners in: "A very good people, Ma'am, very clever people; but *terribly aff for a lANGitch*".'[88] The Scottishness of Carlyle's work is not achieved through pedagogic content—he never wrote a history of Scotland or of the Reformation, although he wrote repeatedly of doing so in his letters—but rather through '*lANGitch*': that is, through a performative mode that shatters the kind of organic synthesis of style, form, and content that characterises Macaulay's *History*. With its German affectations, Carlyle's style is more Gothic than Gaelic, a Sassenach, Lowland, or Saxon style rather than one of Celtic exoticism. Yet this 'Scottish' style nonetheless works to deflect the racial association of genius with Englishness, while also seeking to overcome national divisions through the embrace of difference and dissent rather than through 'absorption, assimilation and loss of identity'.[89]

Matthew Arnold's criticism is suggestive of the ambiguity of Victorian Saxonism, with its representation of the Celts as 'a primitive race of underdeveloped aboriginals' who could nonetheless emotionally revitalise English culture.[90] As Leith Davis has put it, Arnold's 'On the Study of Celtic Literature' (1867) provided the 'masterplan' for a conciliatory framework 'based on the assimilation of Romantic Celtic feeling and English rule'.[91] If Carlyle celebrated the dominant, expansionary, and 'civilising' force of Teutonic/Saxon England in *Chartism* (1839) and *On Heroes*, elsewhere his verbal and conceptual irony favours the more synthetic terms of Arnold's schema, working to disavow the classical standards of aesthetic unity in favour of the 'regenerative force of the vernacular'.[92] Infusing his written style with indigenous Scottish idioms that are *just* idiosyncratic enough to be considered a mark of 'universal genius' rather than backward, primitive, or provincial, Carlyle's use of vernacular language in *French Revolution* and elsewhere is best understood as part of a wider reconsideration of national character and the philosophy of style in the early to mid-nineteenth century.

In its blurring of past and present, its prophetic mode, its present tense, and the prominence of Carlyle's own narrative persona, *French*

Revolution radically breaks with the protocols of historical style established in the reviewing culture of the period in order to resituate the springs of human nature in deep irrational passions. This was an approach that, as Hedva Ben-Israel has shown, partly grew out of Carlyle's immersion in ongoing discussions of Burke's *Reflections* in the periodical press. Despite Carlyle's rejection of Burkean prescriptivism, he is indebted to Burke both for the dynamic immediacy of his style and for his emphasis on the passional structures of feeling that produced the Revolution: 'The French Revolution itself had something higher in it than cheap bread and a Habeas-corpus act. Here, too, was an Idea; a Dynamic, not a Mechanic force.'[93]

The idea that historical writing should capture and express the dynamical processes of emerging structures of feeling is the fundamental insight of *French Revolution*. Yet as Chris Vanden Bossche has reminded us, while Carlyle's 'presentness' or immediacy is performative and rhetorical in that it is intended to be persuasive, it is not sentimental or sympathetic in the domesticated or ordinary sense of those words; nor is his view of history a Burkean one. Carlyle's approach is neither teleological nor dialectical in its attitude towards change and authority, instead 'hypostatiz[ing] the elements of cultural consensus of certain eras in order to posit epochs of "nature", "belief", or "culture"' while treating 'historical change as characteristic only of intermediate periods of "transition" ... "unbelief", or "anarchy"'.[94] Influenced by the theories of Saint-Simon, Carlyle believed that history progresses in alternative ways to the Scottish enlightenment stadial theorists: that is, through periods of expansion and contraction, inertia and progression, and faith and disbelief. Carlyle thus shares with Burke a sense of revolutions as discontinuous, irregular, or 'out of nature'. However, his appeal is not to a Burkean conservative 'return from revolution to authority' but rather to a more radical 'return to authority through revolution'.[95]

Unlike Burke's ultimately predictive view of the French Revolution and his belief in the ability of the *ancien régime* to evolve and restore itself, Carlyle emphasises 'the utter inexplicability' of the French Revolution to its main actors and eyewitness observers, charting a movement from inertia to chaos and frenzy.[96] Carlyle's account thus differs both from Burkean prescription and from Wollstonecraft's emphasis on the logical explicability of the Revolution's violence, even if that violence can sometimes occasion from her a response laden with sensibility. The dynamism of the Revolution's conflict also requires Carlyle to downplay the importance of a centralising hero figure: with Mirabeau dying too early to sustain the role of hero and Robespierre an anti-hero who only feigns or adopts the 'machinery' of 'Priest and Prophet', Carlyle is forced to question whether the history of great men can provide order or resolution to social life in the face of the deterioration of the labouring bodies that ultimately sustain it.[97] He therefore deliberately subjugates the category of 'character' in *French Revolution*, turning the would-be protagonists of the French Revolution into 'vehicles of collective and transindividual forces' rather than producing the deep character studies that would later emerge in *Cromwell*.[98]

With the people harnessing collective emotions of anger and resentment, social consensus is not for Carlyle, as for Burke, an unchanging civic emotion tied to the embodied representatives of the nation; nor is it, as for Wollstonecraft, a means of depicting concrete acts of collective agency. Rather, it is something more like the animal magnetism of 'action and reaction', one that characterises the ominous natural 'magic' of the guillotine as the most public theatre of them all: 'here is still a real magic in the action and reaction of minds on one another. The casual deliration of a few becomes, by this mysterious force, the frenzy of many; men lose the use, not only of their understandings, but of their bodily senses.'[99] Unlike Wollstonecraft's orderly, composed, yet agential crowds, Carlyle's crowds are made up of irrational actors who forfeit both mind and feelings to 'unagencied action' in a way that recalls those theories of mesmerism and other spiritualist practices that were so popular in late eighteenth-century France.[100] The people, as Vanden Bossche notes, are humanised and have a kind of authority in Carlyle's account: 'the masses consist all of units. Every unit of whom has his own heart and sorrows; stands covered there with his own skin, and if you prick him, he will bleed.' However, it is ultimately 'an inverse authority capable of producing only an "inverse order," an "organised ... Anarchy', with both the old order and the new incapable of understanding the material and transcendental needs of the starving masses.[101]

John Plotz has discussed the distinction in Carlyle's work between discursive understandings of the relationship between massed people and written petition-making to understandings of the declarative 'clamour and struggle' of crowds as speech with 'competing forms of possible speech-act'. While focusing on *Chartism*, Plotz's insight—that Carlyle appropriates the language and actions of the Chartists in order to wrest control of and reduce Chartist speech to speechlessness—is equally applicable to *French Revolution*, where the restoration of agency to the revolutionary crowd emerges not from their own speech or actions but rather from the promise of explication, wholeness, and legitimacy through and within Carlyle's own writing.[102] Like Burke, Carlyle self-consciously places the political crisis of the French Revolution within a linguistic one, understanding the crisis in kingship as one of representation. The French Constitution thus becomes, as Mary Desaulniers has argued, both a thematic and 'self-reflexive constituent of the linguistic process', with language forming part of a wider 'economics of representation' that demonstrates 'man's abstraction from a natural and holistic materialism'. L. M. Findlay, too, sees Carlyle as reflexively 're-constitut[ing] political convulsions as the rending and repair of language as cultural fabric' or, in other words, as a 'process of rupture/suture in the rhetoric of temporality', while Mark Cumming has characterised the history as a 'disemprisoned' epic or a 'pastiche of epic', in which literary allusions are built into 'a hybrid and unstable makeshift construct'.[103] For Patricia McCallum, Carlyle's 'fresh' style, which she characterises as a sort of 'double articulation' of language that reinvigorates the 'long-extinct forms and archetypes' of 'earlier vocabularies', performs a dual task: it simultaneously re-enacts 'the new reality of worldwide, international class struggle' and 'records the lived experience of the English political situation'.[104]

In his 1828 review of Walter Scott's *Life of Napoleon Buonaparte* (1827), J. S. Mill anticipates McCallum's argument when he recognises the extent to which the French Revolution requires a new type of historian, one who will give a prominent role to the people as political subjects and agents, and thus redirect discussions of the body politic to the social body.[105] Understanding that Carlyle's protagonist is not Mirabeau or Robespierre but rather the 'general will', Mill concedes in his 1837 review of *French Revolution* that, whatever his reservations about its hyper-metaphorical and rhapsodical style, Carlyle's history allows the reader to experience the 'mass protagonist' with the full force of its immediacy: rather than providing 'plausible talk *about* a thing', it provides 'an image of the thing itself'. Mill thus recognises the extent to which Carlyle's style rejects the 'characterless uniformity' of the Anglo-British prose style in order to match the visceral nature of the social convulsions that mark the Revolution itself, collapsing historical distance in favour of the 'bodily concrete coloured presence of things'.[106] David Sorensen and Ruth Scurr have both demonstrated that Carlyle's style emerged from the 'deep intellectual and empathetic engagement with the form, content, and spirit of his sources' in *French Revolution*, with much of the history's rhetorical effect emerging from a dramatic weighing of sources, and a foregrounding of the process of source criticism. Carlyle's immersive engagement with his sources is, for Scurr, a spiritual act of 'historical re-creation', one in which any form of 'invention' or 'true fiction' is closely tied to a reproduction of the anecdotal style and language of eyewitness accounts from the

Histoire parlementaire.[107] Carlyle's dynamic style is thus tightly bound to the 'real' historical time of eyewitness accounts rather than simply being an ornamental device.

As the discussion of Wollstonecraft's *Historical and Moral View* in Chapter 1 of this book suggests, Carlyle was not the first to write a history of the French Revolution based on eyewitness accounts or one that centres on the people's collective will. Yet his history deploys a rebelliously Calvinist style that more substantively than Wollstonecraft casts off the stadial, philosophic view of the Scottish enlightenment. That Carlyle considered his *French Revolution* to be a 'stylistic watershed' is evident in his own characterisation of it as 'a queer book … one of the queerest published in this Century' and as 'a wild savage book, itself a kind of French Revolution'.[108] Herman Merivale's 1840 review of *French Revolution* in the *Edinburgh Review* insightfully, if aggressively, attacks Carlyle's poetic language in ethnolinguistic terms by arguing that Carlyle's 'barbarian' and 'bastard English' lacks the formal acquisition of 'British discipline':

> Self-educated, we believe, and nurtured on the very quintessence of German transcendentalism, with little ordinary British discipline to counteract it, he could only clothe his own thoughts in the same uncouth foreign livery in which the parent thoughts had been clothed when first his mind received and appropriated them.[109]

The stylistic idiom that permeates the history is rejected by Merivale as both insufficiently 'purified' and as a 'foreign livery', with Carlyle himself characterised as a 'foreigner' in much the same way as Macaulay's seventeenth-century Irishman:

> He seemed a solitary or rare example of one who, in his native country, had unlearned his native language; and was as much a stranger among us as Jean Paul or Ludwig Tieck might have been, if suddenly transferred from their own metaphysical cloud-land to our matter-of-fact atmosphere.[110]

Merivale's intuition that Carlyle had both 'unlearned his native language' and 'acquired his particularities in the school of journal and essay writing' resonates with Carlyle's own narrative of rejecting the British expository style, even if Merivale attributes Carlyle's newly appropriated style more to German transcendentalism than to the vernacularisms of his Scottish inheritance. Rejecting a 'fallen' language that has grown old and tired, Carlyle's un-English 'corporeal idiom' maintains a view of language that is indebted to the Scottish Irving's spiritual 'logic of incarnation' or 'word-become-flesh'. In discarding desacralising phenomenological and scientifically materialist understandings of language origins, Carlyle seeks to restore the noumenal 'inner life' of historical facts through a process that John Lamb has called 'convertibility' or the linguistic approximation of ideals.[111] Carlyle thus argues for an understanding of cultural life in *French Revolution* that is both material and ideational, both feeling and thinking, reflecting his gradual movement away from the idealist separation of ideas and social materiality towards an understanding that culture is experiential or 'built into our living', as Raymond Williams has put it.[112] This, Carlyle recognises, is ultimately what the study of history has taught him: 'How such Ideals do realise themselves; and grow, wondrously, from amid the incongruous ever-fluctuating chaos of the Actual: this is what World-History, if it is to teach anything, has to teach us.'[113]

The Scottish Calvinist idioms that permeate the history do not, however, manifest themselves in any straightforwardly positive or productive way. Carlyle's history is not, as some critics have suggested, a naive return to an earlier, typological Scottish historiography along the lines of Knox's *History of the Reformation* (1559–66). While the doctrine of incarnation is central to the 'somatic idiom' of *French Revolution*, Carlyle's depiction of the 'cloud-capt fire-breathing Spectre of DEMOCRACY' can be read as a parody rather than an endorsement of Puritan apocalyptic beliefs.[114] Not only does Carlyle draw explicit parallels between the revolutionaries and the Scottish Covenanters, but the French ideologues implicitly attempt to usurp the divine prophetic calling, only to end up replicating the quackery of Irving's 'Babel-like confusion of tongues' in a noisy confusion of 'endless debating' 'about the Rights of Man, Right of Peace and War, *Veto suspensif*, *Veto absolu*, what are they but so many Pedant's-curses, "May God confound you for your *Theory of Irregular Verbs!*"'. Linking illegitimacy with pedantry and a 'radically devalued language', Carlyle's National Assembly falls into the anarchic, dissonant, and illegible cant of the 'babbler' and 'pamphleteer', where words circulate without intelligible meaning.[115] Unable to name the new realities they are producing, the fanatical ideologues lapse into a loudly dissonant sansculottism rather than a curative or 'healthy silence'.[116]

Replicating Diogenes Teufelsdröckh's project of writing the Clothes Volume and the *Palingenesia* in *Sartor Resartus* (1836), Carlyle replaces the metaphor of clothes—itself reminiscent of Burke's understanding of 'decent drapery' as a system reproducing social distinctions—with the metaphor of paper or the 'Paper Age', as Book 2 of *French Revolution* is titled. Focusing on paper as a simulacrum of value and linking 'Bank-paper' and 'Book-paper' to an indictment of laissez-faire economics and anatomising individualism, Carlyle echoes debates about fiscal policy and economic value contemporary to the Revolution itself.[117] Like the values of those speculative financiers detached from the land, the illusory values of the French Constitution are 'all paper', even 'wastepaper', 'a simulacre, the graven image of revolutionary idolatry'.[118] Partly modelled on the self-deluded Irving and his extreme version of Scottish Calvinism, Teufelsdröckh's frenzied making and remaking in *Sartor Resartus* is therefore matched in *French Revolution* by the Constituent Assembly's 'whirling' and 'grinding' project of making the new constitution, a revealing process of artificial national construction that acts only as a substitute or proxy for the feeling of 'the true Constitution . . . grown, unconsciously, out of the wants and efforts of these Twenty-five Millions of men'.[119]

Situated alongside these artificial acts of constitutional creation is an imagery of 'endless circling', which ultimately encircles the very text itself, as metaphors of natural disaster such as 'whirlwinds of military fire and of human passions, and tornados of fatalism "spin" through the pages of the history'. The 'topos of impossible closure' comes full circle at the end of the history, as the declamatory conclusion, a 'fictitious *ex post facto* prophecy', ironically predicts what has already been the subject of the history itself, circling the reader back to the very 'moment at which the older order disintegrated', back to the 'Fire-Sea; crackling with new dislocated timber': 'The World is black ashes; which, ah, when will they grow green? . . . This Prophecy, we say, has it not been fulfilled, is it not fulfilling?' Aware that his own history may be little more than a simulacrum or 'Flame-Picture', the Scottish pulpit style that Carlyle employs in *French Revolution* paradoxically works both to unhinge and to consolidate meaning, acting as a marker of the impossibility of the 'nineteenth-century preoccupation with recovering linguistic holism': 'Any approximation to the right name has value: were the right Name itself once here, the Thing is known henceforth; the Thing is then ours, and can be dealt with.'[120]

Given Carlyle's interest in ethnonational identity and his argument that European culture would be enveloped by the fiery blaze of a 'Gaelic fire' until it kindled a more long-lasting 'Teutonic kind', it is perhaps unsurprising that the latent ideal of a holistic British nation lurks behind the style and content of his representation of the chaos of revolutionary France.[121] As Richard Altick has noted, Carlyle's topical allusions to recent British history in *French Revolution* are a reflection of the ways in which the Revolution could hold up a mirror to the British nation state and its own divisive constitutionalist discourse, issuing a warning to those who would ignore the 'Condition of England' question, 'swallowed up in the barren Chaos of Politics'.[122] Carlyle references Paine's time in France, French immigrants in England, British missionaries in

France, and French animosity towards Pitt, as well as drawing implicit parallels between the French insurgents and the destitute and working poor in 1830s Britain.[123] Even, then, as Carlyle disavows his own complicity in the 'national fetish', he endorses and naturalises 'fictions of national wholeness' by co-opting and sublimating the revolutionary project of national regeneration into one of British national reconstitution. Carlyle's irregular '*l*ANG*itch*' ironically argues for the possibility of effective authority and national self-regeneration, the 'green' that will arise from the 'black ashes', through a stylistic principle that consistently resists standardisation into the mechanistic refinement of the British 'national' language.[124] Recuperating referential failure, Carlyle's style demonstrates what Plotz has called 'an irrationalist account of what language can do as it circulates in the public sphere', displaying all of the underlying 'logic of a style that strives to mark itself as illogical'.[125]

Professionalisation and the Man of Letters

In her landmark study of the rise of the professional historian, Philippa Levine absents Carlyle and Macaulay on the basis that they considered themselves part of an older tradition of essayists and reviewers rather than as specialist historians.[126] Owen Dudley Edwards likewise argues that neither man was ready to call himself a historian, and that, for Macaulay, 'the term itself signified an impossibility': 'A historian, such as we have been attempting to describe, would indeed be an intellectual prodigy ... We shall sooner see another Shakespeare or another Homer.'[127] The idea that Macaulay and Carlyle essentially 'wrote [themselves] out of the history of history' is by now a well-rehearsed trope in studies of nineteenth-century historiography. Macaulay is dismissed as Whiggish, naively progressivist, and novelistic, while Carlyle's ambivalence towards archival research, his hero worship and authoritarianism, and his irregular, illogical, or queer style remain problematic for present-day historians, who tend to depict him either as a proto-postmodernist who pre-empts current concerns with the subjective origins of empirical data or as a 'hopelessly outdated' Victorian sage.[128]

The first of these narratives seeks to rescue Carlyle from the naivety of Macaulay's Whig progressivism by arguing for his 'preservation of a spiritual sense of the past that resisted rationalist attempts to classify and codify human experience'.[129] Macaulay, on the other hand, is generally considered valuable as a progenitor of social history and thick description, albeit one whose commitment to a picturesque style and to Whig progressivism ultimately prevents any serious social analysis. This second narrative essentially reproduces the judgments of later historians about the literary qualities of their predecessors. For Seeley, writing in 1877, Macaulay and Carlyle had 'spoiled the public taste' to the extent that 'to the general public no distinction remains between history and fiction', producing a history so 'radically unscientific', so dependent 'upon interesting and thrilling the reader', that it was no kind of history at all.[130] Seeley's famous condemnation of Macaulay's florid style—history should be 'ordinary' and 'monotonous', 'ruled by routine', 'acts of parliament, budgets and taxation'—is only the most aggressive example of a generation of boundary work that attempted to close the apparently porous boundaries between history and fiction, and resituate the 'possibilities of [authorial] selfhood along the professional/amateur axis'.[131]

The question of historical specialisation is, however, far more complex and multilayered than Seeley's distinctions intimate. As Edward Adams has pointed out, both Macaulay and Carlyle were dismissive of popular or fashionable novels even as they sought, to varying degrees, to write popular or epic history. Writing history conferred on them a higher cultural status than that of the popular novelist and ensured that they could overcome the novelist's 'double-bind': high financial reward but a loss of status and authorial control in the literary marketplace. Yet the relative success of Macaulay and Carlyle as men of letters, as opposed to, say, Thackeray's sorry decline in sales and reputation, must itself be set against their declining reputation and status as historians as the century progressed. While it is certainly true that mid-century England continued to 'elevate and reward epic histories ... despite the novel's apparent dominance', it did not take long for that cultural valorisation to begin a rapid descent, demarcating 'men of letters' from 'men of science', and ultimately from 'scholars'.[132]

From as early as the 1860s, Carlyle and Macaulay are characterised by critics such as Morley as essayists rather than as historians, as cultural figures who are at once 'engaged in a project of anxious self-construction' and eager to 'transfigure the space of cultural authority left vacant by the waning of traditional models'.[133] Richard Salmon has rightly argued that Carlyle's understanding of the social and disciplinary stratifications of literary labour must be situated in the context of a literary marketplace that allows for the democratic 'dissemination of prophetic speech on an enlarged scale' but also 'produces the anomaly of a disorganic Literary Class' left 'at the mercy of blind Chance'. Sacrificed to this marketplace, Carlyle's literary heroes—Johnson, Rousseau, and Burns—are victims of its 'corrosion of heroism and hero-worship' and its degeneration into the idolatry or 'Lionism' that accompanies literary celebrity.[134] At the same time, Carlyle's call to organise the 'disorganic Literary Class' was not immune to emerging forces of professionalisation and specialisation, drawing on the example of literary guilds and academic appointments in France and Prussia. Carlyle himself tried several times, albeit somewhat half-heartedly, to gain a permanent appointment at a university, and thus to distinguish his own work from the amateurism of antiquarian publishing societies and the market-driven approaches of periodical culture.[135]

While Carlyle was concerned with the cultural visibility of the man of letters as a class or collective group, both he and Macaulay were more comfortable with the term 'historian' than we now tend to allow. Macaulay is explicit in his claims to historical expertise in his review essays, noting in a review of William Mitford's *History of Greece* (1784–1810) in the *Edinburgh Review* for 1824 that Mitford had 'almost succeeded in mounting unperceived by those whose office it is to watch such aspirants, to a high place among historians'. Characterising himself as a custodian or gatekeeper who could 'reduce an overpraised writer to his proper level', Macaulay is not afraid to call himself a historian or to dismiss those whose claims to that status were undeserved. In his 1832 *Edinburgh Review* essay 'Burleigh and his Times', he refers to the Regius Professor of History at Oxford, the Reverend Edward Nares, as 'a man of great industry and research' but utter incompetence, proving so ill-fit 'to arrange the materials which he has collected that he might as well have left them in their original repositories'.[136]

Carlyle, too, saw himself as something of a gatekeeper in relation to historical publications, dismissing the work of antiquarians and publishing societies as piecemeal and insubstantial. For all his dependence on antiquaries and librarians such as David Davy, David Laing, John Bruce, and John Harland, part of Carlyle's frustration with 'Dryasdust' book clubs and their editors was, as Heather Henderson has pointed out, his 'exasperation as a professional historian trapped in the accepted publishing system and compelled to use the incompetent works of clubbable amateurs locked in mutual admiration'. For Carlyle, book-club members were amateurs because of their dilettantism, elitism, monopolistic tendencies, and mistaken idealism.[137] Even worse than the bibliomaniac's fetishisation of the rarefied book-object as collectible was the antiquarian's disinclination to print what was useful rather than just what was old or curious, a position that, as Ina Ferris has noted, 'hinged on citation rather than translation in the act of transmitting the past'. If clubs like the Bannatyne marked a shift from the old book club sponsored by private individuals to a new and more cooperative form of group subscription printing, their corporate middle ground was not sufficient to appease Carlyle's annoyance at the indiscriminate nature of their publications.[138]

Carlyle thus sought to redefine his own work against that of the antiquarian, claiming that the dramatic intersection of past and present was more important than a study of historical particulars. Yet, as Chapter 2 has considered in more detail, he took a more fastidiously documentary approach to his sources than is generally credited. Like the publications of Scott's Bannatyne Club, Carlyle sought to retain vernacular language as much as possible, incorporating its peculiar idioms and antiquated phraseology into his own style.[139] Contemporary critics recognised the extent to which Carlyle's queer style emerged from his desire to recapture the original language of his sources. As Leslie Stephen put it in an unsigned obituary of Carlyle in *Cornhill Magazine* for 1881:

> whatever the accuracy of the colouring in his historical studies, they at least imply the most thorough going and conscientious labour ... It is, indeed, a subsidiary pleasure, in reading all Carlyle's writings, to feel that the artist is always backed up by the conscientious workman.[140]

Stephen draws here on Carlyle's own distinction, in his 1830 essay 'On History', between the 'Artisan' (who deals 'mechanically with discrete phenomena') and the 'Artist' (who can envisage 'a sense of the organic whole'), but he rightly sees these two historiographical types as 'mutually reinforcing' in Carlyle's work.[141] In *French Revolution*, as in *Cromwell*, Carlyle immerses himself in sources not just to represent the world from their particular viewpoint, but to relive in the present the multiple experiences and clashing perspectives of the past.[142]

For all the claims that Carlyle and Macaulay were generalists or men of letters, they both self-identified to some extent as specialist historians. Far from writing themselves out of the history of history, they played a pivotal role in the making of the modern, professional historian, both in the sense of developing inductive and hermeneutic methodologies, and in the sense of participating in the shift towards new evidence-based methods of source criticism.[143] Focusing on their stylistic practice and its reception means acknowledging not just the extent to which literary or narrative paradigms remained pervasive in British historical writing in the nineteenth and early twentieth centuries, but also that stylistic virtuosity did not negate the gradual and ongoing process of historical specialisation. This insight suggests, first, that we should understand historical writing as an activity and practice as much as a profession; and second, that we require a looser definition of the 'professional' historian in the nineteenth century, one that is detached from the attainment of academic or institutional positions. While essayists such as Macaulay and Carlyle are often seen as incompatible with later scholarly types, the following chapter argues that they were central, rather than incidental, to how specialisation emerged in historical discourse.

Chapter 5

Historical Reviewing: Specialisation and Periodical Culture

The first half of the nineteenth century undoubtedly saw the rise of the man of letters and the emergence of the popular historian, who attempted to situate his or her work in a literary marketplace newly dominated by the novel.[1] Yet the idea that 'generalists' and 'popularisers' rejected learned discourse, and that specialised study stagnated over the course of the late eighteenth and early nineteenth centuries, has rightly been met with increasing scepticism. Historians of academic disciplines have demonstrated the extent to which popularisation and specialisation could be complementary rather than antagonistic in certain fields, from physics and biology to philosophy and poetry.[2] Early nineteenth-century history-writing is usually seen as impervious, if not actively resistant, to specialisation. However, practitioners in the period could take a different view. The sense that technicity, jargon, and opacity were already pervasive in written history led T. B. Macaulay to contend repeatedly in review essays in the 1820s and 1830s that the historian needed to reclaim those aspects of the past that the novelist had appropriated following history's turn to its 'present narrow limits'. If Macaulay urges his fellow historians to 'assert the rights of history over every part of her natural domain' and to return to those vernacular sources that historians had wrongly declared 'beneath their dignity', it is precisely because he found the histories of the period so technical and so dry.[3]

Even as he rejects history's narrowing field, Macaulay presciently recognises that several forces were converging in Britain to encourage historical specialisation and the bureaucratisation of historical study, including the expansion of science and the elevation of scientific research models, the university reform movement and the institutionalisation of disciplines, and changes to cultural criticism and conceptions of intellectual elites.[4] The period from the 1820s to the 1850s witnessed agitation for changes to proprietary and copyright laws, as well as attempts to organise the 'disorganic Literary Class' into guilds and other professional bodies.⁵ History, too, had its own protocol-generating organisations in the form of cooperative printing societies such as the Roxburghe Club and the Bannatyne Club. These societies and book clubs originated in the 1810s and 1820s in Scotland but soon sprang up across the British Isles to organise antiquarians and bibliophiles into working associations, and to fill the gap in printing and preserving historical documents not yet undertaken by the long-awaited Public Record Office (1838).⁶ Subjected to charges of amateurism and elitism, book clubs generated what we would now call technical vocabulary, scholarly protocols, and field knowledge, representing an early model of that kind of cooperative association that Clifford Siskin has identified as a prerequisite for disciplinary specialisation and the development of autonomous professional fields.⁷

Contrary to the institutional or bureaucratic contexts of professionalisation, specialisation is ordinarily defined as a deepening and narrowing of the scope of knowledge, resulting in a division of labour that promotes the tendency to 'occupy a particular niche in an environment by "performing a few activities well" instead of "many activities poorly"'.⁸ It is, however, perhaps more fruitful in the context of historiographical developments to understand specialisation as an alteration in the relationship between theory and practice, and increasingly between philosophical and empirical impulses in history-writing. Nicholas Dames has usefully drawn attention to the significance of the 'protocol' for understanding various kinds of disciplinary and generic practice. As 'an unstated, uncodified aspect of professional or generic *techne*', whose 'procedures are not so much taught as absorbed', the protocol operates between the 'material constraints of a given practice and the kinds of theoretical propositions that fit those constraints', expressing the 'difference between doing something appropriately and inappropriately'. If, as Siskin has argued, specialisation is best characterised as a shift in emphasis from doctrine (or abstract theory) to discipline (or practice, exercise, or craft), it is reasonable to assume that the normative protocols and epistemic virtues we now associate with history as a modern discipline emerged as much from the style, technê, and praxis of working historians and their commercial publishers, distributors, and reviewers as it did from more overt institutional endeavours to organise and define the identity of the historical profession from the 1850s onwards.⁹

This chapter examines those earlier, more dynamic attempts at boundary-making in reviews of historical works published in the early nineteenth-century periodical press, arguing that reviewers worked in tandem with commercial publishing practices to establish new historical protocols surrounding specialisation, archival research, and source criticism.[10] Given the extent to which 'style' is used as a shorthand by reviewers to mask 'deeper divergences in structure and content', review essays can provide a unique insight into how and why certain aspects of historical writing became normative as the century progressed, allowing for an examination of the rhetoric of specialisation within its commercial context.[11] Acknowledging that written history is a commodity form within a professional and commercial knowledge industry is especially important in a period that has been called a 'new media moment', one characterised by a greater number of periodical publications, the conventions of anonymous reviewing, and the 'changing identity of print as a medium'.[12] By promoting fewer but longer and more selective reviews ('review-like essay[s]' and 'essay-like review[s]'), the quarterly format initiated by the *Edinburgh Review*, and adopted by many other review journals, allowed editors to blend market-oriented approaches with the pedagogic entertainment of an ambitious bourgeois reading audience, making accessible that kind of useful and expert knowledge 'which was then beyond the reach of the ordinary reader'.[13]

This chapter focuses on the *Edinburgh Review* and, to a lesser extent, other organs of higher journalism, such as the *Quarterly Review* and the *Athenaeum*, for three reasons: first, because of the pedagogical nature of the texts they select for review; second, because of their appeal to an ambitious, upwardly mobile set of middle-class readers; and finally, because of the new journalistic strategies, styles, and formats that such journals inaugurate. Combining instruction with entertainment, the 'information genre' of the longer, quarterly review essay could be said to instantiate in its very form the tensions between specialisation, generalisation, and popularisation that early nineteenth-century historians were attempting to negotiate, offering an important, if overlooked, way of illuminating the processes of protocol formation and the attribution of value in the field of written history.[14] To study historical protocol formation alongside the more explicit contestations of historical theory and method in the periodical press is to study the process of defining and attributing historical value as it was emerging in the period, as well as to attend to the complex, networked acts of valuation that constitute that process. Book reviews and essays can therefore help us to recover dynamic 'modes of emergence' in both periodical and historiographical culture, and to rethink the nineteenth-century historical field as one that developed gradually from within a commercial knowledge industry rather than as one inherently divided between amateurs and professionals.[15]

Historical Specialisation and the Review Essay

By the 1830s, reviewers were complaining about the tendency of the British book trade to commission popular authors to write works of history, resulting in a deluge of histories with very little to recommend them beyond an engaging literary style. Reviewing Francis Palgrave's *History of England (Anglo-Saxon Period)* (1831) anonymously in the *Athenaeum* for 1831, Hannah Lawrance derides the ongoing inclination of market-conscious and profit-driven publishers to commission 'men of talent' to compile historical works for which their abilities are 'wholly inadequate': 'The writer of poetry was considered surely competent to take an extensive view of the progress of society—the humorous novel-writer to paint the manners and customs of past times—and the brilliant essayist to do "all and everything".' In arguing that 'not every writer ... can write history' and that 'not every writer of history ... deserves the name of an historian', Lawrance draws attention to an ideal type of 'competent' historian with 'a peculiar character of mind' and an 'intimate acquaintance with a peculiar line of study', one whose '[h]abits of patient research, careful inquiry, and cautious induction' will 'bring one obscure fact to bear upon another – a nice discrimination that will weigh, and duly estimate, the many conflicting statements of ... contemporary writers'.[16]

Advocating for a more specialised or stratified division of literary labour than the demand for cheap books currently allows, Lawrance's *Athenaeum* review introduces two conceptual categories that are relevant to the emergence of modern history as a specialised field: the first is 'technicality' or the extent to which the writer has access to a discrete body of knowledge, which is then used in ways that accord with emerging standards of competency or expertise; and the second is 'indetermination' or the establishment of the ideological bases of an occupation or profession via qualities distinct to that occupation.[17] Since all of the putative 'historians' are paid or professional writers, a standard of 'competence' is used to imbue the specialist historian with an added sense of vocational integrity and prestige, attempting to regulate the market for historical works by imposing a series of normative values, such as depth of knowledge or an 'intimate acquaintance with a peculiar line of study' over 'a long course of years'. A second value determines that the specialist historian will have a 'peculiar character of mind', including the ability to discriminate between the 'conflicting statements' of historical sources—qualities which are not yet associated with systematic study or training on source criticism within the university system but that nonetheless illuminate a kind of 'cognitive exclusiveness'.[18]

Herself the prospective author of well-researched historical biographies of illustrious women, it is perhaps ironic that Lawrance should make the case for historical specialisation in relation to a history published in John Murray's popular and affordable *Family Library* series. Unlike his later *Rise and Progress of the English Commonwealth* (1832), Palgrave's *History of England* was intended for a wide audience, including children. While conceding that it was not an 'elementary work', Henry Hallam sneered at its 'popular manner' and '"Family" style' in the *Edinburgh Review*, arguing that it occasionally veered into the excesses of Walter Scott's *Tales of a Grandfather* and displayed a 'proneness to credulity' that operated 'at the expense of the author's critical reputation'.[19] In a review of Connop Thirwall's *History of Greece* (1835–47), itself published in Longman's *Cabinet Cyclopaedia*, Herman Merivale similarly concludes in the *Edinburgh Review* that 'popular' and 'superficial' works commissioned for identifiably mass-market 'cabinet miscellanies' tend to narrate little more than 'the chief occurrences in national annals', making it unreasonable to expect, in a book 'prepared for general circulation', the 'indefatigable labours' and 'original historical research' of German scholars.[20] Edward Lytton Bulwer was more sanguine, noting in *England and the English* (1837) that publishers' series were not so much 'proof of degeneracy in the knowledge of authors' as 'proof of the increased number of readers'.[21]

The idea that an appeal to a broad or general readership might work against primary research, critical acuity, and professional reputation was increasingly widespread across review journals of all political persuasions in the 1830s, when the use of the term 'popular' acquired a more pejorative tone. While the inverse relationship between esteem and popularity has a long history, the indeterminate status of popular history was both governed and mitigated by the rise of mass culture and a newly industrialising commercial publishing system. Despite increasingly negative attitudes towards popular history, Leslie Howsam has demonstrated that, even by the middle of the century, mainstream publishers like Macmillan were turning down 'worthy but dry' manuscripts, with the university presses equally uninterested.[22] Notwithstanding the widening gap between the amateur and professional historian, Howsam documents the extent to which publishers were imbricated in the demands and practices of the mass market, attempting to combine accurate and well-documented historical narratives by specialist historians with a compelling and accessible narrative style. Knowing that an 'impenetrable boundary between the popular and the professional would be bad for business' and potentially cost them around 12 per cent of their trade's annual output, mainstream publishers such as Macmillan worked hard to adapt to the movement towards academic specialism while still catering for an expanding middle-class market.[23]

In their endeavour to combine specialisation with an accessible narrative style, commercial publishers were assisted by periodical reviewers, who praised artistic flair at the same time as they distinguished between works of history prepared for a general market and those that were modelled on the German school's ideals of specialised research.[24] Authors, too, began to position their historical writing for specific reading audiences and markets, sometimes including the word 'popular' in titles and prefaces to signal their appeal to a broad, non-specialist audience. The preface to the first volume of James Mackintosh's *History of England*, commissioned for the *Cabinet Cyclopaedia*, emphasises that it is an 'abridged' version of English history aimed at busy 'general' readers who require 'a particularly accessible manual for reference'.[25] Yet if works such as Mackintosh's *History* explicitly proclaim their desire to reach a mass market, other authors are equally determined *not* to write popular history. The *Athenaeum* notes that the popular historical novelist G. P. R. James's 'erudite', 'correct', and 'dignified' *History of Charlemagne* (1832) is deliberately 'as unlike a *romance* as possible', concluding that 'if the work ... was not so strictly a history, it might perhaps be less instructive, but would certainly be more popular'.[26]

Debates about the relative value of popular and specialised history were thus already proliferating in periodical discourse by the 1830s and did not emerge ready-made with J. R. Seeley's dismissal of 'literary' historians in the 1860s and 1870s. Unlike Seeley's more trenchant complaints, Lawrence's 1831 *Athenaeum* review does not align the distinction between the generalist and the specialist with what Seeley would later characterise as the 'literary' and the 'scientific' historian.[27] Combining antiquarian detail and accuracy with stylistic virtuosity, Lawrence deems Palgrave's history engaging *and* specialised: his content is detailed, accurate, and well documented, and his style is 'clear, unaffected, remarkably well suited to historical narrative' while still being vivid, pictorial, and picturesque in the style of the 'early chronicle'.[28] Lawrence thus makes some concessions to the stylistic qualities that would satisfy the demands of a popular or general readership, while also recognising that an engaging narrative style is an insufficient measure of historical value.

Articulating claims to historical specialisation that cut across the levelling effects of the British book trade, other reviewers in the higher journals of the 1820s and 1830s tend to agree in affirming that the 'standard' qualities of a historian are what T. B. Macaulay characterised in the *Edinburgh Review* for 1833 as 'great diligence in examining authorities', 'great judgment in weighing testimony', and 'great impartiality in estimating characters', while simultaneously retaining the importance of literary assets such as concision, perspicuity, vigour, and picturesqueness.[29] Reviewers are certainly able to distinguish between stylistic qualities and invention or make-believe: a historian could be highly proficient in the 'literary arts' while nonetheless remaining a 'writer of scrupulous veracity' since historical narrative required 'not the talent of inventing, but the gift of discerning'.[30] As John Allen put it in the *Edinburgh Review* for 1825, without a 'critical examination' of sources and an appeal to a 'multitude of authorities' 'a work professing to be historical ... is not more deserving of credit than the romances of Waverley or Ivanhoe'.[31] At the same time, G. B. Niebuhr's work upheld the idea that literary evidence could have historical value, and this view allowed Liberal Anglican historians such as Thomas Arnold, Charles Merivale, and Charles Kingsley to maintain 'literary attitudes' well into the second half of the nineteenth century.[32]

Notwithstanding the persistence of literary or picturesque history, the demands of early nineteenth-century reviewers for more specialised histories marks a change from an earlier periodical reviewing culture that tended to select for review histories that either were aimed at a broad market and written in an accessible style, or were more universal in their scope. Before the nineteenth century, the periodical press was more likely to review a general, universal, or synthetic narrative history than it was to review eyewitness accounts or 'coterie publications', such as antiquarian tracts.[33] By the early nineteenth century, antiquarian studies and publications of original material were receiving renewed attention. Despite Francis Jeffrey's noted aversion to antiquarian enthusiasm, some twenty reviews appeared on antiquarian subjects in the *Edinburgh Review* in the early part of the nineteenth century, half of which were written by Walter Scott.[34] In the 1820s and 1830s, this interest in antiquarian material was largely redirected towards reviews of publications by book societies and clubs, with Scott's Bannatyne Club setting a 'furious pace' of publication, particularly between 1823 and 1832.[35] Once slighted by periodical reviewers as scraps or fragments without any exchange value in the literary marketplace, specialist publications of manuscripts and rare printed books were increasingly lauded by the *Edinburgh Review*, with the journal seeing itself as a counter-force to the 'vulgar spirit of economy' that would allow historical records to perish and prevent serious historical scholarship in Britain.[36]

Historical Reviewing in the *Edinburgh Review*, 1820–40

It is well known that the *Edinburgh Review* openly professed a Whig political agenda and corporate identity, as well as developing its own way 'of thinking and writing historically': the progressive, teleological 'Whig interpretation of history', as it is now known. Party biases notwithstanding, the selectivity of the journal and its aspiration to review those serious and weighty works that had gained 'a certain portion of celebrity' make it a valuable case study for the history of historical reviewing culture.[37] Whereas *Blackwood's* actively capitalised on a commodified industry of celebrity, the *Edinburgh Review*, perhaps more than any other review journal in the early nineteenth century, attempted to reconcile the tension between the specialism of learned discourse and the education and entertainment of bourgeois reading audiences. It is therefore especially useful in excavating the emerging protocols attaching to specialised history, as well as enabling a better understanding of what was classified and valued as 'history' by reviewers. The journal's editorial policy of using anonymous, male-only reviewers illuminates, too, the 'remasculinisation' of literary culture in the early nineteenth century and the ongoing gendering of historical protocol formation and scholarly merit.[38]

In the twenty-year period from 1820–40 examined in this instance, the *Edinburgh Review* reviews 68 out of 648 histories listed in the journal for potential review. Aside from volumes 43 and 44 in 1826 and volume 52 in 1831, the journal published a quarterly list of new publications at the end of each of volume, listing under the heading 'History' a total of approximately 198 printed works between 1820 and 1825, and approximately 456 works from the final quarter of 1826 to January 1840.[39] This is around half the number of 'Novels, Tales, and Romances', 'Biographies', and 'Travels and Voyages' listed in the same period, respectively.[40] Works classified as 'History' include compilations and chronicles; local histories; histories for children; constitutional histories; ancient and classical histories; antiquarian histories and publications of original documents; histories of empire; religious histories; military histories; philosophies of history; histories of literature; and various histories by German, French, Italian, and Spanish historians (both in original languages and in translation). History is distinguished from biography, travel writing, and antiquities and architecture, all of which have their own separate listings, while histories of imperial dominions tend to be separated from travel literature and emigration guides based on the depth and breadth of their information.[41]

The granularity of these classifications suggests that a degree of historical specialisation had already been established by the 1820s and 1830s. There are, for instance, very few universal histories in the *Edinburgh Review* lists along the lines of the Scottish historian Alexander Fraser Tytler's *Universal History, from the Creation of the World to the Beginning of the Eighteenth Century* (1839) or the Irish historian Edward Quin's *Universal History from the Creation* (1838). While J. A. Roebuck's review of, among other publications, the first volume of William Napier's controversial six-volume *History of the War in the Peninsula* (1828–40) derides those who approach military history as 'a mere bookselling speculation', there was a burgeoning field of specialised naval and military histories, memoirs, and biographies published just after the Peninsular War.[42] Based on the available publications listed for review, other subfields such as local history, constitutional history, and antiquarian history also experienced something of a resurgence in the 1820s and 1830s.[43]

What, then, are the qualities that led the *Edinburgh Review* to single out some works of history from their list of new publications and not others? The social status, celebrity, party affiliation, and authority of the author are certainly relevant. Yet while historical works by prominent Whig statesmen such as James Mackintosh and Charles James Fox receive due attention, party affiliation appears to be less important than intellectual renown and authority.[44] Acclaimed continental historians such as Guizot, Sismondi, and Niebuhr receive multiple reviews of their work on the basis of merit, currency, and reputation, including formal merit such as academic degrees and appointments. James Mackintosh notes that Sismondi is 'already well known to his readers', with his 'talents', 'principles' and 'peculiar qualifications' making him the 'undisputed authority' on the early history of European nations, while the origin of Niebuhr's *History of Rome* (1827–8; 1832) in a series of lectures at the University of Berlin is considered appropriate for a work of 'serious' history.[45] The journal thus tends to review high-status or authoritative works that are either considered standard works in various fields or draw on previously unpublished sources.[46]

Within the realm of 'higher-order' history, the journal often selects for review those histories that have generated a certain amount of notoriety, such as Lingard's eight-volume *History of England* (1819–30) and Niebuhr's *History of Rome*, the latter of which sold more copies (in translation) in England than in Germany.[47] Thomas Jefferson Hogg's 1830 review of the first volume of the *History of Rome*, translated by John Julius Hare and Connop Thirlwall, maintains that 'it has attracted so much attention, and drawn forth so many critical notices, both in

Britain and on the Continent' that it requires a reviewer almost as diligent as the historian himself. Roman history is, moreover, considered to be a field of 'active controversy', ensuring a measure of public interest.[48] As Fiona Stafford has noted, there was a certain topicality to the *Edinburgh Review*'s choices, with the journal selecting publications for review that would allow 'direct and broadly Whiggish comment on the contemporary political situation' while seemingly distancing itself from the 'vulgarity of "news" and "journalism"'.[49] Coverage of histories of Ireland, for instance, allowed reviewers to discuss the case for Catholic Emancipation and repeal of the Union, while reviews of constitutional histories provided opportunities to discuss reform and Whig party self-definition.[50] Histories of ancient Greece and Rome similarly enabled reflections on governance, republicanism, and democratic franchise in the years leading up to the Reform Acts, invoking the *topos* of Roman decadence and decline, and generating Athenian and anti-Athenian discourse.[51]

The journal's topical interests are reflected in a more detailed breakdown of the historical texts selected for review. Of the approximately sixty-eight review essays that met the journal's own criteria for 'history', around twenty relate to antiquarian publications of primary documents. There are four reviews of antiquarian histories and six review essays on religious or ecclesiastical history. On the history of England, there are eight review essays (three of which relate to Lingard's history), with an additional four review essays on English legal and constitutional history. Histories of ancient Greece and Rome make up four review essays (three of which are on Niebuhr's *History of Rome*), and there are two review essays on histories of Ireland, four reviews on histories of Spain and/or the Spanish Empire, and two reviews of histories on Britain's colonies. During this period, the *Edinburgh Review* did not tend to select for review works of local history, histories of Scotland, or histories written by women.[52] The journal's failure to review more general histories of Scotland (as opposed to antiquities or illustrations) is perhaps related to an editorial desire to avoid parochialism, while the absence of reviews of local histories suggests a certain fastidiousness towards a local history community made up of amateur organisations and writers of all classes.

Unlike the *Athenaeum*, *Blackwood's*, and even the Tory *Quarterly Review*, the *Edinburgh Review* did not employ women reviewers and adopted a pervasively 'masculinist rhetorical stance'.[53] More generally, Siskin has noted the extent to which a 'gender-conscious economy of print' elevated certain kinds of writing above others and contributed to the remasculinisation of literature in Britain at the turn of the nineteenth century. At the *Edinburgh Review*, a male-only network of reviewers worked alongside 'newly specialized treatments of traditionally masculine subjects' such as economics, politics, and history to re-emphasise the 'feminized identity of the literary and aesthetic'.[54] The few women writers who did receive critical notice in the journal tended to be moulded into 'traditional female stereotypes'. While Jeffrey was supportive of writers such as Joanna Baillie, Maria Edgeworth, and Felicia Hemans in the early part of the century, there were no notices of women writers between November 1825 and October 1829, until Jeffrey signalled his retirement as editor with a notice on Hemans as an example of the 'female poetic virtues' of the poetess.[55]

While some works by women historians appear under 'History' in the journal's new publications lists (including those by Charlotte West, Madame de Staël, Frances Milton Trollope, C. A. Davies, Barbara Allen Simon, Hannah Lawrance, Emma Roberts, and Elizabeth Blacket), the relative lack of female historians in the lists is partly the result of gender bias and partly of the generically hybrid forms in which women wrote and published, which were often not considered authoritative enough for inclusion under the category of history. While the more progressive journals and newspapers such as the *North British Review*, the *Westminster Review*, and the *Athenaeum* more readily reviewed works of history by women, it is perhaps not surprising that only one historical text by a woman is reviewed by the *Edinburgh Review* in a twenty-year period: Lucy Aiken's *Memoirs of the Court of Charles I* (1833), which, along with her previous *Memoirs of the Court of Queen Elizabeth* (1818) and *Memoirs of the Court of James I* (1822), is described by the novelist and biographer Thomas Henry Lister in 1834 as an 'agreeable' and 'acceptable addition[s] to our literature'. Published by the reputable Longmans, Aiken's work was well regarded by the *Edinburgh Review*, but in this case it falls short of the new standards required for specialist history. The genre in which Aiken writes—the 'modern memoir'—is deemed a 'difficult' one, occupying an unsettled generic space somewhere between 'political history and historical romance'. However, the problem lies primarily with Aiken's research methods: despite her 'tenor of easy narration', which is 'attractive to the general reader', she has not extensively availed herself 'of the mass of curious and valuable materials, still unpublished, which lie in our public repositories'.[56] Aiken is therefore framed as an agreeable writer but not as an able historian with the requisite technical and research skills.

It is by now well known that nineteenth-century women undertook pioneering documentary research into various aspects of what we would today call social history, including fashion, diet, and maternity. The dearth of reviews of their work in the *Edinburgh Review* coincides with the very moment when 'authorial momentum began to turn Britain into an information culture', one that relied heavily on word of mouth and on the social dissemination of information emanating from circulating reviews.[57] The reformulation of the theory, methods, and protocols of historical writing in periodical reviews not only meant that the hybrid genres favoured by women, such as a travelogues and memoirs, increasingly found themselves outside of specialised definitions of history as a genre and vocation, but also that the reading public was trained to interpret and view women's writing as non-technical. The charge levelled at Aiken—that she has 'not enough of the spirit of the antiquary'—suggests the extent to which her strengths as a writer were explicitly tied to attributes of femininity and domesticity. It also, however, reflects changing attitudes towards antiquarian knowledge within the *Edinburgh Review* circle.[58]

Antiquarianism was an important discourse for the journal, partly because it was a non-threatening way of examining Scottish national difference in the context of post-Union assimilation and partly because of its 'affective pull' for a wide readership.[59] Increasingly, however, antiquarian interest became entangled with questions of historical specialisation. In the twenty-year period under consideration, over twenty review essays pertain to historical source material or publications of historical documents by printing societies. Many of these reviews involve a reassessment of antiquarian methodologies. Henry Brougham's review of *Original Letters, Illustrative of English History* (1825) by Henry Ellis, Keeper of Manuscripts in the British Museum, for instance, describes Ellis as a new sort of antiquarian who has given up the elite dilettantisms of the private club and the 'abstruse speculations' of the mere 'editor' in favour of providing free public access to records to 'mankind at large'.[60] Allen's review of Palgrave's *Parliamentary Writs and Writs of Military Summons* (1827) more explicitly argues that without the antiquarian publication of primary sources, including those with 'sufficient indexes, glossaries, and chronological tables', 'no satisfactory history' of the legal and constitutional history of England could emerge.[61]

Reviews of antiquarian publications also encouraged an interest in archival or primary documents, in particular memoirs of family or domestic life such as that of the royalist Lady Fanshawe, which Jeffrey declares able to provide a glimpse into the 'living character of bygone ages' and thus to disclose 'the true springs of [historical] action'.[62] If these publications stimulated a change in the whole idea of biographical exemplarity, establishing a new genre of domestic life-writing, they also tended to place women writers outside of the bounds of specialised history and into the generic realm of biography and memoir.⁶³ Charges of 'domesticating' history were not, however, directed only at women: the antiquarian and director of the Camden Society, John Bruce, writing in the *Edinburgh Review* for 1840, equally disparaged Patrick Fraser Tytler's attempt in his *England under the Reigns of Edward VI and Mary* (1839) to 'popularize ... historical documents, and render a collection of letters three centuries old a book for the drawing room and the circulating library'. While not objecting to the publication of historical documents, Bruce wishes to prevent the too prevalent error of mistaking 'history' for its 'materials', a mistake compounded by attempts by editors to correct errors and to modernise the peculiar idioms, antiquated language, and orthography of historical texts for the general reader, thereby destroying the historical identity and authenticity of the original documents.⁶⁴

Source Criticism and Neo-Antiquarianism

If the *Edinburgh Review* inaugurated the movement towards more extensive analyses and evaluations in book reviews, neither it nor the other quarterlies abandoned the extraction method altogether. The ongoing propensity among reviewers in nineteenth-century journals to quote lengthy passages from historical texts—the so-called 'abstract and extract' style of 'quotation and paraphrase'—was not just a signal that the text in question was capable of imparting useful knowledge to its readers or even simply a 'system of authentication' that used source material of various kinds to establish authority via a kind of 'calculated antiquarianism': it was also evaluative in its selection and abridgement of material. Unlike extracts from fictional texts, which, as Dames has shown, aimed to mimic the durational experience of reading longer narratives in order to elicit affective immersion, selected extracts from historical works tended to illuminate for the reader two key aspects of the relevant text: first, the accessibility and lucidity of its prose style; and second, its religious and/or party-political affiliations. The primary aim of extraction in reviews of historical works was therefore to enable the reader to self-assess the suitability of a selected text on the basis of religious and political biases, as well as implicitly to direct or adjudicate readerly appraisal.⁶⁵

A characteristic example can be found in Henry Hallam's 1831 *Edinburgh Review* article on Lingard's Cisalpinist and revisionist challenge to Protestant readings of English history, which sets out extracts from Lingard's *History of England* to show his 'powers of historical narration in a very favourable light', while nonetheless condemning his 'sneering' Gibbonesque style in relation to Protestant religious beliefs.[66] The accusation that religious or other forms of controversy might overtake historical content was a common one. The charge levelled at Mitford, a Country Tory, by T. B. Macaulay in the *Edinburgh Review* for 1824, for instance, is that he has become a celebrity by privileging 'singularity' of content over historical argument: 'An exploded opinion, or an unpopular person, has irresistible charm for him'. Mitford's quest for novelty is matched by a style 'distinguished by harsh phases, strange collocations, occasional solecisms, frequent obscurity, and . . . a peculiar oddity'; namely, Mitford anglicises ancient and foreign names, 'mangling' them 'in defiance of both reason and custom'.[67] Macaulay makes a similar complaint in relation to Lord Mahon, who he describes as 'so bigoted a purist' that he 'transforms the Abbe d'Estrees into an Abbot'.[68] Likewise Fox, nervous of sliding into parliamentary slang, is characterised as over-zealous in purifying his vocabulary: 'He would not allow Addison, Bolingbroke, or Middleton to be sufficient authority for an expression. He declared that he would use no word which was not to be found in Dryden.'[69]

The value of a purified over a vernacular, idiomatic, or colloquial style was still very much under debate in the 1820s and 1830s. As discussed in the previous chapter, debates over the purification of language were politically charged, with histories by Scottish or Irish Catholic authors often facing heightened stylistic and linguistic criticism. In a review of John O'Driscol's *History of Ireland* (1827) in the *Edinburgh Review*, Jeffrey declares O'Driscol, 'like most of his countrymen', 'not particularly scrupulous about the purity or dignity of his diction', particularly in relation to the 'orthography of proper names'.[70] While Mitford, Mahon, and Fox are *over-scrupulous* in their approach to language and style, O'Driscol and Lingard have not attained the level of 'purity' of language that the *Edinburgh Review* deems desirable.[71] Lingard's 'contaminated' language is never explicitly related to his views on the 'Catholic Question'. However, Hallam sets out extracts in his 1831 review in the *Edinburgh Review* relating to the most controversial passages of Lingard's work, particularly passages from volume four on the Tudor dynasty which draws on primary sources to present the Protestant Reformation 'unfavourably', albeit 'dispassionately'.[72] While Hallam condemns Lingard's 'want of candour' on the Reformation, he nonetheless concedes that the *History* is comparatively free of party prejudice and praises Lingard's 'neutrality' and 'good sense'.[73]

As Hallam's review intimates, the staple values addressed and promoted by the extraction method (literary style and impartiality) were increasingly supplemented by a third value: source criticism. Practising historians such as Hallam tend to foreground the importance of consulting and testing primary historical documents. While Hallam begins his review of Lingard by defending Hume's lack of original research, he ultimately prefers Lingard's account of Cromwell's expulsion of Parliament because of Lingard's more rigorous evaluation of eyewitness accounts. Moreover, Hallam takes on the task of source criticism himself in his review, testing Lingard's history by scrupulously consulting primary sources to resolve differences between competing accounts. As Hallam puts it in a brief reflection on his own reviewing practice, he knows 'not how to review a general history of England, except by adverting to some of the facts which are not contained, or which are differently related, in other books, and to some of the author's opinions on disputable points'.[74]

In Hallam's review, Lingard's merits as a specialist historian are given their due, with Hallam concluding that Lingard has corrected a longstanding propensity towards partisanship in written history through a renewed attention to primary historical sources.[75] Lingard's antiquarian background—in particular, his *Antiquities of the Anglo-Saxon Church* (1806)—is increasingly deemed a benefit rather than a detriment to his more explicitly narrative historical work. In his 1825 review of volumes two and three of the *History of England* in the *Edinburgh Review*, Allen notes that Lingard demonstrates 'the rare merit of having collected his materials from original historians and records' rather than being 'copied at secondhand from other compilers', giving his history a 'stamp of originality, not to be found in any general history of England in common use'.[76] By the 1830s, Lingard is said to embody the standards of 'research and erudition' to which the *Edinburgh Review* holds all other modern historians of Britain, adding to this learning 'a talent for narration which we rarely find in authors distinguished for antiquarian research'.[77]

While it was often continental historians such as Sismondi and Niebuhr who were held up by the British periodical press as pioneers of innovative historical methods, Lingard and Palgrave are increasingly declared the standard bearers for a 'new type' or 'school' of historical writing in Britain.[78] Lawrance's association of Palgrave with the 'competent' historian in the *Athenaeum*, and the almost universal praise among reviewers for his history of the Anglo-Saxon period, revolved around his modification of the realm of antiquarian scholarship based on his pioneering work as an archivist in the Public Record Office.[79] Palgrave's journey from the author of 'some very learned articles in periodical publications' and the 'editor of the Parliamentary Writs, under the Commissioners of Public Records' to 'the personal character of an original author'—in other words, from antiquarian to historian—is one that reconciled erudition with narrative appeal and situated the 'raw materials' of the national past within wider frameworks of social development.[80] As Palgrave put it in an 1844 essay in the *Quarterly Review* that makes palpable his desire to reposition himself as an archival historian rather than an antiquary, '[o]ur attention is in danger of being engrossed by the archaeology of the curiosity shops. Unless this tendency be corrected, we shall be overwhelmed with literary dealers in the *rococo* of history'. For Palgrave, archaeology—in the sense of the study of 'manners and customs', 'incident and romance', and 'art or decoration'—is 'secondary and subordinate' to history's 'sound instruction', which must substitute the 'illuminated miniature' for 'the real view of the state of society'.[81]

Palgrave's desire to distance himself from his antiquarian roots is suggestive of an emerging demarcation between the historian, the antiquary, and the archivist.[82] Yet while attitudes towards the 'the chill technicality of the antiquary' remained ambivalent for much of the century, Palgrave's blend of antiquarian accuracy and historical narrative contributed to the rise of what Guy Beiner calls 'neo-antiquarianism', which was central both to the development of source-based historical criticism and to the regional forms of national feeling discussed in Chapter 3 of this book.[83] By 1837, when Palgrave published his inventive *Truths and Fictions of the Middle Ages*, he was already known as a populariser, who sought to render even his more 'formal works' accessible to 'hasty and indolent readers'.[84] At the same time, reviewers favourably note Palgrave's 'zeal and diligence' in 'the careful examination of our ancient sources' and consider him a corrective to the 'errors of chroniclers', with Allen declaring his *Rise and Progress* the 'most luminous work' ever produced on England's early institutions and jurisprudence, even when compared to Sharon Turner's 'valuable history'.[85]

The older style of antiquarianism that Palgrave had left behind was one considered 'dry, hard, and repulsive' to the general reader. Writing in the *Edinburgh Review*, the lawyer and specialist in Scottish history James Browne notes of John Gardner Wilkinson's *Manners and Customs of the Ancient Egyptians* (1837) that 'the nature of his earlier productions' was 'little suited to the taste of readers in this country'. Wilkinson's *Materia Hieroglyphica* (1828) is deemed 'devoid of method or arrangement' and 'lacking a connected view' of the state of knowledge of his subjects. His *Topography of Thebes* (1835) is an improvement but also betrays 'a singular want of sequence and connexion in many of its parts'. Yet in producing these kinds of dry and disconnected specialist endeavours, Wilkinson is nonetheless slowly, albeit 'unconsciously', 'qualifying himself' for a new kind of work, which could combine 'ancient learning and modern discovery' with a 'philosophical spirit'.[86] The then Professor of Ecclesiastical History at the University of Edinburgh, David Welsh, writing in the *Edinburgh Review* for 1835, thus praises as exemplary those historians like Wilkinson who successively publish specialised works of smaller scope before attempting a larger compilation or general history:

> Without any exception of moment, the best general histories have been produced by individuals who commenced their literary career by collecting materials for special departments, and who proceeded by degrees in this manner, publishing works upon separate branches ere they ventured to attempt an exhibition of the vast whole.[87]

The idea that the historian should work gradually by accretion, building on his or her specialist knowledge before publishing a more expansive general history, points both to the rise of historical specialism and to the ongoing value accorded to more synthetic works of general history. As reviewers became increasingly willing to engage with questions of source criticism, and as the focus of historical protocol formation shifted from philosophic theory to historical praxis, the popular historian was negatively compared to the antiquarian specialist, even as general narrative history remained the highest form of historical writing. Lawrance's 1831 *Athenaeum* review of volume two of James Mackintosh's *History of England*, for instance, 'regret[s] to find Sir James following so closely in the footsteps of … preceding historians, who compiled their narratives of these fierce conflicts and obscure but important events chiefly from the "lying chronicles" of others'.[88] Similarly, Robert Southey's *History of the Peninsular War* (1823–32) is criticised by the *Athenaeum* for deriving its knowledge principally from secondary sources, in contrast to those historians who have consulted state papers and other records.[89]

Once influential French historians, too, are increasingly subjected to scrutiny by British reviewers. Mackintosh's glowing review of Sismondi's *History of France* in the *Edinburgh Review* attributes the decline of historical talent in France to 'the want of habits of research' and 'critical examination' of sources and facts 'among their late popular writers', which cannot be remedied by 'ingenious speculation', 'ostentatious ornament', or 'vivacity' of style. History, as Sismondi remarks, must be 'contemplated at its source'.[90] Even here, however, the historian must not succumb too fully to antiquarian enthusiasm. In a review of *Histoire de la Réforme* or *History of the Reformation* (1834–5), also in the *Edinburgh Review*, Allen describes the French historian Jean-Baptiste Capefigue as 'ransacking archives' and 'accumulating' material. '[S]educed by the success of Sir Walter Scott', Capefigue obsessively replicates the 'minute and circumstantial details from contemporary writers who witnessed and participated in the scenes they describe' without 'tracing and explaining causes'. Capefigue thus provides too much antiquarian detail without selection, refinement, or explanation, resulting in something like a category error: 'He has not the vivid imagination of Victor Hugo, but he is a labourer in the same vineyard.'[91] Guizot, on the other hand, demonstrates both 'an indefatigable industry' in collecting research materials and 'a rigid severity in discarding unnecessary detail', successfully placing the 'brilliant colours' and 'harmonizing tints' of picturesque descriptions within a broader framework of 'large and general views'.[92]

The extent to which antiquarian detail had begun to merge with scientific methods of source criticism is most evident in reviews of Niebuhr's *History of Rome*, which resituated the interpretative battles over the symbolic power of Rome following Gibbon's *Decline and Fall* (1776–88) within a more scholarly and source-oriented framework. While there is still a tendency in British reviews to deride Niebuhr's antiquarian tendencies, he is nonetheless perceived to have pioneered a form of 'sceptical' or 'critical history' of which 'probability' is 'the keystone'.[93] The expertise with which Niebuhr is able to reconcile conflicting testimony, his scepticism towards both his predecessors and ancient eyewitnesses, and his privileging of 'doubt' over 'dogmatism' render him a historian of 'great sobriety'.[94] Hogg recognises in the *Edinburgh Review* for 1830 that Niebuhr's *History of Rome* is not a popular history but rather a specialist 'work of difficult comprehension', one requiring the reader to be a 'good scholar' and, as the classical historian Henry Malden put it, one presupposing 'a considerable degree of learning, and a more than ordinary power of attention and reflection'.[95]

By 1833, Niebuhr is described by Malden as having given 'birth to a new school of historical enquiry', one that can bring discordant facts and testimony 'within the compass of one probable theory'. While Niebuhr is disproportionately excited by Roman antiquities, he has nonetheless introduced an alternative methodology to the stadial, hypothetical, and conjectural methods of philosophic historians by refusing 'fanciful theories of the origin and progress of human society' and the 'imaginary process[es] by which savages are supposed to be civilized, and civilized communities to be corrupted'. There is, in other words, nothing speculative about Niebuhr's methodology, which applies the laws of science to the raw material of experience in order to construct an internally coherent social world, rather than superimposing *a priori* philosophic generalisations on to human history. His conclusions are gathered from the events of history and the experiences of nations: that is, from an examination of 'human feelings, and passions, and interests'.[96]

From the 1830s onwards, historians and periodical reviewers are keen to distinguish the new 'scientific' history from philosophic history, suggesting the extent to which German historicist thought 'leaked' into Britain through periodical reviewers, as well as more explicitly through the work of Carlyle, Arnold, and others.[97] As Jeffrey recognised in the *Edinburgh Review* for 1824, the emerging distinction between factual or empirical 'narrative histories' and conjectural 'philosophical essays' was critical to changing standards of historical discourse in England: in particular, to the difference between analytical/scientific and speculative/philosophic history. While 'more philosophical, discriminating, and concise histories' had largely taken the place of 'diffuse complications' in England, Jeffrey concludes that this exchange has come at the cost of partiality, particularly when historians speculatively attribute motives to historical actors in the manner of Hume.[98] Lingard, too, is critical of philosophic history, deeming it 'the philosophy of romance' because of its conjectural and unscientific application of general laws. As Allen notes in the *Edinburgh Review* for 1825, Lingard 'compares the philosophic historian to the novelist "whose privilege," he tells us, it is "to be always acquainted with the secret motives of those whose conduct and character he delineates"'. In privileging hypothesis, speculation, and theory over empirical fact, the philosophic historian is increasingly deemed no more objective or impartial than the novelist.[99]

Party Politics and Impartiality

In 1833, Malden declares Niebuhr's desire 'to ascertain and make known the facts of Roman history' an indication of the great task and 'morality' at the heart of historical writing: to write without prejudice. Unlike Mitford, who writes on ancient history with 'perpetual allusion to modern politics' and thus with 'all the anxiety of a pamphleteer', Niebuhr is free from 'furious and blind partisanship'.[100] The charge of 'prejudice' or 'partiality' is a common one in the 1830s, relating primarily to party-political affiliations, religious belief, and other forms of personal bias. If partisan reviewing reached its apotheosis in the ideological divisions that marked the decade following the French Revolution, the events leading up to Catholic Emancipation and the

1828–32 Reform Acts ensured that reviewing culture remained strongly divided on party-political lines. As T. B. Macaulay put it in his review of Hallam's *Constitutional History* in the *Edinburgh Review* for 1828, the accession of George III had ended 'a perfect cycle' or 'great year of the public mind' by reintroducing a period of cultural struggle, sectarianism, and political unrest after the American and French Revolutions.[101]

Macaulay's characterisation of Hallam as one of the few impartial historians in Britain suggests that, in a period of continuing political unrest, there was capital to be gained in making impartiality seem atypical of written history: focusing on a historian's partiality allowed the reviewer to forward his or her own party-political position at the same time as bolstering his or her authority as an unbiased expert and mediator of learned discourse.[102] Notwithstanding such rhetoric, there had already been a marked shift towards what we would today call 'objectivity' from the early to mid-eighteenth century onwards. If, in the seventeenth century, projective or partisan histories were grounded in the ethos, character, or virtue of the historian, the rhetorical efforts of eighteenth-century historians to achieve impartiality involved a movement away from 'consciously held and explicitly articulated political agendas'.[103] Despite being characterised as partisan, Hume had drawn on Clarendon's pro-royalist *History of the Rebellion* when writing his *History of England* not so much because he wanted to construct an overtly Tory historiography of the Civil Wars, but rather to redress what he saw as Whig party-political biases in histories of his own time.[104]

Yet while historians such as Hume and Robertson appear, to a large extent, to have dismissed the 'idealizing and demonizing passions', there were nonetheless serious limits to their purported objectivity, with both historians using rhetorical techniques to mask their ideological agendas.[105] The eighteen-year-old John Stuart Mill, reviewing George Brodie's *History of the British Empire* in the *Westminster Review* for 1824, sees Hume primarily as a sceptic and rhetorician rather than as a historian, accusing him of being enslaved by the sort of literature that seeks to 'excite emotion', and going so far as to call the last two volumes of his *History of England* a 'romance', of which Charles I is the hero.[106] Palgrave, too, thought that Hume was a '*consummate Rhetor*' who perverts '*history* into a panegyric of infidelity', noting that Hume had failed to 'translate' the 'history of remote times' and to capture its 'idiomatic peculiarities'. Like Mill, Palgrave, writing in the *Quarterly Review*, sees Hume's philosophic scepticism, and his desire to nullify and banish 'religious fictions', as barriers to his accuracy: 'He constantly labours to suppress any *belief in belief*, as an efficient cause of action.'

Hume's sentimental character portraits are an especial and 'constant source of falsification', and a lack of original research only adds to this superstructure of falsity: formed out of the 'cast of a cast', 'all the sharpness of the original has been lost' and 'denaturaliz[ed]'.[107]

While partly the product of Whig revisionism, early nineteenth-century responses to Hume suggest that historians and reviewers took charges of partiality and partisanship seriously, seeking to distance themselves from the imputation of writing polemic rather than history. Allen's review of the early volumes of Lord Mahon's *History of England from the Peace of Utrecht* (1836–53) in the *Edinburgh Review*, for instance, complains not only of Mahon's Tory party bias, but of his 'propensity to view every subject with a reference to modern politics'. In advising Mahon to expunge these passages, Allen distinguishes between the temporal depth models associated with history and the ephemeral nature of newspaper writing: 'He who aspires to write a history for posterity, should not lower his work to the standard of newspapers and party pamphlets.'[108] The idea that newspaper writing and pamphlets were shallow or ahistorical is also reflected in attitudes to quasi- or parahistorical genres such as biographies, with Brougham declaring the lives of public men to be 'peculiarly exposed to the danger only of becoming party pamphlets'.[109] Macaulay likewise notes of Mitford's *History of Greece* that the tendency to represent historical figures allegorically as 'heroes and villains' rather than as complex human agents was still largely unchecked in the period's written history.[110]

Like the histories of Greece and Rome, histories of the English Commonwealth enabled reflections on partiality, with Mackintosh condemning the 'slavish fear' to talk freely and impartially about the Civil Wars and Restoration as one of the 'most disgraceful novelties to have infected the English character'.[111] Nineteenth-century reviewers were also alert to the ways in which a seemingly dispassionate or objective stance could be weaponised. In his 1830 piece in the *Edinburgh Review*, Hallam attributes the critical and commercial success of Lingard's *History of England* to the latter's ability to conceal his ideological position effectively:

> No angry expression, no arrogance or indignation betrays the writer's intention; a placid neutrality, and almost an affected indifference to the whole subject, seems to guide his pen: aware of the propensity of mankind ... he prefers lowering his adversaries to exalting his friends.

Yet while Hallam attempts to expose Lingard's strategic misuse of rhetorical neutrality, he also 'sincerely congratulate[s] our author, as well as the public, on the manifest signs of increased candour and impartiality' which distinguish the later volumes of Lingard's history, at least in relation to political, if not religious, questions.[112]

The extent to which reviewers in the 1830s saw impartiality as a defining trait of the 'new historian' is evident in an 1838 review of William H. Prescott's *The History of the Reign of Ferdinand and Isabella the Catholic of Spain* (1838) by the Spanish scholar and orientalist Pascual de Gayangos in the *Edinburgh Review*. The so-called 'Boston Brahmin' historians that gathered around Prescott, such as Henry Adams, George Bancroft, and Francis Parkman, were highly lauded within Britain as epic historians and meticulous researchers. As an American and 'the inhabitant of another world', Prescott seems to 'have shaken off all the prejudices of ours; he has written a history without party-spirit, and without bias of any sort'.[113] Similarly, the Scottish novelist and travel writer Leitch Ritchie, reviewing Scott's *Tales of a Grandfather* in the *Athenaeum* for 1831, is pleasantly 'surprised to find a man of such fierce party spirit as Sir Walter Scott, writing history for the rising generation with the temper and impartiality of a philosopher'. Scott's *Life of Napoleon Buonaparte*, on the hand, is seen by most reviewers as partisan in intent and overly emotive in style. Despite Scott's research trip to Paris, John Ryley in the *Eclectic Review* considered it 'extremely superficial', showing 'no signs of severe research . . . [or] of patient and protracted investigation'.[114]

More so even than histories of Scotland and France, histories of Ireland occasioned historiographical reflections on the vexed question of impartiality. In 1827, Jeffrey claimed in the *Edinburgh Review* that a good history of Ireland was 'still a desideratum in our literature', noting that party rancour and religious animosity 'have made impartiality almost hopeless'. Denigrating the Catholic O'Driscol's tendency to 'exaggerate' ancient Ireland's antiquarian golden age of civilisation, Jeffrey urges a more realistic view of an ancient Ireland of 'unreclaimed bogs', 'polygamy', and 'other savage vices', claiming that O'Driscol's 'partiality for the *ancient* Irish . . . is truly a mere peculiarity of taste or feeling'.[115] Jeffrey's concern to discredit the identarian claims of Irish antiquaries and to reduce historical arguments to national partialities was a common response to nationalist histories of Ireland, which were often written and reviewed on ideological lines, even by commentators like Jeffrey who favoured Catholic Emancipation and wrote for Cardinal Nicholas Wiseman and Daniel O'Connell's Catholic *Dublin Review*. A review of the Whig historian W. C. Taylor's *History of the Civil Wars in Ireland* (1831), for instance, is highly praised in the British press for its 'non-partisan' view of contentious events, particularly the 'insurrection' of 1798, an impartiality not apparently achieved by the Catholic

Dennis Taaffe's earlier *An Impartial History of Ireland* (1809) or later histories such as Patrick O'Kelly's *General History of the Rebellion of 1798* (1842). William Hamilton Maxwell's popular *History of the Irish Rebellion in 1798* (1844), too, is lauded in the English press for its 'realistic' depictions of the United Irishmen. The Irish nationalist press, on the other hand, note that its apparently objective attention towards new manuscripts masks 'a distinct loyalist bias'.[116]

The same ideological approach applied to the controversies surrounding the Peninsular War. The third volume of Napier's *History of War in the Peninsula* is declared by the Spanish émigré Mateo Seoane in the *Athenaeum* to be 'dangerous to the character of history – dangerous to the fair repute of literature – and dangerous to the friendly feeling which Spain ought to nourish towards England'. Another notice by Seoane emphasises even more clearly Napier's 'strong personal prejudices' against the Spanish, characterising them as unhealthy and diseased: 'From a sort of anti-Spanish malady of mind the Colonel commits many mistakes, which, in a healthy state of impartiality, he would have avoided.' The *Quarterly Review* concurred, with John Wilson Croker and George Murray complaining of Napier's partiality to the French, factual distortions, and Whig party bias in a series of reviews. Southey, on the other hand, is said by the *Athenaeum* to evince the 'narrow prejudices of ultra-Toryism' in volume three of his *History of the Peninsular War*, particularly in his apparent whitewashing of the Jesuits.[117]

Reviewers also increasingly condemn histories written from a preconceived religious position, arguing for the importance of contextual interpretations of Scripture and drawing on a tradition of Biblical exegesis that viewed religious texts as historical sources. A review of Thomas Lathbury's *History of the English Episcopacy* (1836) by the Evangelical minister and biographer Joseph Sortain in the *Edinburgh Review* argues for the need to consider church history from a historical perspective, and, in particular, to acknowledge that the Anglican Church is a 'human church' and not the preordained product of divine intervention.[118] Similarly, William Empson's review of George Miller's *Lectures on the Philosophy of Modern History* (1820–4) rejects that idea that church history should demonstrate 'a strict unity of action', tracing out the parts 'of one great system of moral order' into a 'drama of the Divine Providence'. This, Empson argues, is more a 'theology than a philosophy of history', a view later taken up at greater length by Seeley in his anonymously published bestseller *Ecce Homo* (1865).[119] Arguing that natural theory is not a progressive science, T. B. Macaulay's review of Leopold von Ranke's *History of the Popes* (1840), translated by

Sarah Austin, likewise makes the case for the special importance of a 'spirit of impartiality' in religious history, bestowing Ranke's unbiased research a special 'place among the English classics'.[120]

Polemic, Feeling, and Gendered Reviews

Reflecting on English constitutional history in the *Edinburgh Review* for 1835, Macaulay notes the 'vehement, contentious, replying manner' of Charles Fox's *History of England from the Accession of James II* (1808), maintaining that almost every statement is an 'interrogation, an ejaculation, or a sarcasm', as if responding to 'an imaginary Tory'. While there are some fine passages in Fox's history 'made red hot by passion', Macaulay concludes that 'this is not the kind of excellence proper to history', noting that it is 'hardly too much to say, that whatever is strikingly good in Mr Fox's Fragment is out of place'. Macaulay's criticism of Fox's passionate style leads him to reassert the value of alternative Whig party histories written by Hallam and Mackintosh: whereas nearly all other eminent historians of English history write as 'advocates', Hallam and Mackintosh 'alone are entitled to be called judges'.[121]

Banishing advocacy and representing an overly passionate style as 'out of place' within normative historical protocol, a rhetorical or oratorical style ('Mr Fox wrote debates') is frequently used as a shorthand by reviewers for bias, affective involvement, and excessive emotion, whereas impartiality or objectivity is associated with a detached, neutral, and sober style. Despite his own vivid techniques, Macaulay's comments suggest that a general uniformity of style was becoming increasingly critical to the ways in which history was written. Yet the appeal to neutrality did not always amount to a dismissal of the historian's or the reader's emotions. In his review of Sismondi's *History of France*, Mackintosh argues that a 'fellow-feeling' with the emotions in original sources and experiences is critical to the 'moral effect' of history and indeed all narrative: the effect of a work, 'whether it be historical or what is called fictitious, is in proportion to the degree in which it exercises and thereby strengthens the social feelings and moral principles of the reader'.[122]

Notwithstanding these ongoing valorisations of sentimental immersion, Macaulay's objections to Fox's 'emotional' style form part of a more general distinction between history and polemic in the early nineteenth century. The so-called 'common style' promoted by Blair, Smith, and other belletrists (and roundly rejected by Carlyle) had already partially given way to a 'split between vulgar and refined language' in the decade following the French Revolution. By the 1820s, style is used as a way of policing both political and generic boundaries.[123] William Cobbett's emotional recoil from industrialism and individualism in his *History of the Protestant Reformation in England and Ireland* (1824–7), for instance, is dismissed by reviewers across party lines as a polemical text culled from Lingard's more rigorous *History of England*.[124] Allen similarly deems R. Plumer Ward's *Historical Essay on the Revolution of 1688* 'a Conservative Pamphlet in the disguise of an Historical Essay'.[125] On the same basis, both Whig and conservative critiques of industrial capitalism, such as Southey's *Colloquies* (1829), Augustus Pugin's *Contrasts* (1836), and Carlyle's *Past and Present* (1843), are distinguished from history because of their emotional style, amounting to examples of works that Macaulay considers 'splendid and affecting' but lacking in political instruction.[126]

While Macaulay did not go so far as to use the colloquy format, he himself faced similar criticism from Tory reviewers. His *History of England* is praised by the *Edinburgh Review* for its 'felicity of style' and picturesque evocation, but Croker in the *Quarterly Review* argues in a scathing piece that it does not sufficiently distinguish history from fiction, and displays a poisonous 'rancour more violent than even the passions of the time':

> Mr. Macaulay deals with history, evidently, as we think, in imitation of the novelists—his first object being always picturesque effect [. . .] For this purpose he would not be very solicitous about contributing any substantial addition to history, strictly so called.[127]

Too little picturesque evocation could also be met with hostile reviews. A review of Edward Lytton Bulwer's *Athens, its Rise and Fall* (1837) by the classical scholar Daniel Keyte Sandford expects from the 'graphic narrator' of stories of imperial decadence, such as *Rienzi* and *Pompeii*, 'a series of elaborate and brilliant scenes', and is disappointed that 'continuous narrative' takes over from picturesque evocation.[128] Similarly, Hallam in the *Edinburgh Review* complains that the style of Godwin's *History of the Commonwealth* is 'frigid and deficient in picturesque liveliness', lacking the 'great power of delineation' that characterises his fiction.[129]

Picturesque evocation is, however, more likely to be tolerated by reviewers than either direct authorial intrusion or speculative invention. Palgrave's *Truths and Fictions*, for instance, is listed under 'Novels, Tales, and Romances' in the *Edinburgh Review*. Described as shallow and contrived in its attempt to introduce the author's general reflections, the narrative portion of that work, which imagines a visit to England by

Marco Polo in the company of Friar Roger Bacon, is dismissed as speculative in content and 'exaggerated and peremptory' in tone.[130] Godwin, too, is criticised in an 1831 review of his *Thoughts on Man* (1831) in the *Athenaeum* for the 'candid manner in which the writer comes personally forward'.[131] Godwin's earlier *Life of Geoffrey Chaucer* (1804) was even more roundly dismissed by Walter Scott, Robert Southey, and others for combining history, biography, and criticism in a 'heterogeneous mixture', with Scott derisively suggesting that this type of speculative, counter-factual, and 'whimsical' historical project involves 'hooking in the description and history of every thing that existed upon the earth at the same time as Chaucer'.[132]

Positioning personal feelings as adverse to historical knowledge, reviewers increasingly characterise a polemical or emotional style as outside of the conventions or norms for written history, as well as linking it to the speculative use of invention and other fictionalising techniques that sought to address the feelings rather than the judgment. While the charge of an emotional style was not always gender-directed, female historians are more frequently portrayed as lacking the qualities required for historical competence and serious study, such as emotional restraint, impartiality, and political insight.[133] Other than Catherine Macaulay and Mary Wollstonecraft, few women historians in the late eighteenth and early nineteenth centuries were considered successful in the 'higher departments' of philosophic history. While the hostile *British Critic* maintained that Wollstonecraft's *Historical and Moral View* had mixed together the roles of novelist and historian, and the *Critical Review* argued that she had achieved 'not so much a *history* of the revolution but a *critique* upon it', most reviewers saw her work as sufficiently serious and philosophical.[134]

The 'manly' qualities of the work of the 'female philosophers' thus tend to be portrayed by reviewers as the exceptions that prove the rule about the masculine cast of official history. As the 1834 assessment of Lucy Aiken in the *Edinburgh Review* suggests, reviews of women historians imply that they lack the technical knowledge of the specialist or serious historian and should confine their studies to 'homely', 'feminine', and 'domestic' genres. Palgrave, writing in the notoriously conservative *Quarterly Review* for 1843, went so far as to argue that 'the whole clique ... of living Clios' 'ought to be contented with marking pinafores and labelling pots of jam'.[135] Despite the dramatic expansion of historical subject matters and social groups achieved by women historians, Palgrave, Carlyle, and Macaulay identify their own endeavours to broaden and widen historical research as uniquely innovative and regenerative.[136]

The gendering of history as masculine was partly effected through the gender biases inherent to nineteenth-century education, training, and formal qualifications. However, it was also a product of the genres women tended to favour, with many women writing in the mixed or hybrid modes of life-writing, memoir, biography, and travel writing, or supplementing the lives of public figures with accounts of their domestic and private experiences.[137] Lawrance's *Historical Memoirs of the Queens of England* (1838), for instance, explicitly seeks to 'unite[s] the fields of male history and female memoir'.[138] By the late 1840s, more women were engaging in political history, including Harriet Martineau's *History of the Thirty Years' Peace* (1849) and Anne Marsh's *The Protestant Reformation in France and the Huguenots* (1847), but the most prominent genre for women remained historical biographies of celebrated women produced by writers such as Agnes Strickland, Elizabeth Ogilvy Benger, Julia Kavanagh, and Caroline Halstead.[139]

As the negative reviews of Godwin's mixing of genres intimate, the hybridity of the genres in which women wrote left them open to charges of category error, polemic, bias, and emotional excess. A favourite means of policing the boundaries between women's writing and serious history was to use gender-specific terms to label their work 'anecdotal', 'sketchy', and 'gossipy' in both style and subject matter.[140] Reviews of Maria Graham's *Journal of a Voyage to Brazil* (1824) fuse partisan opposition with a scepticism towards the ability of women to acquire and synthesise certain types of knowledge. Despite the long historical essays with which she opens her travel journals and notwithstanding her having spent several years in Brazil, the *Quarterly Review* declares Graham 'unqualified to write *political* disquisitions on Brazil' due to 'her slight knowledge of the characters with whom she mixed, her ignorance of the language in which they conversed, and her imperfect acquaintance with the customs and manners of the people'. Similarly, John Barrow's review of her *Journal of a Residence in India* (1812) labels the work little more than a 'literary curiosity'.[141]

While her friendship with Lord Cochrane granted her privileged access to local dignitaries and Brazil's royal family, Graham could be publicly self-deprecating about her work and abilities, claiming that her 'opportunities of information were too few; my habits as a woman and a foreigner never led me into situations where I could acquire the necessary knowledge'.[142] If this (incorrectly) led to allegations that her *Journal of a Voyage to Brazil* was a 'hasty and ill-arranged abridgement of Southey', the practice of history in the nineteenth century was not an entirely masculine enterprise divided into separate spheres.[143] While some women sought to differentiate their work from official history by focusing on the alternative discourses of domestic and private life, others such as Wollstonecraft engaged in acts of historical self-fashioning within the masculine and public domain. Still others, like Lawrance, were anonymously policing the boundaries between competent and incompetent historians in periodical reviews, capitalising on publishing conventions to create 'spaces of agency and meaning' within male-dominated publishing industries.[144] Excluded from formal qualifications such as academic degrees and appointments, women also increasingly appropriated history's gendered authority and the ideal of scholarly excellence through alternative paratextual strategies such as title pages, dedications, and prefaces. As the second half of the nineteenth century progressed and more women entered a field of historical writing newly characterised by merit-based standards, they used these strategies to 'sanction their scholarly competence' in ways that suggest they were not isolated from either the specialisation or the professionalisation of history.[145]

From Opinion to Expertise

In his 1830 review of Niebuhr's *History of Rome* in the *Edinburgh Review*, Hogg argues that the expertise demanded of the critical reviewer is one of 'compression', 'distillation', and 'microscopic penmanship': a review, in other words, is the work of 'a sharply pointed pen' that can distil a historical work to its essence in the same way that the chemist can distil compounds. Correctly identifying that the work of the reviewer is a type of information management involving the reduction or distillation of knowledge, Hogg notes the extra pedagogic burden of adding 'additional value to the elaborate compound', grafting the reviewer's own expertise on to that of the author and reducing some of the 'abstruseness and obscurity of the original'. The point of a historical review essay is not, therefore, simply to summarise the contents of the work under review or to 'paint a historical subject in miniature', but rather to provide 'an intellectual and historical context for the work under review' and to 'show the spirit of the author, and the school to which he belongs', while also generating greater intellectual wealth by increasing the accessibility and circulation of historical knowledge.[146]

The didactic claim that the reviewer is both a decoder and a purveyor of knowledge who must strike the right balance between 'summary and evaluation' is a response to an early nineteenth-century periodical culture that aimed to navigate the reader through an almost overwhelming superabundance of print and to make more accessible increasingly specialised forms of knowledge, such as Niebuhr's difficult and learned histories.[147] On the one hand, the review essay enshrined 'a rational mode of "philosophical criticism"' drawn from a Scottish enlightenment inheritance; on the other hand, it wielded 'a lively "slashing" style'. In combining these two seemingly conflicting approaches in the *Edinburgh Review*, Jeffrey ascribed to the periodical project 'a responsibility to be "dispassionate"' and to avoid 'extravagance' and 'absurdity', while at the same time being lively, entertaining, and accessible.[148] Jeffrey thus saw the anonymity of the reviewer as a 'means of projecting a disinterested voice of impartiality' while simultaneously allowing the reviewer to be more candid and independent.[149]

The 1820s and 1830s mark out the consolidation of the review essay 'as a distinct critical discourse' for modern times. As Ina Ferris has pointed out, the periodical essay became much more than an 'auxiliary form' over the course of the nineteenth century; it became *the* 'discursive form in which culture itself was increasingly defined for an expanding middle-class public', allowing for a quasi-encyclopaedic reorganisation of knowledge in the public domain.[150] The review essay also increasingly developed into a commodity or what Samuel Taylor Coleridge called a 'saleable article' to be collected, repackaged, and attributed to its author: for example, Macaulay's popular *Critical and Historical Essays Contributed to the Edinburgh Review* (1843). The saleability of the review essay eventually led to a shift from a periodical marketplace dominated by anonymous reviews to attributed pieces revolving around the critical expertise and character of the reviewer.[151] While reviews largely remained anonymous or pseudonymous until the 'star system' emerged in the 1870s and 1880s, it was not unknown for reviewers in the first half of the century to acknowledge authorship, either publicly or privately, in particular cases, or to develop a pseudonymous critical persona beyond the corporate identity of the journal.[152] Notwithstanding the conventions of anonymity, the development of the long review essay was key to the creation of the professional critic and to the perceived discourse of authority and expertise that, its proponents claimed, distinguished the quarterly from the weekly and even the monthly review.[153]

As William Christie has noted, the priorities of book reviewing changed in the early nineteenth century, 'as the reviewer and his ideas on the topic in question took more and more precedence over the publication under review, which often became merely the occasion for the reflective article or essay'.[154] If, at the turn of the century, periodical writing was regarded as a trade rather than as a gentlemanly profession, the new review essay 'underwrote the transformation of the lowly reviewer into the cultural critic' and later into the public intellectual.[155]

This occurred partly because quarterly journals like the *Edinburgh Review* were able to offer 'unprecedentedly high fees', investing in their reviewers' 'status as gentlemen' and in the qualities of intellectual leadership, but also because, as Macaulay was to discover, review essays had a permanency and longevity beyond their 'natural life' of 'only six weeks'.[156]

Self-reflections on the occupational codes of historical reviewing are relatively rare in the early nineteenth century. However, reviews of historical texts in the period's organs of higher journalism can profitably be seen as a distinct subcategory within a more general culture of historical reviewing, increasingly adopting for the review format emerging historical protocols relating to objectivity that go beyond the opinion-based discourse of reviewing culture. With these reviews often, although not always, written by what we would today call 'practitioners' of history (such as Lawrance, Allen, Macaulay, Hallam, Palgrave, and Mackintosh), reviewers sought to appropriate the impartial authority of historical discourse by adopting methods of source criticism in their reviews, as well as condemning religious dogma, party system, polemic, emotion, invention, and other perceived prejudices.[157] If the intent of the reviewer in engaging in party self-critique was usually to promote a specific version of party history (rather than to abandon the party position altogether), standards of neutrality and objectivity nonetheless increasingly permeated historical reviewing culture and provided it with a level of historical expertise.

While there is no 'direct line' of descent from the antiquarian to the professional historian—with the new university-based professionals eventually side-lining antiquarianism to 'the [unsalaried] fringes of historical enterprise'—review essays by Jeffrey, Allen, and others demonstrate the extent to which antiquarian scholarship was central, rather than incidental, to the development of historical specialisation and source criticism in Britain.[158] Attitudes towards feeling also played a key role in articulating the changing protocols of history as scientific as opposed to literary writing.[159] As a new orientation towards objectivity emerged in tandem with an appreciation of historical source material, to be affecting was increasingly less important than to be accurate, although the two were not always considered mutually exclusive. Sceptical attitudes towards the place of imagination, feeling, and intuition in historical texts were thus heavily entangled with questions of method and style: just as being a good historian depended on suppressing personal bias, restraining feeling, and writing in a non-polemical style, being a good reviewer of historical texts increasingly meant adopting the same kind of rhetorical restraint. Far from promoting what Macaulay called a 'bold, dashing, scene-painting manner', reviews of serious historical works such as Niebuhr's increasingly reflect the author's scholarly intentions.[160]

Nurtured in an environment of concern over Britain's reputation for record-keeping and a new respect for the documentary aspects of historical writing, the rhetorical restraint identified in reviews of historical text increasingly came to permeate the *Edinburgh Review* and reviewing culture more generally. By the end of Macvey Napier's editorship of the *Edinburgh Review* in 1847, the reviewing scene 'had altered beyond recognition': the tone was 'decidedly more sober and statesmanlike', with the *Edinburgh Review* approaching the 1840s as 'a solid and respectable organ of public opinion'.[161] While reviewing culture was still primarily anonymous and multidisciplinary in its approach to knowledge formation, closer attention to reviews of historical texts demonstrates the extent to which reviewers invested in the standards of impartiality, self-restraint, and source criticism that increasingly came to define specialised history. If, to this day, 'the culture of knowledge (scholarly research) and the culture of informed opinion (journalism) remain in an uneasy . . . overlapping, and inextricable relationship', historical reviews in the 1820s and 1830s map out the emergence of the specialist practitioner and critic of history well before historical reviewing culture was dominated by specialised and dedicated academic journals such as the *English Historical Review* (1886), and even before agitation for such a journal in the 1860s.[162]

Epilogue: A Romantic Return?

Against the conception of romantic-era historicism as primarily sentimental or feeling, this book has identified an alternative type of counter-sentimental historicism: one that foregrounds an ethical and representational ambivalence towards sentimentalism without necessarily disavowing it altogether. Both working historians and post-structuralist philosophers of history have tended to pit romantic-era historians against their more scientific successors. This book has argued instead that the written history of the period—usually represented as anomalous, alternative, or transitional in historiographical accounts—is critical to understanding how the history of modern history-writing developed. Despite persistent fears (then and now) that late eighteenth- and early nineteenth-century Britain had not produced a 'grand history' in the continental style, the period is unique in providing a diverse set of historiographical alternatives to empirical and positivist history based on investments in certain types of feeling, sympathetic, or sentimental history, while simultaneously proving integral to the rise of empirical history through its incorporation of antiquarianism, its emphasis on documentary and material research, and its inauguration of inductive and hermeneutic methodologies.

Adapting both to the ascent of the novel and to a rapidly industrialising print-media and publishing landscape, romantic-era historians negotiated and synthesised prior modes of antiquarian, philosophical, and sentimental history in the context of newly historicised understandings of character and subjectivity. Acknowledging that 'reactive behaviour' shapes the motives and actions of historical individuals is a conceptual intervention in written history that had its first extended airing in the historical moment we now call 'romantic', one in which 'situational narratives' increasingly privileged dynamic internal processes and their unanticipated or unintended consequences over philosophical metanarratives of progress and decline.[1] At the same time, the recognition that feelings could and should be studied historically resulted in a certain distance from sentimental modes of representation and from the subjective experience of the historical witness and/or interpreter. Situating romantic-era written history within the history (or pre-history) of the history of emotions has therefore ironically meant focusing not so much on sentimental historicism or 'feeling history', but rather on the objectification and even suppression of feeling in nineteenth-century historical writing. More specifically, I have argued that the period's written history played an important role in the movement towards reifying feeling into a historically contingent object of study with its own history and process of development; or, in other words, in making feeling amenable to objectification.

In focusing on the history *of* feelings and on the larger structural relationships between self and society that so many romantic-era histories explore, I have no wish to deny that there were other historiographical modes circulating in the period or that these modes were central to some of its most important conceptual and political developments, from individualism to nationalism. Yet an understanding of romantic-era historical writing that focuses only or even primarily on feeling as a technique, mood, or modality cannot, I have argued, adequately account either for the diversity of the period's official history, or for the kind of socio-psychological understanding of the past that replaced the abstractions of philosophic causation as one of the period's primary historical paradigms. Seeing sentimental history as one type of history among several options available to romantic-era historians allows us to foreground influences other than sympathetic identification and intersubjectivity in written history, particularly those relating to the complex dynamics of reactive human behaviour. Put simply, David Hume's behaviouralist philosophy of human understanding rather than Adam Smith's sympathetic theory of moral sentiments has been the overriding point of reference (but also sometimes of departure) for this book.[2]

While I have primarily focused on the written history of the late eighteenth and early nineteenth centuries, one of the book's aims has been to think about the ways in which we understand historical vocabularies in relation to both that period and our own, and therefore to reassess the stories we have been told about the rise of empirical history and modern history's disciplinary origins in the late nineteenth century. I have heeded, in particular, Joan Wallach Scott's injunction that historiographical study should be concerned 'not with lineages for difference, but with *processes of differentiation*', and that it should attempt to historicise historical interpretation, 'understanding it not as a distortion of objectivity, but as the very source of knowledge itself'.[3] The emergent processes of differentiation uncovered in this book suggest that we must resist the either/or binaries of modern and premodern, subjective and objective, disciplinary and pre-disciplinary, and amateur and professional in our approaches to historical protocol formation. Focusing only or even primarily on the evolution of history as a discipline and profession risks the 'pitfalls of teleology' and forecloses both the diversity of earlier forms of official history and 'the fertile particularity of bygone intellectual life', including those so-called historiographical 'dead ends' that can provide a window into the values that underpin the historical writing of the past.[4]

Mark Salber Phillips has rightly argued that it is more productive to consider historical writing as being on a spectrum of presence and distance than to divide it into two fundamentally incompatible types of knowledge and representation: 'literary' and 'scientific', or 'subjective' and 'objective'. While the professionalisation of history has hardened and deepened the distinction between subjective and objective history, these two views of history do not, in any event, so much exclude each other as divide historical territory between them, marking out a distinction between narrative interpretation and investigative evidence.[5] The idea that historical narrative and rhetoric should be demarcated from historical knowledge and research in this way is suggestive of a 'non-discursive and non-historical definition of knowledge'.[6] Moreover, it encourages historiographers to carve up periods artificially into those that were primarily rhetorical and narrative in approach (sixteenth, seventeenth, and eighteenth centuries), those that were transitional (nineteenth century), those that were primarily empirical and archival (twentieth century), and those that could be said to mark something of a return to earlier anti-empirical modes and methodologies (late twentieth and twenty-first centuries).

If we accept Phillips's argument that eighteenth-century abstraction, irony, detachment, and distance were, to some extent, myths created by romantic historians as a foil for their own type of vivid history, we can instead see romantic historiography as part of a long-standing shift over three centuries towards actuality and immediacy rather than as a completely new type of history.[7] Such a view rightly rejects the idea of a sharp divide between romantic inwardness and enlightenment abstraction, so often promoted by the romantics' own narratives about themselves. However, it also risks presenting romantic-era historical writing as a now defunct type of history superseded by empiricism and objectivity and only currently making its return after a long period of 'desublimation' by the romantics' 'chastened, prosaic' successors.[8] According to this account, romantic-era historical writing belatedly appropriates the innovations of other genres (such as memoir, biography, and the novel) before being emancipated by a new positivist and professional agenda in the later nineteenth century, which is itself now increasingly repudiated by poststructuralist philosophers of history. Certainly, there is a tendency among intellectual historians either to read historical writing to the extent that it evinces this teleology, or to argue that late eighteenth- and early nineteenth-century historians were 'wiser poststructuralists' than their late Victorian successors.[9]

In some ways, it is true that the increasingly anti-philosophic and agent-centred historicism collectively developed by Wollstonecraft, Godwin, Carlyle, Macaulay, and other historians in the early to mid-nineteenth century prefigures the linguistic, narrativist, and culturalist turns away from causal or structural history in the late twentieth century, as well as pre-empting the more recent emphasis on emotions and social experience as primary sites of historical investigation. Yet seeing romantic history as the 'other' of empirical history and aligning it with an alternative tradition to empirical and structural approaches has led to a disjunction between working historians and philosophers of history. The resurfacing of the term 'romantic' in current philosophies of history has tended to draw even deeper divisions between a scientific history that follows Ranke's apparent 'objectification of the protocols of historical reconstruction' and a literary or rhetorical history that models itself upon Carlyle's 'passionate evocation of subjective responses to the past'.[10] As Chris Lorenz has pointed out, the linguistic and narrativist turns in the philosophy of history may even have inadvertently promoted an inverted form of positivism by maintaining 'a deep conceptual dichotomy . . . between "objective" empirical observation and "subjective" interpretation'.[11]

Periodising Feeling

In our periodising of the history of history, the long eighteenth century is often said to have a special relationship to feeling and in particular to the 'cult of sensibility'.[12] Historians and literary scholars are by now wary of origin narratives, which suggest that modernity, and thus modern historical consciousness, emerged in western Europe in the 1790s. However, there are few who would deny that a shift in historical sensibility occurred over the course of the eighteenth century or that the American and French Revolutions brought this shift into sharper focus.[13] The French Revolution has certainly held its own as 'a key moment in emotional history', one in which '*sensibilité* was seen to animate a post-Enlightenment generation in France' and 'arguably provided one of [its] central experiential motors'.¹⁴ The period following the Revolution witnessed a transformation in understandings of feeling as essentially private to understandings of feeling as transmissible, collective, and public, extending more fully into the public domain forms of *patrie* identification 'founded in the private intimate sphere of the conjugal family'.¹⁵ This newly public or collective understanding of feeling depended on the mobilisation—and masculinisation—of an ideology of intimacy, making shared emotions increasingly central to the historian's duty to provide what Carlyle called 'a scientific revelation of the whole secret mechanism whereby men cohere together in society'.¹⁶

If the Revolution later prompted a suspicion towards 'the French fashion for tears, sensibility and revolution' and a scepticism towards the idea that feelings are a marker of an authentic or transparent self, it is no coincidence that much of the formative work surrounding the new history of emotions as a distinct historical subdiscipline—for example, that of Lynn Hunt, William Reddy, and Sophia Rosenfeld—has centred on the French and American Revolutions, or that the recent emphasis on historical experience by David Andress, Peter McPhee, and others has taken its cue from agent-centred and lived accounts of revolutionary trauma, temporality, and subjectivity.¹⁷ While not confined to the study of late eighteenth-century France, these exploratory approaches represent a sharp turn away from an ideologically driven historiography of the French Revolution that sees it as 'a rebellion so self-defeating as to render the notion of "agency" make-believe or imaginary' towards the experiential worlds of its participants, thereby transfiguring the still influential arguments of François Furet and others that the Revolution 'determined the political composition of its participants' and was little more than an 'illusion of creating the future'.¹⁸

In recent studies of selfhood and subjectivity, the emotional and agential experiences of revolutionary actors have also proved central to periodisations of the so-called 'rising "modernity" of social experience' or what Daniel M. Gross has called the distinctive 'emotional complex of modernity'. In this view, the 'stratified' post-revolutionary self is understood as emerging from psychological and socio-political confrontations with a new political moment, relocating 'within the self conflicts which Hobbes and Rousseau [had previously] distributed across regimes'.¹⁹ As the modern theory of the subject shifted accounts of political conflict to a location within the individual self, a closely related issue was how identity could be understood and maintained in the face of the perceived temporal rupture or radical discontinuity of modernity.

By situating affect-logic within systems theory, Niklas Luhmann has drawn our attention to some of the underlying reasons why feeling was so central to post-revolutionary understandings of selfhood, noting that the experiencing subject is key to our encounter with modernity more generally: not only is an individual required to perform his or her individuality within a repertoire of 'codes of affect' and a 'culture of affect-management' that delimits and forecloses the expression of raw emotion, but the trend towards functional differentiation in modern societies means that individuals interpret 'the difference between themselves and their environment (and in the temporal dimension, the history and future of this difference) in terms of their own person', so that the subject or ego becomes 'the focal point of all their inner experiences'. Modernity, in other words, increases the need for a world that is 'understandable, intimate and close', a world that one can internalise or 'learn to make one's own'.[20]

The internalising temporalisations of modernity are closely related to its historicist foundations. As Luhmann's socio-psychological understanding of affect suggests, historicism does not situate feeling as the naive obverse of modernity but rather positions it as central to modern historical time and the creation of the modern self. Zoltán Boldizsár Simon has accordingly argued that the 'historical sensibility' that emerged in the late eighteenth century was one designed to mitigate the temporal and psychic ruptures that modernity is said to unfold: 'it served to inoculate us against the terror of novelty by embedding it in one rational, continuous process [so that] even the most dramatic experience of rupture could be "tamed" and rationalised'.[21] The sublime 'rupture with tradition' that is said to define modern temporality was therefore tempered and even normalised by the compensatory ability of historicism to explain its novelty and to contextualise it within a longer historical continuum while simultaneously remaining dependent on the separation of the modern from the premodern self.

Barbara Rosenwein has rightly argued that modernity is a problematic periodising category in the history of emotions (and, indeed, in the history of political development more widely).[22] Yet any post-revolutionary understanding of the role of feeling in historical discourse must account for the nineteenth century's deep and abiding association with modernity as a political and social project, as well as with the persistent sense among philosophers of history that the French Revolution marked an 'irreparable rupture' from a pre-revolutionary identity—one that effected 'a decisive rearrangement in the set of truths needed for a proper comprehension of the social and political world one was living'.[23] My own interest in this book has been less in arguing for the validity of rupture narratives, which themselves have a long history dating back to the new calendrical system of 1789, than in understanding why revolutionary narratives of radical historical discontinuity have proved so pervasive in both historiographical accounts of the nineteenth century and understandings of the modern, experiential self.[24]

Historicising Experience

Intellectual historians such as Reinhart Koselleck, Craig Ireland, and Martin Jay have argued that experience has been central to formations of self, time, and history since at least the beginning of the eighteenth century. For Koselleck, modernity's distinctive sense of temporality is characterised by an increased divide between the past and the present, between the space of historical experience (memory) and the open-ended horizon of expectation (futurity); and this divide is evident in textual and aesthetic forms of various kinds.[25] Although Koselleck's work is sometimes considered to exist independently of the hermeneutic tradition, his double-rupture argument—a rupture in our sense of temporality and a rupture in the forms in which temporality is represented—is part of a genealogy of western historical thought invested in questions of hermeneutic experience that runs from Wollstonecraft, Carlyle, Burckhardt, Huizinga, Dilthey, Dewey, Benjamin, Husserl, and Gadamer right up to American pragmatists such as Rorty.

Experience is, however, a notoriously 'slippery' or difficult concept in the philosophy of history.[26] As discussed in the introduction to this book, Williams declines to use it in his definition of structures of feeling, and definitional questions surrounding the term are at the heart of the 'poverty of theory debate' between E. P. Thomson and Louis Althusser.[27] Ever since Joan Scott declared experience to be one of those 'foundationalist discourses' that reproduces the gendered and racialised 'workings of the system' in her essay 'The Evidence of Experience' (1991), it has seemed conceptually inadequate to account for the ways in which power and political difference are 'relationally constituted'. As Scott points out, experience has several conflicting meanings. On the one hand, it has come to mean 'a particular kind of consciousness', one that Williams defines in *Keywords* (1976) as 'a full and active "awareness"' of a subjective witness' and is 'offered not only as truth, but as the most authentic kind of truth', as 'the ground for all (subsequent) reasoning and analysis'. On the other hand, experience can refer to 'influences external to individuals – social conditions, institutions, forms of belief or perception – "real" things outside that they react to, and does not include their thought or consideration'.[28] Drawing on Teresa de Laurentis's redefinition of experience as 'the process ... by which subjectivity is constructed', Scott asks us to denaturalise the 'ground zero' space of experience by asking 'how conceptions of selves ... are produced'.[29]

The concept of experience has been more controversially resurrected in Frank Ankersmit's *Sublime Historical Experience* (2005), which rejects both the kind of dialectic relationship between experience and the experiencing subject promoted by Gadamer, and Rorty's critique of linguistic transcendentalism. Ankersmit outlines three types or categories of historical experience: the first is 'objective' historical experience, which he seems to understand as something like *l'histoire des mentalités*; the second is 'subjective' historical experience, which he uses to describe the distance between the observer's present and the historical past; and the third is 'sublime' historical experience, which he suggests is born out of the historian's 'traumatic experience of having entered a new world'.[30] Ankersmit describes his own approach as 'a plea in favour of a Romantic conception of our relationship to the past—a conception seeing in moods, feelings, and the experience of the past the highest stage of historical consciousness'. He later continues the analogy with romanticism by comparing the tortuous route taken by contemporary philosophers of history from theory to experience to the route taken from enlightenment rationalism to the romantic sublime experience 'two centuries ago', arguing that we must replace the 'intellectual bureaucracy of "theory"' with the '"Romanticism" of an approach to the past involving all of the historian's personality and not just (or even primarily) the formation of his or her cognitive faculties'.[31]

Like Williams, Ankersmit tries to free history from fixed conventions and social forms and to reintegrate it within wider structures of feeling. Yet he also seeks to divorce experience from the perceived stranglehold of language and tropological representations of the past: 'Language is where experience is not, and experience is where language is not.' For Ankersmit, the central question instead becomes the 'authenticity' of the historical experience, by which he seems to mean an immediate, direct, or unmediated experience with historical reality. Drawing on Herder and Huizinga, Ankersmit sees the problem of how to represent this authentic experience in language as arising later and in a separate way from the feeling itself. He thus assumes an anti-cognitive approach to historical feeling and experience in that sublime experience does not result in truth or knowledge about the past: 'Sublimity will, by its very nature, teach us no truths about the past, for from the perspective of cognitive truth this kind of encounter with the past simply does not and cannot exist.'[32]

In separating experience from an empiricist epistemology, Ankersmit's definition of sublime historical experience has been the subject of much criticism, with some seeing it as a 'lost cause', a withdrawal from narrativism, and as a rejection of the philosophy of history itself. Objections to Ankersmit's notion of an authentic, unmediated experiential past disconnected from language have been comprehensively documented, not least in book-length form by Peter Icke.[33] In a partial defence of Ankersmit's position, Keith Jenkins, Anton Froeyman, and others have argued that the point of Ankersmit's focus on sublime experience is not to reject his own pioneering work on narrativism but rather to ask a different set of questions: that is, to distinguish the past 'as it constitutes us' (experience) from the past 'as we constitute it' (representation), and thus to promote a non-linguistic and non-discursive understanding of the past that is similar to Huizinga's conception of 'historical sensation' or the 'feeling of experience'.[34]

My issue in this instance is not so much with Ankersmit's separation of experience from representation (although my position remains a narrativist one), but rather with his 'return of a tradition' argument. If, according to Ankersmit, poststructural and postmodern philosophies of history play out strategies already embedded in romantic approaches to the past, the problem with this view is two-fold: first, it falls back on older, now defunct, understandings of the relationship between enlightenment and romanticism, defining the enlightenment as a period of 'icy formalism' and romanticism as providing 'something of the warmth of the human heart'; and second, it posits the romantic relationship to the historical past as anti-cognitive and unmediated—that is, as primarily determined by the emotionalism of 'moods and feelings'. As discussed in Chapter 1 of this book, the charge of unmediated emotional aestheticism was one faced by Edmund Burke following the publication of *Reflections on the Revolution*. Unsurprisingly, Ankersmit frequently cites Burke as an example of the kind of romantic historical consciousness to which he wishes to stage a return.[35]

For Ankersmit, romanticism is a movement determined almost solely by emotional expressivism, by the 'spontaneous overflow of powerful feelings', rather than being 'recollected in tranquility' and mediated by a variety of other influences, from the institutional and social to the motivational, behavioural, and psychological, all of which, as Marilyn Butler has reminded us, attempt to chasten the romantic egotistical sublime by putting 'rational thought, moral intention and social utility above the subjective, emotional side of the mind, and above the claims of self-expression'.[36] Ironically, then, philosophers of history have 'tended to account for historiographical changes in the late eighteenth and early nineteenth centuries largely in aesthetic terms': that is, by invoking the term 'romantic' and designating to that term the attributes of an ideology that privileges the irrational and the emotive.[37] Without denying that sentimentalism and the sublime were important developments in romantic-era historical consciousness, the view of romantic-era historicism as one of 'moods and feelings' is one that this book has worked to qualify, seeing sentimental or feeling historicism as operating in negotiation with the emergence of documentary historical protocols and with the increasing objectification of feeling itself.

Anachronisms of the Present

John Schwarzmantel has argued that the enlightenment inaugurated the polarisation of ideological thinking on a mass scale, particularly after the large-scale social transformations of the American and French Revolutions.[38] Without necessarily or inevitably seeing romanticism as a form of counter-enlightenment, one of the ways in which romanticism could be said to remediate enlightenment thinking is by casting a particularist suspicion on the fixities of ideology. The elevation of the local and particular over the general and systematic identifiable in many of the histories considered in this book brings to the surface the tension between macro (large-scale social processes) and micro (small-scale interactions between individuals or groups) levels of analysis that Raymond Williams's theory of 'structures of feeling' attempts to mediate or resolve. As Kevis Goodman has noted, Williams's emphasis on nascent social and subjective formations 'in *solution*' allows us to acknowledge the 'presentness' of those feelings, beliefs, and experiences that are in the process of emerging out of moments of individual or collective social consciousness, and accordingly to resist the temptation to study the past retroactively as a fixed form or finished product.[39] Williams's concept helps, too, to illuminate the concerted effort by romantic-era historians to use the historically locatable phenomena of eyewitness accounts to understand both the dynamic evolution of the historical subject and its institutional contexts: that is, to understand the subject as simultaneously situated, emergent, and experiential.[40]

For eighteenth-century philosophic historians, the point of historical enquiry was both to establish a causal continuity between the past and present via the generalising principles of 'human nature' and to set out a 'succession of distinct cultural stages, each of which cancels the one preceding it'. By the mid-nineteenth century, however, the colliding temporalities of 'modernity's rupture with tradition' had begun to reconfigure themselves through the analogical practices of 'comparative historicism', which saw each epoch of the past as a closed totality that could nonetheless be analysed in relation to each other. This type of historicism manifested itself in various forms, from the explicit comparativism of Carlyle's *Past and Present* to the cross-sectional approach of Jacob Burkhardt's *The Civilization of the Renaissance in Italy* (1860). As Devin Griffiths has noted, comparativism is a 'historical epistemology ... organized through analogies drawn between the past and the present'. At the same time, the inherent disjunction between past and present that underpins comparativism (and ontological realism more generally) encourages attempts to resurrect or re-enact the past via sentimental, evocative, and picturesque techniques that function as 'allegories of the present'.[41]

In the epilogue to *Provincializing Europe* (2000), Dipesh Chakrabarty argues that historicism's 'capacity to see the past as gone and reified into an object of investigation', as something 'separate from the time of the observer', has given rise to utopian and hermeneutic (that is, 'romantic') struggles to 'try to get inside the skin of the past, to try and see it "as it really was", to try to re-enact it in the historian's mind'. The seemingly contrary or conflicting processes of empirical 'objectification', on the one hand, and idealist 'resurrection', on the other, are therefore equally part of the project of historicism, which ultimately depends on both maintaining and mitigating qualities of temporal distance. The historicist subject of political modernity wishes to objectify the past in order to be free of the past, to postulate the true present as a 'radically new departure'. Yet, for Chakrabarty, this sense of anachronism or uneven development 'stops us from confronting the temporal heterogeneity of the "now" in thinking about history'.[42] Chakrabarty thus reframes what Jonathan Crimmins, following Michel de Certeau, has called the 'historicist's dilemma'—that is, the tension between the 'fullness of lost time and its corollary empty freedom'—as one centred in the principle of anachronism.[43]

While anachronism is generally seen as fatal to the spirit of historicism, Chakrabarty places anachronism at the heart of historicist time and thus of western historical consciousness: 'Historical evidence (the archive) is produced by our capacity to see something that is contemporaneous with us ... as a relic of another time or place.' These objects or relics of the past become objectified 'in the observer's time as a "bit" of that past', denying 'the lived relations the observing subject already has with that which he or she identifies as belonging to a historical or ethnographic time and space separate from the ones he or she occupies as the analyst'.[44] Jacques Rancière, too, has argued that anachronism is not a horizontal problem of the order of time but a vertical problem of the order of time in the hierarchy of beings. It is a problem in the division (*partage*) of time, in the sense of 'what one receives as one's share'.[45]

For both Rancière and Chakrabarty, historical accounts of the past should be responsible to the present and the future on the basis that there is no clear ontological division between past and present: the past, as Chakrabarty puts it, is 'already constitutive of the present' and 'oriented to the future'.[46]

The dialogical nature of the relationship between past, present, and future in many of the histories discussed in this book—variously dismissed by later historians as unscientific, anachronistic, prophetic, or presentist—may be the period's greatest contribution to western philosophies of history, simultaneously historicising and calling attention to the limits of historicising; objectifying feeling and critiquing the objectivist desire to hide or purge the historian's own intentionality; illuminating the otherness of the past only to provide a greater sense of its persistent relationship to the present and future.[47] This kind of 'romantic' history is not, or at least not always, a history of resurrection, reanimation, and presence, but rather an extended and evolving sense of 'how and why the past inheres in the present' and, by extension, the future.[48] If, as Crimmins has argued, we must 'banish the spectre of a transcendentally lost past' and 'understand history as "*that which persists into the future*"', the interpenetration between past, present, and future in romantic-era written history provides one way of understanding why romantic historicism continues to stage various 'returns'.[49] Carlyle's interest in the logic of the trace and his acceptance of the non-linear and palimpsestic nature of the past; Wollstonecraft's 'human' causation and her acknowledgement of the temporal momentaneousness of revolutionary experience; Godwin's rejection of mechanical causality and his recovery of the particular and contingent possibilities of the past; Macaulay's 'double vision' and his emphasis on local knowledge, social texture, and thick description; and Moore's utopian refusal of the category of post-history: all of these historians make room for the unruly and active relationship of the past to the present and future even as they increasingly seek to objectify or rationalise feeling in written history.

Notes

Introduction

1. William Godwin, *History of the Commonwealth of England. From its Commencement to the Restoration of Charles the Second*, 4 vols (London: Henry Colburn, 1824–8), 4:579, 580, abbreviated as *HC*.
2. On Godwin's revisions, see, e.g., Mark Philp, *Godwin's Political Justice* (London: Gerald Duckworth & Co., 1986), p. 202. On Godwin's turn to collaborative modes of knowledge exchange, see Victoria Myers, 'Godwin and the *Ars Rhetorica*', *Studies in Romanticism*, 41.3 (2002), 415–44; and Jon Mee, *Conversable Worlds: Literature, Contention, and Community 1762 to 1830* (Oxford: Oxford University Press, 2011). On Godwin's professional reorientation towards fiction and history, see Rowland Weston, 'Introduction: William Godwin and Political Justice', *Nineteenth-Century Prose*, 41.1/2 (2014), 1–26; and John-Erik Hansson, 'The Genre of Radical Thought and the Practices of Equality: The Trajectories of William Godwin and John Thelwall in the mid-1790s', *History of European Ideas*, 43.7 (2017), 776–90.
3. David Hume, *A Treatise of Human Nature*, ed. L. A. Selby-Bigge, 2nd edn, rev. P. H. Nidditch (Oxford: Clarendon Press, 1978), pp. 415, 456, abbreviated as *T*. See also *An Enquiry Concerning the Principles of Morals* (1751), in *Enquiries Concerning Human Understanding and Concerning the Principles of Morals*, ed. L. A. Selby-Bigge, 3rd edn, rev. P. H. Nidditch (Oxford: Clarendon Press, 1975), p. 172. Godwin was reading Hume's *Treatise* before the first edition of *Political Justice* appeared. On Hume's influence, see Pamela Clemit, *The Godwinian Novel: The Rational Fictions of Godwin, Brockden Brown, Mary Shelley* (Oxford: Clarendon Press, 1993), esp. p. 75; and Peter Marshall, *William Godwin* (New Haven, CT: Yale University Press, 1984), pp. 160–2, 199–200. For a more sceptical view, see Peter Howell, 'Godwin, Contractarianism, and the Political Dead End of Empiricism', *Eighteenth-Century Life*, 28.2 (2004), 61–86. For Godwin's attitude towards Hume as historian, see Eliza O'Brien, '"The most inconsistent of men": William Godwin and the "Apology" of Sir Thomas More', *Nineteenth-Century Prose*, 41.1/2 (2014), 79–110.
4. Feelings, for Hume, arguably are primarily a way of heightening the

experience of writing and reading history, of providing it with a kind of imaginative momentum, without usually being in themselves a way of explaining the complex causality of past actions and events. See, e.g., *History of England by Hume and Smollett with a Continuation by the Rev. T. S. Hughes* (London: Valpy, 1834–6), p. 402. Hume's 'Of the Study of History' (1741) suggests that he was trying to appeal to female readers, *Essays Moral, Political, and Literary*, ed. Eugene F. Miller (1758; Indianapolis: Liberty Fund, 1994), pp. 563–9 (esp. 564). On Hume's sentimentalism, see Mark Salber Phillips, *Society and Sentiment: Genres of Historical Writing in Britain, 1740–1820* (Princeton: Princeton University Press, 2000), esp. pp. 66–70. On Hume's behaviouralism, see, e.g., Elizabeth S. Radcliffe, 'Hume on the Generation of Motives: Why Beliefs Alone Never Motivate', *Hume Studies*, 25.1–2 (1999), 101–22. On Hume's approach to the imagination and sympathy, see Jennifer A. Herdt, 'Artificial Lives, Providential History, and the Apparent Limits of Sympathetic Understanding', and Douglas Long, 'Hume's Historiographical Imagination', both in *David Hume: Historical Thinker, Historical Writer*, ed. Mark G. Spencer (University Park, PA: Penn State University Press, 2013), pp. 37–60 and 201–4. More generally, see Timothy M. Costelloe, *The Imagination in Hume's Philosophy: The Canvas of the Mind* (Edinburgh: Edinburgh University Press, 2018).
5. William Godwin, 'Of History and Romance' (wr. 1797), in *Caleb Williams, or Things as they Are*, ed. Maurice Hindle (Harmondsworth: Penguin, 1988), pp. 359–73 (362, 363, 363–4, 368), abbreviated as HR. See also 'On the Composition of History: An Occasional Reflection', MS. Abinger c.29, undated, watermarked 1808.
6. HC, 3:v; 4:531; 1:vii. On necessity and contingency, see Jon Klancher, 'Godwin and the Genre Reformers: On Necessity and Contingency in Romantic Narrative Theory', in *Romanticism, History, and the Possibilities of Genre: Re-forming Literature 1789–1837*, ed. Tilottama Rajan and Julia M. Wright (Cambridge: Cambridge University Press, 1998), pp. 21–38.
7. HC, 1:84; 3:v.
8. Ina Ferris, 'Transformations of the Novel – II', in *The Cambridge History of English Romantic Literature*, ed. James K. Chandler (Cambridge: Cambridge University Press, 2008), pp. 473–89 (477).
9. Ann Rigney, *Imperfect Histories: The Elusive Past and the Legacy of Romantic Historicism* (Ithaca, NY: Cornell University Press, 2001), pp. 9–10.
10. Peter Hanns Reill, *The German Enlightenment and the Rise of Historicism* (Berkeley: University of California Press, 1975), pp. 161, 165.
11. Lucien Febvre, 'Sensibility and History: How to Reconstitute the Emotional Life of the Past', in *A New Kind of History: From the Writings of Febvre*, ed. Peter Burke, trans. K. Folca (New York: Harper & Row, 1973), pp. 12–26 (15). On romantic-era historicism in the context of literary history, see Mike Goode, *Sentimental Masculinity and the Rise of History 1790–1890* (Cambridge: Cambridge University Press, 2009); Christopher M. Bundock, *Romantic Prophecy and the Resistance to Historicism* (Toronto: University of Toronto Press, 2016); and Jonathan

Crimmins, *The Romantic Historicism to Come* (London: Bloomsbury Academic, 2018).

12. Claudia M. Schmidt, 'David Hume as a Philosopher of History', in *David Hume: Historical Thinker, Historical Writer*, ed. Mark G. Spencer (University Park, PA: Penn State University Press, 2013), pp. 163–180 (172, 173); William Godwin, *The Enquirer: Reflections on Education, Manners, and Literature in a Series of Essays* (London: G. G. and J. Robinson, 1797), pp. x, vi.
13. See, e.g., Damian Walford Davies (ed.), *Counterfactual Romanticism* (Manchester: Manchester University Press, 2020).
14. Thomas Carlyle, *Critical and Miscellaneous Essays*, 4 vols (Boston: James Monroe & Co., 1838–9), 2:249, 247, abbreviated as *CME*.
15. See the arguments about psychology, emotion, and neuroscience in Rob Boddice, *The History of Emotions* (Manchester: Manchester University Press, 2018), p. 34.
16. See, e.g., Lionel Gossman, 'History as Decipherment: Romantic Historiography and the Discovery of the Other', *New Literary History*, 18.1 (1986), 23–57; Stephen Bann, *The Clothing of Clio: A Study of the Representation of History in Nineteenth-Century Britain and France* (New York: Cambridge University Press, 1984), p. 60; Ann Rigney, *The Rhetoric of Historical Representation: Three Narrative Histories of the French Revolution* (Cambridge: Cambridge University Press, 1990); and Rosemary Mitchell, *Picturing the Past: English History in Text and Image, 1830–1870* (Oxford: Oxford University Press, 2000).
17. Gossman, 'History as Decipherment', 24. See also Gossman, 'Towards a Rational Historiography', *Transactions of the American Philosophic Society*, 79.3 (1989), 1–68 (16); and David Simpson, *Romanticism and the Question of the Stranger* (Chicago: University of Chicago Press, 2013), p. 134.
18. Phillips, *Society and Sentiment*, p. 19; Goode, *Sentimental Masculinity*, p. 149.
19. On ethics, see, e.g., Laura Mandell, 'Virtue and Evidence: Catherine Macaulay's Historical Realism', *Journal for Early Modern Cultural Studies*, 4.1 (2004), 127–57; and Ildiko Csengei, *Sympathy, Sensibility and the Literature of Feeling in the Eighteenth Century* (Basingstoke: Palgrave Macmillan, 2012), esp. pp. 1–3.
20. J. G. A. Pocock, 'Adam Smith and History', in *The Cambridge Companion in Adam Smith*, ed. Knud Haakonssen (Cambridge: Cambridge University Press, 2006), pp. 270–87 (272); Phillips, *Society and Sentiment*, p. xii.
21. John Burrow, *A Liberal Descent: Victorian Historians and the British Past* (Cambridge: Cambridge University Press, 1981), p. 4.
22. Carl Thompson, 'Sentiment and Scholarship: Hybrid Historiography and Historical Authority in Maria Graham's South American Journals', *Women's Writing*, 24.2 (2017), 185–206 (185).
23. See, e.g., Devoney Looser, *British Women Writers and the Writing of History, 1670–1820* (Baltimore: Johns Hopkins University Press, 2000); Lisa Kasmer, *Novel Histories: British Women Writing History, 1760–1830* (Madison, NJ: Fairleigh Dickinson University Press, 2012); and Mary Spongberg, *Women Writers and the Nation's Past*,

1790–1860: Empathetic Histories (London: Bloomsbury Academic, 2020).
24. Jennifer L. Fleissner, 'Is Feminism a Historicism', *Tulsa Studies in Women's Literature*, 21.1 (2002), 45–66 (57, 60); Spongberg, *Women Writers*, p. 24. On the period's 'barrenness', see, e.g., T. P. Peardon, *The Transition in English Historical Writing, 1760–1830* (New York: Columbia University Press, 1933), p. 9; and Burrow, *Liberal Descent*, pp. 117, 119.
25. See, e.g., Frank R. Ankersmit, *Sublime Historical Experience* (Stanford: Stanford University Press, 2005), and *Historical Representation* (Stanford: Stanford University Press, 2001).
26. See, e.g., Peter Burke, *What is Cultural History?* (Cambridge: Polity Press, 2008), pp. 111–12. On boundary studies, see Thomas F. Gieryn, 'Boundary-Work and the Demarcation of Science from Non-Science: Strains and Interests in Professional Ideologies of Scientists', *American Sociological Review*, 48.6 (1983), 781–95.
27. For an overview, see Alon Confino, Ute Frevert, Uffa Jensen, and Lyndal Roper, 'Forum: History of Emotions', *German History*, 28.1 (2010), 67–80.
28. Samuel Johnson, *A Dictionary of the English Language*, 4th edn (Dublin: Thomas Ewing, 1775), cited in David Dwan, 'Edmund Burke and the Emotions', *Journal of the History of Ideas*, 72.4 (2011), 571–93 (576). On the nineteenth-century position, see Thomas Dixon, *From Passions to Emotions: The Creation of a Secular Psychological Category* (Cambridge: Cambridge University Press, 2003), p. 72. For the pre-history, see Adela Pinch, *Strange Fits of Passion: Epistemologies of Emotion, Hume to Austen* (Stanford: Stanford University Press, 1996), esp. pp. 18–19.
29. Dixon, *From Passions to Emotions*, p. 24; Aleksondra Hultquist, 'New Directions in History of Emotion and Affect Theory in Eighteenth-Century Studies', *Literature Compass*, 13.12 (2016), 762–70 (764); Mary Wollstonecraft, *A Vindication of the Rights of Men*, 2nd edn (London: J. Johnson, 1792), p. 96, abbreviated as *VM*. As Dixon notes, the emotions 'conceived as a set of morally disengaged, bodily, non-cognitive and involuntary feelings, is a relatively recent invention', *From Passions to Emotions*, p. 72.
30. Annette C. Baier, 'What Emotions are About', *Philosophical Perspectives*, 4 (1990), 1–29 (5). See also Ronald de Sousa, *The Rationality of Emotion* (Cambridge, MA: MIT Press, 1987). On feelings as collective phenomena, see, e.g., William M. Reddy, *The Navigation of Feeling: A Framework for the History of Emotions* (Cambridge: Cambridge University Press, 2009).
31. See Daniel Wickberg, 'What is the History of Sensibilities? On Cultural History, Old and New', *The American Historical Review*, 112.3 (2007), 661–84.
32. Raymond Williams, 'Structures of Feeling', in *Marxism and Literature* (Oxford and New York: Oxford University Press, 1977), pp. 128–35 (129). See, e.g., Sean Matthews, 'Change and Theory in Raymond Williams's Structure of Feeling', *Pretexts: Literary and Cultural Studies*, 10 (2001), 179–94; and David Simpson, 'Raymond Williams: Feeling for Structures, Voicing "History"', *Social Text*, 30 (1992), 9–26.

33. Williams, *Marxism and Literature*, p. 132. Williams rejects the term 'experience' because of its implied 'pastness', but considers it in a more positive light in *Keywords: A Vocabulary of Culture and Society* (1976; New York: Oxford University Press, 1983), p. 126.
34. Matthews, 'Change and Theory', 179. On 'experience', see, e.g., David Andress, 'Introduction: Revolutionary Historiography, Adrift or at Large?', in *Experiencing the French Revolution*, ed. David Andress (Oxford: Oxford University Press, 2013), pp. 1–15; Joan Wallach Scott, 'The Evidence of Experience', *Critical Inquiry*, 17.4 (1991), 773–97; and Teresa de Lauretis, 'Eccentric Subjects: Feminist Theory and Historical Consciousness', *Feminist Studies*, 16.1 (1990), 115–50.
35. Williams, *Marxism and Literature*, pp. 131, 129, 133–4 (his emphasis). See Kevis Goodman, *Georgic Modernity and British Romanticism: Poetry and the Mediation of History* (Cambridge: Cambridge University Press, 2004), p. 3.
36. William M. Reddy, 'Against Constructionism: The Historical Ethnography of Emotions', *Current Anthropology*, 38.3 (1997), 327–51 (327, 331, 332).
37. Jane Lydon, *Imperial Emotions: The Politics of Empathy Across the British Empire* (Oxford: Oxford University Press, 2019), p. 4.
38. See Claire Hemmings, 'Invoking Affect: Cultural Theory and the Ontological Turn', *Cultural Studies*, 19.5 (2005), 548–67 (552); and Catherine A. Lutz, 'The Language and Politics of Emotion', *Journal of Linguistic Anthropology*, 1.1 (1995), 115–17.
39. Seth T. Reno, 'Introduction: Romanticism and Affect Studies', *Romantic Circles*. Available at <https://romantic-circles.org/praxis/affect/praxis.2018.affect.introduction.html> (last accessed 5 January 2020).
40. For pioneering works, see, e.g., Carolyn Dinshaw, *Getting Medieval* (Durham, NC: Duke University Press, 1999); Lauren Berlant, *Intimacy* (Chicago and London: University of Chicago Press, 2000); Sara Ahmed, *The Cultural Politics of Emotions* (Edinburgh: Edinburgh University Press, 2004); and Brian Massumi, *Politics of Affect* (London: Polity Press, 2015).
41. This position resonates with 'economies of affect' perspectives. See, e.g., Jean McAvoy, 'From Ideology to Feeling: Discourse, Emotion, and an Analytic Synthesis', *Sociology*, 12.1 (2015), 22–33 (22); and Paul Ricoeur, 'The Metaphorical Process as Cognition, Imagination, and Feeling', *Critical Inquiry*, 5.1 (1978), 143–59 (esp. 156).
42. See, e.g., Peter N. Stearns with Carol Z. Stearns, 'Emotionology: Clarifying the History of Emotions and Emotional Standards', *The American Historical Review*, 90.4 (1985), 813–36.
43. Barbara H. Rosenwein, 'Worrying about Emotions in History', *The American Historical Review*, 107.3 (2002), 821–45.
44. Barbara H. Rosenwein, 'Problems and Methods in the History of Emotions', *Passions in Context: Journal of the History and Philosophy of the Emotions*, 1.1 (2010), n.p. Available at <http://www.passionsincontext.de/%3e/> (last accessed 24 April 2017). See also Rosenwein's *Generations of Feeling: A History of Emotions, 800–1700* (Cambridge: Cambridge University Press, 2015), esp. pp. 8–9.

45. Daniel Woolf, 'Disciplinary History and Historical Discourse. A Critique of the History of History: The Case of Early Modern England', *Cromohs*, 2 (1997), 1–25.
46. See Friedrich Meinecke, *Die Entstehung des Historismus*, 2 vols (Berlin and Munich: R. Oldenbourg, 1965); and Friedrich Jaeger and Jörn Rüsen, *Geschichte des Historismus* (Munich: Beck, 1992).
47. Stephen Bann, *The Inventions of History: Essays on the Representation of the Past* (Manchester: Manchester University Press, 2000), pp. 8, 16; Michael Bentley, 'Past and "Presence": Revisiting Historical Ontology', *History and Theory*, 45.3 (2006), 349–61 (353).
48. Bann, *Inventions of History*, p. 6. On idealist and materialist historicism, see James Connelly, 'Philosophising History: Distinguishing History as a Discipline', in *The Edinburgh Critical History of Nineteenth-Century Philosophy*, ed. Alison Stone (Edinburgh: Edinburgh University Press, 2011), pp. 146–67 (148).
49. Karen O'Brien, 'History and the Novel in Eighteenth-Century Britain', in *The Uses of History in Early Modern England*, ed. Paula Kewes (San Marino, CA: Huntington Library, 2006), pp. 389–406 (389). See also Ceri Crossley, 'History, Nature and National Identity in France, 1800–30', *Literature and History*, 10.1 (2001), 18–27.
50. Leslie Howsam, 'Academic Discipline or Literary Genre? The Establishment of Boundaries in Historical Writing', *Victorian Literature and Culture*, 32.2 (2004), 525–45 (525). See also Ian Hesketh, 'Diagnosing Froude's Disease: Boundary Work and the Discipline of History in Late-Victorian Britain', *History and Theory*, 47 (2008), 373–95; and Mark Bevir, 'Anglophone Historicism: From Modernist Method to Post-Analytic Philosophy', *Journal of the Philosophy of History*, 3 (2009), 211–24.
51. Mark Salber Phillips, *On Historical Distance* (New Haven, CT: Yale University Press, 2013), p. 80.
52. See Judith Surkis, 'When was the Linguistic Turn? A Genealogy', *American Historical Review*, 117.3 (2012), 700–22.
53. Michel Foucault, *Society Must Be Defended: Lectures at the Collège de France 1975–76*, ed. Mauro Bertani and Alexandro Fontana, trans. David Macey (New York: Picador, 2003), p. 66. See also Arnaldo D. Momigliano, 'Gibbon's Contribution to Historical Method', *Contributo alla storia degli studi classici* (Rome: Edizioni di storia e letteratura, 1955), esp. p. 198.
54. Blair Worden, 'Historians and Poets', in *The Uses of History in Early Modern England*, ed. Paula Kewes (San Marino, CA: Huntington Library, 2005), pp. 69–78 (71); William Blake, *A Descriptive Catalogue of Pictures, Poetical and Historical Inventions* (London: D. N. Shury for J. Blake, 1809), pp. 43–4. On the fact, see, e.g., Anthony Grafton, 'The Footnote from De Thou to Ranke', *History and Theory*, 33.4 (1994), 53–76, and *The Footnote: A Curious History* (Cambridge, MA: Harvard University Press, 1997); and Mary Poovey, *A History of the Modern Fact: Problems of Knowledge in the Sciences of Wealth and Society* (Chicago: University of Chicago Press, 1998).
55. See, e.g., Fleissner, 'Is Feminism a Historicism?', 46, 48, cited in Gary Kelly, 'Romanticism and the Feminist Uses of History', in *Romanticism,*

History, Historicism: Essays on an Orthodoxy, ed. Damian Walford Davies (New York and London: Routledge, 2009), pp. 163–81 (167); Keith Jenkins and Alun Munslow (eds), *The Nature of History Reader* (London and New York: Routledge, 2004), pp. 14–15; and Joan Wallach Scott, 'After History?', *Common Knowledge*, 5.3 (1996), 8–26.

56. Dipesh Chakrabarty, *Provincializing Europe: Postcolonial Thought and Historical Difference*, rev. edn (Princeton: Princeton University Press, 2000), pp. 6, 7, 12. See also Timothy Mitchell, 'The Stage of Modernity', in *Questions of Modernity*, ed. Timothy Mitchell (Minneapolis: University of Minnesota Press, 2000), pp. 1–34.
57. Chakrabarty, *Provincializing Europe*, pp. 35, 73.
58. Friedrich Meinecke, 'Kausalitäten und Werte in der Geschichte', *Historische Zeitschrift*, 137 (1928), 1–27 (8), cited in Robert A. Pois, 'Two Poles Within Historicism: Croce and Meinecke', *Journal of the History of Ideas*, 31.2 (1970), 253–72 (260).
59. Pois, 'Two Poles', 260. On the mischaracterisation of Ranke, see Peter Novick, *That Noble Dream: The 'Objectivity' Question and the American Historical Profession* (Cambridge: Cambridge University Press, 1988), p. 28.
60. Jerry Szacki, 'On the So-Called Historicism in the Social Sciences', *The Polish Sociological Bulletin*, 22 (1970), 36–46 (37).
61. Jacques Bos, 'Nineteenth-Century Historicism and its Predecessors: Historical Experience, Historical Ontology and Historical Method', in *The Making of the Humanities: Vol. II From Early Modern to Modern Disciplines*, ed. Rens Bod, Jaap Maat, and Thijs Weststeijn (Amsterdam: Amsterdam University Press, 2012), pp. 131–48 (140).
62. Ferris, 'Transformations of the Novel', p. 484.
63. Bos, 'Nineteenth-Century Historicism', p. 140. On the related rise of 'corporate persons', see Daniel M. Stout, *Corporate Romanticism: Liberalism, Justice, and the Novel* (New York: Fordham University Press, 2017).
64. Michel Foucault, 'What is Enlightenment?', in *The Foucault Reader*, ed. Paul Rabinow (New York: Pantheon Books, 1984), pp. 32–50 (49); Christopher Bundock, '"A feeling that I was not for that hour / Nor for that place": Wordsworth's Modernity', *European Romantic Review*, 21.3 (2010), 383–9 (384).
65. Foucault, *Society Must Be Defended*, pp. 167–8. See also Ericka L. Tucker, 'The Subject of History: Historical Subjectivity and Historical Science', *Journal of the Philosophy of History*, 7.2 (2013), 205–29.
66. Eric J. Hobsbawm, *Nations and Nationalism Since 1780: Programme, Myth, Reality* (Cambridge: Cambridge University Press, 1990), p. 11, cited in Ben Dew and Fiona Price, 'Introduction: Visions of History', in *Historical Writing in Britain, 1688–1830: Visions of History*, ed. Ben Drew and Fiona Price (Basingstoke: Palgrave Macmillan, 2014), pp. 1–17 (9, 3).
67. Clifford Siskin, *The Historicity of Romantic Discourse* (Oxford: Oxford University Press, 1988), p. 92.
68. Nancy Armstrong, *How Novels Think: The Limits of Individualism from 1719–1900* (New York: Columbia University Press, 2005), p. 3. For an alternative view that sees history as 'the paradigmatic form of knowledge'

in the nineteenth century, see Stephen Bann, *Romanticism and the Rise of History* (New York: Twayne, 1995), p. 4.
69. Nancy Armstrong, *Desire and Domestic Fiction: A Political History of the Novel* (New York and Oxford: Oxford University Press, 1987), p. 5.
70. On ontological consistency, see Ian Baucom, *Spectres of the Atlantic: Finance Capital, Slavery, and the Philosophy of History* (Durham, NC: Duke University Press, 2005), pp. 67–72. On formal realism in history, see Roland Barthes, 'L'Effet de réel' (1968), reprinted as 'The Reality Effect', in *The Rustle of Language*, trans. Richard Howard (Berkeley: University of California Press, 1989), pp. 141–8. More generally, see Frank R. Ankersmit, *The Reality Effect in the Writing of History: The Dynamics of Historiographical Topology* (Amsterdam: Koninklijke Nederlandse Akademie van Wetenschappen: Noord-Hollandsche, 1989).
71. Roger Maioli, 'David Hume, Literary Cognitivism, and the Truth of the Novel', *Studies in English Literature 1500–1900*, 54.3 (2014), 625–48 (635, 635–6); *T*, p. 122.
72. Idealist defences of poetry, in turn, tended to rest on the argument that poetry provides a 'more privileged version of the real', Crossley, 'National Identity', 18.
73. Catherine Gallagher, 'The Rise of Fictionality', in *The Novel: History, Geography and Culture, Vol. 1*, ed. Franco Moretti (Princeton: Princeton University Press, 2006), pp. 336–63 (336, 337, 343). On the historical novel, see Ian Duncan, 'Edinburgh and Lowland Scotland', in *The Cambridge History of English Romantic Literature*, ed. James Chandler (Cambridge: Cambridge University Press, 2009), pp. 159–81 (173–4). For anti-fiction statements, see Hume's comparison of poetic logic with madness in *T*, pp. 630–1.
74. Duncan, 'Lowland Scotland', p. 172; Robert Mayer, 'The Illogical Status of Novelistic Discourse: Scott's Footnotes for the Waverley Novels', *English Literary History*, 66 (1999), 911–38 (911–12). See also Mayer's *History and the Early English Novel* (Cambridge: Cambridge University Press, 1997). On Scott's empirical realism, see, e.g., Ina Ferris, '"Before Our Eyes": Romantic Historical Fiction and the Apparitions of Reading', *Representations*, 121.1 (2013), 60–84 (esp. 61, 70–1, 74). On Scott's role as mediator between history and literature, see Ina Ferris, 'Re-Positioning the Novel: "Waverley" and the Gender of Fiction', *Studies in Romanticism*, 28.2 (1989), 291–301; and Joep T. Leerssen, 'Literary Historicism: Romanticism, Philologists, and the Presence of the Past', *Modern Languages Quarterly*, 62 (2004), 221–43.
75. Michael McKeon, 'Prose Fiction: Great Britain', in *The Cambridge History of Literary Criticism. Volume IV: The Eighteenth Century*, ed. H. B. Nisbet and Claude Rawson (Cambridge: Cambridge University Press, 1997), pp. 238–63. See also McKeon's *The Origins of the English Novel, 1600–1740* (1987; repr. Baltimore and London: Johns Hopkins University Press, 2002).
76. Roger Maioli, *Empiricism and the Early History of the Novel: Fielding to Austen* (Basingstoke: Palgrave Macmillan, 2016), p. 11.
77. Frederick Burwick, *Poetic Madness and the Romantic Imagination* (University Park, PA: Penn State University Press, 1996), pp. 8, 22–7. See

also Timothy Milnes, 'Is it true? . . . What is the meaning of it?': Bentham, Romanticism, and the Fictions of Reason', in *Bentham and the Arts*, ed. Anthony Julius, Philip Schofield, and Malcom Quinn (London: UCL Press, 2020), pp. 140–59 (esp. 151–5), and *The Testimony of Sense: Empiricism and the Essay from Hume to Hazlitt* (Oxford: Oxford University Press, 2019).
78. William Wordsworth, 'Preface', to William Wordsworth and Samuel Taylor Coleridge, *Lyrical Ballads, 1798 and 1802*, ed. Fiona Stafford (Oxford: Oxford University Press, 2013), p. 105. On Wordsworth and utility, see Rowan Boyson, *Wordsworth and the Enlightenment Idea of Pleasure* (Cambridge: Cambridge University Press, 2012). For Hume's analysis of truth-directed versus pleasure-directed feelings, see Kelly Martin, 'On the Origin of Hume's Philosophy in the Passions', 1–33 (16). Available at <http://econfaculty.gmu.edu/klein/PdfPapers/SHLE_paper/Martin%20Kelly%20Hume8.pdf> (last accessed 3 March 2019). For the idea that the origins of historiography can likewise be found in wonder and pleasure, see Marnie Hughes-Warrington, *History as Wonder: Beginning with Historiography* (New York: Routledge, 2019).
79. *The Collected Letters of Thomas and Jane Welsh Carlyle*, ed. C. R. Sanders et al., 24 vols (Durham, NC: Duke University Press, 1970–), 7:24, abbreviated as *CL*. See, e.g., Bann, *Inventions of History*, pp. 36–7.
80. Rigney, *Imperfect Histories*, p. 86.
81. Herman Paul and Ethan Kleinberg, 'Are Historians Ontological Realists? An Exchange', *Rethinking History*, 22.4 (2018), 546–67 (552); Tilottama Rajan, *Romantic Narrative: Shelley, Hays, Godwin, Wollstonecraft* (Baltimore: Johns Hopkins University Press, 2010), p. xii. On language, see, e.g., Robin Valenza, *Literature, Language, and the Rise of the Intellectual Disciplines in Britain, 1680–1820* (Cambridge: Cambridge University Press, 2009), esp. pp. 47–9; and Andrew Elfenbein, *Romanticism and the Rise of English* (Stanford: Stanford University Press, 2008), esp. pp. 118, 127. On the sensitive nature of belief, see Hume's first *Enquiry* (1748): 'the difference between *fiction* and *belief* lies in some sentiment or feeling, which is annexed to the latter, not to the former, and which depends not on the will, nor can it be commanded by pleasure' (*Enquiries*, pp. 78–9).
82. *HR*, p. 372; Tilottama Rajan, 'Between Individual and General History: Godwin's Seventeenth-Century Texts', *Nineteenth-Century Prose*, 41.1/2 (2014), 111–60 (115, 119); Weston, 'Political Justice', 4–5.
83. *HR*, p. 370.
84. Jon Klancher, 'Godwin and the Republican Romance: Genre, Politics, and Contingency in History', *Modern Language Quarterly*, 56.2 (1995), 145–66 (146).
85. Tilottama Rajan, 'Uncertain Futures: History and Genealogy in William Godwin's *The Lives of Edward and John Philips, Nephews and Pupils of Milton*', *Milton Quarterly*, 32.3 (1998), 75–86. On Baillie, see Mary Jacobus, '"The science of herself": Scenes of Female Enlightenment', in *Romanticism, History, and the Possibilities of Genre*, pp. 240–69; and Porscha Fermanis, 'Countering the Counterfactual: Joanna Baillie's

Metrical Legends of Exalted Characters (1821) and the Paratexts of History', *Women's Writing*, 19.3 (2012), 333–50.
86. Julie Carlson, *England's First Family of Writers: Mary Wollstonecraft, William Godwin, Mary Shelley* (Baltimore: Johns Hopkins University Press, 2007), p. 293; Rajan, *Romantic Narrative*, p. xii; Joel Faflak, 'Speaking of Godwin's *Caleb Williams*: The Talking Cure and the Pyschopathology of Enlightenment', *English Studies in Canada*, 31.2–3 (2005), 99–122 (esp. 99, 108).
87. See, e.g., Anne C. Vila, *Enlightenment and Pathology: Sensibility in the Literature and Medicine of Eighteenth-Century France* (Baltimore: Johns Hopkins University Press, 1998); and Jessica Riskin, *Science in the Age of Sensibility: The Sentimental Empiricists of the French Enlightenment* (Chicago: University of Chicago Press, 2002).
88. Febvre, 'Sensibility and History', 19; Dixon, *From Passions to Emotions*, p. 12. See also Carol Z. Stearns and Peter N. Stearns (eds), *Emotional and Social Change: Towards a New Psychohistory* (New York: Holmes and Meier, 1988).
89. Fernando Vidal, *The Sciences of the Soul: The Early Modern Origins of Psychology* (Chicago: University of Chicago Press, 2011), pp. 410–41.
90. Isaiah Berlin, *The Age of Enlightenment* (1956; repr. New York: New American Library, 1984), p. 19.
91. Jenny Davidson, 'Recent Studies in the Restoration and Eighteenth Century', *Studies in English Literature*, 56.3 (2016), 671–725 (681), reviewing Brad Pasanek, *Metaphors of Mind: An Eighteenth-Century Dictionary* (Baltimore: Johns Hopkins University Press, 2015), esp. p. 252.
92. Cathy Gere, *Pain, Pleasure, and the Greater Good: From the Panopticon to the Skinner Box and Beyond* (Chicago: University of Chicago Press, 2017), p. 143. For earlier conceptions of the 'feeling body', see, e.g., Antonio Damasio, *Looking for Spinoza: Joy, Sorrow and the Feeling Brain* (London: Heinemann, 2003).
93. T, pp. 417, 214; see also 418–19. See John Deigh, 'Concepts of Emotions in Modern Philosophy and Psychology', in *The Oxford Handbook of the Philosophy of Emotion*, ed. Peter Goldie (Oxford: Oxford University Press, 2010), pp. 17–40 (22, 33).
94. Daniel M. Gross, *The Secret History of Emotions: From Aristotle's Rhetoric to Modern Brain Science* (Chicago: University of Chicago Press, 2006), pp. 7, 8; Neil Saccamano, 'Parting with Prejudice: Hume, Identity, and Aesthetic Universality', in *Politics and the Passions, 1500–1850*, ed. Victoria Kahn, Neil Saccamano, and Daniela Coli (Princeton: Princeton University Press, 2006), pp. 217–30; T, p. 360. On rhetoric, see Jean Nienkamp, *Internal Rhetorics: Toward a History and Theory of Self-Persuasion* (Carbondale: Southern Illinois University Press, 2001).
95. S. K. Wertz, 'Moral Judgments in History: Hume's Position', *Hume Studies*, 22.2 (1996), 339–67 (344). See also Henri Ellenberger, *The Discovery of the Unconscious: The History and Evolution of Dramatic Psychiatry* (New York: Basic Books, 1970).
96. On sympathy, see, e.g., Michael Frazer, *The Enlightenment of Sympathy: Justice and the Moral Sentiments in the Eighteenth Century and*

Today (Oxford: Oxford University Press, 2012); James Chandler, *An Archaeology of Sympathy: The Sentimental Mode in Literature and Cinema* (Chicago: Chicago University Press, 2013); and Rob Boddice, *The Science of Sympathy: Morality, Evolution and Victorian Civilization* (Urbana: University of Illinois Press, 2016).

97. Hume, *Enquiries*, p. 336. See Long, 'Hume's Historiographical Imagination', p. 208. On the 'science of character', see Timothy M. Costelloe, 'Hume on History', in *The Continuum Companion to Hume*, ed. Alan Bailey and Dan O'Brien (London and New York: Continuum, 2012), pp. 364–76 (365); Phillips, *On Historical Distance*, p. 88.

98. *HR*, p. 363; see also William Godwin, *Enquiry Concerning Political Justice, and its Influence on Morals and Happiness*, 3rd edn, 2 vols (London: G. G. and J. Robinson, 1798 [1793, 1796]), 1:160, abbreviated as *PJ* and distinguished by date. On Godwin's suspicion towards sympathy, see Michael Edson, 'Godwin's Anti-Mass Politics Revisited: Sympathy, Retirement, and Epistemic Diversity', *Nineteenth-Century Prose*, 41.1/2 (2014), 161–94; and Suzi Asha Park, '*Caleb Williams* and the Smithian Spectator: Reading the "Reasonable Demand"', *Nineteenth-Century Prose*, 41.1/2 (2014), 195–224.

99. Wilhelm Dilthey, *Ideas Concerning a Descriptive and Analytic Psychology* (1894), in *Descriptive Psychology and Historical Understanding*, trans. Kenneth Heiges and Richard Zaner (The Hague: Martinus Nijhoff, 1977), pp. 21–120.

100. Dilthey, *Descriptive and Analytic Psychology*, pp. 81–2.

101. Klancher, 'Republican Romance', 147.

102. See, e.g, Rosemary Jann, *The Art and Science of Victorian History* (Athens: Ohio State University Press, 1985); and Philippa Levine, *The Amateur and the Professional: Antiquarians, Historians and Archeologists in Victorian England, 1838–1886* (Cambridge: Cambridge University Press, 2003).

103. On boundary studies, see, e.g., George Levine, *The Boundaries of Fiction: Carlyle, Macaulay, Newman* (Princeton: Princeton University Press, 1968); Lionel Gossman, *Between History and Literature* (Cambridge, MA: Harvard University Press, 1990); Suzanne Gearhart, *The Open Boundaries of History and Fiction* (Princeton: Princeton University Press, 1984); and Everett Zimmerman, *The Boundaries of Fiction* (Ithaca, NY: Cornell University Press, 1996). On the transgressive nature of the historical novel, see, e.g., Richard Maxwell, *The Historical Novel in Europe, 1650–1950* (Cambridge: Cambridge University Press, 2009), 2; and Ann Rigney, 'Relevance, Revision, and the Fear of Long Books', in *A New Philosophy of History*, ed. Frank R. Ankersmit and Hans Kellner (Chicago: University of Chicago Press, 1995), 127–47.

104. Karen O'Brien, *Narratives of Enlightenment: Cosmopolitan History from Voltaire to Gibbon* (Cambridge: Cambridge University Press, 1997), p. 6.

105. Emily Allen, *Theatre Figures: The Production of the Nineteenth-Century Novel* (Columbus: Ohio State University Press, 2003), pp. 6, 9, 12, 13.

106. O'Brien argues that such debates were usually conducted within the novel rather than across the novel/history border, 'History and the Novel', p. 390.

107. Clara Tuite, *Romantic Austen: Sexual Politics and the Literary Canon* (Cambridge: Cambridge University Press, 2002), p. 10.
108. Dew and Price, 'Introduction', p. 6; Phillips, *Society and Sentiment*, pp. 22–3.
109. Angela Keane, 'The Importance of Elsewhere: Romantic Subjectivity and the Romance of History', *Wordsworth Circle*, 27.1 (1996), 16–21; Paul and Kleinberg, 'Are Historians Ontological Realists?', 550; Stout, *Corporate Romanticism*, p. 10.
110. Phillips, *Society and Sentiment*, p. 19.
111. Dew and Price, 'Introduction', p. 2.
112. See O'Brien, 'History and the Novel'.
113. See, e.g., Walter Scott, 'Godwin's *Life of Chaucer*', *Edinburgh Review*, 3 (Jan. 1804), 437–52, hereafter abbreviated as *ER*. Hume was accused of everything from scepticism to atheism. See, e.g., Peter Jones (ed.), *The Reception of David Hume in Europe* (London and New York: Thoemmes Continuum, 2005).
114. Bann, *The Clothing of Clio*, p. 60.
115. See Porscha Fermanis and John Regan, 'Introduction', in *Rethinking British Romantic History, 1770–1845*, ed. Porscha Fermanis and John Regan (Oxford: Oxford University Press, 2014), pp. 1–34. As Worden notes, '[t]he art of narrative developed in fiction alongside, even in collaboration with, its progress in history', 'Historians and Poets', p. 91.
116. Goode, *Sentimental Masculinity*, p. 4; Tilottama Rajan and Julia M. Wright, 'Introduction', in *Romanticism, History, and the Possibilities of Genre*, pp. 1–21 (1).
117. Mary Poovey refers to differentiation as 'the gradual elaboration of sets of conventions and claims about method', *Genres of the Credit Economy: Mediating Value in Eighteenth- and Nineteenth-Century Britain* (Chicago: University of Chicago Press, 2008), p. 1. See also Clifford Siskin, *The Work of Writing: Literature and Social Change in Britain, 1700–1830* (Baltimore: Johns Hopkins University Press, 1998); and Michael McKeon, *The Secret History of Domesticity: Private, Public, and the Division of Knowledge* (Baltimore: Johns Hopkins University Press, 2005).
118. Devin Griffiths, *The Age of Analogy: Science and Literature Between the Darwins* (Baltimore: Johns Hopkins University Press, 2016), p. 16.
119. Herman Paul, 'Scholarly Personae: What They Are and Why They Matter', in *How to Be a Historian: Scholarly Personae in Historical Studies, 1800–2000*, ed. Herman Paul (Manchester: Manchester University Press, 2019), pp. 1–14 (11).
120. See, e.g., Thomas Haskell, *Objectivity is not Neutrality: Explanatory Schemes in History* (Baltimore: Johns Hopkins University Press, 1998), pp. 145–73, 174–224; and L. D. Burnett, 'The Sensibility of Historians', *S-USIH* (2012). Available at <http://s-usih.org/2012/06/sensibility-of-historians.html> (last accessed 24 April 2017).
121. Peter Gay, *Style in History: Gibbon, Ranke, Macaulay, Burckhardt* (New York: Basic Books, 1974), cited in Bann, *Clothing of Clio*, p. 5.
122. Bann, *Clothing of Clio*, p. 13. On objectivity, see, e.g., Alan Munslow, *The New History* (Edinburgh: Pearson, 2003); and Marek Tamm, 'Truth,

Objectivity and Evidence in History Writing', *Journal of the Philosophy of History*, 8 (2014), 265–90.
123. See Frank R. Ankersmit, *Narrative Logic: A Semantic Analysis of the Historian's Language* (The Hague, Boston, and London: Martin Nijhoff, 1983).
124. Hayden White, *Metahistory: The Historical Imagination in Nineteenth-Century Europe* (Baltimore: Johns Hopkins University Press, 1973), pp. x, xii. For a less tropological approach, see Dominick LaCapra, *Rethinking Intellectual History: Texts, Contexts, Language* (Ithaca, NY: Cornell University Press, 1983).
125. Rigney, *Imperfect Histories*, pp. 9–10.
126. David Carr, *Time, Narrative, and History* (Bloomington: Indiana University Press, 1986), p. 176; Hans Kellner, *Language and Historical Representation: Getting the Story Crooked* (Madison: University of Wisconsin Press, 1989), p. xi.

Chapter 1

1. Edmund Burke, *Reflections on the Revolution in France, and on the Proceedings of Certain Societies in London Relative to that Event*, 10th edn (1790; London: James Dodsley, 1791), pp. 11, 11–12, abbreviated as *R*.
2. Mary Wollstonecraft, *Historical and Moral View of the Origin and Progress of the French Revolution; and the Effect it has Produced in Europe* (London: J. Johnson, 1794), pp. 289–90, abbreviated as *HMV*; *VM*, pp. 25, 60; Edmund Burke, *Thoughts on the Prospect of a Regicide Peace, in a Series of Letters* (London: J. Owen, 1796), p. 6. On the ways in which the 'didactic distance' between Burke and his objects collapses, see Linda Zerilli, 'Text/Woman as Spectacle: Edmund Burke's "French Revolution"', *The Eighteenth Century*, 33.1 (1992), 47–72 (esp. 56, 63); and Tom Furniss, *Edmund Burke's Aesthetic Ideology: Language, Gender and Political Economy in Revolution* (Cambridge: Cambridge University Press, 1993), p. 140. On non-coherence in *Reflections*, see Angela Keane, 'Reflections and Correspondences: The Familiarity of Burke's Unfamiliar Letter', in *Edmund Burke's Reflections on the Revolution in France: New Interdisciplinary Essays*, ed. John Whale (Manchester: Manchester University Press, 2000), pp. 193–218. On the ways in which 'Burke's language performs the principles of his political thought', see Timothy Michael, *British Romanticism and the Critique of Political Reason* (Baltimore: Johns Hopkins University Press, 2016), esp. 74–83.
3. Paul Hamilton, *Metaromanticism: Aesthetics, Literature, Theory* (Chicago: University of Chicago Press, 2003), p. 122; Steven Blakemore, *Burke and the Fall of Language: The French Revolution as Linguistic Event* (Hanover, NH: University Press of New England, 1988), p. 293; *R*, p. 99. Thomas Paine's well-known admonishment that 'Mr. Burke should recollect that he is writing History, and not *Plays*' more explicitly characterises *Reflections* as a category or boundary error, *Rights of Man: Being an Answer to Mr. Burke's Attack on the French Revolution* (London: J. S. Jordan, 1791), pp. 21, 43, 36. On medial forms, see Randall Sessler,

'Recasting the Revolution: The Media Debate between Edmund Burke, Mary Wollstonecraft, and Thomas Paine', *European Romantic Review*, 25.5 (2015), 611–26.
4. For the 'romantic' view of Burkean historiography, see, e.g., Blakemore, *Fall of Language*, esp. p. 105; F. Locke, 'Rhetoric and Representation in Burke's *Reflections*', in *Edmund Burke's Reflections on the Revolution in France*, ed. John Whale (Manchester: Manchester University Press, 2000), pp. 19–20; and Ian Ward, 'The Perversions of History: Constitutionalism and Revolution in Burke's Reflections', *Liverpool Law Review*, 31 (2010), 207–32 (esp. 214). For an approach focused on ethical character, see Paddy Bullard, *Edmund Burke and the Art of Rhetoric* (Cambridge: Cambridge University Press, 2011). For Scottish enlightenment influences, see J. G. A. Pocock, 'Burke and the Ancient Constitution: A Problem in the History of Ideas', *The Historical Journal*, 3 (1960), 125–43; and Daniel I. O'Neill, *The Burke–Wollstonecraft Debate: Savagery, Civilization, and Democracy* (University Park, PA: Penn State University Press, 2007). For an overview, see Sora Sato, *Edmund Burke as Historian: War, Order and Civilisation* (Basingstoke: Palgrave Macmillan 2018).
5. Lynn Hunt, *The Family Romance of the French Revolution* (Berkeley: University of California Press, 1992), p. 4.
6. Hamilton, *Metaromanticism*, p. 129.
7. Zerilli, 'Text/Woman', 47; Mary Wollstonecraft, *A Vindication of the Rights of Woman: With Strictures on Political and Moral Subjects* (London: J. Johnson, 1792), p. 9, abbreviated as *VW*. As G. J. Barker-Benfield has argued, both *Vindications* were contributions to the revolutionary debate, 'Mary Wollstonecraft: Eighteenth-Century Commonwealthwoman', *Journal of the History of Ideas*, 50.1 (1989), 95–115. On the 'scientising' nature of Wollstonecraft's view of history, see Fiona Price, '"Experiments Made by the Airpump": Jane West's *The Loyalists* (1812) and the Science of History', *Women's Writing*, 19 (2012), 315–32.
8. *VM*, pp. 53, 111.
9. Burke nonetheless admits that 'a different plan' might have been 'more favourable to a commodious division and distribution of his material', *R*, pp. iv, 11; Burke to W. C. Smith, 22 July 1971, *Correspondence of Edmund Burke*, ed. T. W. Copeland, 10 vols (Chicago: University of Chicago Press, 1963–71), 6:303–4. This defence was in relation to Burke's *Appeal from the New to the Old Whigs* (1791).
10. *R*, pp. 11, 209. Burke wrote *Reflections* in 'a mood of agitation' following the public severing of his friendship with Charles James Fox, Ward, 'Perversions of History', 212. On Burke's historical pessimism, see Katy Castellano, 'Burke's "Revolutionary Book": Conservative Politics and Revolutionary Aesthetics in the *Reflections*', *Romanticism on the Net*, 45 (2007). Available at <https://www.erudit.org/en/journals/ron/1900-v1-n1-ron1728/015818ar/> (last accessed July 2019).
11. *R*, pp. 210, 209; Frank R. Ankersmit, *Political Representation* (Stanford: Stanford University Press, 2002), p. 47; Zerilli, 'Text/Woman', 49.
12. *R*, pp. 105, 106. William Selinger sees *Reflections* as a 'postmortem', 'Patronage and Revolution: Edmund Burke's "Reflections on the Revolution in France" and his Theory of Legislative Corruption', *The*

Review of Politics, 76.1 (2014), 43–67 (61). On Burke's 'proleptic' tendencies, see Claire Connolly, 'Reflections on the Act of Union', in *Edmund Burke's Reflections on the Revolution in France*, ed. John Whale, pp. 168–92. See also Burke's earlier *Abridgement of English History* (1757–c.1763), which effectively embraces 1688 as the high point of constitutional progress.

13. *R*, pp. 33, 128, 106, 171; O'Neill, *The Burke-Wollstonecraft Debate*, p. 156.
14. See Lauren Berlant, 'The Subject of True Feeling: Pain, Privacy, and Politics', in *Cultural Pluralism, Identity Politics, and the Law*, ed. A. Sarat and T. Kearns (Ann Arbor: University of Michigan Press, 1999), pp. 49–84.
15. On Burke's emphasis on the faculty of emotional response in conjoining public history and private romance, see Elizabeth D. Samet, 'Spectacular History and the Politics of Theatre: Sympathetic Arts in the Shadow of the Bastille', *PMLA*, 118.5 (2005), 1305–19. On crowd psychology, see George Rude, *The Crowd in the French Revolution* (Oxford: Oxford University Press, 1967); Vanessa Smith, *Intimate Strangers: Friendship, Exchange and Pacific Encounters* (Cambridge: Cambridge University Press, 2010), esp. pp. 39, 42–3; and Mary Fairclough, *The Romantic Crowd: Sympathy, Controversy and Print Culture* (Cambridge: Cambridge University Press, 2013).
16. *R*, pp. 22, 7, 130; Dwan, 'Edmund Burke and the Emotions', 571–93.
17. O'Neill, *Burke-Wollstonecraft Debate*.
18. *R*, pp. 91, 209; Ankersmit, *Political Representation*, p. 48.
19. *R*, pp. 114, 11.
20. Blakemore, *Fall of Language*, pp. 286, 290.
21. Jason Frank, '"Delightful Horror": Edmund Burke and the Aesthetics of Democratic Revolution', in *The Aesthetic Turn in Political Thought*, ed. Nikolas Kompridis (New York and London: Bloomsbury, 2014), pp. 3–28 (20, 21); *R*, p. 119. See also Jason Frank, *The Democratic Sublime: On Aesthetics and Popular Assembly* (Oxford: Oxford University Press, 2021).
22. *R*, pp. 38, 69, 29, 49. See J. G. A. Pocock, 'Burke and the Ancient Constitution'; and David Craig, 'Burke and the Constitution', in *The Cambridge Companion to Edmund Burke*, ed. David Dwan and Christopher Insole (Cambridge: Cambridge University Press, 2012), pp. 104–16 (esp. 105–6).
23. Daniel Woolf, 'Getting Back to Normal: On Normativity in History and Historiography', *History and Theory*, 60.3 (2021), 469–512 (474). On Burke and novelty, see Frank, 'Aesthetics of Democratic Revolution', esp. pp. 10–11.
24. See Jonathan Sachs, *The Poetics of Decline in British Romanticism* (Cambridge: Cambridge University Press, 2018).
25. *R*, pp. 271, 270, 114, 143, 287. On Burke's obsession with 'money-jobbers', see J. G. A. Pocock, 'The Political Economy of Burke's Analysis of the French Revolution', *Historical Journal*, 25.2 (1982), 331–49.
26. *R*, pp. 269, 70, 96, 102. On Burke's pathologising of legislative assemblies, see Selinger, 'Patronage and Revolution', 43–67.

27. *R*, pp. 144, 326, 29, 49, 68–9; Pocock, 'Burke and the Ancient Constitution', p. 131.
28. Frank, 'Aesthetics of Democratic Revolution', pp. 8, 29; Yoon Sun Lee, *Nationalism and Irony: Burke, Scott, Carlyle* (Oxford and New York: Oxford University Press, 2004), p. 3; *R*, pp. 144, 326, 29, 49, 68–9, 115, 360, 132.
29. Koen Vermeir and Michael Funk Deckard, 'Preface', in *The Science of Sensibility: Reading Burke's Philosophical Enquiry*, ed. Koen Vermeir and Michael Funk Deckard (Dordrecht: Springer, 2011), pp. v–xx (vi). On Burke's relative pluralism and respect for difference in India, see Richard Bourke, *Empire and Revolution: The Political Life of Edmund Burke* (Princeton: Princeton University Press, 2015). Yet see also Burke's Eurocentrism and universalism, as discussed in Spurgeon Thompson, 'Edmund Burke's *Reflections on the Revolution in France* and the Subject of Eurocentrism', *Irish University Review*, 33.2 (2003), 245–62.
30. Frank, 'Aesthetics of Democratic Revolution', p. 12; Deidre Lynch, 'Nationalizing Women and Domesticating Fiction: Edmund Burke and the Genres of Englishness', *The Wordsworth Circle*, 25.1 (1994), 45–9. On Burke's debt to Montesquieu, see Ian McBride, 'Burke and Ireland', in *The Cambridge Companion to Edmund Burke*, pp. 181–94.
31. Terry Eagleton, 'Aesthetics and Politics in Edmund Burke', *History Workshop*, 28 (1989), 53–62 (54). On the psychology of the sublime, see David Bromwich, *A Choice of Inheritance: Self and Community from Edmund Burke to Robert Frost* (Cambridge, MA: Harvard University Press, 1989), esp. p. 288.
32. Daniel I. O'Neill, 'The Sublime, The Beautiful, and the Political in Burke's Work', in *The Science of Sensibility: Reading Burke's Philosophical Enquiry*, ed. Koen Vermeir and Michael Funk Deckard (Dordrecht: Springer, 2011), pp. 193–224 (195).
33. Ankersmit, *Political Representation*, pp. 39, 44.
34. Richard A. Barney, 'Burke, Biomedicine, and Biobelligence', *The Eighteenth Century*, 54.2 (2013), 231–43 (233).
35. *R*, p. 46; Ankersmit, *Political Representation*, pp. 91–2; Frank, 'Aesthetics of Democratic Revolution', pp. 11, 12.
36. Frank, 'Aesthetics of Democratic Revolution', p. 16.
37. *R*, p. 115; Zaki Nahaboo, 'Subverting Orientalism: Political Subjectivity in Edmund Burke's India and Liberal Multiculturalism', *Citizenship Studies*, 15.5-6 (2012), 587–603 (594); Daniel I. O'Neill, 'Edmund Burke, the "Science of Man," and Statesmanship', in *Scientific Statesmanship, Governance, and the History of Political Philosophy*, ed. Kyriakos N. Demetriou and Antis Loizides (New York and London: Routledge, 2015), pp. 174–92 (178); Michael, *Critique of Political Reason*, p. 83.
38. Goodman, *Georgic Modernity*, pp. 3, 4; Gross, *Secret History of Emotions*, pp. 6, 7.
39. *R*, p. 139; Anne Mallory, 'Burke, Boredom, and the Theatre of Counterrevolution', *PMLA*, 118.2 (2003), 224–38; Lee, *Nationalism and Irony*, p. 32.

40. Burkean feelings of revulsion are linked to gendered and racialised representations of cannibalism, nakedness, and savagery, Thompson, 'Eurocentrism', 246–55. However, Burke's wariness towards majority rule was also related to his desire for accountability. See, e.g., David Bromwich, *The Intellectual Life of Edmund Burke: From the Sublime and Beautiful to American Independence* (Cambridge, MA: Harvard University Press, 2014), pp. 209–10, 424–5.
41. Mike Goode, 'The Man of Feeling History: The Erotics of Historicism in *Reflections on the Revolution in France*', *English Literary History*, 74.4 (2007), 829–57 (851, 848). See also Blakemore, *Fall of Language*, p. 250. Paine's attack on Burke in *Rights of Man* is similarly constructed via the 'topos of life' versus 'the written or printed word of the past', Ronald Paulson, 'Burke's Sublime and the Representation of Revolution', in *Culture and Politics: From Puritanism to the Enlightenment*, ed. Perez Zargorin (Berkeley and Los Angeles: University of California Press, 1980), pp. 241–69 (244).
42. Blakemore, *Fall of Language*, pp. 9–10; Claudia L. Johnson, *Equivocal Beings: Politics, Gender, and Sentimentality in the 1790s, Wollstonecraft, Radcliffe, Burney, Austen* (Chicago and London: University of Chicago Press, 1995), p. 6. It is worth noting these codes are also, for Burke, a means of preventing 'the most cruel oppression on the minority' (*R*, p. 186).
43. Luke Gibbons, *Edmund Burke and Ireland: Aesthetics, Politics, and the Colonial Sublime* (Cambridge: Cambridge University Press, 2003), p. 99; James T. Boulton, *The Language of Politics in the Age of Wilkes and Burke* (1963; repr. Abingdon: Routledge, 2010), p. 121.
44. Lee, *Nationalism and Irony*, p. 114; *R*, p. 112; Nahaboo, 'Subverting Orientalism', 593–4. On physiology and the sublime, see Aris Sarafianos, 'Pain, Labour, and the Sublime: Medical Gymnastics and Burke's Aesthetics', *Representations*, 91.1 (2005), 58–83.
45. *VM*, pp. 9, 111, 68.
46. *VM*, pp. 29, 70. See also Karen Green, 'The Passions and the Imagination in Wollstonecraft's Theory of Moral Judgement', *Utilitas*, 9.3 (1997), 271–90 (271, 278); and Alex Schulman, 'Gothic Piles and Endless Forests: Wollstonecraft Between Burke and Rousseau', *Eighteenth-Century Studies*, 41.1 (2007), 41–54. 'Virtues', as Alasdair MacIntyre has put it, 'are dispositions not only to act in particular ways, but also to feel in particular ways. To act virtuously is not to act against inclination; it is to act from inclination formed by the cultivation of the virtues', *After Virtue: A Study in Moral Theory*, 2nd edn (Notre Dame, IN: University of Notre Dame Press, 1984), p. 149.
47. *VM*, pp. 70, 96, 77. On this point, see David Bromwich, 'Wollstonecraft as a Critic of Burke', *Political Theory*, 23.4 (1995), 617–34 (626).
48. Shane Greentree, 'The "Equal Eye" of Compassion: Reading Sympathy in Catherine Macaulay's *History of England*', *Eighteenth-Century Studies*, 52.3 (2019), 299–318. See also Barbara Taylor, *Mary Wollstonecraft and the Feminist Imagination* (Cambridge: Cambridge University Press, 2003), p. 129; and Karen Green, 'Will the Real Enlightenment Historian Please Stand Up? Catherine Macaulay versus David Hume', in *Hume*

and the Enlightenment, ed. Craig Taylor and Stephen Buckle (London: Pickering & Chatto, 2011), pp. 39–51.
49. Wollstonecraft arguably sees feelings as a kind of mobilising practice that can result in virtuous action. See Monique Scheer, 'Are Emotions a Kind of Practice (and is That What Makes Them Have a History)? A Bourdieuian Approach to Understanding Emotion', *History and Theory*, 51.2 (2012), 193–220. For the argument about virtue as a mediating discourse, see Fiona Price, *Reinventing Liberty: Nation, Commerce and the Historical Novel from Walpole to Scott* (Edinburgh: Edinburgh University Press, 2016), pp. 76, 198.
50. *VM*, p. 110; Frances Ferguson, 'Envy Rising', *ELH*, 69.4 (2002), 889–905 (889).
51. Mandell, 'Virtue and Evidence', 124, 128. See also Virginia Sapiro, *A Vindication of Political Virtue: The Political Theory of Mary Wollstonecraft* (Chicago: University of Chicago Press, 1992). On ethos, see Bullard, *Art of Rhetoric*; and Ann L. George, 'Grounds of Assent in Joseph Priestley's *A Course of Lectures on Oratory and Criticism*', *Rhetoric*, 16 (1998), 81–109 (esp. 106).
52. Mandell, 'Virtue and Evidence', 128.
53. J. G. A. Pocock, 'Catherine Macaulay: Patriot Historian', *Women Writers and the Early Modern British Political Tradition*, ed. Hilda L. Smith (Cambridge: Cambridge University Press, 1998), pp. 243–58 (252–4); Angela Maione, 'Over the Centuries: A History of Wollstonecraft Interpretation', *Journal of Gender Studies*, 28.7 (2019), 777–88 (780).
54. Barker-Benfield, 'Mary Wollstonecraft', 97; Pocock, 'Catherine Macaulay'; *VM*, p. 78.
55. See, e.g., Marisa Linton, *The Politics of Virtue in Enlightenment France* (Basingstoke: Palgrave Macmillan, 2001); and Jack R. Censer, *Debating Modern Revolution: The Evolution of Revolutionary Ideas* (London: Bloomsbury, 2016).
56. Bromwich, 'Wollstonecraft as a Critic of Burke', 628, 629; *VM*, pp. 134, 135.
57. *VM*, pp. 134, 28.
58. Ann Laura Stoler, 'Affective States', in *A Companion to the Anthropology of Politics*, ed. David Nugent and Joan Vincent (Oxford: Blackwell, 2007), pp. 4–20 (9–10); *VM*, p. 73.
59. *VM*, pp. 42, 43, 145; Paine, *Rights of Man*, p. 24; Lee, *Nationalism and Irony*, p. 34. For Burke 'the theatre is a better school of moral sentiments than churches' (*R*, p. 120), but Wollstonecraft tends to represent theatre as a sterile, performative, and fleeting spectacle. See Lisa Plummer Crafton, *Transgressive Theatricality, Romanticism, and Mary Wollstonecraft* (Farnham: Ashgate, 2011).
60. *VM*, p. 121; Zerilli, 'Text/Woman', 55; Mandall, 'Virtue and Evidence', 137; Frank, 'Aesthetics of Democratic Revolution', pp. 5, 10.
61. *VM*, p. 12; Spongberg, *Women Writers*, p. 45. See also O'Neill, *Burke–Wollstonecraft Debate*, p. 194.
62. *VM*, p. 127; Bromwich, 'Wollstonecraft as a Critic of Burke', 632; Zerilli, 'Text/Woman', 57.

63. Blakemore, *Fall of Language*, pp. 297, 305; Zerilli, 'Text/Woman', 57; *R*, p. 144; Michael, *Critique of Political Reason*, pp. 94–5.
64. *VM*, p. 127; *R*, p. 128; *VM*, pp. 2, 5; Chandler, *Archaeology of Sympathy*, pp. xv–xvi, 176. Bromwich has noted the 'contradiction' that Burke's argument 'engenders from within', 'Wollstonecraft as a Critic of Burke', 623–4.
65. *VM*, p. 5.
66. *VM*, p. 35. On Price's own self-effacing yet 'feeling' style, see Barker-Benfield, 'Mary Wollstonecraft', 114. Cf. Catherine Macaulay's attack in *Observations on the Reflections of the Right Hon. Edmund Burke* (London: C. Dilly, 1790).
67. *VM*, pp. 1, 6; Nienkamp, *Internal Rhetorics*, p. 132
68. On the reception of Wollstonecraft's work, see, e.g., Elaine Hunt Botting, 'Wollstonecraft in Europe: A Revisionist Reception History, 1792–1904', *History of European Ideas*, 39.4 (2013), 503–27; and Isabelle Bour, 'A New Wollstonecraft: The Reception of the *Vindication of the Rights of Woman* and of *The Wrongs of Woman* in Revolutionary France', *Journal for Eighteenth-Century Studies*, 36.4 (2013), 575–87.
69. Rajan, *Romantic Narrative*, pp. 197, 198; William Godwin, *Memoirs of the Author of a Vindication of the Rights of Woman* (London: J. Johnson, 1798), pp. 75–7.
70. See, e.g., Mitzi Myers, 'Godwin's *Memoirs* of Mary Wollstonecraft: The Shaping of Self and Subject', *Studies in Romanticism*, 20.3 (1981), 299–316; and Harriet Guest, *Unbounded Attachment: Sentiment and Politics in the Age of the French Revolution* (Oxford: Oxford University Press, 2013), pp. 88–122.
71. Susan Khin Zaw, 'The Reasonable Heart: Mary Wollstonecraft's View of the Relation Between Reason and Feeling in Morality', *Hypatia*, 13.1 (1998), 78–117 (84); Susan Gubar, 'Feminist Misogyny: Mary Wollstonecraft and the Paradox of "It Takes One to Know One"', *Feminist Studies*, 20 (1994), 452–73.
72. Wollstonecraft's dedication to Talleyrand notes the great flaw in the French constitution: its exclusion of women 'from participation in the natural rights of mankind', *VW*, p. xi. See Deborah Weiss, *The Female Philosopher and her Afterlives: Mary Wollstonecraft, the British Novel, and the Transformation of Feminism, 1796–1811* (Basingstoke: Palgrave Macmillan, 2017), p. 3.
73. *VM*, pp. 78, 137; Barker-Benfield, 'Mary Wollstonecraft', 95–115 (esp. 100). As Katherine O'Donnell notes, Wollstonecraft's 'sexualization of virtue' allows her to represent Burke as an 'unnatural male': oriental, sodomitical, quasi-French, pseudo-papist, and Jesuitical, 'Effeminate Edmund Burke and the Masculine Voice of Mary Wollstonecraft', *Journal of Gender Studies*, 28.7 (2019), 789–801. See also Taylor, *Feminist Imagination*, esp. p. 67. On Burke's perceived Celtic temperament, see Emily Jones, *Edmund Burke and the Invention of Modern Conservatism, 1830–1914: An Intellectual History* (Oxford: Oxford University Press, 2017), esp. pp. 56–80.
74. Bromwich, 'Wollstonecraft as a Critic of Burke', 623, 620; Price, *Reinventing Liberty*, p. 198; Barker-Benfield, 'Mary Wollstonecraft', 111, 113; *VW*, pp. ix, v.

75. *VW*, pp. 224, 249; Barker-Benfield, 'Mary Wollstonecraft', 111.
76. *VW*, p. 224; Barker-Benfield, 'Mary Wollstonecraft', 107.
77. Johnson, *Equivocal Beings*, pp. 24, 60; Spongberg, *Women Writers*, p. 40.
78. Wendy Gunther-Canada, 'The Politics of Sense and Sensibility: Mary Wollstonecraft and Catherine Macaulay Graham on Edmund Burke's *Reflections on the Revolution in France*', in *Women Writers and the Early Modern British Political Tradition*, ed. Hilda L. Smith (Cambridge: Cambridge University Press, 1998), pp. 126–47 (127).
79. Poovey, *The Proper Lady and the Woman Writer: Ideology as Style in the Works of Mary Wollstonecraft, Mary Shelley, and Jane Austen* (Chicago and London: University of Chicago Press, 1984), p. 68. emphasis in original; Gunther-Canada, 'Sense and Sensibility', p. 140.
80. *VM*, pp. 153, 7, 154, 155; Poovey, *The Proper Lady*, pp. 53, 54, 68.
81. Smith, *Intimate Strangers*, p. 146.
82. Julie Ellison, *Cato's Tears and the Making of Anglo-American Emotion* (Chicago: Chicago University Press, 1999), p. 70. See also Thomas Dixon, *Weeping Britannia: Portrait of a Nation in Tears* (Oxford: Oxford University Press, 2015).
83. Lauren Berlant, *The Female Complaint: The Unfinished Business of Sentimentality in American Culture* (Durham, NC: Duke University Press, 2008), pp. 55, 56.
84. Berlant, *Female Complaint*, p. 56; Michael, *Critique of Political Reason*, p. 101.
85. *HMV*, p. vi; Ashley Tauchert, 'Maternity, Castration and Mary Wollstonecraft's *Historical and Moral View of the French Revolution*', *Women's Writing*, 4.2 (1997), 173–99 (177).
86. *HMV*, pp. v, 25, 26, 296; Isabelle Bour, 'Mary Wollstonecraft as Historian in *An Historical and Moral View of the Origin and Progress of the French Revolution*', *Études Épistémè*, 17 (2010). Available at <https://journals.openedition.org/episteme/668#abstract> (last accessed 5 January 2020), para. 16; Tauchert, 'Maternity, Castration', 181. In its preliminary form, the *Historical and Moral View* was entitled 'Letters on the Present Character of the French Nation' (1793), providing an enhanced sense of the importance of national character to Wollstonecraft's representation of history.
87. *HMV*, pp. 105, 104–5.
88. Mike Goode, 'Feeling History', 852, 834; Phillips, *Society and Sentiment*, p. 92. On Burke's performative style, see, e.g., Jane Hodson, *Language and Revolution in Burke, Wollstonecraft, Paine, and Godwin* (Aldershot: Ashgate, 2007); and Kevin Gilmartin, *Writing against the Revolution: Literary Conservatism in Britain, 1790–1832* (Cambridge: Cambridge University Press, 2007).
89. *HMV*, pp. 62, 104, 105, 522.
90. Bour, 'Mary Wollstonecraft as Historian', paras 17, 18–19, 5.
91. Jane Rendell, '"The grand causes which combine to carry mankind forward": Wollstonecraft, History and Revolution', *Women's Writing*, 4.2 (1997), 155–72 (esp. 164–6). See also Daniel I. O'Neill, 'Shifting the Scottish Paradigm: The Discourse of Morals and Manners in Mary

Wollstonecraft's *French Revolution*', *History of Political Thought*, 23.1 (2002), 90–116.
92. Price, *Reinventing Liberty*, p. 76.
93. *HMV*, pp. 8, 17, 16, 22, 23.
94. *HMV*, p. 16.
95. *HMV*, pp. 7, 21, 309, 247, 27, 521, 485, 5, 1, 4, 232–4, 19; Price, *Reinventing Liberty*, p. 193.
96. *VM*, p. 109. Wollstonecraft is alert to the fact that, as Furniss puts it, 'radicalism might represent an uncanny reflection of [Burke's] own *Reflections*', *Burke's Aesthetic Ideology*, p. 11.
97. *HMV*, pp. 459–60, 76, 489, 490, 8, 249.
98. *HMV*, pp. 24, 225; Macaulay, *Observations*, p. 42.
99. *HMV*, pp. 406–7, 467, 520.
100. *HMV*, pp. 107, 59, 374–5, 375, 375–6, 124; Barker-Benfield, 'Mary Wollstonecraft', 101; Crafton, *Transgressive Theatricality*, p. 96.
101. *HMV*, pp. 33, 35–6, 421, 132, 133, 135.
102. Spongberg, *Women Writers*, p. 2.
103. Crafton, *Transgressive Theatricality*, pp. 104, 104–5. See also Saba Bahar, *Mary Wollstonecraft's Social and Aesthetic Philosophy* (New York: Palgrave Macmillan, 2002), p. 125.
104. *HMV*, pp. 131, 256, 470. Wollstonecraft differentiates the 'people', even when they are in thrall to the monarchy or 'easy of belief', from the degeneracy of the aristocracy: 'How different was this frankness of the people, from the close hypocritical conduct of the cabal!' (131).
105. *HMV*, pp. 422, 246, 196; see also 426, 430–1; Fairclough, *Romantic Crowd*, p. 84. The Duke of Orleans similarly personifies those aristocratic artifices that have corrupted republican feeling. See Michelle Callander, '"The grand theatre of political changes": Marie Antoinette, the Republic, and the Politics of Spectacle in Mary Wollstonecraft's *An Historical and Moral View of the French Revolution*', *European Romantic Review*, 11.4 (2000), 375–92.
106. For a detailed, historicist consideration of revolutionary electricity, see Samantha Wesner, 'Revolutionary Electricity in 1790: Shock, Consensus, and the Birth of a Political Metaphor', *BJHS*, 54.3 (2021), 257–75.
107. Hunt, *Family Romance*, p. 2; *HMV*, p. 32.
108. *HMV*, p. 522.
109. Callander, 'Politics of Spectacle', 376, 377. On questions of 'maternal thinking', see Tauchert, 'Maternity, Castration'. On matriphobic culture, see Angela Keane, 'Mary Wollstonecraft's Imperious Sympathies: Population, Maternity, and Romantic Individualism', in *Body Matters: Feminism, Textuality, Corporeality*, ed. Avril Horner and Angela Keane (Manchester: Manchester University Press, 2000), pp. 29–42.
110. Crafton, *Transgressive Theatricality*, pp. 93–4; Mona Ozouf, *Festivals and the French Revolution*, trans. Alan Sheridan (Cambridge, MA: Harvard University Press, 1988), pp. 9–10.
111. Thomas Carlyle, *The French Revolution: A History*, introd. John D. Rosenberg (New York: The Modern Library, 2002), pp. 1407–8; *HMV*, pp. 54, 245; Lee, *Nationalism and Irony*, pp. 120, 121.

112. Price, *Reinventing Liberty*, pp. 17–19. On Rousseau and revolutionary festivals, see Crafton, *Transgressive Theatricality*, esp. p. 46.
113. Amy Mallory-Kani, '"A Healthy State": Mary Wollstonecraft's Medical Politics', *The Eighteenth Century*, 56.1 (2015), 21–40 (23).
114. Crafton, *Transgressive Theatricality*, p. 9; HMV, pp. 58, 113–14; Bour, 'Mary Wollstonecraft as Historian', para. 12.
115. Harry Harootunian, 'Shadowing the Past: National History and the Persistence of the Everyday', *Cultural Studies*, 18.2/3 (2004), 181–200.
116. See Rowan Boyson on Barbara Ehrenreich's conception of 'collective joy', *Enlightenment Idea of Pleasure*, p. 15.
117. HMV, pp. 344, 72; 356; see also 361.
118. Sophie Wahnich, *In Defence of the Terror: Liberty or Death in the French Revolution*, trans. David Fernbach (New York and London: Verso, 2012), p. 83, discussed in Tristan Donal Burke, 'From Terror to Terrorism in *Bleak House*: Writing the Event, Representing the People', *The London Journal*, 45.1 (2020), 17–38 (31).
119. HMV, pp. 487, 426, 386 206, 449–50, 460, 484. Wollstonecraft does, however, condemn gendered accounts that classify the storming of the Queen's boudoir as 'merely the rage of women, who were supposed to be actuated only by the emotions of the moment' (426).
120. Mahesh Ananth, 'A Cognitive Interpretation of Aristotle's Concepts of Catharsis and Tragic Pleasure', *International Journal of Art and Art History*, 2.2 (2014), 1–33 (esp. 6). On the limitations of Rousseau's conflation of popular sovereignty and constituent power, see Eoin Daly, 'Alchemising Peoplehood: Rousseau's Lawgiver as a Model of Constituent Power', *History of European Ideas*, 47.1 (2021), 1278–91.
121. HMV, p. 486.
122. HMV, pp. 474, 475.
123. Viven Jones, 'Women Writing Revolution: Narratives of History and Sexuality in Wollstonecraft and Williams', *History of European Ideas*, 16 (1991), 299–305.
124. Tauchert, 'Maternity, Castration', 192; Janet Todd, *Gender, Art and Death* (Cambridge: Polity Press, 1993), p. 143; HMV, p. 163.
125. Gary Kelly, *Revolutionary Feminism: The Mind and Career of Mary Wollstonecraft* (New York: St Martin's Press, 1992), pp. vi, 153; Jones, 'Women Writing Revolution'; Rendell, 'Wollstonecraft, History and Revolution', 155.
126. Crafton, *Transgressive Theatricality*, p. 98. On the radical sensibility of the first-person voice, see Gregory Dart, *Rousseau, Robespierre, and English Romanticism* (Cambridge: Cambridge University Press, 1999), p. 38.
127. Zerilli, Text/Woman', 67; R, p. 112.
128. Nahaboo, 'Subverting Orientalism', 594; Hume, *Essays Moral, Political and Literary*, pp. 465–87; Ernest Renan, *Qu'est-ce qu'une nation?*, trans. and annot. Martin Thom, in *Nation and Narration*, ed. Homi K. Bhabha (London and New York: Routledge, 1990), pp. 8–22; R, p. 95.
129. Ina Ferris, *The Romantic National Tale and the Question of Ireland* (Cambridge: Cambridge University Press, 2004), p. 84.
130. See, e.g., Peter McPhee, *Living the French Revolution, 1789–99* (Basingstoke: Palgrave Macmillan, 2006); David Andress (ed.),

Experiencing the French Revolution (Oxford: Voltaire Foundation, 2013); and Jan Goldstein, *The Post-Revolutionary Self: Politics and Psyche in France, 1750–1850* (Cambridge, MA: Harvard University Press, 2005).

131. Howard Zinn, *A People's History of the United States* (New York: HarperPerennial, 1980), pp. 9–11.
132. Chris R. Vanden Bossche, *Carlyle and the Search for Authority* (Columbus: Ohio State University Press, 1991), p. 63; Mary Desaulniers, *Carlyle and the Economics of Terror: A Study of Revisionary Gothicism in The French Revolution* (Kingston, Ontario: McGill-Queens University Press, 1995), p. 7; Martin Meisel, *Realizations: Narrative, Pictorial, and Theatrical Arts in Nineteenth-Century England* (Princeton: Princeton University Press, 1984), p. 211. On Carlyle's crowds, see also John Plotz, 'Crowd Power: Chartism, Carlyle, and the Victorian Public Sphere', *Representations*, 70 (2000), 87–114.
133. Jonathan Sachs, 'History Writing', *Mary Wollstonecraft in Context*, ed. Nancy E. Johnson and Paul Keen (Cambridge: Cambridge University Press, 2020), pp. 305–13 (305). On the utopian trope, see Dan Edelstein, 'Future Perfect: Political and Emotional Economies of Revolutionary Time', in *Power and Time: Temporalities in Conflict and the Making of History*, ed. Dan Edelstein, Stefanos Geroulanos, and Natasha Wheatley (Chicago: University of Chicago Press, 2020), pp. 357–78.
134. Fairclough, *Romantic Crowd*, esp. pp. 87–90.
135. Wollstonecraft wrote her *Historical and Moral View* while in France from December 1792 to April 1795. The work was based on eyewitness sources, including Mirabeau's *Courrier de Provence*, the Assemblée Nationale's *Journal des débats et des décrets* (1789–91), the *Gazette nationale ou le Moniteur universel* (1789–99), and the Marquis de Lally-Tollendal's *Mémoire* (1790). See Bour, 'Mary Wollstonecraft as Historian', para. 2.
136. Étienne Balibar, *Politics and the Other Scene*, trans. Christine Jones, James Swenson, and Chris Turner (London: Verso, 2002), p. 165. See also Crimmins's discussion of futurity and the ways it 'need not sever its connection to causality' to remain 'open to radical change', *Romantic Historicism*, p. 26.

Chapter 2

1. Paul Hamilton, 'Inexhaustible Fertility: Contemporary Re-figurations of the French Revolution', *Comparative Critical Studies*, 15.2 (2018), 153–68.
2. On the *History*'s chronology and composition, see Don Locke, *A Fantasy of Reason: The Life and Thought of William Godwin* (London: Routledge & Kegan Paul, 1980), pp. 305, 313–15.
3. Henry Hallam, *The Constitutional History of England, from the Accession of Henry VII, to the Death of George II*, 2 vols (London: John Murray, 1827), 2:85. On party identities, see John Morrow, 'Republicanism and Public Virtue: William Godwin's *History of the Commonwealth of England*', *The Historical Journal*, 34.3 (1991), 645–64; and R. C. Richardson, *The Debate on the English Revolution Revisited* (London and New York: Routledge, 1988), pp. 4–5, 36–64, 65–86.

4. *HR*, pp. 373, 371. Godwin had also shown himself to be disinterested in party conflict in his earlier *The History of the Life of William Pitt, Earl of Chatham* (London: G. Kearsley, 1783), pp. x, 5.
5. *HC*, 3:17. On the Whigs' rejection of classical republicanism, see Burrow, *Liberal Descent*, pp. 33, 55–8.
6. Thomas Carlyle, *Oliver Cromwell's Letters and Speeches*, 5 vols, 3rd edn (London: Chapman & Hall, 1872), 1:13, 14, abbreviated as *C*.
7. Mary Spongberg notes that whether one identified as a 'Cavalier' or a 'Roundhead' was a 'defining feature' of nineteenth-century English history, *Women Writers*, p. 3.
8. *C*, 4:189; T. B. Macaulay, *Critical and Historical Essays Contributed to the Edinburgh Review*, 3 vols (London: Longman, Brown, Green and Longman, 1843), 1:183, abbreviated as *CHE*. For Southey's review of four books on Cromwell, see 'Life of Cromwell', *Quarterly Review*, 25 (July 1821), 279–347.
9. *HC*, 3:v. See David Eastwood, 'Robert Southey and the Meaning of Patriotism', *Journal of British Studies*, 31.3 (1992), 265–87 (284).
10. On Godwin's biographies, see Jared McGeough, '"Imperfect, Confused, Interrupted": Biography, Nationalism, and Generic Hybridity in William Godwin's *Life of Chaucer*', *European Romantic Review*, 30.4 (2019), 367–82. On the rhizomatic model, see Rajan, 'Between Individual and General History', 118–19, and 'Uncertain Futures', 78.
11. Günter Gödde, 'The Unconscious in the German Philosophy and Psychology of the Nineteenth Century', trans. Ciaran Cronin, in *The Edinburgh Critical History of Nineteenth-Century Philosophy*, ed. Alison Stone (Edinburgh: Edinburgh University Press, 2011), pp. 204–22.
12. Nienkamp, *Internal Rhetorics*, p. 11.
13. See, e.g., Dror Wahrman, *The Making of the Modern Self: Identity and Culture in Eighteenth-Century England* (New Haven, CT: Yale University Press, 2004).
14. See, e.g., Erich Neumann, *Depth Psychology and a New Ethic*, trans. Eugene Rolfe (New York: Putnam, 1969).
15. Adam Smith, *Lectures on Rhetoric and Belles Lettres*, ed. J. C. Bryce (Oxford: Oxford University Press, 1983), p. 95, abbreviated as *LR*. On affective communication, see J. Michael Hogan, 'Historiography and Ethics in Adam Smith's Lectures on Rhetoric, 1762–1763', *Rhetorica*, 2.1 (1984), 75–91 (esp. 75). On indirect narration, see Mark Salber Phillips, 'Reconsiderations on History and Antiquarianism: Arnaldo Momigliano and the Historiography of Eighteenth-Century Britain', *Journal of the History of Ideas*, 57.2 (1996), 297–316 (esp. 311), and 'Adam Smith, Belletrist', in *The Cambridge Companion to Adam Smith*, ed. Knud Haakonssen (Cambridge: Cambridge University Press, 2006), pp. 57–78.
16. *LR*, pp. 99, 100. Smith divides these effects, in turn, into internal and external ones (107).
17. *LR*, pp. 99, 148.
18. Pocock, 'Adam Smith and History', p. 273.
19. *LR*, pp. 124, 114. On the 'ethical turn' in rhetoric, see Bullard, *Art of Rhetoric*, pp. 25–51. On character, see Vincent M. Bevilacqua, 'Adam

Smith's Lectures on Rhetoric and Belles Lettres', *Studies in Scottish Literature*, 3.1 (1965), 41–60 (esp. 55).
20. *LR*, p. 112; Phillips, 'Adam Smith, Belletrist', pp. 73, 64, 66; Nienkamp, *Internal Rhetorics*, pp. 281, 282.
21. *T*, pp. 252, 252–3. See Alan Schwerin, *Hume's Labyrinth: A Search for the Self* (Newcastle upon Tyne: Cambridge Scholar Publishers, 2012), pp. 248, 261.
22. *T*, p. 252; Schwerin, *Hume's Labyrinth*, pp. 276, 261.
23. David A. Reisman, *Adam Smith's Sociological Economics* (London: Croom Helm, 1976), p. 27.
24. *LR*, pp. 113, 93–4, 99.
25. *LR*, pp. 114, 132.
26. Sharon Crowley, *The Methodical Memory: Invention in Current-Traditional Rhetoric* (Carbondale and Edwardsville: Southern Illinois University Press, 1990), p. 49.
27. Pocock, 'Adam Smith and History', pp. 277–8; Phillips 'Adam Smith, Belletrist', p. 86; Dugald Stewart, *Elements of the Philosophy of the Human Mind* (London and Edinburgh: Strahan, Cadell and Creech, 1792), pp. 10, 29.
28. David Norbrook, 'The English Revolution and English Historiography', in *The Cambridge Companion to Writing of the English Revolution*, ed. N. H. Keeble (Cambridge: Cambridge University Press, 2001), pp. 233–50 (242).
29. See, e.g., Norbrook, 'The English Revolution', pp. 242–4.
30. Deidre Shauna Lynch, *The Economy of Character: Novels, Market Culture, and the Business of Inner Meaning* (Chicago: Chicago University Press, 1998), pp. 6, 30, 48, 133–4; Jonathan Arac, *Impure Worlds: The Institution of Literature in the Age of the Novel* (New York: Fordham University Press, 2010), p. 43. Cf. Andrea Henderson, who has unsettled the depth model of romantic interiority by looking at commercial identity, context-based identity, and body-based identity in *Romantic Identities: Varieties of Subjectivity, 1774–1830* (Cambridge: Cambridge University Press, 1996), pp. 2, 6–10.
31. *CME*, 4:179. On Carlyle and character, see Gavin Budge, 'The Hero as Seer: Character, Perception and Cultural Health in Carlyle', *Romanticism and Victorianism on the Net*, Special Issue 'Science, Technology and the Senses', 52 (2008). Available at <doi.org/10.7202/019805ar/> (last accessed 15 October 2021).
32. See, e.g., Neil K. Hargraves, 'National History and "Philosophical" History: Character and Narrative in William Robertson's History of Scotland', *History of European Ideas*, 26.1 (2000), 19–33 (22–3).
33. Fiona Price, 'Resisting "the Spirit of Innovation": The Other Historical Novel and Jane Porter', *Modern Language Review*, 101.3 (2006), 638–51 (638); Phillips, *Society and Sentiment*, p. 120. On Shakespeare biography and the *Bildungsroman*, see James Shapiro, 'Unravelling Shakespeare's Life', in *On Life-Writing*, ed. Zachary Leader (Oxford: Oxford University Press, 2015), pp. 7–24 (13–15, 18).
34. Stefan Collini, *Public Moralists: Political Thought and Intellectual Life in Britain, 1850–1930* (Oxford: Oxford University Press, 1992), pp. 108–10.
35. Phillips, *Society and Sentiment*, p. 98.

36. Phillips, *Society and Sentiment*, pp. 98, 136. See also William St. Clair, 'Romantic Biography: Conveying Personality, Intimacy, and Authenticity in an Age of Ink on Paper', in *On Life-Writing*, pp. 48–71.
37. O'Brien, 'History and the Novel', p. 398. On the fate of the epistolary novel, see, e.g., Nicola J. Watson, *Revolution and the Form of the British Novel, 1790–1825: Intercepted Letters, Interrupted Seductions* (Oxford: Oxford University Press, 1994).
38. D. J. Trela, 'The Writing of "An Election to the Long Parliament": Carlyle, Primary Research and the Book Clubs', *Carlyle Studies Annual*, 14 (1994), 71–82.
39. For examples of Godwin's various sources for the *History of the Commonwealth*, see, e.g., the footnotes at HC, 1:10–16, 19–20, 77–5; 3:vii, viii. Blair Worden has rightly described Godwin as an 'archival pioneer', *Roundhead Reputations: The English Civil Wars and the Passions of Posterity* (London: Penguin, 2002), p. 323.
40. Blair, *Lectures on Rhetoric and Belles Lettres*, 2 vols (London: W. Strahan, 1783), 2:280.
41. Nienkamp, *Internal Rhetorics*, p. 128.
42. Rebecca Tierney-Hynes, 'Shaftesbury's "Soliloquy": Authorship and the Psychology of Romance', *Eighteenth-Century Studies*, 38.4 (2005), 605–21 (605, 607).
43. Nienkamp, *Internal Rhetorics*, pp. 44, 54.
44. Nienkamp, *Internal Rhetorics*, pp. 74, 70, 71.
45. Nienkamp, *Internal Rhetorics*, pp. 77, 74, 73.
46. Angela Esterhammer, 'Godwin's Suspicion of Speech Acts', *Studies in Romanticism*, 39.4 (2000), 553–78 (554, 555, 556, 557). See also Myers, 'William Godwin and the *Ars Rhetorica*'.
47. William Godwin, *Letters of Mucius*, in *The Political and Philosophical Writing of William Godwin: Volume 1*, ed. Martin Fitzpatrick (London: Pickering and Chatto, 1993), pp. ix, 36–8.
48. Esterhammer, 'Godwin's Suspicion', 573, 562.
49. HC, 3:v; 4:531; Damian Walford Davies, 'Counterfactual Obstetrics: Mary Wollstonecraft's *Frankenstein*', in *Counterfactual Romanticism*, ed. Damian Walford Davies (Manchester: Manchester University Press, 2019), pp. 155–201 (163); Phillips, *On Historical Distance*, pp. 96, 232, cited in Davies.
50. HC, 1:viii. Cf. Godwin's *Enquirer* essay 'Of Difference in Opinion' (1797), which questions the possibility of impartiality (305–6, 308); and Gary Handwerk, 'Of Caleb's Guilt and Godwin's Truth: Ideology and Ethics in *Caleb Williams*', *English Literary History*, 60.4 (1993), 939–60 (951).
51. HC, 1:vi. The quotation is from Edmund Burke's eulogy on John Howard's visits to European prisons, *The Works and Correspondence of the Right Honourable Edmund Burke*, 8 vols (London: F. & J. Rivington, 1852), 3:422.
52. HR, p. 366; HC, 2:220–1. Godwin's emphasis on the moral character of public men is partly classical in origin, but it is also a product of his Dissenting education. His *Sketches of History, in Six Sermons* (1784), written not long after leaving Hoxton Academy, maintains, along the lines

of Bolingbroke and Priestley, that history serves 'to enlarge and ennoble the human mind' by teaching through example. Similarly, in his *Account of the Seminary . . . at Epsom* (1783) Godwin argues that history is the best way to study and teach human nature in ways that resonate with his later *Essay on Sepulchers* (1809), in which he emphasises the moral qualities of exemplary men and their role in the civic life of the nation. See William Godwin, *Sketches of History in Six Sermons* (London: T. Cadell, 1784), pp. 67, 69; and Rowland Weston, 'History, Memory, Knowledge: William Godwin's *Essay on Sepulchres* (1809)', *The European Legacy*, 14.6 (2009), 651–66.

53. *HC*, 1:6; Davies, 'Counterfactual Obstetrics', p. 164.
54. *HC*, 3:332; see also 4:88, 388; 2:405. For Godwin's criticism of party bias by Clement Walker and Ludlow, see *HC*, 1:210; 3:463–4.
55. *HC*, 1:84; see also 2:76–7; Morrow, 'Republicanism and Public Virtue', 649. See also Godwin, *Life of Geoffrey Chaucer, The Early English Poet*, 4 vols (London: Richard Phillips, 1804), 1:261, 352–3.
56. *HC*, 3:189–90; 1:lx, vii, viii. See Phillips, 'Relocating Inwardness: Historical Distance and the Transition from Enlightenment to Romantic Historiography', *PMLA*, 118.3 (2003), 436–49 (441–2); Mandell, 'Virtue and Evidence', 133.
57. *HC*, 2:111; Klancher, 'Godwin and the Republican Romance', p. 78.
58. *HR*, pp. 361, 364, 363–4. See also Ab MSS b. 228/9 (2b), p. 3.
59. *HC*, 1:407–8; 2:199–201; 4:17–18. Lilburne and Cromwell also represent 'striking examples of two opposing forms of public conduct' (2:7; 3:46). This is a methodology that colours Godwin's archival research methodology, which centred on uncovering the private records of historical actors either individually or in pairs.
60. *Congregational Magazine*, 8 n.s. (Feb. 1825), 94–8; *Literary Chronicle and Weekly Review*, 8.376 (29 July 1826), 456–9; 8.377 (5 Aug. 1826), 488–92; 8.379 (19 Aug. 1826), 520–3. For a critique of Godwin's structural plan, see *Christian Moderator*, 1 (1826), 378–82, 423–5; and *Monthly Critical Gazette*, 1 (June 1824), 7–9, all reprinted in Kenneth W. Graham, *William Godwin Reviewed: A Reception History, 1783–1834* (New York: AMS Press, 2001), pp. 449–50, 277, 472, 560.
61. *HC*, 2:30; 1:viii.
62. *HC*, 2:671, 674. Godwin's 'stoical harshness' is noted by the *National Magazine and General Review*, 1 (March 1827), 309–12, reprinted in Graham, *Godwin Reviewed*, p. 484.
63. *HC*, 4:574. Godwin also rejects claims that on Cromwell's death a great storm arose, thus recording portents and marvels while simultaneously indicting his scepticism towards such narratives (4:575).
64. Ireland is a theme that runs throughout Godwin's career as a whole, from his friendship with Irish patriots such as John Philpot Curran, to his six-week visit to Ireland in 1800, to his reading of Irish revisionist historians such as John Curry and Thomas Leland. See David O'Shaughnessy, 'Godwin, Ireland, and Historical Tragedy', in *New Approaches to William Godwin: Forms, Fears, Futures*, ed. Eliza O'Brien, Helen Stark, and Beatrice Turner (Cham: Palgrave Macmillan, 2021), pp. 13–36.

65. *HC*, 3:436–7n. The *Monthly Critical Gazette* accuses Godwin of 'more of the obtrusion of the first person than is usual or consistent with the dignity of history', but Godwin's use of the first person is, in fact, limited, *Monthly Critical Gazette*, 1 (June 1824), 7–9 (8), reprinted in Graham, *Godwin Reviewed*, p. 560.
66. *HC*, 3:435n, 438–41.
67. *HC*, 3:146, 147, 150.
68. O'Shaughnessy, 'Historical Tragedy', p. 34 n57.
69. Catherine Macaulay, *The History of England, from the Accession of James I to that of the Brunswick Line*, 8 vols (London: J. Nourse, 1763–83), 5:383; *HC*, 1:18; 4:597; 2:409. On Cromwell as a Machiavellian figure, see Blair Worden, 'Classical Republicanism and the Puritan Revolution', in *History & Imagination: Essays in Honor of H. R. Trevor-Roper*, ed. Hugh Lloyd-Jones, Valerie Pearl, and Blair Worden (London: Duckworth, 1981), pp. 196–8.
70. Godwin was accused by reviewers of exercising the 'talents of an apologist' and panegyrist. See, e.g., the review of *Life of Pitt* in the *English Review*, 1 (Feb. 1783), 141–4 (142), and the review of *History of the Commonwealth* in the *Athenaeum*, 54 (5 Nov. 1828), 850–1, reprinted in Graham, *Godwin Reviewed*, pp. 20, 499.
71. Godwin, *Life of Pitt*, 1:46–7, 50, 57; *HC*, 3:436–7.
72. *Monthly Magazine*, 7 n.s. (Jan. 1829), 82–4, reprinted in Graham, *Godwin Reviewed*, p. 504.
73. As Esterhammer notes, there is 'an ongoing parallel [in Godwin's work] between the imaginative process of creating identity and character' and 'the institutional process of establishing identity', 'Godwin's Suspicion', 574–5.
74. *PJ* (1793), 3:12–18. For Godwin's (often negative) depiction of Dissenting religious groups, see Morrow, 'Republicanism and Public Virtue'.
75. *HC*, 3:18.
76. *HC*, 1:77.
77. *PJ* (1793), 3:122; *HC*, 2:204–5; Rajan, *Romantic Narrative*, p. 119.
78. Edson, 'Godwin's Anti-Mass Politics Revisited', 162, 163, 164, 166, 163.
79. *PJ* (1796), 1:259; *HC*, 3:120.
80. *HC*, 4:579, 528, 530–1, 531.
81. *HR*, p. 362. See also an unpublished 'Preface' written in January 1830, Ab MSS b. pp. 226/7, and the preface to *Cloudesley, A Tale*, 3 vols (London: Henry Colburn and Richard Bentley, 1830), which argues that 'fictitious history ... comprises more of the science of man, than whatever can be exhibited by the historian' (1:xi).
82. *CL*, 2:94; *The Norman and Charlotte Strouse Edition of the Writings of Thomas Carlyle: Historical Essays*, ed. Chris R. Vanden Bossche (Berkeley: University of California Press, 2003), p. xxxv.
83. *CL*, 2:70, 81, 94.
84. Carlyle's will of 1873, cited in *Historical Sketches of Notable Persons and Events in the Reigns of James I and Charles I*, ed. Alexander Carlyle (London: Chapman and Hall, 1898), p. vii.
85. Folio 95 and v, cited in Vanden Bossche, *Search for Authority*, p. 103. For a detailed study, see D. J. Trela, *A History of Carlyle's 'Oliver Cromwell's*

Letters and Speeches' (Lewiston, NY: Edwin Mellon Press, 1992), and *Cromwell in Context: The Conception, Writing and Reception of Carlyle's Second History* (Edinburgh: Carlyle Newsletter, 1986).
86. See, e.g., *C*, 2:88–90, 93; 3:184.
87. Vanden Bossche, *Search for Authority*, pp. 103–4. See also K. J. Fielding, 'Carlyle and Cromwell: The Writing of History and "Dryasdust"', in *Lectures on Carlyle and his Era*, ed. Jerry D. James and Rita D. Bottoms (Santa Cruz: University Library, University of California, 1985), pp. 45–68.
88. Ann Rigney, 'The Untenanted Places of the Past: Thomas Carlyle and the Varieties of Historical Ignorance', *History and Theory*, 35.3 (1996), 338–57 (349). On Carlyle's working methods as a historian, see Budge, 'The Hero as Seer', para. 13.
89. *CME*, 2:255.
90. *C*, 1:65, 3.
91. *C*, 1:239, 11.
92. *C*, 1:11, 2; 'Baillie the Covenanter', *CME*, 6:215.
93. *CME*, 3:97, 110, 105. In his 'Essay on Burns' (1828), Carlyle's preference for eighteenth-century novels is based on their relationship to reality, including their concrete detail, their conviction and sincerity, and their didacticism and emphasis on moral instruction, *CME*, 3:304.
94. *C*, 3:231; 1:11.
95. See, e.g., Thomas O. Beebee, *Epistolary Fiction in Europe 1500–1850* (Cambridge: Cambridge University Press, 1999), p. 3.
96. *C*, 1:68; see also 1:239; 4:253.
97. Vanden Bossche, *Search for Authority*, p. 120.
98. Budge, 'Hero as Seer', para. 33.
99. Thomas Carlyle, *On Heroes, Hero-Worship, and the Heroic in History* (New York: Charles Scribner's Sons, 1841), p. 217.
100. *CME*, 6:224.
101. James Eli Adams, 'The Hero as Spectacle: Carlyle and the Persistence of Dandyism', in *Victorian Literature and the Victorian Visual Imagination*, ed. Carol T. Christ and John O. Jordan (Berkeley: University of California Press, 1995), pp. 213–32 (217).
102. Adams, 'Hero as Spectacle', 215, 218; *C*, 4:80–1.
103. Adams, 'Hero as Spectacle', 219, 220; W. J. Fox, 'On the Study of History. No. 2', *People's Journal*, 1 (1846), 187–93 (191).
104. *C*, 1:271; see also 2:137; 3:133; McKeon, *Secret History of Domesticity*, pp. 228–9.
105. *C*, 1:11; John D. Rosenberg, *Carlyle and the Burden of History* (Oxford: Clarendon Press, 1985), pp. 18–19. See also Christine Persak, 'Rhetoric in Praise of Silence: The Ideology of Carlyle's Paradox', *Rhetoric Society Quarterly*, 21.1 (1991), 38–52.
106. *C*, 4:193–4, 197. See, e.g., Joseph W. Childers, 'Carlyle's *Past and Present*, History, and a Question of Hermeneutics', *Clio*, 13.3 (1984), 247–58. On Carlyle's 'stereoscopic' time-effects, see Rosemary Jann, 'Changing Styles in Victorian Military History', *Clio*, 11.2 (1982), 159–60. On Carlyle's 'physiognomic' history, see Michael K. Goldberg, 'Gigantic Philistines:

Carlyle, Dickens, and the Visual Arts', in *Lectures on Carlyle and his Era*, pp. 17–43 (31).
107. Richard Salmon, *The Formation of the Victorian Literary Profession* (Cambridge: Cambridge University Press, 2013), p. 50; Paul Barlow, 'The Imagined Hero as Incarnate Sign: Thomas Carlyle and the Mythology of the "National Portrait" in Victorian Britain', *Art History*, 17.4 (1994), 517–45; and Julian North, 'Portraying Presence: Thomas Carlyle, Portraiture, and Biography', *Victorian Literature and Culture*, 43.3 (2015), 465–88.
108. Barlow, 'The Imagined Hero', 542; Salmon, *Victorian Literary Profession*, pp. 47, 50.
109. North, 'Portraying Presence', 465, 466, 467; Paul White, 'Darwin Wept: Science and the Sentimental Subject', *Journal of Victorian Culture*, 16.2 (2011), 195–213 (200); *C*, 5:10.
110. *C*, 5:19; 'Baillie, Robert', in Mark Cumming (ed.), *The Carlyle Encyclopedia* (Cranbury, NJ: Associated University Presses, 2004), p. 24; Vanden Bossche, *Search for Authority*, p. 122.
111. Adams, 'Hero as Spectacle', 229.
112. O'Brien, 'History and the Novel', p. 392, and 'History and Literature 1660–1780', in *The Cambridge History of English Literature, 1660–1780*, ed. John Richetti (Cambridge: Cambridge University Press, 2005), pp. 363–90 (368).
113. *C*, 2:20; 3:155; 2:125.
114. *C*, 5:147.
115. Rosenberg, *Burden of History*, p. 146.
116. Gillian Beer, *Arguing with the Past: Essays in Narrative from Woolf to Sidney* (Cambridge: Cambridge University Press, 1989); Chris R. Vanden Bossche, 'Fictive Text and Transcendental Self: Carlyle's Art of Biography', *Biography*, 10 (1987), 116–28 (116).
117. *HR*, p. 368. See Ann Rigney, 'Semantic Slides: History and the Concept of Fiction', in *History-Making: The Intellectual and Social Formation of a Discipline*, ed. Irmline Veit-Brause and Rolf Thorstendahl (Stockholm: Kungl. Vitterhets Historie och Antikvitets Akademien, 1996), pp. 31–46 (32).
118. *C*, 3:33–4; Phillips, *Society and Sentiment*, p. 141. On Carlyle's antiquarian methods and sources, see D. J. Trela, 'Dryasdust's Revenge: Carlyle, *Cromwell* and John Harland', *Bibliotheck*, 27.1–3 (1991), 45–56.
119. Childers, 'Carlyle's *Past and Present*', 242. Cf. White, *Metahistory*, p. 14.
120. Jann, *The Art and Science of Victorian History*, p. xii. An unsigned obituary in the *Saturday Review* for 1881 argued that Carlyle had *improved* the 'chaotic' speeches of the Protector, *Saturday Review* (12 Feb. 1881), 199–301, reprinted in Jules Paul Seigel (ed.), *Thomas Carlyle: The Critical Heritage* (London and New York: Routledge & Kegan Paul, 1971), p. 470.
121. *C*, 3:231; Vanessa L. Ryan, 'The Unreliable Editor: Carlyle's *Sartor Resartus* and the Art of Biography', *The Review of English Studies*, 54.215 (2003), 287–307 (291).
122. Yoon Sun Lee, 'A Divided Inheritance: Scott's Antiquarian Novel and the British Nation', *English Literary History*, 64.2 (1997), 537–67 (545, 539).

123. *C*, 1:2; Rosenberg, *Carlyle and the Burden of History*, p. 140. See also Daniela Garafolo, 'Communities in Mourning: Making Capital out of Loss in Carlyle's *Past and Present* and *Heroes*', *Texan Studies in Literature and Language*, 45.3 (2003), 293–314.
124. *C*, 1:65–6, 290, 317; 2:141, 224
125. *C*, 2:143, 141. See also 1:99, 107; 2:141.
126. John Morrow, 'Thomas Carlyle, "Young Ireland", and the "Condition of Ireland Question"', *The Historical Journal*, 51.3 (2008), 643–67 (esp. 650, 665–7). See also Roger Swift, 'Thomas Carlyle, *Chartism* and the Irish in Early Victorian England', *Victorian Literature and Culture*, 29.1 (2001), 67–83.
127. *C*, 1:459–60, 462; Thomas Carlyle, *Reminiscences of my Irish Journey in 1849* (London: S. Low, Marston, Searle, & Rivington, 1882), p. v. Carlyle travelled to Ireland twice between 1846 and 1849, sometimes in the company of the Irish nationalist Charles Gavan Duffy.
128. Rigney, 'Untenanted Places', 351; Jason B. Jones, *Lost Causes: Historical Consciousness in Victorian Literature* (Columbus: Ohio State University Press, 2006), p. 2.
129. *C*, 1:99, 107; see also 1:165.
130. *C*, 1:206; Ian Campbell, 'Carlyle: Style and Sense', *Carlyle Studies Annual*, 14 (1994), 13–24 (22).
131. Barton Swaim, '"Our own periodical pulpit": Thomas Carlyle's Sermons', *Christianity and Literature*, 52.2 (2003), 137–58 (146); Jones, *Lost Causes*, pp. 19, 20. On Carlyle, textual exegesis, and hermeneutic interpretation, see Suzy Anger, *Victorian Interpretation* (Ithaca, NY: Cornell University Press, 2005), pp. 61–84.
132. Nienkamp, *Internal Rhetorics*, pp. 5, 4.
133. Nienkamp, *Internal Rhetorics*, pp. 82, xii.
134. Nienkamp, *Internal Rhetorics*, pp. xii, 82.
135. Karen O'Brien, 'The History Market in Eighteenth-Century England', in *Books and their Readers in Eighteenth-Century England: New Essays*, ed. Isabel Rivers (London: Continuum, 2001), pp. 105–33 (109); 'History and the Novel', p. 391.
136. O'Brien, 'History and the Novel', p. 405.
137. Vanden Bossche, 'Fictive Text', 124, 121–2. As Rosenburg has noted, for Carlyle, the opposite or contrary of history is not fiction, but oblivion, *Burden of History*, p. 15.
138. *CME*, 2:248; Vanden Bossche, *Search for Authority*, p. 58.
139. Grafton, 'The Footnote from De Thou to Ranke', 58; Leopold von Ranke, *The Theory and Practice of History*, ed. Georg G. Iggers (London: Routledge, 2011), p. 13.
140. For a different view, see Griffiths, *Age of Analogy*, p. 3.
141. Ethan Kleinberg, *Haunting History: For a Deconstructive Approach to the Past* (Stanford: Stanford University Press, 2017), pp. 202, 283; Dominic LaCapra, *History and Criticism* (Ithaca, NY: Cornell University Press, 1984), pp. 92 n17, cited and discussed in Kleinberg. See also Peter Fritzsche, 'The Archive', *History and Memory*, 17.1/2 (2005), 15–44.

Chapter 3

1. Stefan Berger, 'Introduction: Towards a Global History of National Historiographies', in *Writing the Nation: A Global Perspective*, ed. Stefan Berger (Basingstoke: Palgrave Macmillan, 2007), pp. 1–29 (4, 9); Silvia Sebastini, 'National Characters and Race: A Scottish Enlightenment Debate', in *Character, Self, and Sociability in the Scottish Enlightenment*, ed. Thomas Ahnert and Susan Manning (Basingstoke: Palgrave Macmillan, 2011), pp. 187–205.
2. Joep T. Leerssen, 'Englishness, Ethnicity, and Matthew Arnold', *European Journal of English Studies*, 10.1 (2006), 63–79 (74); Anthony D. Smith, 'A Europe of Nations – or a Nation of Europe?', *Journal of Peace Research*, 30.2 (1993), 129–35 (130). See also John Hutchinson, 'Myth against Myth: The Nation as Ethnic Overlay', *Nations and Nationalism*, 10.1–2 (2004), 109–23.
3. See, e.g., Anne Frey, *British State Romanticism: Authorship, Agency, and Bureaucratic Nationalism* (Stanford: Stanford University Press, 2009); and Francesco Crocco, *Literature and the Growth of British Nationalism: The Influence of Romantic Poetry and Bardic Criticism* (Jefferson, NC: McFarland, 2014).
4. Catherine Hall, 'Macaulay's Nation', *Victorian Studies*, 51.3 (2009), 505–23; Guy Beiner, *Forgetful Remembrance: Social Forgetting and Vernacular Historiography of a Rebellion in Ulster* (Oxford: Oxford University Press, 2018), pp. 6, 15.
5. Thomas Moore, 'Prefatory Letter on Music' to *Irish Melodies* (1807–28), in *The Poetical Works of Thomas Moore* (London: Frederick Warne, n.d.), p. 194, discussed in Luke Gibbons, 'Romantic Ireland: 1750–1845', in *The Cambridge History of English Romantic Literature*, ed. James K. Chandler (Cambridge: Cambridge University Press, 2009), pp. 182–203 (196). For a reassessment of Moore's 'imperial sentimentality', see Emer Nolan, *Catholic Emancipations: Irish Fiction from Thomas Moore to James Joyce* (Syracuse, NY: Syracuse University Press, 2007), p. 3.
6. For a reassessment of the 'hot' nationalism associated with emotionally based ethnic nationalism and the 'cold' nationalism associated with civic or liberal nationalism, see Jonathan G. Heaney, 'Emotions and Nationalism: A Reappraisal,' in *Emotions in Politics: The Affect Dimension in Political Tension*, ed. Nicolas Demertzis (New York: Palgrave Macmillan, 2013), pp. 243–63, esp. 247.
7. See Sharon Crozier-De Rosa, 'Anger, Resentment, and the Limits of Historical Narratives in Protest Politics: The Case of Early Twentieth-Century Irish Women's Intersectional Movements', *Emotions: History, Culture, Society*, 5 (2021), 68–86.
8. Richard Price, 'Historiography, Narrative, and the Nineteenth Century', *Journal of British Studies*, 35.2 (1996), 220–56 (222, 224).
9. See, e.g., Mark Storey, '"Bob Southey! – Poet Laureate": Public and Private in Southey's Poems of 1816', in *Robert Southey and the Contexts of English Romanticism*, ed. Lynda Pratt (Aldershot: Ashgate, 2006), pp. 87–100 (91); and David Simpson, 'Review: Locating Southey', *Eighteenth-Century Studies*, 41.4 (2008), 565–8 (566). More generally,

see Linda Colley, *Britons: Forging the Nation, 1707–1837* (New Haven, CT, and London: Yale University Press, 1992).

10. See, e.g., J. R. Seeley, *Expansion of England: Two Courses of Lectures* (London: Macmillan, 1883), esp. p. 9. On diasporic, settler, and exilic nationalism, see Benedict Anderson, *Long-Distance Nationalism: World Capitalism and the Rise of Identity Politics* (Amsterdam: Centre for Asian Studies Amsterdam, 1992).
11. Oded Y. Steinberg, *Race, Nation, History: Anglo-German Thought in the Victorian Era* (Philadelphia: University of Pennsylvania Press, 2019); Gibbons, 'Romantic Ireland', p. 185. On Anglo-Saxonism, see Dustin M. Frazier Wood, *Anglo-Saxonism and the Idea of Englishness in Eighteenth-Century Britain* (Woodbridge: Boydell, 2020).
12. See, e.g., Hall, 'Macaulay's Nation'; and Benedikt Stuchtey, 'Literature, Liberty and Life of the Nation: British Historiography from Macaulay to Trevelyan', in *Writing National Histories: Western Europe since 1800*, ed. Stefan Berger, Mark Donovan, and Kevin Passmore (London and New York: Routledge, 1999), pp. 30–46. For an earlier example, see Catherine Macaulay, who located English liberty in 'the Saxon institutions, on which the common law of England is grounded', *History of England*, 1:387n.
13. Charles W. Mills, *The Racial Contract* (Ithaca, NY, and London: Cornell University Press, 1997), esp. pp. 7–14; Onni Gust, *Unhomely Empire: Whiteness and Belonging, c. 1760–1830* (London: Bloomsbury, 2020), pp. 12, 17, 39. See also Nicholas Hudson, 'From "Nation" to "Race": The Origin of Racial Classification in Eighteenth-Century Thought', *Eighteenth-Century Studies*, 29.3 (1996), 247–64.
14. Colin Kidd, '"The Strange Death of Scottish History" Revisited: Constructions of the Past, c. 1790–1914', *The Scottish Historical Review*, 76.201 (1997), 86–102 (93). On Pinkerton's Anglocentric assertion of Scotland's Gothic origins, see Dale Townsend, *Gothic Antiquity: History, Romance, and the Architectural Imagination, 1760–1840* (Oxford: Oxford University Press, 2019), pp. 3, 5. On the racial history of constitutional liberty on both sides of the Atlantic, see Laura Doyle, *Freedom's Empire: Race and the Rise of Novel in Atlantic Modernity, 1640–1940* (Durham, NC: Duke University Press, 2008).
15. Katie Trumpner, *Bardic Nationalism: The Romantic Novel and the British Empire* (Princeton: Princeton University Press, 1997).
16. Susan Manning, 'Antiquarianism, Balladry and the Rehabilitation of Romance', in *The Cambridge History of English Romantic Literature*, ed. James Chandler (Cambridge: Cambridge University Press, 2008), pp. 45–70 (56); Colin Kidd, *Subverting Scotland's Past: Scottish Whig Historians and the Creation of an Anglo-British Identity, 1689–c. 1830* (Cambridge: Cambridge University Press, 1993), p. 270; and 'North Britishness and the Nature of Eighteenth-Century Patriotisms', *The Historical Journal*, 39.2 (1996), 361–82; Onni Gust, 'Empire, Exile, Identity: Locating Sir James Mackintosh's Histories of England' (PhD thesis, University College London, 2010), p. 49. On 'anglopetal' and 'anglofugal' representations of Scotland's place within the British polity, see Murray Pittock, *Scottish and Irish Romanticism* (Oxford: Oxford University Press, 2008), p. 7.

17. Manning, 'Rehabilitation of Romance', 63–4.
18. David Lloyd, 'Adulteration and the Nation: Monologic Nationalism and the Colonial Hybrid', in *An Other Tongue: Nation and Ethnicity in the Linguistic Borderlands*, ed. Alfred Artega (Durham, NC: Duke University Press, 1994), pp. 53–92 (54). More generally, see Clare O'Halloran, *Golden Ages and Barbarous Nations: Antiquarian Debate and Cultural Politics in Ireland, 1750–1800* (Cork: Cork University Press, 2004).
19. Kidd, 'Constructions of the Past', 87, 88; Lee, *Nationalism and Irony*, pp. 7, 91, 8; Homi K. Bhabha, 'DissemiNation: Time, Narrative, and the Margins of the Modern Nation', in *Nation and Narration*, pp. 291–322 (294).
20. Julia M. Wright, *Ireland, India, and Nationalism in Nineteenth-Century Literature* (Cambridge: Cambridge University Press, 2007), pp. 30, 31; Price, *Reinventing Liberty*, p. 3. See also Joep T. Leerssen, *Remembrance and Imagination: Patterns in the Historical and Literary Representation of Ireland in the Nineteenth Century* (Cork: Cork University Press, 1996).
21. Townsend, *Gothic Antiquity*, p. 4; Wright, *Ireland, India, and Nationalism*, pp. 36, 35.
22. Rosemary Sweet, *Antiquaries: The Discovery of the Past in Eighteenth-Century Britain* (London: Bloomsbury Academic, 2004), p. xiv.
23. Manning, 'Rehabilitation of Romance', p. 46.
24. Manning, 'Rehabilitation of Romance', p. 49.
25. Paul Ricoeur, *Time and Narrative, Volume 3*, trans. Katherine Blarney and David Pellauer (Chicago: Chicago University Press, 1988), p. 124, cited in Clare Pettitt, *Serial Forms: The Unfinished Project of Modernity, 1815–1848* (Oxford: Oxford University Press, 2020), p. 239.
26. See Levine, *The Amateur and the Professional*.
27. Manning, 'Rehabilitation of Romance', p. 45. More generally, see Arnaldo Momigliano, *Studies in Historiography* (New York and London: Weidenfeld & Nicolson, 1966).
28. O'Brien, 'History and the Novel', p. 400; Duncan, 'Edinburgh and Lowland Scotland', p. 172.
29. Walter Scott, 'Essay on Romance', in *The Miscellaneous Prose Works of Sir Walter Scott*, 6 vols (Boston: Wells and Lilly, 1829), 6:100–63 (esp. 129, 134–7); Richard Marsden, 'In Defiance of Discipline: Antiquarianism, Archaeology and History in Late Nineteenth-Century Scotland', *Journal of Scottish Historical Studies*, 40.2 (2020), 103–33; Beiner, *Forgetful Remembrance*, pp. 7, 12, 13, 16. See also Norman Vance, 'Celts, Carthaginians and Constitutions: Anglo-Irish Literary Relations, 1780–1830', *Irish Historical Studies*, 22.87 (1981), 216–38; and Alain Schnapp, *Discovery of the Past: The Origins of Archaeology* (London: British Museum Press, 1996).
30. Thomas Carlyle, *Two Notebooks of Thomas Carlyle from 23 March, 1822 to 16 May, 1832*, ed. Charles Eliot Norton (New York: The Grolier Club, 1898), p. 168; Walter Scott, *History of Scotland*, 2 vols (London: Longman, Rees, Orme, Brown, and Green, 1829–30), 2:76–150, 227–302, abbreviated as *HS*; Hargraves, 'National History', 29.
31. *HS*, 2:375.
32. *HS*, 1:v.

33. See, e.g., Peter D. Garside, 'Scott and the "Philosophical" Historians', *Journal of the History of Ideas*, 36 (1975), 497–512; David Daiches, 'Sir Walter Scott and History', *Études anglais*, 24 (1971), 458–77; and Duncan Forbes, 'The Rationalism of Sir Walter Scott', *Cambridge Journal*, 7 (1953), 20–35. For alternative influences, see, e.g., Edward Adams, *Liberal Epic: The Victorian Practice of History from Gibbon to Churchill* (Charlottesville: University of Virginia Press, 2011), esp. pp. 89–103.
34. HS, 1:49, 50.
35. William Robertson, *History of Scotland During the Reigns of Queen Mary and King James VI*, 3 vols (Edinburgh: A. Millar, 1759), 1:5; HS, 1:13, 16.
36. HS, 1:1, 6, 7, 53.
37. Kidd, 'Constructions of the Past', 87, 99.
38. Hargraves, 'National History', 20 21, 22. See also O'Brien, *Narratives of Enlightenment*, pp. 93–128; and Colin Kidd, 'The Ideological Significance of Robertson's *History of Scotland*', in *William Robertson and the Expansion of Empire*, ed. S. J. Brown (Cambridge: Cambridge University Press, 1997), pp. 122–44.
39. HS, 1:68, 69, 70, 71, 166.
40. Hargraves, 'National History', 26.
41. James I is praised by Scott for recognising that 'the royal authority was the best means by which the general peace could be preserved', HS, 2:204; 1:276; 2:277.
42. HS, 1:33, 54, 57, 58.
43. HS, 1:52, 350, 54, 58.
44. HS, 1:156–7; 2:400.
45. See Saree Makdisi, *Romantic Imperialism: Universal Empire and the Culture of Modernity* (Cambridge: Cambridge University Press, 1998), pp. 79–80. On Mackintosh's 'dis-identification' with the Highlanders, see Onni Gust, 'Remembering and Forgetting the Scottish Highlands: Sir James Mackintosh and the Forging of a British Imperial Identity', *Journal of British Studies*, 52.3 (2014), 615–37; and James Mackintosh, *History of the Revolution in England in 1688* (London: Longman, Rees, Orme, Brown, Green, & Longman, 1834), p. 101.
46. See, e.g., James Watt, 'Scott, the Scottish Enlightenment, and Romantic Orientalism', in *Scotland and the Borders of Romanticism*, ed. Leith Davis, Ian Duncan, and Janet Sorensen (Cambridge: Cambridge University Press, 2004), pp. 94–112.
47. HS, 1:1. For Scott's anti-centralisation position, see, e.g., HS 1:94–8 and his *Letters of Malachi Malagrowther* (1826).
48. Murray Pittock, *The Myth of the Jacobite Clans: The Jacobite Army in 1745* (Edinburgh: Edinburgh University Press, 2009), p. 112, and *The Invention of Scotland: The Stuart Myth and the Scottish Identity, 1638 to the Present* (London: Routledge, 1991), pp. 84–90; Adams, *Liberal Epic*, p. 91.
49. See Scott's reference to Tytler's views on the existence of a third estate in Scotland, in HS, 1:56, and other references at HS, 1:166, 178, 202. For Scott's review, in which he notes the difficulty of writing a popular or marketable history of Scotland, see '*History of Scotland*. By Patrick Fraser Tytler', *Quarterly Review*, 41 (Nov. 1829), 328–59. On Scottish

nationalism and empire, see, e.g., John M. MacKenzie, 'Empire and National Identities: The Case of Scotland', *Transactions of the Royal Historical Society*, 8 (1998), 215–31.
50. Kidd, 'Constructions of the Past', 98; *HS*, 2:204, 208, 204, 209, 74.
51. *HS*, 1:32, 33, 54.
52. *HS*, 1:33, 122, 217, 128, 345, 218, 176–83, 341–4. On the fated nation, see Pittock, *Invention of Scotland*, pp. 33–4.
53. See Jane Stabler, '1830: Time for Change', in *Burke to Byron, Barbauld to Baillie, 1790–1830* (Basingstoke: Palgrave Macmillan, 2002), pp. 211–64.
54. Hamilton, *Metaromanticism*, pp. 131, 130.
55. *HS*, 1:59, 283; 2:55–7, 63; 1:59.
56. *HS*, 1:5, 163. On 'unionist nationalism', see Kidd, 'Constructions of the Past', 91.
57. Duncan, 'Edinburgh and Lowland Scotland', pp. 160–1.
58. *HS*, 2:402, 405, 425, 426, 427.
59. Duncan, 'Edinburgh and Lowland Scotland', pp. 160, 168.
60. Kidd, 'Constructions of the Past', 96; Gust, 'Empire, Exile, Identity', p. 262. See also John Foster, 'Nationality, Social Change and Class: Transformations of National Identity in Scotland', in *The Making of Scotland*, ed. D. McCrone, S. Kendrick, and P. Strow (Edinburgh: Edinburgh University Press, 1989), pp. 31–52.
61. Letter to Mary Shelley dated 10 April 1834, in Thomas Moore, *The Letters of Thomas Moore*, ed. Wilfred S. Dowden, 2 vols (Oxford: Clarendon Press, 1964), 1:783, abbreviated as *L*. See also letter to Dionysius Lardner dated 1 September 1833, in *L*, 1:78. For Moore's remuneration, see letter to Lord John Russell dated 9 May 1835, in *L*, 1:793. On the process of writing the *History of Ireland*, see Ronan Kelly, *Bard of Erin: The Life of Thomas Moore* (Dublin: Penguin Ireland, 2008), pp. 506–26.
62. Wednesday, 11 February 1835, in *The Journal of Thomas Moore*, ed. Wilfred S. Dowden, 6 vols (Newark: University of Delaware Press; London and Toronto: Associated University Presses, 1983–92), 4:1174, abbreviated as *J*.
63. Tuesday, 1 January 1839, in *J*, 5:2039, and Friday, 15 March to Wednesday, 27 March 1839, in *J*, 5:2046. Moore saw the completion of the *History* as a rebirth, *J*, 5:2430.
64. Letter to Thomas Longman dated 30 October 1843, in *L*, 1:879. Moore saw the advance proofs of Scott and Mackintosh's histories. See Saturday, 20 February 1829 and Saturday, 3 October 1829, in *J*, 3:1253, 1291. Moore commenced his second volume in 1835, his third in 1837, and his fourth in 1841, *J*, 4:1681; 5:2205.
65. On Scott's methods, see *J*, 5:2191. For Moore's scrupulousness towards his sources, see, e.g., Wednesday, 30 October 1833, *J*, 4:1562. For the works Moore read, see, e.g., Friday, 19 September 1823, *J*, 2:676; Thursday, 11 October 1823, *J*, 2:681; Saturday, 4 April 1832, *J*, 4:1472; Wednesday, 17 May 1833, *J*, 4:1536; Tuesday, 8 August 1837, *J*, 5:1906; Wednesday–Friday, 15, 16, 17 &c July 1840, *J*, 5:2141; and Monday, 24 January 1842, *J*, 6:2315. For Moore's archival consultations in London, see, e.g., Tuesday, 17 December 1833, *J*, 4:1579; Wednesday, 4 March 1835, *J*, 4:1672; Wednesday, 2 March 1836, *J*, 5:1786; Wednesday,

21 November 1838, *J*, 5:2022; Tuesday, 8 August 1837, *J*, 5:1906; and Monday, 7 August 1837, *J*, 5:1904. In 1838, Moore travelled to Dublin to consult manuscripts at the libraries of Trinity College Dublin and the Royal Irish Academy, including a life of the chieftain Hugh O'Donnell. See, e.g., Tuesday, 4 September 1838, *J*, 5:1997; Saturday, 22 September 1838, *J*, 5:2004; and Monday, 24 September 1838, *J*, 5:2006.
66. Tuesday, 12 November 1833, *J*, 4:1572–3. On Hume and Lingard, see, e.g., Tuesday, 17 December 1833, *J*, 4:1579; and Wednesday, 2 March 1836, *J*, 5:1786.
67. Saturday, 30 September 1830, *J*, 3:1316; Tuesday–Thursday, 15, 16, 17 &c July 1834, *J*, 4:1611. For Moore's treatment of this question, see *The History of Ireland*, 4 vols (London: Longman, Brown, Green, and Longmans, 1835–46), 1:78ff, abbreviated as *HI*.
68. Wednesday, 14 September 1842, *J*, 5:2263. Moore's review of Henry O'Brien's *The Round Towers of Ireland* (1834) appeared in *ER*, 59 (April 1834), 143–54.
69. *HI*, 1:88, 89; Wednesday, 14 September 1842, *J*, 5:2263.
70. *HI*, 1:88.
71. See Karen Tongson, 'The Cultural Transnationalism of Thomas Moore's *Irish Melodies*', *Repercussions*, 9.1 (2001), 5–31; and Leith Davis, 'Irish Bards and English Consumers: Thomas Moore's "Irish Melodies" and the Colonized Nation', *ariel*, 24.2 (1993), 7–25 (11, 12).
72. *HI*, 2:336; 3:1.
73. *HI*, 4:146, 151, 162, 169, 170, 172.
74. *HI*, 3:14, 29, 65, 87; 4: 84–5, 125, 142.
75. *HI*, 3:142, 145, 152.
76. *HI*, 4:11; 3:159, 164; 4:11; Seán Patrick Dolan, '"They put to the torture all the ancient monuments": Glib Reflections on Making Eighteenth-Century Irish Legal History', in *Making Legal History: Approaches and Methodologies*, ed. Anthony Musson and Chantal Stebbings (Cambridge: Cambridge University Press, 2012), pp. 146–63 (162).
77. Thomas Osbourne Davis, 'Literary and Historical Essays', in *Thomas Davis: Selections from his Poetry and Prose* (1842; repr. New York: AMS Press, 1982), p. 191, discussed in Tongson, 'Cultural Transnationalism', 11 n5.
78. Julia M. Wright, 'Irish Literary Theory: From Politeness to Politics', in *Irish Literature in Transition, 1780–1830*, ed. Claire Connolly (Cambridge: Cambridge University Press, 2020), pp. 69–84 (69). On the politics of Gaelophilia, see also Joep Leerssen, *Mere Irish and Fíor-Ghael: Studies in the Idea of Irish Nationality* (Cork: Cork University Press, 1986), pp. 341–78; and Oliver MacDonagh, *States of Mind: A Study of Anglo-Irish Conflict 1780–1980* (Boston: Allen & Unwin, 1983), esp. Chapter 7. On the problematic nature of romantic nationalism in an Irish context, see David Dwan, 'Romantic Nationalism: History and Illusion in Ireland', *Modern Intellectual History*, 14.3 (2017), 717–45.
79. See James Quinn, *Young Ireland and the Writing of Irish History* (Dublin: UCD Press, 2015).
80. MacDonagh, *States of Mind*, pp. 1, 6. See also Guy Beiner, 'Irish Historical Studies *Avant la Lettre*: The Antiquarian Genealogy of Interdisciplinary

Scholarship', in *Routledge International Handbook of Irish Studies*, ed. Reneé Allyson Fox, Mike Cronin, and Brian Ó Conchubhair (London: Routledge, 2021), pp. 47–58. Before Ledwich, the revisionist work of Thomas Leland and John Curry had already gone some way to refuting propagandist accounts of Irish history. See Roy Foster, 'History and the Irish Question', *Transactions of the Royal Historical Society*, 33 (1983), 169–92.

81. *HI*, 1:72, 73, 157, 168.
82. *HI*, 1:136, 138 142. Moore's German translator, August Schäfer, praised the *History*'s 'depth of research and "etudes historiques"', *J*, 5:1848. The first German translation was the two-volume *Die Geschichte von Irland*, translated by Schäfer and published by Stahel in 1835, followed by another translation by Carl Uckens published by D. R. Marx in 1846. There were two French translations of Moore's work in 1835 and 1836. On *Ossian*'s elevation of 'authenticity' 'in the conceptualization of culture', see Duncan, 'Edinburgh and Lowland Scotland', p. 168.
83. See O'Halloran, *Golden Ages*, pp. 97–126; and Vance, 'Celts', 221–2.
84. *HI*, 1:72, 73, 74.
85. *HI*, 1:106–7, 16, 19, 27, 29.
86. Gibbons, 'Romantic Ireland', p. 183.
87. *HI*, 1:3, 8, 13, 15, 11.
88. *HI*, 1:187, 183, 183–4, 186–7. On the replication of classical dichotomies in representations of Ireland, see Leerssen, *Mere Irish*, p. 42.
89. James Kelly, 'Dreaming the Future while Arguing the Past: Temperaments and Temporalities in Irish Writing', in *Dreams of the Future in Nineteenth-Century Ireland*, ed. Richard J. Butler (Liverpool: Liverpool University Press, 2021), pp. 19–36; Patrick O'Malley, *Liffey & Lethe: Paramnesiac History in Nineteenth-Century Anglo-Ireland* (Oxford: Oxford University Press, 2017), p. 1.
90. 'Moore's History of Ireland', *Nation* (27 June 1846), n.p.; *HI*, 1:32, 23, 28, 47–8n51, 54, 111–12.
91. *HI*, 1:112, 113, 114; Kidd, 'Gaelic Antiquity', 1208. Even in relation to the more recent past, Moore poignantly reiterates the 'sad sameness of Irish history' in the form of the insurrections of 1798 and 1803 (1:160): 'still to this day, after a lapse of 300 years, Ireland continues to be the spot through which the whole English empire may be most easily as well as most fatally wounded' (4:6).
92. *HI*, 2:289, 296, 297.
93. *HI*, 2:13, 25, 26.
94. *HI*, 1:117, 165, 118, 315; Gibbons, 'Romantic Ireland', p. 194. See also the lack of resistance to the Anglo-Norman invasion led by Henry in the twelfth century, *HI*, 2:212, 250, 287.
95. *HI*, 1:180, 183.
96. *HI*, 2:288, 233.
97. *HI*, 1:187, 187–8, 188, 194.
98. *HI*, 1:170, 171, 317. Moore adopts an anti-feudal position, but he follows Henry Hallam in understanding Ireland's political state as more federal than feudal, *HI*, 1:173.
99. Moore argues repeatedly that Ireland is a 'special case', *HI*, 2:141.

On anachronism, see Mary Mullen, *Novel Institutions: Anachronism, Irish Novels and Nineteenth-Century Realism* (Edinburgh: Edinburgh University Press, 2019).

100. *HI*, 2:130, 142, 142–3, 171, 172. Moore notes that Irish marriage contracts were distinct in form and meaning from English ones, although he is sceptical of exceptionalist accounts of Irish religious distinctiveness, *HI*, 2:192. Moore thus rejects accounts by James Ussher and others about the uniqueness of the Irish Church. On the link between Gaelic antiquary, religious tolerance, and bridges between Catholic and Protestant traditions in the eighteenth century, see Colin Kidd, 'Gaelic Antiquity and National Identity in Englightenment Ireland and Scotland', *English Historical Review*, 434 (1994), 1197–214.
101. *HI*, 2:129, 31, 76, 127.
102. *HI*, 1:199, 120.
103. Crozier-De Rosa, 'Protest Politics', 75.
104. *HI*, 3:91, 108, 105, 124.
105. Dolan, 'Reflections', p. 161.
106. Murray Pittock, 'History and the Teleology of Civility in the Scottish Enlightenment', in *Enlightenment and Emancipation*, ed. Peter France and Susan Manning (Lewisburg, PA: Bucknell University Press, 2006), pp. 81–96 (p. 81); *HI*, 3:295, 296; 4:22, 26, 59.
107. *HI*, 4:69, 75, 76. By the reign of Charles I in the seventeenth century, the Earl of Strafford proceeds on the basis that Ireland is a conquered country and available for English colonisation, *HI*, 4:184; see also 4:208, 209, 215. See recent studies of plantation settlement in Ireland, which emphasise the fallacy of the 'civilising' programme of benign cooperation, e.g., Gerard Farrell, *The 'Mere' Irish and the Colonisation of Ulster, 1570–1641* (Basingstoke, Palgrave Macmillan, 2017).
108. *HI*, 4:225, 222, 223, 227–8, 230.
109. *HI*, 3:165, 166, 207.
110. *HI*, 4:11; 3:159, 164; 4:11.
111. Raised a Catholic, Moore's Catholicism was nominal by adulthood. His *Letter to the Roman Catholics of Dublin* (1810) expresses a compromise position, arguing that checks on papal authority were part of Ireland's Gallican tradition. See, e.g., John B. Roney, 'Negotiating the Middle Ground: Thomas Moore on Religion and Irish Nationalism', in *Representing Irish Religious Histories: Histories of the Sacred and Secular, 1700–2000*, ed. Jacqueline Hill and Mary Ann Lyons (Cham: Palgrave Macmillan, 2017), pp. 151–64.
112. *HI*, 4:260, 267, 271, 281, 282.
113. Gibbons, 'Romantic Ireland', pp. 184, 185.
114. Propagandism', *Nation* (16 Sept. 1843), n.p.; 'Moore's History of Ireland', *Nation* (27 June 1846), n.p.; 'Ecclesiastical Antiquities of Ireland', *Nation* (19 July 1845), n.p., cited in Quinn, *Young Ireland*, pp. 24, 28, 30; Gibbons, 'Romantic Ireland', pp. 184, 185. On the *Nation*, see Francesca Benatti, 'Young Ireland and the Superannuated Bard: Rewriting Thomas Moore in The Nation', in *The Reputations of Thomas Moore: Poetry, Music, and Politics*, ed. Sarah McCleave and Triona O'Hanlon (New York and London: Routledge, 2019), pp. 214–34. On Moore and Polish

nationalism, see Eoin MacWhite, 'Thomas Moore and Poland', *Proceedings of the Royal Irish Academy*, 72 (1972), 49–62; and Róisín Healy, *Poland and the Irish National Imagination, 1772–1922: Anti-Colonialism within Europe* (Basingstoke: Palgrave Macmillan, 2017). Moore had the benefit of consulting in person with antiquarians such as Thomas Crofton-Croker, Eugene O'Curry, and George Petrie but their later work, particularly Petrie's *Ecclesiastical Architecture of Ireland* (1845) on the Round Towers controversy, was generally published too late to be of use to him. See, e.g., Sunday, 14 November 1841, in *J*, 5:2208.

115. See Robert Southey, 'The Roman Catholic Question', *Quarterly Review*, 38 (Oct. 1828), 535–96; 'Inquiry into the Poor Laws, &c.', *Quarterly Review*, 8 (Dec. 1812), 319–56 (35); and 'Transactions of the Missionary Society', *Annual Review, and History of Literature; for 1803*, ed. Arthur Aiken, 2 vols (London: Longman, 1804), 2:189–201 (199).

116. Brazil imported nearly half of its consumer goods from Britain. See Rebecca Cole Heinowitz, *Spanish America and British Romanticism, 1777–1826: Rewriting Conquest* (Edinburgh: Edinburgh University Press, 2010), p. 4; Jessie Reeder, *The Forms of Informal Empire: Britain, Latin America, and Nineteenth-Century Literature* (Baltimore: Johns Hopkins University Press, 2020); and Nigel Leask, 'Southey's *Madoc*: Reimagining the Conquest of America', in *Robert Southey and the Contexts of English Romanticism*, ed. Lynda Pratt (Aldershot: Ashgate, 2006), pp. 133–50 (142). On the impact of the Peninsular War, see Robert Southey, *History of the Peninsular War*, 3 vols (London: John Murray, 1823–32), 1:1–2.

117. Diego Saglia, 'Nationalist Texts and Counter-Texts, Southey's *Roderick* and the Dissensions of the Annotated Romance', *Nineteenth-Century Literature*, 53.4 (1991), 421–51 (422); Nigel Leask, *British Romantic Writers and the East: Anxieties of Empire* (Cambridge: Cambridge University Press, 1992), pp. 97–8; Robert Southey, *History of Brazil*, 3 vols (London: Longman, Hurst, Rees, and Orme, 1810–19), 1:1, abbreviated as *HB*. See also Carol Bolton, *Writing the Empire: Robert Southey and Romantic Colonialism* (London: Pickering & Chatto, 2007), p. 179.

118. See Mônica Yumi Jinzenji and Maria de Oliveira Galvão, 'History of Brazil for the "fair sex": Appropriations of the Foreign Perspective for Nineteenth-Century Female Readers', *Revista Brasileira de Histórica*, 30 (2010), 119–36 (121); and Leslie Bethell, *Brazil by British and Irish Authors* (Oxford: Centre for Brazilian Studies, 2003).

119. Mary Louise Pratt, *Imperial Eyes: Travel Writing and Transculturation* (London and New York: Routledge, 1992), pp. 119, 121–3; Carol Bolton, '"Green Savannahs" or "savage lands": Wordsworth's and Southey's Romantic America', in *Robert Southey and the Contexts of English Romanticism*, ed. Lynda Pratt, pp. 115–32 (115–16); *HB*, 3:284–5; 1:262–3.

120. *HB*, 1:32.

121. *HB*, 1:52, 64, 80, 171, 104, 156. *Orsua* was initially intended as part of Southey's *History of Brazil*. See Rebecca Nesvet, 'Robert Southey, Historian of El Dorado', *Keats–Shelley Journal*, 61 (2012), 116–21.

122. *HB*, 2:44. Southey draws on 'four-stages' theory but he also emphasises anthropophagic rituals such as witchcraft, infanticide, promiscuity, and

cannibalism, *HB*, 1:34–5, 118–19, 224–51; 2:681; 3:398–401, 421, 773, 831; 1:218–23. On stadial theory, see Flávia Florentino Varella, 'Robert Southey, William Robertson e a teoria dos quatro estágios na construção da macronarrativa da história dos autóctones americanos', *Revista de História*, 175 (2016), 349–84. On Southey's reliance on narratives by Hans Staden and Jean de Léry, see Jinzenji and Galvão, 'History of Brazil', 122.

123. *HB*, 1:640 n66, 642 n73, 3:831; David M. Craig, *Robert Southey and Romantic Apostasy: Political Argument in Britain, 1780–1840* (Suffolk: Boydell Press, 2007), p. 146.

124. *Monthly Review*, 69 n.s. (Dec. 1812), 337–52, cited in Lionel Madden (ed.), *Robert Southey: The Critical Heritage* (London and Boston: Routledge & Kegan Paul, 1972), p. 152.

125. Pratt, *Imperial Eyes*, pp. 87, 204. On the ways in which sentimentalism has historically been co-opted to uphold dominant racial ideologies, see, e.g., Lynn Festa, *Sentimental Figures of Empire in Eighteenth-Century Britain and France* (Baltimore: Johns Hopkins University Press, 2006).

126. Tim Fulford, 'Blessed Bane: Christianity and Colonial Disease in Southey's *Tale of Paraguay*', *Romanticism on the Net*, 24 (2001), n.p., paras 9–12. Available at <https://id.erudit.org/iderudit/005998ar> (last accessed 12 June 2019). Southey is, however, less hostile to the Jesuits than his rabid anti-Catholicism would suggest: religious institutions are central to civilisation, and he therefore gives the Jesuits their due as religious pioneers in Brazil, *HB*, 1:214; 2:171; 1:251; 2:252, 268, 278; 3:372–3. In largely vindicating the Jesuits, Southey was treading a well-worn path established by Montesquieu in *De l'esprit des loix* (1748) and Robertson in his *History of America* (1777), but unlike Las Casas and Robertson, who argue against religious conversion, he insists on the superiority of Christian values, offering a critique of Jesuit behaviour only to the extent that it is dehumanising and/or ineffectual.

127. On anti-Spanish sentiment, see Diego Saglia, *Poetic Castles in Spain: British Romanticism and Figurations of Iberia* (Amsterdam and Atlanta: Rodopi, 2000), pp. 40–52 (esp. 43).

128. *HB*, 1:354, 355; 2:57; 1:373; 2:299, 694, 675; see also 2:784–5.

129. *HB*, 1:1–2, 258; Marcus Wood, *Slavery, Empathy, and Pornography* (Oxford: Oxford University Press, 2002), p. 211. On savage practices, see 1:218–23.

130. *HB*, 2:334, 362.

131. *Eclectic Review*, 6 (Sep. 1810), 788–800, cited in Madden, *Critical Heritage*, p. 149; *HB*, 3:831.

132. *HB*, 3:773; 1:318–22, 329; 2:305, 329, 376.

133. *HB*, 3:376–7; 1:326–8, 327, 329.

134. *HB*, 2:260, 261, 380, 450–504. On Southey's representation of feudalism, see R. J. Smith, *The Gothic Bequest: Medieval Institutions in British Political Thought, 1688–1863* (Cambridge: Cambridge University Press, 1987), pp. 540–8.

135. *HB*, 3:21, 773; see also 2:3471; 3:41–5, 362.

136. *HB*, 1:330; 2:643; 3:729–30; 1:330; 2:186–7, 304; see also 2:643.

137. See, e.g., *HB*, 3:878. On this point, see Valentina P. Aparicio, 'Intermarriage

in the *Quilombo*: Southey's Republic of Runway Slaves', *European Romantic Review*, 32.4 (2021), 399–418; and Karen O'Brien, 'Uneasy Settlement: Wordsworth and Emigration', in *Romanticism's Debatable Lands*, ed. Claire Lamont and Michael Rossington (Basingstoke: Palgrave Macmillan, 2007), pp. 121–35 (127).

138. See Nesvet, 'Historian of El Dorado', 120–1; *HB*, 3:128, 798.
139. Luke Gibbs, 'Great Britain and Latin America: The Romantics and Informal Empire' (PhD thesis, University of Missouri, 2013), p. 101. Southey is scathing about the greedy materialism of the Dutch West India Company, whose sole aim in Brazil is commercial speculation; and for this reason, he supports the Portuguese patriots over the Dutch in the seventeenth century, *HB*, 1:538; 2:104, 138, 658.
140. *HB*, 2:662, 186–7; Southey, *History of the Peninsular War*, 1:86; 2:503–4, 709–11; Diego Saglia, '"O My Mother Spain!": The Peninsular War, Family Matters, and the Practice of Romantic Nation-Writing', *ELH*, 65.2 (1998), 363–93 (364–5).
141. Wood, *Slavery*, pp. 210, 212, 213; Gibbs, 'Latin America', p. 92; *HB*, 2:27; 3:24.
142. *HB*, 3:29; Gibbs, 'Latin America', p. 92.
143. *HB*, 3:24.
144. Wood, *Slavery*, p. 212; *HB*, 3:696, 831; Gibbs, 'Latin America', pp. 93, 103.
145. *HB*, 3:878.
146. See, e.g., *HB*, 3:223.
147. *HB*, 3:128, 550, 294, 553.
148. See, e.g., the marriage of Goervyl to Malinal (*Madoc*, Part 2, Book 17, l:3400–7); and the possible interracial union between Madoc and Erillyab (Part 2, Book 24, l:4313–17), *Madoc*, 2 vols (London: Longman, Reese, and Orme, 1805). In many ways, Koster and Southey's accounts pre-empt the utopianism of Gilberto Freyre's later theory of 'lusotropicalismo' or the idea of successful European acclimatisation to the tropics. See, e.g., Gilberto Freyre, *New World in the Tropics: The Culture of Modern Brazil* (New York: Alfred A. Knopf, 1959), p. 6.
149. Henry Koster, *Travels in Brazil* (London: Longman, Hurst, Rees, Orme, and Brown, 1816), p. 209.
150. See Aparicio, 'Intermarriage', 399–418.
151. Ulla D. Berg and Ana Y. Ramos-Zayas, 'Racializing Affect: A Theoretical Proposition', *Current Anthropology*, 56.6 (2015), 654–77 (657). On the Brazilian ideal of whitening, see the classic Thomas E. Skidmore, *Black into White: Race and Nationality in Brazilian Thought* (New York: Oxford University Press, 1974).
152. *HB*, 3:877; Manoel Cardozo, 'England's Fated Ally', *Luso-Brazilian Review*, 7 (1970), 46–56 (46–7).
153. *Eclectic Review*, 6 (Sep. 1810), 788–800; and *Monthly Review*, 69 n.s. (Dec. 1812), 337–52, reprinted in Madden, *Critical Heritage*, pp. 148, 151. For Southey's access to manuscripts, see Robert Arthur Humphreys, *Robert Southey and his History of Brazil* (London: Hispanic and Luso Brazilian Council, 1978), p. 9.
154. Madden, *Critical Heritage*, p. 149.

155. Madden, *Critical Heritage*, p. 151; *British Critic*, 10 (March 1818), 225–45 (227).
156. Leask, 'Southey's *Madoc*', 144. See also Manuela Mourão, 'Robert Southey on Portugal: Travel Narrative and the Writing of History', *Nineteenth-Century Contexts*, 37.1 (2015), 43–60; and Maria Zulmira Castanheira, '"The best laid schemes sometimes turn out the worst": Robert Southey's Success and Failure', *Via Panorâmica*, 2 (2009), 89–100.
157. Leask, 'Southey's *Madoc*', 144. On Gibbon, see Southey's letter to Charles Wynn, 30 April 1801, in *Journals of a Residence in Portugal 1800–1801 and a Visit to France 1838*, ed. Adolfo Cabral (Oxford: Clarendon Press, 1960), p. 166. More generally, see Stuart Andrews, 'Before the Laureateship: Robert Southey as Historian', *Romanticism*, 21.1 (2015) 72–9, and *Robert Southey: History, Politics, and Religion* (Basingstoke: Palgrave Macmillan, 2011).
158. Letter to John May, 16 December 1800, in *Journals*, pp. 144–5.
159. Southey probably meant Palaye's three-volume *Histoire littéraire des troubadours* (1774), a copy of which he owned, *Journals*, p. 141n. *Selections from the Letters of Robert Southey*, ed. J. W. Warter, 4 vols (London: Longman, Brown, Green, and Longmans, 1856), 4:220.
160. *Selections from the Letters of Robert Southey*, 4:220; Nesvet, 'El Dorado', 118.
161. Tom Duggett, 'Southey's "Colloquies" and Romantic History', *The Wordsworth Circle*, 44.2/3 (2013), 87–93 (88, 91); Robert Southey and Edward Edwards, 'Hallam's *Constitutional History of England*', *Quarterly Review*, 37 (Jan. 1828), 194–260 (195).
162. Southey and Edwards, 'Hallam's Constitutional History of England', 194, cited in Craig, *Romantic Apostasy*, p. 137; Southey's letter to Thomas Southey of 23 March 1800 and his letter to William Taylor of 26 March 1800, in *Journals*, pp. 68, 69. Southey explicitly notes that he plans 'to resemble the old chroniclers' rather than 'the modern historians', *Journals*, p. 69.
163. See, e.g., Stefan Berger with Christof Conrad, *The Past as History: National Identity and Historical Consciousness in Modern Europe* (Basingstoke: Palgrave Macmillan, 2015).
164. Miranda Burgess, 'Nationalisms in Romantic Britain and Ireland: Culture, Politics, and the Global', in *A Concise Companion to the Romantic Age*, ed. Jon Klancher (Oxford: Blackwell, 2009), pp. 77–98 (95–6).

Chapter 4

1. Michael D. Hurley and Marcus Waithe, 'Introduction: Thinkers, Thinking, Style, Stylists', in *Thinking Through Style: Non-Fiction Prose of the Long Nineteenth Century*, ed. Michael D. Hurley and Marcus Waithe (Oxford: Oxford University Press, 2018), pp. 1–10 (1).
2. John Morley, 'Essay on Macaulay' (1876), in *Critical Miscellanies, Vol. 1* (London and New York: Macmillan, 1904), p. 19; Thomas De Quincey, 'Style I', *Blackwood's Edinburgh Magazine*, 48 (July 1840), 1–17. On De Quincey's 'organology', see Markus Iseli, *Thomas De Quincey and the*

Cognitive Unconscious (Basingstoke: Palgrave Macmillan, 2015), esp. p. 84.
3. Elfenbein, *Rise of English*, p. 183.
4. Michael Goldberg, '"Demigods and Philistines": Macaulay and Carlyle – A Study in Contrasts', *Studies in Scottish Literature*, 24.1 (1989), 116–28 (126). For the ways in which Carlyle mined but then subverted Macaulay's key metaphors, see Saul Isaacson, 'Carlyle and Macaulay in the Journals: Towards a New Historiography', *Carlyle Annual*, 10 (1989), 21–30; and Owen Dudley Edwards, 'Carlyle Versus Macaulay? – A Study in History', *Carlyle Studies Annual*, 27 (2011), 177–206. For the phrase 'Gothic and Gaelic confection', see *Letters of Thomas Carlyle to John Stuart Mill, John Sterling and Robert Browning*, ed. Alexander Carlyle (London: T. Fisher Unwin, 1924), p. 192.
5. Elfenbein, *Rise of English*, pp. 116, 78. See also Robert Crawford, *Devolving English Literature* (Oxford: Clarendon Press, 1992), pp. 16–44. Cf. Macaulay's own Evangelical Scottish lineage, discussed in Edwards, 'Carlyle Versus Macaulay'.
6. On Macaulay's periodical style, see, e.g., William A. Davis, Jr, '"This Is My Theory": Macaulay on Periodical Style', *Victorian Periodicals Review*, 20.1 (1987), 12–22; and G. S. Fraser, 'Macaulay's Style as an Essayist', *Review of English Literature*, 1.4 (1960), 9–19. More generally, see Peter F. Morgan, *Literary Critics and Reviewers in Early Nineteenth-Century Britain* (London: Croom Helm, 1983).
7. Jason Camlot, *Style and the Nineteenth-Century British Critic: Sincere Mannerisms* (Aldershot: Ashgate, 2008), pp. 84, 81. As Alex Watson notes, the footnote is, for De Quincey, a 'redundancy', a 'textual prosthesis' that brings to the surface uncomfortable ideological questions of absorption, wholeness, and integrity, *Romantic Marginality: Nation and Empire on the Borders of the Page* (London and New York: Routledge, 2012), esp. pp. 5–6.
8. Macaulay to Macvey Napier, 25 January 1830, *Letters of Thomas Babington Macaulay*, 1:261; Francis X. Roellinger, Jr, 'The Early Development of Carlyle's Style', *PMLA*, 72.5 (1957), 936–51 (936); Davis, '"This is My Theory"', 14, 13. Macaulay's *ER* colleagues considered his periodical style to be too contentious, which was one of the reasons that he abandoned periodical writing in favour of his *History of England*.
9. Peter Gay, *Style in History*, p. 10. Hall argues that Macaulay's essays on Robert Clive and Warren Hastings were a sort of 'clearing the decks for his *History*' for topics and people that did not belong in 'history proper', 'Macaulay's Nation', 513. See also Macaulay's comments in his letter to Napier of 1 December 1841, *Letters of Thomas Babington Macaulay*, 4:27–8.
10. David Sorensen, 'Carlyle, Macaulay, and the "Dignity of History"', *Carlyle Studies Annual*, 11 (1990), 41–52 (42, 46); Davis, '"This is My Theory"', 13–14.
11. Morley, 'Essay on Macaulay', in *Critical Miscellanies*, p. 33.
12. Morley, *Critical Miscellanies*, pp. 21, 22.
13. Morley, *Critical Miscellanies*, p. 25.

14. John Guillory, 'The Memo and Modernity', *Critical Inquiry*, 31.1 (2004), 108–32 (esp. 129–30).
15. See John L. Kijinski, 'John Morley's "English Men of Letters" Series and the Politics of Reading', *Victorian Studies*, 34.2 (1991), 205–25 (esp. 206). This view of popular writing is a more middle-brow form of the Gramscian conceptualisation of popular culture. See, e.g., Peter Burke, *Popular Culture in Early Modern Europe* (Aldershot: Ashgate, 1978), p. 1; and Niall Ó Ciosáin, *Print and Popular Culture in Ireland, 1750–1850* (Basingstoke: Palgrave Macmillan, 1997), p. 4.
16. Warren Staebler, *The Liberal Mind of John Morley* (Princeton: Princeton University Press, 1943), p. 167.
17. Elfenbein, *Rise of English*, pp. 16, 182. This was by no means the consensus among Macaulay's *Edinburgh Review* colleagues, who criticised his digressive and overly florid style. See, e.g., Joanne Shattock, 'Politics and Literature: Macaulay, Brougham, and the *Edinburgh Review* under Napier', *The Yearbook of English Studies*, 16 (1986), 32–50 (esp. 40). On the emergence of high and low cultures, see Andreas Huyssen, *After the Great Divide: Modernism, Mass Culture, Postmodernism* (Bloomington: Indiana University Press, 1986).
18. Morley, *Critical Miscellanies*, p. 22; Salmon, *Victorian Literary Profession*, p. 9; Borislav Knezevic, *Figures of Finance Capitalism: Writing, Class and Capital in Mid-Victorian Narratives* (New York and London: Routledge, 2003), p. 44. See also Marco de Waard, '"The Morality of Style": John Morley as Essayistic Liberal', *Nineteenth-Century Prose*, 43.1–2 (2016), 227–44.
19. T. B. Macaulay, 'Hallam's *Constitutional History*', *ER*, 48 (Sep. 1828), 96–169; *CHE*, 1:116, 117, 118. On Hallam's mischaracterisation as a 'rationalist Voltairean hangover', see Burrow, *Liberal Descent*, pp. 30–3.
20. Letter from Hallam to Lord Webb Seymour, 5 November 1813, in Guendolen Ramsden (ed.), *Correspondence of Two Brothers: Edward Adolphus, Eleventh Duke of Somerset, and his Brother, Lord Webb Seymour, 1800–1819 and After* (London: Longmans Green, 1906), p. 124.
21. Michael Bentley, 'Henry Hallam Revisited', *The Historical Journal*, 55.2 (2012), 453–73 (462). For a different view, see Duncan Forbes, *The Liberal Anglican Idea of History* (Cambridge: Cambridge University Press, 1952), pp. vii–viii, 15, 124.
22. Bentley, 'Henry Hallam Revisited', 467; *CHE*, 1:115.
23. Rex W. Mixon, Jr, 'Bentham, Science and Utility', *Revue d'études benthamiennes*, 18 (2020). Available at <https://journals.openedition.org/etudes-benthamiennes/8127> (last accessed 1 January 2021).
24. T. B. Macaulay, 'Mill's Essay on Government', *ER*, 49 (June 1829), 273–99 (287). On J. S. Mill's response to this debate, see Rosario López, 'John Stuart Mill's Idea of History: A Rhetoric of Progress', *Res Publica*, 27 (2012), 63–74.
25. *CHE*, 3:39, 33–4; *Selections from the Edinburgh Review*, ed. Maurice Cross, 4 vols (London: Rees, Orme, Brown, Green, & Longman, 1833), 2:139, 140, abbreviated as *S*. On Mill's *British India*, see Javed Majeed, *Ungoverned Imaginings: James Mill's "History of British India" and Orientalism* (Oxford: Clarendon Press, 1992).

26. Michael Stuckey, 'Francis Palgrave's Historico-Legal World of Science and Theology', *Legal Roots*, 3 (2015), 297–312, and 'The Study of English National History by Sir Francis Palgrave: The Original Use of the National Records in an Imaginative Historical Narrative', *Law, Culture and Humanities*, 15.2 (2019), 421–47 (436).
27. *CHE*, 1:115. Hallam's emphasis on the practical lessons of history also points to the influence of German intellectual life on his work. See, e.g., Rosemary Ashton, *The German Idea: Four English Writers and the Reception of German Thought 1800–1860* (Cambridge: Cambridge University Press, 1980).
28. *CHE*, 3:35.
29. James Mackintosh, 'Sismondi's *History of France*', *ER*, 35 (July 1821), 488–509 (492). Thomas Moore noted that Mackintosh defended novel reading, describing Mackintosh's 'way of putting things' as *'feelosophic'*, Sunday, 22 October 1837, *J*, 5:1927.
30. *S*, 2:118, 124; see also *CHE*, 1:113.
31. O'Brien, *Narratives of Enlightenment*, p. 7; *CHE*, 2:209; *S*, 2:123.
32. Bann, *Clothing of Clio*, p. 121; Meisel, *Realizations*, p. 211; Walter Scott, 'Ellis and Ritson', *ER*, 7 (Jan. 1806), 387–413; *S*, 2:143, 141.
33. E. P. Thompson, 'History from Below', *TLS*, 3345 (7 April 1966), pp. 279–80.
34. *S*, 2:143, 124; White, *Metahistory*, p. 67; Barthes, 'The Reality Effect'. Foteini Lika demonstrates the extent to which Macaulay drew on fiction as an evidentiary source, 'Fact and Fancy in Nineteenth-Century Historiography and Fiction: The Case of Macaulay and Roidis', in *The Making of the Humanities*, pp. 149–66 (155). See also Beverley Southgate, 'Macaulay 1828: History, Biography, and Portraiture', *Rethinking History*, 20.4 (2016), 544–55 (547).
35. *S*, 2:124.
36. *S*, 2:118.
37. *S*, 2:124.
38. *The History of England, from the Accession of James II*, 5 vols (Philadelphia: Porter & Coates, n.d.), Project Gutenberg EBook #1468, produced by Ken West and David Widger, 3:12n, abbreviated as *HE*.
39. Knezevic, *Finance Capitalism*, p. 55; Hall, 'Macaulay's Nation', 507, 506, 519. See also Jane Rendell, 'Scottish Orientalism: From Robertson to James Mill', *The Historical Journal*, 25.1 (1983), 43–69.
40. Francis Jeffrey qtd in Hall, 'Macaulay's Nation', 519.
41. J. S. Mill, *Collected Works of J. S. Mill*, ed. J. A. Robson et al. 31 vols (Toronto: University of Toronto Press, 1963–1991), 14:6, 27; Walter Bagehot, *The Works: Volume 2*, ed. Mrs Russell Barrington (London: Longmans, Green & Co., 1915), pp. 106, 122; Harriet Martineau, 'Lord Macaulay', *Daily News* (31 Dec. 1859), p. 5; Morley, *Critical Miscellanies*, p. 32.
42. *HE*, 3:601–2; 2:550. On Macaulay's character sketches, see, e.g., 'The History of England', *North American Review*, 93 (Oct. 1861), 418–56.
43. Bagehot, *The Works: Volume 2*, pp. 99, 100, 103.
44. Charles Firth, *A Commentary on Macaulay's History of England* (1938; repr. Abingdon: Frank Cass & Co., 1964), pp. 34, 35. Macaulay sought

to mitigate polemic by replacing classical orations with what he called 'declamatory disquisitions' or a written summary of arguments. See, e.g., *HE*, 1:165–6.
45. Macaulay's revival of 'straightforward narration' was a response to Gibbon, who Macaulay believed had brought into fashion 'an unpleasant trick of telling a story by implication and allusion', *CHE*, 1:115.
46. Elizabeth van Dendem Lecky, *A Memoir of the Right Honourable William Edward Hartpole Lecky* (London: Longmans, Green and Co., 1909), p. 130; J. R. Seeley, *Lectures and Essays* (London: Macmillan, 1870), pp. 98–9; Herman Merivale, 'Carlyle, *The French Revolution*', *ER*, 71 (July 1840), 411–45 (412).
47. Knezevic, *Finance Capitalism*, p. 48.
48. Levine, *Boundaries of Fiction*, p. 126.
49. 'Hallam', *CHE*, 1:117.
50. Rohan Amanda Maitzen, '"This Feminine Preserve": Historical Biographies by Victorian Women', *Victorian Studies*, 38.3 (1995), 371–93 (380).
51. James Moncreiff, 'Macaulay's History of England', *ER*, 90 (July 1849) 249–92 (253); Archibald Alison, 'Macaulay's History of England', *Blackwood's Edinburgh Magazine*, 65 (April 1849), 383–405 (402); Gay, *Style in History*, p. 117; John Clive, *Not by Fact Alone: Essays on the Writing and Reading of History* (New York: Alfred Knopf, 1989), p. 10. Bagehot was a dissenting voice, objecting to 'small men' being 'so largely described' and arguing against 'the superficies of circumstance, the scum of events', *The Works: Volume 2*, p. 125.
52. Alison, 'Macaulay's History of England', 402.
53. Knezevic, *Finance Capitalism*, p. 47.
54. Bagehot, *The Works: Volume 2*, p. 119.
55. Bagehot, *The Works: Volume 2*, p. 120; Knezevic, *Finance Capitalism*, p. 47.
56. *HE*, 3:133–4. On epic structure, see Adams, *Liberal Epic*, esp. pp. 161–3.
57. *HE*, 1:57, 54, 52, 180.
58. *HE*, 2:416–7.
59. James Mackintosh, *The History of England, Vol. I* (London: Longman, Rees, Orme, Brown & Green and J. Taylor, 1830), p. 109. See Gust, 'Empire, Exile, Identity', pp. 232–3.
60. *HE*, 1:143–4, 144.
61. See Mary Mullen, 'How the Irish Became Settlers: Metaphors of Indigeneity and the Erasure of Indigenous People', *New Hibernia Review*, 20.3 (2016), 81–96.
62. Joep Leerssen, 'Ethnography and Ethnicity: English'. Available at <https://ernie.uva.nl/viewer.p/21/56/object/122-160545> (last accessed 2 July 2020); Roberto Romani, 'British Views on Irish National Character, 1800–1846. An Intellectual History', *History of European Ideas*, 23.5–6 (1997), 193–219 (197, 202, 209). See also John Clive, *Thomas Babington Macaulay. The Shaping of the Historian* (London: Knopf, 1973), pp. 105–24.
63. Romani, 'British Views on Irish National Character', 209. See Mill's stadialist view of the 'Irish Question' in 'State of Ireland', *ER*, 21 (July 1813),

340–64, and *The History of British India*, 3 vols (London: Baldwin, Cradock and Joy, 1817), 1:312–15. More generally, see Robert Phillipson, *Linguistic Imperialism* (Oxford: Oxford University Press, 1992).
64. CME, 2:229.
65. On the 'novelistic' nature of Macaulay's style, see Levine, *Boundaries of Fiction*, pp. 109–22; David Fong, 'Macaulay: The Essayist as Historian', *Dalhousie Review*, 51 (1971), 38–48; and William A. Madden, 'Macaulay's Style', in *The Art of Victorian Prose*, ed. George Levine and William A. Madden (New York: Oxford University Press, 1968), pp. 127–53.
66. Knezevic, *Finance Capitalism*, p. 44.
67. 7 December 1849, *The Journals of Thomas Babington Macaulay*, ed. William Thomas, 5 vols (London: Pickering & Chatto, 2008), 2:180.
68. *New Letters of Thomas Carlyle*, ed. Alexander Carlyle, 2 vols (London: J. Lane, 1904), 2:120.
69. Salmon, *Victorian Literary Profession*, pp. 64–5; CL, 7:264. Carlyle and his friends characterised the early failure of *Sartor Resartus* as one of audience rather than of merit. See, e.g., Emerson to Carlyle, 14 May 1834, CL, 8:135. On 'Carlylese', see Malcolm Ingram, 'Carlylese', *Occasional Papers 26: The Carlyle Society* (Edinburgh: Carlyle Society, 2013), pp. 5–20. Available at <https://www.ed.ac.uk/files/atoms/files/carlyle_papers_no._26.pdf> (last accessed 19 November 2020).
70. Campbell, 'Carlyle: Style and Sense', 19; Lee, *Nationalism and Irony*, pp. 106, 107n.
71. *Letters of Thomas Babington Macaulay*, ed. Thomas Pinney, 6 vols (Cambridge: Cambridge University Press, 1981), 2:113.
72. For Wordsworth's comments, see W. H. Wylie, *Thomas Carlyle: The Man and his Books* (London: Marshall Japp, 1881), p. 381; and Ralph Waldo Emerson, *The Works of Ralph Waldo Emerson in 12 Volumes, Fireside Edition, Vol. 5 English Traits* (Boston and New York: n. pub., 1909), p. 279.
73. Charles Richard Sanders, 'Carlyle and Wordsworth', *Browning Institute Studies*, 9 (1981), 115–22.
74. Joanna Malecka, 'Thomas Carlyle's Calvinist Dialogue with the Nineteenth-Century Periodical Press', *History of European Ideas*, 45.1 (2019), 15–32 (29). Barton Swaim, Ian Campbell, Ralph Jessop, and others have made a strong case for the Scottishness of Carlyle's style and thought. See, e.g., Campbell, 'Carlyle: Style and Sense'; Barton Swaim, 'Thomas Carlyle's Sermons', 137–58, and *Scottish Men of Letters and the New Public Sphere, 1802–1834* (Lewisburg, PA: Bucknell University Press, 2009), esp. pp. 162–5; and Ralph Jessop, *Carlyle and Scottish Thought* (Basingstoke: Palgrave Macmillan, 1997).
75. Malecka, 'Calvinist Dialogue', 15, 17.
76. See Joanna Malecka, 'The Ethics, Aesthetics and Politics of Thomas Carlyle's "French Revolution"' (PhD thesis, University of Glasgow, 2017), esp. p. 148. Available at <http://theses.gla.ac.uk/8182/1/2016MaleckaPhD.pdf> (last accessed 12 November 2020). See also J. G. A. Pocock, *Virtue, Commerce, and History: Essays on Political Thought and History, Chiefly in the Eighteenth Century* (Cambridge:

Cambridge University Press, 1985), p. 236; Burrow, *Liberal Descent*, p. 47; and Kidd, *Subverting Scotland's Past*, p. 200.
77. Lowell T. Frye, '"Leaving Blair's Lectures Quite Behind": Thomas Carlyle's Rhetorical Revolution', *Occasional Papers 26: The Carlyle Society* (Edinburgh: Carlyle Society, 2013), pp. 21–43 (26). Available at <https://www.ed.ac.uk/files/atoms/files/carlyle_papers_no._26.pdf> (last accessed 19 November 2020). See also Kidd, 'North Britishness', 361–82; and Gust, 'Empire, Exile, Identity', pp. 17–18.
78. See Carlyle's own rejection of Friedrich Althaus's description of his 'Germanized, Jean Paulized style' in *Unsere Zeit* in 1866: 'Edward Irving and his admiration of the Old Puritans & Elizabethans . . . played a much more important part than Jean-Paul on my poor "style"; – & the most important part by far was that of Nature, you would perhaps say, had you ever heard my Father speak, or very often heard my Mother & her inborn melodies of heart and of voice!,' cited in *Two Reminiscences of Thomas Carlyle*, ed. John Clubbe (Durham, NC: Duke University Press, 1974), pp. 58–60, 59.
79. Carlyle to Sterling, 4 June 1835, *CL*, 8:134. On 'making words', see Carlyle to Mill, *CL*, 9:16; Carlyle to Sterling, *CL*, 8:135; and Carlyle to Emerson, *CL*, 7:264.
80. Crawford, *Devolving English Literature*, esp. p. 18. See also Janet Sorensen, *The Grammar of Empire in Eighteenth-Century British Writing* (Cambridge: Cambridge University Press, 2000).
81. Elfenbein, *Rise of English*, pp. 20, 21, 22, 30.
82. 'On the Styles of Hume, Gibbon, and Robertson', *Gentleman's Magazine*, 102 (Jan., Feb., and April 1832), 17–23 (23), 121–6, 313–17.
83. William Makepeace Thackeray, 'Carlyle's *French Revolution*', *Times* (3 Aug. 1837), p. 6, repr. in *Thomas Carlyle: The Critical Heritage*, pp. 69–75.
84. As Frye notes, Carlyle's early letters reveal 'a young writer experimenting with a voice and style very much in the mode Blair advocated', 'Carlyle's Rhetorical Revolution', p. 23.
85. Carlyle to Robert Mitchell, *Early Letters of Thomas Carlyle*, ed. Charles E. Norton (New York and London: Macmillan & Co., 1886), pp. 20–1.
86. Carlyle to James Johnstone, *Early Letters*, p. 144.
87. Cited in Lee, *Nationalism and Irony*, p. 18.
88. *CL*, 9:15.
89. Leerssen, 'Englishness', 66, 67; Carlyle, 'The Repeal of the Union', *Examiner* (29 April 1848), 275–6. It is notable that Carlyle imbues his discussions of Scottish culture with a cultural relativism that he fails to extend to Ireland in 'The Repeal of the Union'. See Lee, *Nationalism and Irony*, p. 145.
90. Leerssen, 'Englishness', 65. See also Seamus Deane, *Celtic Revivals: Essays in Modern Irish Literature, 1880–1890* (London: Faber and Faber, 1985), p. 14.
91. Davis, 'Irish Bards and English Consumers', 22.
92. Oded Y. Steinberg, '"Contesting Teutomania": Robert Gordon Latham, "Race", Ethnology and Historical Migrations', *Journal of European Ideas*, (2021), 1–17 (6–7). Available at <https://doi.org/10.1080/01916599.2021.1894592> (last accessed 7 October 2021); Leerssen, 'Englishness', 63.

93. Hedva Ben-Israel, *English Historians on the French Revolution* (Cambridge: Cambridge University Press, 1968), pp. 4, 8–18; Carlyle, 'Signs of the Times', *CME*, 2:159. On Carlyle's prophetic and providential mode, see also Marylu Hill, '"History is a Real Prophetic Manuscript": Reason and Revelation in Thomas Carlyle's Historical Essays', *Literature and Belief*, 25.1 (2005), 1–16.
94. Vanden Bossche, *Search for Authority*, p. 59.
95. *R*, p. 11; Vanden Bossche, *Search for Authority*, p. 11; Raymond Williams, *Culture and Society: 1780–1950* (Harmondsworth: Penguin, 1963), p. 87. For Carlyle's similar attitude to the English Civil Wars, see John Morrow, 'Heroes and Constitutionalists: The Ideological Significance of Thomas Carlyle's Treatment of the English Revolution', *History of Political Thought*, 14.2 (1993), 205–23.
96. Malecka, 'Carlyle's Calvinist Dialogue', 30.
97. See John M. Ulrich, *Signs of Their Times: History, Labor, and the Body in Cobbett, Carlyle, and Disraeli* (Athens: Ohio University Press, 2002).
98. Pamela McCallum, 'Misogyny, the Great Man, and Carlyle's *The French Revolution*: The Epic as Pastiche', *Cultural Critique*, 14 (1989–90), 153–78 (160).
99. 'Signs of the Times', *CME*, 2:14, cited in Lee, *Nationalism and Irony*, pp. 123, 133.
100. See, e.g., Robert Darnton, *Mesmerism and the End of the Enlightenment in France* (New York: Schocken Books, 1968).
101. Chris R. Vanden Bossche, 'Chartism, Class Discourse, and the Captain of Industry: Social Agency in *Past and Present*', in *Thomas Carlyle Resartus: Reappraising Carlyle's Contribution to the Philosophy of History, Political Theory, and Cultural Criticism*, ed. Paul E. Kerry and Marylu Hill (Madison, NJ: Fairleigh Dickinson University Press, 2010), pp. 30–48; Thomas Carlyle, *The French Revolution: A History*, introd. John D. Rosenberg (New York: The Modern Library, 2002), p. 97, abbreviated as *FR*; see also Marylu Hill, 'Of Bricklayers and Kings: Burke, Carlyle, and the Defense of Monarchy', in *Thomas Carlyle Resartus*, ed. Kerry and Hill, pp. 18–105.
102. Plotz, 'Crowd Power', 90, 97.
103. Barbara Barrow, 'Speaking the Social Body: Language-Origins and Thomas Carlyle's *The French Revolution*', *Journal of Victorian Culture*, 19.1 (2014), 79–92 (87); Desaulniers, *Carlyle and the Economics of Terror*, p. 8; L. M. Findlay, '"Maternity must forth": The Poetics and Politics of Gender in Carlyle's *French Revolution*', *Dalhousie Review*, 66.1&2 (1986), 130–54 (130); Mark Cumming, *A Disimprisoned Epic: Form and Vision in Carlyle's "French Revolution"* (Philadelphia: Pennsylvania University Press, 1988), p. 157.
104. McCallum, 'Misogyny', 156, 157, 159.
105. J. S. Mill, 'French Revolution – Scott's *Life of Napoleon*', *London and Westminster Review*, 9 (April 1828), 313–28 (326). More generally, see Mary Poovey, *Making a Social Body: British Cultural Formation 1830–1864* (Chicago: University of Chicago Press, 1995), pp. 7–8.
106. J. S. Mill, '*The French Revolution*', *London and Westminster Review*, 27

(July 1837), 17–53 (18, 17, 22); Meisel, *Realizations*, pp. 212–13; Lee, *Nationalism and Irony*, p. 118.
107. David Sorensen, '"Natural Supernaturalism": Carlyle's Redemption of the Past in *The French Revolution*', *Revue LISA*, 7.3 (2009), para. 5. Available at <https://journals.openedition.org/lisa/132> (last accessed 3 July 2019); Ruth Scurr, '"The greatest irregular": Thomas Carlyle's Re-creative Purpose in *The French Revolution*', in *Thinking Through Style*, pp. 87–105 (93).
108. CL, 8:209; 9:116.
109. Merivale, 'Carlyle on the *French Revolution*', 412, 411.
110. Merivale, 'Carlyle on the *French Revolution*', 412.
111. Barrow, 'Speaking the Social Body', 79, 81, 82; John B. Lamb, 'The Paper Age: Currency, Crisis, and Carlyle', *Prose Studies*, 30.1 (2008), 27–44 (41).
112. Williams, *Marxism and Literature*, p. 59.
113. FR, p. 48.
114. Barrow, 'Speaking the Social Body', 83; Malecka, 'Ethics, Aesthetics and Politics', p. 138; FR, p. 73.
115. FR, pp. 484, 244.
116. Barrow, 'Speaking the Social Body', 87.
117. See, e.g., John Shovlin, *The Political Economy of Virtue: Luxury, Patriotism, and the Origins of the French Revolution* (Ithaca, NY: Cornell University Press, 2006).
118. Lee, *Nationalism and Irony*, pp. 113–4; Lamb, 'The Paper Age', 28–9, 29.
119. FR, p. 1171; Desaulniers, *Economics of Terror*, p. 17. This 'true Constitution' is something different to the unthinking Burkean allegiance to habit, that formulaic 'unwritten Code' that Carlyle rejects as little more than artifice (FR, p. 107).
120. Vanden Bossche, *Search for Authority*, pp. 63–4, 81–2, 82; Desaulniers, *Economics of Terror*, p. 8; FR, p. 1745.
121. FR, p. 1944.
122. Richard D. Altick, 'Carlyle's Past and Present: Topicality as Technique', in *Writers, Readers, and Occasions: Selected Essays on Victorian Literature and Life* (Columbus: Ohio State University Press, 1989), pp. 38–51; Carlyle to Emerson, 1835, CL, 8:123. As in Burke's *Reflections*, the national chaos in *French Revolution* is a both an emotional and a gendered one, with the destabilising effects of famine and hunger, feminised in Book 7, 'The Insurrection of Women', contained within a larger 'patriarchal narrative economy' that ultimately promises to restore the male-dominated balance of gender relations. See McCallum, 'Misogyny', 141–2; and Henriette M. Morelli, '"An Incarnated Word": A Revisionary Reading of "The Insurrection of Women" in Thomas Carlyle's *The French Revolution*', *Women's Studies*, 34.7 (2005), 533–50.
123. See Catherine Heyrendt-Sherman, 'Re-presenting the French Revolution: The Impact of Carlyle's Work on British Society and its Self-representation', *French Journal of British Studies*, 15.4 (2010), n.p. Available at <https://doi.org/10.4000/rfcb.6118> (last accessed 2 June 2019).
124. FR, p. 1997; Lee, *Nationalism and Irony*, pp. 32, 103, 112, 118, 115.
125. Plotz, 'Crowd Power', 97, 98.
126. Levine, *The Amateur and the Professional*, p. 3.

127. Cited in Edwards, 'Carlyle Versus Macaulay?', 184.
128. Perez Zagorin, 'Thomas Carlyle and Oliver Cromwell', in *Historians and Ideologues: Essays in Honour of Donald R. Kelley*, ed. Anthony Grafton and J. H. M. Salmon (Rochester, NY: University of Rochester Press, 2001), pp. 231–58 (231, 233). For an excellent rebuttal of the idea that Carlyle's position is proto-postmodernism focusing on his hermeneutic perspectivism, see Anger, *Victorian Interpretation*, esp. pp. 74–5, 83.
129. Sorensen, 'Natural Supernaturalism', para. 3.
130. J. R. Seeley, 'History and Politics I', *Macmillan's Magazine*, 40 (Aug. 1879), 289–99 (292, 291–2).
131. Seeley, 'History and Politics I', 291–2; Siskin, *Work of Writing*, p. 114; Hesketh, 'Froude's Disease', 374–5.
132. Adams, *Liberal Epic*, pp. 142, 143, 155–6, 98; Jon Klancher, 'The Vocation of Criticism and the Crisis of the Republic of Letters', in *The Cambridge History of Literary Criticism, Vol. 5: Romanticism*, ed. Marshall Brown (Cambridge: University of Cambridge Press, 2000), pp. 296–320 (312).
133. Salmon, *Victorian Literary Profession*, pp. 214–15.
134. Salmon, *Victorian Literary Profession*, pp. 56, 55, 56, 59.
135. Carlyle was interested in the chair of moral philosophy at the University of London in 1827, as well as considering the Regius Professorship of Rhetoric and Belles Lettres at the University of St Andrews. In 1834, he unsuccessfully applied for a position as Professor of Astronomy at the University of Edinburgh, and was ultimately elected to the honorary position of Lord Rector at Edinburgh University in 1866. See Frye, 'Carlyle's Rhetorical Revolution', p. 34.
136. Valenza, *Intellectual Disciplines*, pp. 5, 4; CHE, 1:138; 2:3, 4.
137. Trela, 'Carlyle, Primary Research and the Book Clubs', esp. 76; Rosenberg, *Carlyle and the Burden of History*, p. 16; Heather Henderson, 'Carlyle and the Book Clubs: A New Approach to Publishing?', *Publishing History*, 6 (1979), 37–62 (46); Foster MS cited in Henderson, 'Book Clubs', 44.
138. Ina Ferris, 'Printing the Past: Walter Scott's Bannatyne Club and the Antiquarian Document', *Romanticism*, 11.2 (2005), 143–60 (144, 146, 148).
139. Trela, *A History*, pp. 120, 81. On Carlyle's documentary research, see John Morrow, *Thomas Carlyle* (London: Hambledon Continuum, 2006), p. 166; and Rosenberg, *Burden of History*, pp. 140–1.
140. Leslie Stephen, 'Thomas Carlyle', *Cornhill Magazine*, 43 (March 1881), 349–58.
141. Cumming, *Carlyle Encyclopedia*, p. 362.
142. Sorensen, 'Natural Supernaturalism', para. 11.
143. Levine, *The Amateur and the Professional*, p. 3.

Chapter 5

1. See, e.g., John Gross, *The Rise and Fall of the Man of Letters: Aspects of English Literary Life Since 1800* (London: Weidenfeld and Nicolson, 1969).
2. Valenza, *Intellectual Disciplines*, pp. 1, 4.
3. CHE, 1:154.

4. T. W. Heyck, 'From Men of Letters to Intellectuals: The Transformation of Intellectual Life in Nineteenth-Century England', *Journal of British Studies*, 20.1 (1980), 158–83 (167).
5. See, e.g., Salmon, *Victorian Literary Profession*.
6. See Ina Ferris, *Book-Men, Book Clubs, and the Romantic Literary Sphere* (Basingstoke: Palgrave Macmillan, 2015). On the influence of antiquarian book clubs on 'the organizational revolution in Scottish historiography', see Kidd, *Subverting Scotland's Past*, p. 255.
7. Siskin, *Work of Writing*, p. 98.
8. Valenza, *Intellectual Disciplines*, pp. 6, 5–6.
9. Nicholas Dames, 'On Not Close Reading: The Prolonged Excerpt as Victorian Critical Protocol', in *The Feeling of Reading: Affective Experience and Victorian Literature*, ed. Rachael Ablow (Ann Arbor: University of Michigan Press, 2010), pp. 11–26 (14–15); Siskin, *Work of Writing*, p. 99. For institutional studies that largely ignore the tradition of essayists and reviewers, see, e.g., Levine, *The Amateur and the Professional*, p. 3. For looser definitions of the historian, see, e.g., Jann, *Art and Science*, pp. 126–7, 216; Rolf Torstendahl, *The Rise and Propagation of Professional History* (New York: Routledge, 2015), esp. pp. 7–11, 42–54; and Ian Hesketh, *The Science of History in Victorian Britain: Making the Past Speak* (London: Pickering & Chatto 2006).
10. See the definition of 'discipline' in Valenza, *Intellectual Disciplines*, pp. 5–6. On professionalisation, see, e.g., T. W. Heyck, *The Transformation of Intellectual Life in Victorian England* (New York: St Martin's Press, 1982); Collini, *Public Moralists*; Peter Slee, *Learning and a Liberal Education: The Study of Modern History in the Universities of Oxford, Cambridge and Manchester, 1880–1914* (Manchester: Manchester University Press, 1986); and Reba Soffer, *Discipline and Power: The University, History, and the Making of an English Elite* (Cambridge: Cambridge University Press, 1994).
11. Valenza, *Intellectual Disciplines*, pp. 124, 123, 122; Leslie Howsam, 'Academic Discipline', 526.
12. William Christie, 'The Modern Athenians: The *Edinburgh Review* in the Knowledge Economy of the Early Nineteenth Century', *Studies in Scottish Literature*, 39.1 (2013), 115–18; Elizabeth Carolyn Miller, 'Reading in Review: The Victorian Book Review in the New Media Moment', *Victorian Periodicals Review*, 49.4 (2016), 626–42 (626); Walter Bagehot, 'The First Edinburgh Reviewers' (1855), in *Literary Studies*, ed. Richard Holt Hutton, 2 vols (London: Longmans, Green & Co, 1884), 1:5–6.
13. 'Advertisement', *ER*, 1 (Oct. 1802), n.p.; Henry Hallam, 'Lingard's History of England', *ER*, 53 (March 1831), 1–42 (17).
14. Guillroy, 'The Memo and Modernity', 112. On the inclusion of 'the superior magazines, and the quality newspapers' within the field of 'higher journalism', see Christopher Kent, 'Higher Journalism and the Mid-Victorian Clerisy', *Victorian Studies*, 13.2 (1969), 181–98 (181); and David Blaine Walker, 'Periodicals in Transition: Politics and Style in Victorian Higher Journalism' (PhD Thesis, University of Arkansas, 2018). On readership and circulation, see Alvar Ellegard, *The Readership of the Periodical Press in Mid-Victorian Britain* (Gothenburg: Almqvist and Wiksell, 1957). For

a more inclusive view that argues for the period's emphasis on making history accessible, see Leslie Howsam, 'Mediated Histories: How Did Victorian Periodicals Parse the Past', *Victorian Periodicals Review*, 50.4 (2017), 802–24.
15. Mark Parker, *Literary Magazines and British Romanticism* (Cambridge: Cambridge University Press, 2000), p. 3.
16. Hannah Lawrance, 'Francis Palgrave's *A History of England*', *Athenaeum*, 183 (30 April 1831), 277–9 (277). Lawrance specialised in reviews of early English history. See Joanne Wilkes, *Women Reviewing Women in Nineteenth-Century Britain: The Critical Reception of Jane Austen, Charlotte Brontë and George Eliot* (Farnham: Ashgate, 2010), pp. 58–68.
17. Magali Sarfatti Larson, *The Rise of Professionalism: A Sociological Analysis* (Berkeley: University of California Press, 1979), pp. 41–3, cited in Siskin, *Work of Writing*, p. 116.
18. Larson, *The Rise of Professionalism*, pp. 13, 17.
19. Henry Hallam, 'Francis Palgrave's *Rise and Progress* and *History of England*', *ER*, 55 (Jan. 1832), 305–37 (336).
20. Herman Merivale, 'Thirlwall's *History of Greece*', *ER*, 62 (Oct. 1835), 83–108 (83); David Welsh, 'George Waddington's *History of the Church from the Earlier Ages to the Reformation* (1833)', *ER*, 62 (Oct. 1835), 132–66 (133, 139).
21. Edward Lytton Bulwer, *England and the English* (Paris: Gagliani and Co., 1837), p. 217.
22. Levine, *The Amateur and the Professional*, p. 6; Leslie Howsam, *Past into Print: The Publishing of History in Britain* (London and Toronto: British Library and the University of Toronto Press, 2009), p. 45.
23. Howsam, 'Academic Discipline', 526
24. See, e.g., Welsh, 'Waddington's *History of the Church*', 139.
25. Mackintosh, *History of England, Volume I*, p. v.
26. 'James's *History of Charlemagne*', *Athenaeum*, 247 (21 July 1832), 467–8 (468). All volumes of the *Athenaeum* for 1832 are unmarked and therefore remain unattributed.
27. Seeley, 'History and Politics I', 291–2.
28. Lawrance, 'Palgrave's *History of England*', 278.
29. T. B. Macaulay, '*A History of the War of the Succession in Spain* by Lord Mahon', *ER*, 56 (Jan. 1833), 499–543 (499).
30. James Stephen, '*History of the Great Reformation of the Sixteenth Century, in Germany, Switzerland &c* by J. H. Merle D'Aubigne', *ER*, 68 (Jan. 1839), 273–315 (315).
31. John Allen, 'Lingard's *History of England*', *ER*, 42 (April 1825), 1–31 (2).
32. Linda Dowling, 'Roman Decadence and Victorian Historiography', *Victorian Studies*, 28.4 (1985), 579–607 (589). See also Thomas Arnold, 'Romische Geschichte, von B. G. Niebuhr. History of Rome', *Quarterly Review*, 32 (June 1825), 67–92.
33. Valenza, *Intellectual Disciplines*, p. 97.
34. Susan Manning, 'Walter Scott, Antiquarianism, and the Political Discourse of the *Edinburgh Review*, 1802–11', in *British Romanticism and the Edinburgh Review: Bicentenary Essays*, ed. Massimiliano Demata and

Duncan Wu (Basingstoke: Palgrave Macmillan, 2002), pp. 10–23 (102, 104, 105, 112).
35. Ferris notes that the Bannatyne Club published forty-three volumes between 1823 and 1832, 'Printing the Past', 158 n8.
36. John Allen, '*Documents and Records Illustrating the History of Scotland. Collected and Edited by Francis Palgrave*', *ER*, 66 (Oct. 1837), 36–59 (37).
37. William Christie, *The Edinburgh Review in the Literary Culture of Romantic Britain: Mammoth and Megalonyx* (London and Brookfield: Pickering & Chatto, 2009), p. 7; Massimiliano Demata, 'Prejudiced Knowledge: Travel Literature in the *Edinburgh Review*', in *British Romanticism and the Edinburgh Review*, pp. 85–6; 'Advertisement', *ER*, 1 (Oct. 1802), n.p. On the selectivity of the *Edinburgh Review*, see Ina Ferris, 'The Debut of the *Edinburgh Review*, 1802', *BRANCH: Britain, Representation and Nineteenth-Century History*, ed. Dino Franco Felluga. Available at <http://www.branchcollective.org/?ps_articles=ina-ferris-the-debut-of-the-edinburgh-review-1802> (last accessed 2 July 2019).
38. Miller, 'Reading in Review', 627.
39. There are no new publications listed for these volumes: 43, 44, 52. The following volumes appear to consolidate new titles every six or eight months rather than quarterly: 46, 47, 48, 49, 50, 54, 57, 59, 60. On the mechanism for inclusion in the list, see *ER*, 46 (Oct. 1827), 527.
40. 'Novels, Tales, and Romances' total around 453 texts from 1820 to 1825 and around 907 texts from the final quarter of 1826 to January 1840.
41. William Lane's *Manners of Modern Egypt* (1836) is listed as a historical work primarily because it has 'not the hasty and superficial production of a passing traveller', James Browne, 'Lane's *Manners of Modern Egypt*', *ER*, 65 (April 1837), 146–73 (147).
42. J. A. Roebuck, 'Military Education', *ER*, 49 (June 1829), 388–420 (392).
43. Historical texts are not reviewed as frequently as travelogues in the *ER*. See Demata, 'Prejudiced Knowledge', pp. 82–101. Between 1822 and 1824 there are at least four volumes in which no works of history are reviewed. Between 1825 and 1826, the only works reviewed are the early volumes of Lingard's *History of England*. While more histories are reviewed in the 1830s than in the 1820s, relatively few are considered worthy of notice, with Hallam noting that 'the progress of historical literature, in its higher departments, might long be considered rather slow', 'Lingard's *History of England*', 1.
44. T. B. Macaulay, '*History of the Revolution in England in 1668* by James Mackintosh', *ER*, 61 (July 1835), 265–322 (266). On Fox and Mackintosh's considerable primary research, see J. R. Dinwiddy, 'Charles James Fox as Historian', *The Historical Journal*, 12.1 (1969), 23–34 (esp. 25–8). Access to resources and private papers was still contingent upon networks of patronage and sociability.
45. Mackintosh, 'Sismondi's *History of France*', 488.
46. See, e.g., Welsh, 'Waddington's *History of the Church*', 132. For a definition of a 'standard' work as an 'unchallenged source of authority' and 'History for the Million', see Francis Palgrave, 'Hume and his Influence upon History', ostensibly a review of Augustin Thierry's *Histoire de la*

conquête de l'Angleterre par les normands (1842), *Quarterly Review*, 73 (March 1844), 536–92 (536, 537).
47. Hallam, 'Lingard's *History of England*', 18. On sales of the *History of Rome*, see Peter J. Manning, 'Cleansing the Images: Wordsworth, Rome, and the Rise of Historicism', *Texas Studies in Languages and Literature*, 33.2 (1991), 271–326 (299, 300).
48. Thomas Jefferson Hogg, '*The History of Rome* by B. G. Niebuhr', *ER*, 51 (July 1830), 358–96 (358).
49. Fiona Stafford, 'The *Edinburgh Review* and the Representation of Scotland', in *British Romanticism and the Edinburgh Review*, pp. 33–57 (39); Laurel Brake, 'Periodical Formats: The Changing Review', in *Journalism and the Periodical Press in Nineteenth-Century Britain*, ed. Joanne Shattock (Cambridge: Cambridge University Press, 2017), pp. 47–65 (51).
50. See, e.g., Timothy Webb, 'A "great theatre of outrage and disorder": Figuring Ireland in the *Edinburgh Review*, 1802–29', in *British Romanticism and the Edinburgh Review*, pp. 58–81.
51. William Empson, 'Sismondi's *Italian Republics*', *ER*, 55 (July 1832), 362–97. See, e.g., Simon Goldhill, *Victorian Culture and Classical Antiquity* (Princeton: Princeton University Press, 2012).
52. Quasi-historical texts by women more often appear under 'Biographies' or 'Novels, Tales, and Romances': for example, Agnes Strickland's *Tales and Stories from History* (1836), in *ER*, 62 (Jan. 1836), 229–60. Interestingly, both Tory periodicals such as the *Quarterly Review* and radical ones such as *Taits Edinburgh Magazine* were more likely than the *Edinburgh Review* to review works of local and regional history, such as histories of Scotland and of Durham.
53. Stuart Curran, 'Women and the *Edinburgh Review*', in *British Romanticism and the Edinburgh Review*, pp. 195–208. See also David Stewart, *Romantic Magazines and Metropolitan Literary Culture* (Basingstoke: Palgrave Macmillan, 2011), esp. pp. 56–8.
54. Siskin, *Work of Writing*, pp. 215, 216, 224; David Simpson, *Romanticism, Nationalism, and the Revolt against Theory* (Chicago: University of Chicago Press, 1993), pp. 126–7; Peter Danhay, *The Feminization of the Novel* (Gainesville: University of Florida Press, 1991), p. 47.
55. Curran, 'Women and the *Edinburgh Review*', pp. 195, 198, 206.
56. T. H. Lister, 'Aiken's *Memoirs of the Court of Charles I*', *ER*, 58 (Jan. 1834), 398–442 (398, 399, 425, 422, 400). Even the *Quarterly Review* reviewed more works by women during this time period. See, e.g., John Wilson Croker's review of Lady Anne Hamilton's 'Secret History of the Court of England from the Accession of George III to the Death of George IV', *Quarterly Review*, 61 (April 1838), 425–7.
57. Siskin, *Work of Writing*, p. 218. On women and documentary history, see, e.g., Anne Laurence, 'Women Historians and Documentary Research: Lucy Aikin, Agnes Strickland, Mary Anne Everett Green and Lucy Toulmin Smith', in *Women, Scholarship and Criticism: Gender and Knowledge c. 1790–1900*, ed. Anne Laurence, Joan Bellamy, and Gillian Perry (Manchester: Manchester University Press, 2011), pp. 125–41; and Elise Garritzen, 'Women Historians, Gender and Fashioning the Authoritative

Self in Paratexts in Late-Victorian Britain', *Women's History Review*, 30.4 (2021), 650–68.
58. Lister, 'Aiken's *Memoirs of the Court of Charles I*', 500.
59. Manning, 'Antiquarianism', p. 112.
60. Henry Brougham, 'Ellis's *Letters Illustrative of English History*', *ER*, 41 (Jan. 1825), 427–50 (427, 437, 449). Brougham reviewed the second volume in June 1827.
61. John Allen, 'Palgrave's *Rolls of Parliament*', *ER*, 46 (Oct. 1827), 471–89 (471).
62. Francis Jeffrey, '*Memoirs of Lady Fanshawe*', *ER*, 50 (Oct. 1829), 75–85 (75, 76).
63. McKeon, *Secret History of Domesticity*, pp. 228–9.
64. John Bruce, 'Tytler's *England under the Reigns of Edward VI and Mary*', *ER*, 70 (Jan. 1840), 446–65 (446, 447).
65. Christie, *The Edinburgh Review*, p. 20; Dames, 'On Not Close Reading', pp. 11–26; Mark Schoenfield, *British Periodicals and Romantic Identity: The 'Literary Lower Empire'* (Basingstoke: Palgrave Macmillan, 2009), pp. 107, 108.
66. Hallam, 'Lingard's *History of England*', 18, 33–7, 40. Lingard's *Antiquities of the Anglo-Saxon Church* (1806) had already been attacked as a 'Gibbonesque' 'controversy under the guise of history' by the *Quarterly Review*, 13 (March 1812), 92–107. On Lingard's revisionism, see, e.g., Edwin Jones, *John Lingard and the Pursuit of Historical Truth* (Brighton: Sussex Academic Press, 2001).
67. T. B. Macaulay, 'Mitford's History of Greece', *Knight's Quarterly Magazine*, 3 (Aug. 1824), 285–304 (285, 286).
68. Macaulay, '*War of the Succession in Spain*', 499, 500.
69. Macaulay, '*Revolution in England in 1668*', 267.
70. Francis Jeffrey, 'O'Driscol's *History of Ireland*', *ER*, 46 (Oct. 1827), 433–70 (447).
71. Hallam rejects, for example, Lingard's use of the word 'civilian' as a 'very vile phrase', 'Lingard's *History of England*', 40. Allen's earlier 1825 review is more appreciative of Lingard's style.
72. Hallam, 'Lingard's *History of England*', 18.
73. Lingard passes, for example, the test set by the reign of James the Second, where he 'abstains from anything like invective' towards the Protestant William, Hallam, 'Lingard's *History of England*', 8, 20. For other passages approved by Hallam, see., e.g., 22–25, 39–40.
74. Hallam, 'Lingard's *History of England*', 16, 22, 26
75. Hallam, 'Lingard's *History of England*', 20, 18.
76. Allen, 'Lingard's *History of England*' (1825), 1, 2. Allen nonetheless vehemently refuted Lingard's account of the St Bartholomew Day Massacre. Lingard replied to Allen in *A Vindication of Certain Passages in the Fourth and Fifth Volumes of the History of England* (1826).
77. Allen, 'Lingard's *History of England*' (1825), 2, 3.
78. On the power of the scholarly name, see, e.g., Herman Paul, 'The Virtues of a Good Historian in Early Imperial Germany: Georg Waitz's Contested Example', *Modern Intellectual History*, 15.3 (2018), 681–709; and Ian Hesketh, *Victorian Jesus: J. R. Seeley, Religion, and the Cultural*

Significance of Anonymity (Toronto: University of Toronto Press, 2017), esp. pp. 135–6.
79. Levine, *The Amateur and the Professional*, pp. 101–34.
80. Hallam, *'Rise and Progress'*, 305.
81. Palgrave, 'Hume and his Influence upon History', 568.
82. Levine, *The Amateur and the Professional*, p. 39.
83. 'The Rise and Progress of the English Commonwealth. Anglo-Saxon Period ... By Francis Palgrave', *Athenaeum*, 229 (17 March 1832), 169–70 (169); Manning, 'Rehabilitation of Romance', p. 47. On neo-antiquarianism, see Beiner, *Forgetful Remembrance*, p. 16.
84. T. F. Ellis, *'Truths and Fictions of the Middle Ages. The Merchant and the Friar'*. By Francis Palgrave', *ER*, 66 (Jan. 1837), 465–76 (466, 465, 475).
85. Allen, *'Documents and Records'*, 37.
86. James Browne, 'Wilkinson's *Manners and Customs of the Ancient Egyptians*', *ER*, 68 (Jan. 1839), 315–37 (316, 317, 318).
87. Welsh, 'Waddington's *History of the Church*', 140.
88. Hannah Lawrance, 'Mackintosh's *History of England*', *Athenaeum*, 185 (14 May 1831), 308–10 (309).
89. 'Southey's *History of the Peninsular War*', *Athenaeum*, 234 (21 April 1832), 249–51 (249).
90. Mackintosh, 'Sismondi's *History of France*', 491.
91. John Allen, 'Capefigue's *History of the Reformation*', *ER*, 63 (April 1836), 1–28 (1, 2, 3).
92. Hugh Seymour Tremenheere, *'Lectures on European Civilisation*. By M. Guizot. Translated by Priscilla Maria Beckwith', *ER*, 67 (April 1838), 357–83 (357–8).
93. Hogg, 'Niebuhr's *History of Rome*', 375. See also Henry Malden, 'Niebuhr's *History of Rome*, Volumes I and II', *ER*, 56 (Jan. 1833), 267–312.
94. Hogg, *'The History of Rome* by B. G. Niebuhr', 376, 379. On dogmatism in historical writing, see also Merivale, 'Thirlwall's *History of Greece*', 84.
95. Hogg, *'The History of Rome* by B. G. Niebuhr', 379; Malden, 'Niebuhr's *History of Rome*', 276.
96. Malden, 'Niebuhr's *History of Rome*', 268, 274. The *History of Rome* was a 'classical text' in the two decades before the mid-century. See Dowling, 'Roman Decadence', 582, 580, 585; and Oswyn Murray, 'Neibuhr in Britain', in *Historiographie de l'antiquité et transferts culturels: Les histoires anciennes dans l'Europe des XVIIIe et XIXe siècles*, ed. Chyrssanthi Avlami, Jaime Alvar, and Mirella Romero Recio (Leiden: Brill/Rodolpi, 2010), pp. 239–54.
97. Ashton, *The German Idea*, p. 2. See, e.g., Matthew Arnold's *History of Rome* (1838–43).
98. Francis Jeffrey, 'Brodie's *Constitutional History of the British Empire*', *ER*, 40 (March 1824), 92–146 (95, 96, 97n).
99. Allen, 'Lingard's *History of England*' (1825), 7.
100. Malden, 'Niebuhr's *History of Rome*', 275.
101. *CHE*, 1:97. See also 'The Spirit of Party', *ER*, 46 (Oct. 1827), 415–32.
102. Valenza, *Intellectual Disciplines*, p. 118. Cf. Southey's very different review of Hallam's *History*, written with Edward Edwards, in *Quarterly*

Review, 37 (Jan. 1828), 194–260, where he accuses Hallam of partisanship, sophistry, and misrepresentation.
103. Mandell, 'Virtue and Evidence', 67, 131.
104. As Nicholas Phillipson notes, Hume sought to 'create a more impartial, more polite framework for a history of England', *David Hume: The Philosopher as Historian* (New Haven, CT: Yale University Press, 2012), p. 85. On misreadings of Hume's *History* as Tory propaganda, see Mitchell, *Picturing the Past*, pp. 35, 51; and Duncan Forbes, *Hume's Philosophical Politics* (Cambridge: Cambridge University Press, 1975), pp. 233–307.
105. Mandell, 'Virtue and Evidence', 138, 131.
106. J. S. Mill, 'Brodie's *History of the British Empire*', *Westminster Review*, 2 (Oct. 1824), 346–402 (346). See also Graeme Slater, 'Hume's Revisions of the "History of England"', *Studies in Bibliography*, 45 (1992), 130–57.
107. Palgrave, 'Hume and his Influence upon History', 564, 572, 558. See also Jeffrey's critique of Hume, 'Brodie's *Constitutional History of the British Empire*', 97n.
108. John Allen, 'Lord Mahon's *History of England*', ER, 64 (Oct. 1836), 232–54 (235).
109. Henry Brougham, 'Tucker's *Memoirs, Correspondence and Private Papers of Thomas Jefferson*', ER, 51 (July 1830), 496–525 (503).
110. Macaulay, 'Mitford's *History of Greece*', 285.
111. James Mackintosh, 'Godwin's *Lives of Milton's Nephews*', ER, 25 (Oct. 1815), 435–501 (496).
112. Hallam, 'Lingard's *History of England*', 19, 21, 27. John Allen was less sure of Lingard's impartiality, 'Lingard's *History of England*', ER, 44 (June 1826), 94–155 (94, 95–8).
113. Leitch Ritchie, '*Tales of a Grandfather*', *Athenaeum*, 167 (8 Jan. 1831), 18–20 (18); Pascual de Gayangos, 'Prescott's *The History of the Reign of Ferdinand and Isabella*', ER, 68 (Jan. 1839), 376–405 (404, 405).
114. John Ryley, 'Scott's *Life of Napoleon*', *Eclectic Review*, 28 (July 1827), 148–62 (161).
115. Jeffrey, 'O'Driscol's *History of Ireland*', 433, 446, 445, 454–7, 443, 444, 446.
116. Beiner, *Forgetful Remembrance*, p. 288. Moore's *History of Ireland* received mixed reviews. See, e.g., *Examiner*, 1418 (5 April 1835), 211–12; and *Athenaeum*, 388 (4 April 1835), 257–8.
117. Mateo Seoane, 'Napier's *History of the Peninsular War*', *Athenaeum*, 178 (26 March 1831), 193–5 (195); and 181 (16 April 1831), 247–9 (247); J. W. Croker and George Murray, 'History of the War in the Peninsula &c', *Quarterly Review*, 56 (June 1836), 437–89; '*History of the Peninsular War*. By Robert Southey', *Athenaeum*, 182 (21 April 1832), 249–51 (249).
118. Joseph Sortain, 'Lathbury's *History of the English Episcopacy*', ER, 64 (Oct. 1836), 93–105 (95). See James Kirby, *Historians and the Church of England: Religion and Historical Scholarship, 1870–1920* (Oxford: Oxford University Press, 2016).
119. William Empson, 'Providential and Prophetical Histories', ER, 50 (Jan. 1830), 287–344 (293, 295, 296, 297).

120. Macaulay, 'Leopold von Ranke's *History of the Popes*', *ER*, 72 (Oct. 1840), 227–58 (227). Francis Jeffrey is less sure of Ranke's merits in 'The Ecclesiastical and Political History of the Popes of Rome, during the Sixteenth and Seventeenth Centuries', *Dublin Review*, 14 (May 1843), 321–79.
121. Macaulay, 'Mackintosh's *History of the Revolution*', 267, 268, 270.
122. Mackintosh, 'Sismondi's *History of France*', 492–3.
123. Elfenbein, *Rise of English*, p. 178. See also Olivia Smith, *The Politics of Language* (Oxford: Clarendon Press, 1984).
124. See Peter J. Manning, 'The History of Cobbett's *A History of the Protestant "Reformation"*', *Huntington Library Quarterly*, 64.3/4 (2001), 429–43.
125. John Allen, 'Plumer Ward's *Revolution of 1688*', *ER*, 67 (July 1838), 415–35 (415).
126. Gay, *Style in History*, p. 241; *CHE*, 1:218, 219, 220. Macaulay was also hostile to Southey's neo-feudalist tone, Duggett, 'Southey's "Colloquies"', 87–8.
127. John Wilson Croker, 'Mr Macaulay's *History of England*', *Quarterly Review*, 84 (Dec. 1848), 549–630 (552).
128. Daniel Keyte Sandford, 'Edward Lytton Bulwer's *Athens*', *ER*, 65 (July 1837), 151–77 (152, 151, 152, 165).
129. Hallam, 'Lingard's *History of England*', 22.
130. T. F. Ellis, 'Palgrave's *Truths and Fictions*', *ER*, 66 (Jan. 1838), 464–76 (466, 465, 475).
131. 'Godwin's *Thoughts on Man*', *Athenaeum*, 171 (5 Feb. 1831), 82–4 (83).
132. Robert Southey, 'Godwin's *Life of Geoffrey Chaucer*', *Annual Review and History of Literature; for 1803*, ed. Arthur Aiken, 2 vols (London: Longman, 1804), 2:462–73 (472); Scott, 'Godwin's *Life of Chaucer*', 440, 438.
133. Thompson, 'Sentiment and Scholarship', 185–206.
134. 'Wollstonecraft's *View of the French Revolution*', *British Critic*, 6 (July 1795), 29–36; 'Wollstonecraft's History of the French Revolution', *Critical Review*, 16 (April 1796), 390–6. On Wollstonecraft's 'philosophic eye', see 'Wollstonecraft's *Historical and Moral View*', *Monthly Review*, 16 n.s. (April 1795), 393–402.
135. Francis Palgrave, '*Memoirs of the Queen of France* ... By Mrs Forbes Bush', *Quarterly Review*, 71 (March 1843), 411–16 (416).
136. Rohan Amanda Maitzen, *Gender, Genre, and Victorian Historical Writing* (New York and London: Garland Publishing, 1998), p. 39. On how gender is inscribed in more progressive reviews, see Laurel Brake, 'The *Westminster* and Gender at Mid-Century', *Victorian Periodicals Review*, 33.3 (2000), 247–72.
137. Bonnie G. Smith, *The Gender of History: Men, Women, and Historical Practice* (Cambridge, MA: Harvard University Press, 1998), esp. pp. 71–83.
138. Wilkes, *Women Reviewing Women*, pp. 65, 68.
139. Maitzen, *Victorian Historical Writing*, p. 34.
140. Maitzen, *Victorian Historical Writing*, pp. 50–5.
141. William Jacob, 'Travels in Brazil', *Quarterly Review*, 31 (April 1824), 1–26 (14), cited in Thompson, 'Sentiment and Scholarship', 202; John

Barrow, '*Journal of a Residence in India*. By Maria Graham', *Quarterly Review*, 16 (Sept. 1812), 406–21 (406), cited in Gust, 'Empire, Exile, Identity', p. 61.
142. Maria Graham, *Journal of a Voyage to Brazil and Residence There During Part of the Years 1821, 1822, 1823* (London: Longman and John Murray, 1824), p. 59.
143. Against claims of 'separate spheres', see, e.g., Spongberg, *Women Writers*, esp. pp. 1–17; Rosemary Ann Mitchell, '"The busy daughters of Clio": Women Writers of History from 1820 to 1880', *Women's History Review*, 7.1 (1998), 107–34; Billie Melman, 'Gender, History and Memory: The Invention of Women's Past in the Nineteenth and Early Twentieth Centuries', *History and Memory*, 5.1 (1993), 5–41; and Nadia Clare Smith, *A "Manly Study"?: Irish Women Historians, 1868–1949* (New York: Palgrave Macmillan, 2006). Cf. Christina Crosby, *The Ends of History: Victorians and the 'Woman Question'* (New York and London: Routledge, 1991).
144. See Alexis Easley, *First-Person Anonymous: Women Writers and Victorian Print Media, 1830–1870* (London: Routledge, 2004), and Alexis Easley, Clare Gill, and Beth Rodgers (eds), *Women, Periodicals, and Print Culture, 1830s–1900s: The Victorian Period* (Edinburgh: Edinburgh University Press, 2019). Male reviewers nonetheless capitalised on anonymity to regulate and restrict women writers and readers.
145. Garritzen, 'Fashioning the Authoritative Self', 650.
146. Hogg, '*The History of Rome* by B. G. Niebuhr', 359, 360; Miller, 'Reading in Review', 628; Hogg, '*The History of Rome* by B. G. Niebuhr', 360; Schoenfield, *British Periodicals*, p. 73; Christie, 'Modern Athenians', 122.
147. Christie, 'Modern Athenians', 124; Miller, 'Reading in Review', 628.
148. Ferris, 'Debut of the *Edinburgh Review*', n.p.
149. Miller, 'Reading in Review', 633.
150. Ferris, 'Debut of the *Edinburgh Review*', n.p.; Christie, 'Modern Athenians', 127–9.
151. S. T. Coleridge, *Biographia Literaria*, 2 vols (London: Rest Fenner, 1817), 2:179. See Marilyn Butler, 'Culture's Medium: The Role of the Review', in *The Cambridge Companion to British Romanticism*, ed. Stuart Curran (Cambridge: Cambridge University Press, 2010), pp. 127–52; Derek Roper, *Reviewing Before the Edinburgh, 1788–1832* (London: Methuen, 1978); and Frank Donoghue, *The Fame Machine: Book Reviewing and Eighteenth-Century Literary Careers* (Stanford: Stanford University Press, 1996).
152. Oscar Maurer Jr, 'Anonymity vs. Signature in Victorian Reviewing', *University of Texas Studies in English*, 27.1 (1848), 1–27 (11–12). See also John Mullan, *Anonymity: A Secret History of English Literature* (Princeton: Princeton University Press, 2007), esp. Ch. 6.
153. Valenza, *Intellectual Disciplines*, p. 95.
154. Christie, 'Modern Athenians', 122.
155. Ferris, 'Debut of the *Edinburgh Review*', n.p. See also Joanne Shattock, *Politics and Reviewers: The Edinburgh and the Quarterly in the Early Victorian Age* (London and New York: Leicester University Press, 1989).

156. Duncan, *Scott's Shadow: The Novel in Romantic Edinburgh* (Princeton: Princeton University Press, 2007), p. 25; Macaulay to Macvey Napier, 24 June 1842, *Letters of Thomas Babington Macaulay*, ed. Pinney, 4:40–1. See also Peter Morgan, 'Macaulay on Periodical Style', *Victorian Periodicals Newsletter*, 1 (1968), 26–7 (esp. 27); Davis, '"This is My Theory"', 21, 22; and Shattock, 'Politics and Literature', 47.
157. On reviewing specialisms, see Demata, 'Prejudiced Knowledge', p. 82; and Frank Whitson Fetter, 'The Authorship of Economic Articles in the Edinburgh Review', *Journal of Political Economy*, 61 (1953), 232–59.
158. Levine, *The Amateur and the Professional*, p. 173. See also Heather Ellis, 'Enlightened Networks in Anglo-German Collaboration in Classical Scholarship', in *Anglo-German Scholarly Networks in the Long Nineteenth Century*, ed. Heather Ellis and Ulrike Kirchberger (Leiden: Brill, 2014), pp. 23–8.
159. Gay, *Style in History*, p. 10.
160. Macaulay to Napier, 20 July 1838, *Letters of Thomas Babington Macaulay*, 3:250.
161. Shattock, 'Politics and Literature', 47, 49.
162. Christie, 'Modern Athenians', 124. On agitation for a dedicated historical review from the 1860s onwards, see Howsam, *Past into Print*, 35–7, 59–61.

Epilogue

1. Sarah Knott, 'Narrating the Age of Revolution', *William and Mary Quarterly*, 73.1 (2016), 3–36 (5, 24–5).
2. Despite his emphasis on human motivation in both *The Theory of Moral Sentiments* (1759) and *The Wealth of Nations* (1776), Smith's great legacy in historiography arguably lies in sympathetic approaches to history rather than in behaviouralist approaches.
3. Scott, 'After History?', 263.
4. Kidd, 'Constructions of the Past', 86.
5. Phillips, *On Historical Distance*, p. 14; Gossman, *Between History*, p. 33.
6. Ankersmit, *Narrative Logic*, pp. 8, 11; Gossman, *Between History*, p. 44.
7. Phillips, *Society and Sentiment*, p. 138.
8. For a revised understanding of the enlightenment, see, e.g., Clifford Siskin and William Warner, 'If This is Enlightenment Then What is Romanticism?', *European Romantic Review*, 22.3 (2011), 281–91. Hans Kellner sees the positivist historicism that followed romantic history as a form of 'desublimation', with history turning itself into 'antiliterature, the proponent of the real as against the possible, of experience against fantasy', 'However Imperceptibly: From the Historical to the Sublime', *PMLA*, 118.3 (2003), 591–6 (592); see also Gossman, 'History as Decipherment', p. 28.
9. See, e.g., Gossman, *Between History*, pp. 229–56; Crossley, 'National Identity', 18–27; and Jacques Revel, 'History and the Social Sciences', in *The Cambridge History of Science Vol. 7: The Modern Social Sciences*, ed. Theodore M. Porter and Dorothy Ross (Cambridge: Cambridge University Press, 2008), pp. 391–404 (esp. 391–2).

10. Fermanis and Regan, 'Introduction', p. 2; Stephen Bann, 'The Sense of the Past: Image, Text, and Object in the Formation of Historical Consciousness in Nineteenth-Century Britain', in *The New Historicism*, ed. H. Aram Veeser (London: Routledge, Chapman & Hall, 1989), pp. 102–15 (103–4).
11. Chris Lorenz, 'Can Histories be True? Narrativism, Positivism, and the "Metaphorical Turn"', *History and Theory*, 37.3 (1998), 309–29 (314).
12. See, e.g., Deidre Shauna Lynch, *Loving Literature: A Cultural History* (Chicago: Chicago University Press, 2014), p. 8.
13. On the non-European contexts of modernity, see Mitchell (ed.), *Questions of Modernity*.
14. Andress, 'Introduction', in *Experiencing the French Revolution*, p. 6. See also Sophia Rosenfeld, 'Thinking about Feeling, 1789–1799', *French Historical Studies*, 32.4 (2009), 697–706 (700).
15. Wright, *Ireland, India, and Nationalism*, pp. 30, 38, 30, 44; Ina Ferris, 'Writing on the Border: The National Tale, Female Writing, and the Public Sphere', in *Romanticism, History, and the Possibilities of Genre*, pp. 86–109 (91).
16. Carlyle, *Two Notebooks*, p. 144.
17. Lydon, *Imperial Emotions*, p. 9.
18. Hamilton, *Metaromanticism*, p. 124; Andress, 'Introduction', p. 1; Jacques Rancière, *The Names of History: On the Poetics of Knowledge*, trans. Hassan Melehy, foreword Hayden White (Minneapolis: University of Minnesota Press, 1994), p. 39; François Furet, *Interpreting the French Revolution*, trans. Elborg Forster (Cambridge: Cambridge University Press, 1981), p. 24.
19. Andress, 'Introduction', p. 5; Gross, *Secret History of Emotions*, p. 8; William E. Connolly, *Political Theory and Modernity* (Oxford: Basil Blackwell, 1989), p. 71.
20. Niklas Luhmann, *Love as Passion: The Codification of Intimacy*, trans. Jeremy L. Gaines and Doris L. Jones (Cambridge, MA: Harvard University Press, 1987), pp. 33, 116, 122, 158; *The Differentiation of Society* (New York: Columbia University Press, 1982), pp. 15–17. See also the arguments about an 'affect economy' in Norbert Elias, *The Civilizing Process: Sociogenetic and Psychogenetic Investigations* (1939; repr. Oxford: Blackwell, 2000), esp. pp. 399–402.
21. Zoltán Boldizsár Simon, *History in Times of Unprecedented Change: A Theory for the 21st Century* (London: Bloomsbury, 2019), pp. 46, 50; Marcus Colla, 'The Spectre of the Present: Time, Presentism, and the Writing of Contemporary History', *Contemporary European History*, 30.1 (2021), 124–35 (128). See also Woolf on the modern and postmodern fetishisation of rupture in 'Getting Back to Normal'.
22. Barbara M. Rosenwein, 'Modernity: A Problematic Category in the History of Emotions', *History and Theory*, 53 (2014), 69–78. See also Kathleen Davis, *Periodization and Sovereignty: How Ideas of Feudalism and Secularization Govern the Politics of Time* (Philadelphia: University of Pennsylvania Press, 2008).
23. For the idea that the French Revolution marked changing regimes of historicity, see, e.g., Ankersmit, *Sublime Historical Experience*, p. 57; Rancière, *Names of History*, pp. 33–5, 42; Reinhart Koselleck, *Futures*

Past: On the Semantics of Historical Time, trans. and introd. Keith Tribe (New York: Columbia University Press, 2004), p. 59; François Hartog, *Regimes of Historicity: Presentism and Experiences of Time*, trans. Saskia Brown (New York: Columbia University Press, 2016); and Georg Lukács, *History and Class Consciousness: Studies in Marxist Dialectics*, trans. Rodney Livingstone (Cambridge, MA: MIT Press, 1971), pp. 108, 225–6, 258–9.

24. As Phillips has noted, the 'greatest challenge to historical mimesis in the period ... came from the desire to represent experience as well as action', *Society and Sentiment*, p. 23.
25. Koselleck, *Futures Past*, p. 268. See also Craig Ireland, *The Subaltern Appeal to Experience: Self-Identity, Late Modernity, and the Politics of Immediacy* (Montreal and Kingston: McGill-Queen's University Press, 2004); and Martin Jay, *Songs of Experience: Modern American and European Variations on a Universal Theme* (Berkeley: University of California Press, 2005).
26. Andress, 'Introduction', p. 4.
27. See, e.g., Perry Anderson, *Arguments Within English Marxism* (London: Verso, 1980).
28. Scott, 'Evidence of Experience', 781; Williams, *Keywords*, p. 128.
29. Scott, 'Evidence of Experience', 782.
30. Ankersmit, *Sublime Historical Experience*, pp. 97, 12, 10–11.
31. Ankersmit, *Sublime Historical Experience*, pp. 231–2, 10, 10–11.
32. Ankersmit, *Sublime Historical Experience*, pp. 79, 183, 231–2.
33. See, e.g., Peter P. Icke, *Frank Ankersmit's Lost Historical Cause: A Journey from Language to Experience* (New York and London: Routledge, 2012); and Ewa Domanska, 'Frank Ankersmit: From Narrative to Experience', *Rethinking History*, 13.2 (2009), 175–95.
34. Anton Froeyman, 'Frank Ankersmit and Eelco Runia: The Presence and Otherness of the Past', *Rethinking History*, 15.3 (2012), 393–415; Keith Jenkins, 'Cohen contra Ankersmit', *Rethinking History*, 12.4 (2008), 537–55. For an ontological perspective, see Bentley, 'Revisiting Historical Ontology', 349–61.
35. Ankersmit, *Sublime Historical Experience*, pp. 334–7.
36. Ankersmit, *Sublime Historical Experience*, p. 10; Wordsworth and Coleridge, *Lyrical Ballads*, p. 62; Marilyn Butler, *Romantics, Rebels and Reactionaries: English Literature and its Background 1760–1830* (Oxford: Oxford University Press, 1981), p. 60.
37. Fermanis and Regan, 'Introduction', p. 2.
38. John Schwarzmantel, *The Age of Ideology: Political Ideologies from the American Revolution to Postmodern Times* (New York: New York University Press, 1998) p. 71.
39. Goodman, *Georgic Modernity*, p. 3. Cf. David Simpson, 'Feeling for Structures', 21.
40. Febvre, 'Sensibility and History', p. 16.
41. Duncan, 'Edinburgh and Lowland Scotland', p. 160; Griffiths, *The Age of Analogy*, p. 4. See also Phillips, *On Historical Distance*, pp. 115–39.
42. Chakrabarty, *Provincializing Europe*, pp. 244, 243. On 'presence', see, e.g., Eelco Runia, 'Presence', *History and Theory*, 45.1 (2006), 1–29.

43. Crimmins, *Romantic Historicism*, pp. 13, 20. See also Michel de Certeau, *The Writing of History*, trans. Tom Conley (Columbia: Columbia University Press, 1992).
44. Chakrabarty, *Provincializing Europe*, pp. 238, 239. See also Priya Satia, *Time's Monster: History, Conscience and Britain's Empire* (Cambridge, MA: Harvard University Press, 2020). On anachronism in history more generally, see Jacques Rancière, 'The Concept of Anachronism and the Historian's Truth', *InPrint*, 3.1 (2015), 13–48. Available at <https://arrow.tudublin.ie/cgi/viewcontent.cgi?article=1020&context=inp> (last accessed 2 December 2020); and Harry Harootunian, 'Remembering the Historical Present', *Critical Inquiry*, 33.3 (2007), 471–94.
45. Rancière, 'The Concept of Anachronism', 23.
46. Chakrabarty, *Provincializing Europe*, p. 251.
47. Andress, 'Introduction', p. 7. More broadly, see Renato Rosaldo, *Culture and Truth: The Remaking of Social Analysis* (London: Beacon Press, 1993), p. 21.
48. Antoinette Burton, 'Introduction: When was Brexit? Reading Backward to the Present', *Historical Reflections*, 47.2 (2021), 1–8 (5).
49. Crimmins, *Romantic Historicism*, pp. 15, 20.

Bibliography

Adams, Edward, *Liberal Epic: The Victorian Practice of History from Gibbon to Churchill* (Charlottesville: University of Virginia Press, 2011)
Adams, James Eli, 'The Hero as Spectacle: Carlyle and the Persistence of Dandyism', in *Victorian Literature and the Victorian Visual Imagination*, ed. Carol T. Christ and John O. Jordan (Berkeley: University of California Press, 1995), pp. 213–32
Ahmed, Sara, *The Cultural Politics of Emotions* (Edinburgh: Edinburgh University Press, 2004)
Alison, Archibald, 'Macaulay's History of England', *Blackwood's Edinburgh Magazine*, 65 (April 1849), 383–405
Allen, Emily, *Theatre Figures: The Production of the Nineteenth-Century Novel* (Columbus: Ohio State University Press, 2003)
Allen, John, 'Capefigue's *History of the Reformation*', *Edinburgh Review*, 63 (April 1836), 1–28
—, '*Documents and Records Illustrating the History of Scotland*. Collected and Edited by Francis Palgrave', *Edinburgh Review*, 66 (Oct. 1837), 36–59
—, 'Lingard's *History of England*', *Edinburgh Review*, 42 (April 1825), 1–31
—, 'Lingard's *History of England*', *Edinburgh Review*, 44 (June 1826), 94–155
—, 'Lord Mahon's *History of England*', *Edinburgh Review*, 64 (Oct. 1836), 232–54
—, 'Palgrave's *Rolls of Parliament*', *Edinburgh Review*, 46 (Oct. 1827), 471–89
—, 'Plumer Ward's *Revolution of 1688*', *Edinburgh Review*, 67 (July 1838), 415–35
Altick, Richard D., *Writers, Readers, and Occasions: Selected Essays on Victorian Literature and Life* (Columbus: Ohio State University Press, 1989)
Ananth, Mahesh, 'A Cognitive Interpretation of Aristotle's Concepts of Catharsis and Tragic Pleasure', *International Journal of Art and Art History*, 2.2 (2014), 1–33
Anderson, Benedict, *Long-Distance Nationalism: World Capitalism and the Rise of Identity Politics* (Amsterdam: Centre for Asian Studies Amsterdam, 1992)
Anderson, Perry, *Arguments Within English Marxism* (London: Verso, 1980)
Andress, David, 'Introduction: Revolutionary Historiography, Adrift or at Large? The Paradigmatic Quest versus the Exploration of Experience', in

Experiencing the French Revolution, ed. David Andress (Oxford: Voltaire Foundation, 2013), pp. 1–15
Andrews, Stuart, 'Before the Laureateship: Robert Southey as Historian', *Romanticism*, 21.1 (2015), 72–9
—, *Robert Southey: History, Politics, and Religion* (Basingstoke: Palgrave Macmillan, 2011)
Anger, Suzy, *Victorian Interpretation* (Ithaca, NY, and London: Cornell University Press, 2005)
Ankersmit, Frank R., *Historical Representation* (Stanford: Stanford University Press, 2001)
—, *Narrative Logic: A Semantic Analysis of the Historian's Language* (The Hague, Boston, and London: Martin Nijhoff, 1983)
—, *Political Representation* (Stanford: Stanford University Press, 2002)
—, *The Reality Effect in the Writing of History: The Dynamics of Historiographical Topology* (Amsterdam: Koninklijke Nederlandse Akademie van Wetenschappen: Noord-Hollandsche, 1989)
—, *Sublime Historical Experience* (Stanford: Stanford University Press, 2005)
Aparicio, Valentina P., 'Intermarriage in the *Quilombo*: Southey's Republic of Runway Slaves', *European Romantic Review*, 32.4 (2021), 399–418
Arac, Jonathan, *Impure Worlds: The Institution of Literature in the Age of the Novel* (New York: Fordham University Press, 2010)
Armstrong, Nancy, *Desire and Domestic Fiction: A Political History of the Novel* (New York and Oxford: Oxford University Press, 1987)
—, *How Novels Think: The Limits of Individualism from 1719–1900* (New York: Columbia University Press, 2005)
Arnold, Thomas, 'Romische Geschichte, von B. G. Niebuhr. History of Rome', *Quarterly Review*, 32 (June 1825), 67–92
Ashton, Rosemary, *The German Idea: Four English Writers and the Reception of German Thought 1800–1860* (Cambridge: Cambridge University Press, 1980)
Bagehot, Walter, *Literary Studies*, 2 vols, ed. Richard Holt Hutton, (London: Longmans, Green & Co, 1884)
—, *The Works: Volume 2*, ed. Mrs Russell Barrington, 2nd edn (London: Longmans, Green & Co., 1915)
Bahar, Saba, *Mary Wollstonecraft's Social and Aesthetic Philosophy* (New York: Palgrave Macmillan, 2002)
Baier, Annette, 'What Emotions are About', *Philosophical Perspectives*, 4 (1990), 1–29
Balibar, Étienne, *Politics and the Other Scene*, trans. Christine Jones, James Swenson, and Chris Turner (London: Verso, 2002)
Bann, Stephen, *The Clothing of Clio: A Study of the Representation of History in Nineteenth-Century Britain and France* (New York: Cambridge University Press, 1984)
—, *The Inventions of History: Essays on the Representation of the Past* (Manchester: Manchester University Press, 2000)
—, *Romanticism and the Rise of History* (New York: Twayne, 1995).
—, 'The Sense of the Past: Image, Text, and Object in the Formation of Historical Consciousness in Nineteenth-Century Britain', in *The New Historicism*, ed. H. Aram Veeser (London: Routledge, Chapman & Hall, 1989), pp. 102–15

Barker-Benfield, G. J., 'Mary Wollstonecraft: Eighteenth-Century Commonwealthwoman', *Journal of the History of Ideas*, 50.1 (1989), 95–115
Barlow, Paul, 'The Imagined Hero as Incarnate Sign: Thomas Carlyle and the Mythology of the "National Portrait" in Victorian Britain', *Art History*, 17.4 (1994), 517–45
Barney, Richard A., 'Burke, Biomedicine, and Biobelligerence', *The Eighteenth Century*, 54.2 (2013), 231–43
Barrow, Barbara, 'Speaking the Social Body: Language-Origins and Thomas Carlyle's *The French Revolution*', *Journal of Victorian Culture*, 19.1 (2014), 72–92
Barrow, John, '*Journal of a Residence in India*. By Maria Graham', *Quarterly Review*, 16 (Sept. 1812), 406–21
Barthes, Roland, 'The Reality Effect', in *The Rustle of Language*, trans. Richard Howard (Berkeley: University of California Press, 1989), pp. 141–8
Baucom, Ian, *Spectres of the Atlantic: Finance Capital, Slavery, and the Philosophy of History* (Durham, NC: Duke University Press, 2005)
Beebee, Thomas O., *Epistolary Fiction in Europe 1500–1850* (Cambridge: Cambridge University Press, 1999)
Beer, Gillian, *Arguing with the Past: Essays in Narrative from Woolf to Sidney* (Cambridge: Cambridge University Press, 1989)
Beiner, Guy, *Forgetful Remembrance: Social Forgetting and Vernacular Historiography of a Rebellion in Ulster* (Oxford: Oxford University Press, 2018)
—, 'Irish Historical Studies *Avant la Lettre*: The Antiquarian Genealogy of Interdisciplinary Scholarship', in *Routledge International Handbook of Irish Studies*, ed. Reneé Allyson Fox, Mike Cronin, and Brian Ó Conchubhair (London: Routledge, 2021), pp. 47–58
Ben-Israel, Hedva, *English Historians on the French Revolution* (Cambridge: Cambridge University Press, 1968)
Benatti, Francesca, 'Young Ireland and the Superannuated Bard: Rewriting Thomas Moore in *The Nation*', in *The Reputations of Thomas Moore: Poetry, Music, and Politics*, ed. Sarah McCleave and Triona O'Hanlon (New York and London: Routledge, 2019), pp. 214–34
Bentley, Michael, 'Henry Hallam Revisited', *The Historical Journal*, 55.2 (2012), 453–73
—, 'Past and "Presence": Revisiting Historical Ontology', *History and Theory*, 45.3 (2006), 349–61
Berg, Ulla D., and Ana Y. Ramos-Zayas, 'Racializing Affect: A Theoretical Proposition', *Current Anthropology*, 56.6 (2015), 654–77
Berger, Stefan, 'Introduction: Towards a Global History of National Historiographies', in *Writing the Nation: A Global Perspective*, ed. Stefan Berger (Basingstoke: Palgrave Macmillan, 2007), pp. 1–29
—, with Christof Conrad, *The Past as History: National Identity and Historical Consciousness in Modern Europe* (Basingstoke: Palgrave Macmillan, 2015)
Berlant, Lauren, *The Female Complaint: The Unfinished Business of Sentimentality in American Culture* (Durham, NC: Duke University Press, 2008)
—, *Intimacy* (Chicago and London: University of Chicago Press, 2000)

—, 'The Subject of True Feeling: Pain, Privacy, and Politics', in *Cultural Pluralism, Identity Politics, and the Law*, ed. A. Sarat and T. Kearns (Ann Arbor: University of Michigan Press, 1999), pp. 49–84

Berlin, Isaiah, *The Age of Enlightenment* (1956; repr. New York: New American Library, 1984)

Bethell, Leslie, *Brazil by British and Irish Authors* (Oxford: Centre for Brazilian Studies, 2003)

Bevilacqua, Vincent M., 'Adam Smith's Lectures on Rhetoric and Belles Lettres', *Studies in Scottish Literature*, 3.1 (1965), 41–60

Bevir, Mark, 'Anglophone Historicism: From Modernist Method to Post-Analytic Philosophy', *Journal of the Philosophy of History*, 3 (2009), 211–24

Bhabha, Homi K., 'DissemiNation: Time, Narrative, and the Margins of the Modern Nation', in *Nation and Narration* (London and New York: Routledge, 1990), pp. 291–322

Blair, Hugh, *Lectures on Rhetoric and Belles Lettres*, 2 vols (London: W. Strahan, 1783)

Blake, William, *A Descriptive Catalogue of Pictures, Poetical and Historical Inventions* (London: D. N. Shury for J. Blake, 1809)

Blakemore, Steven, *Burke and the Fall of Language: The French Revolution as Linguistic Event* (Hanover, NH: University Press of New England, 1988)

Boddice, Rob, *The History of Emotions* (Manchester: Manchester University Press, 2018)

—, *The Science of Sympathy: Morality, Evolution and Victorian Civilization* (Urbana: University of Illinois Press, 2016)

Bolton, Carol, '"Green Savannahs" or "savage lands": Wordsworth's and Southey's Romantic America', in *Robert Southey and the Contexts of English Romanticism*, ed. Lynda Pratt (Aldershot: Ashgate, 2006), pp. 115–32

—, *Writing the Empire: Robert Southey and Romantic Colonialism* (London: Pickering & Chatto, 2007)

Bos, Jacques, 'Nineteenth-Century Historicism and its Predecessors: Historical Experience, Historical Ontology and Historical Method', in *The Making of the Humanities: Vol. II From Early Modern to Modern Disciplines*, ed. Rens Bod, Jaap Maat, and Thijs Weststeijn (Amsterdam: Amsterdam University Press, 2012), pp. 131–48

Botting, Elaine Hunt, 'Wollstonecraft in Europe: A Revisionist Reception History, 1792–1904', *History of European Ideas*, 39.4 (2013), 503–27

Boulton, James T., *The Language of Politics in the Age of Wilkes and Burke* (1963; repr. Abingdon: Routledge, 2010)

Bour, Isabelle, 'Mary Wollstonecraft as Historian in *An Historical and Moral View of the Origin and Progress of the French Revolution*', *Études Épistémè*, 17 (2010), <https://journals.openedition.org/episteme/668#abstract> (last accessed 5 January 2020)

—, 'A New Wollstonecraft: The Reception of the *Vindication of the Rights of Woman* and of *The Wrongs of Woman* in Revolutionary France', *Journal for Eighteenth-Century Studies*, 36.4 (2013), 575–87

Bourke, Richard, *Empire and Revolution: The Political Life of Edmund Burke* (Princeton: Princeton University Press, 2015)

Boyson, Rowan, *Wordsworth and the Enlightenment Idea of Pleasure* (Cambridge: Cambridge University Press, 2012)

Brake, Laurel, 'Periodical Formats: The Changing Review', in *Journalism and the Periodical Press in Nineteenth-Century Britain*, ed. Joanne Shattock (Cambridge: Cambridge University Press, 2017), pp. 47–65
—, 'The *Westminster* and Gender at Mid-Century', *Victorian Periodicals Review*, 33.3 (2000), 247–72
Bromwich, David, *A Choice of Inheritance: Self and Community from Edmund Burke to Robert Frost* (Cambridge, MA: Harvard University Press, 1989)
—, *The Intellectual Life of Edmund Burke: From the Sublime and Beautiful to American Independence* (Cambridge, MA: Harvard University Press, 2014)
—, 'Wollstonecraft as a Critic of Burke', *Political Theory*, 23.4 (1995), 617–34
Brougham, Henry, 'Ellis's *Letters Illustrative of English History*', *Edinburgh Review*, 41 (Jan. 1825), 427–50
—, 'Tucker's *Memoirs, Correspondence and Private Papers of Thomas Jefferson*', *Edinburgh Review*, 51 (July 1830), 496–525
Browne, James, 'Lane's *Manners of Modern Egypt*', *Edinburgh Review*, 65 (April 1837), 146–73
—, 'Wilkinson's *Manners and Customs of the Ancient Egyptians*', *Edinburgh Review*, 68 (Jan. 1839), 315–37
Bruce, John, 'Tytler's *England under the Reigns of Edward VI and Mary*', *Edinburgh Review*, 70 (Jan. 1840), 446–65
Budge, Gavin, 'The Hero as Seer: Character, Perception and Cultural Health in Carlyle', *Romanticism and Victorianism on the Net*, Special Issue 'Science, Technology and the Senses', 52 (2008), <doi.org/10.7202/019805ar/> (last accessed 15 October 2021)
Bullard, Paddy, *Edmund Burke and the Art of Rhetoric* (Cambridge: Cambridge University Press, 2011)
Bulwer, Edward Lytton, *England and the English* (Paris: Gagliani and Co., 1837)
Bundock, Christopher M., '"A feeling that I was not for that hour / Nor for that place": Wordsworth's Modernity', *European Romantic Review*, 21.3 (2010), 383–9
—, *Romantic Prophecy and the Resistance to Historicism* (Toronto: University of Toronto Press, 2016)
Burgess, Miranda, 'Nationalisms in Romantic Britain and Ireland: Culture, Politics, and the Global', in *A Concise Companion to the Romantic Age*, ed. Jon Klancher (Oxford: Blackwell, 2009), pp. 77–98
Burke, Edmund, *Correspondence of Edmund Burke*, ed. T. W. Copeland, 10 vols (Chicago: University of Chicago Press, 1963–71)
—, *Reflections on the Revolution in France, and on the Proceedings of Certain Societies in London Relative to that Event. In a Letter Intended to have been Sent to a Gentleman in Paris*, 10th edn (London: James Dodsley, 1791)
—, *Thoughts on the Prospect of a Regicide Peace, in a Series of Letters* (London: J. Owen, 1796)
—, *The Works and Correspondence of the Right Honourable Edmund Burke*, 8 vols (London: Francis & John Rivington, 1852)
Burke, Peter, *Popular Culture in Early Modern Europe* (Aldershot: Ashgate, 1978)
—, *What is Cultural History?* (Cambridge: Polity Press, 2008)

Burke, Tristan Donal, 'From Terror to Terrorism in *Bleak House*: Writing the Event, Representing the People', *The London Journal*, 45.1 (2020), 17–38

Burnett, L. D., 'The Sensibility of Historians', *S-USIH* (2012), <http://s-usih.org/2012/06/sensibility-of-historians.html> (last accessed 24 April 2017)

Burrow, John, *A Liberal Descent: Victorian Historians and the British Past* (Cambridge: Cambridge University Press, 1981)

Burton, Antoinette, 'Introduction: When was Brexit? Reading Backward to the Present', *Historical Reflections*, 47.2 (2021), 1–8

Burwick, Frederick, *Poetic Madness and the Romantic Imagination* (University Park, PA: Penn State University Press, 1996)

Butler, Marilyn, 'Culture's Medium: The Role of the Review', in *The Cambridge Companion to British Romanticism*, ed. Stuart Curran (Cambridge: Cambridge University Press, 2010), pp. 127–52

—, *Romantics, Rebels and Reactionaries: English Literature and its Background 1760–1830* (Oxford: Oxford University Press, 1981)

Callander, Michelle, '"The grand theatre of political changes": Marie Antoinette, the Republic, and the Politics of Spectacle in Mary Wollstonecraft's *An Historical and Moral View of the French Revolution*', *European Romantic Review*, 11.4 (2000), 375–92

Camlot, Jason, *Style and the Nineteenth-Century British Critic: Sincere Mannerisms* (Aldershot: Ashgate, 2008)

Campbell, Ian, 'Carlyle: Style and Sense', *Carlyle Studies Annual*, 14 (1994), 13–24

Cardozo, Manoel, 'England's Fated Ally', *Luso-Brazilian Review*, 7 (1970), 46–56

Carlson, Julie, *England's First Family of Writers: Mary Wollstonecraft, William Godwin, Mary Shelley* (Baltimore: Johns Hopkins University Press, 2007)

Carlyle, Thomas, *The Collected Letters of Thomas and Jane Welsh Carlyle*, ed. Charles Richard Sanders, Clyde de L. Ryals, J. J. Fielding, and Ian Campbell, 24 vols (Durham, NC: Duke University Press, 1970–)

—, *Critical and Miscellaneous Essays by Thomas Carlyle*, 4 vols (Boston: James Munroe & Co., 1838–9)

—, *Early Letters of Thomas Carlyle*, ed. Charles E. Norton (New York and London: Macmillan & Co., 1886)

—, *The French Revolution: A History*, introd. John D. Rosenberg (New York: The Modern Library, 2002)

—, *Historical Sketches of Notable Persons and Events in the Reigns of James I and Charles I*, ed. Alexander Carlyle (London: Chapman and Hall, 1898)

—, *Oliver Cromwell's Letters and Speeches: With Elucidations*, 3rd edn, 5 vols (London: Chapman & Hall, 1872)

—, *Letters of Thomas Carlyle to John Stuart Mill, John Sterling and Robert Browning*, ed. Alexander Carlyle (London: T. Fisher Unwin, 1924)

—, *New Letters of Thomas Carlyle*, ed. Alexander Carlyle, 2 vols (London: J. Lane, 1904)

—, *The Norman and Charlotte Strouse Edition of the Writings of Thomas Carlyle: Historical Essays*, ed. Chris R. Vanden Bossche (Berkeley: University of California Press, 2003)

—, *On Heroes, Hero-Worship, and the Heroic in History* (New York: Charles Scribner's Sons, 1841)

—, *Reminiscences of my Irish Journey in 1849* (London: S. Low, Marston, Searle, & Rivington, 1882)
—, 'The Repeal of the Union', *Examiner* (29 April 1848), 275–6
—, *Two Notebooks of Thomas Carlyle from 23 March, 1822 to 16 May, 1832*, ed. Charles Eliot Norton (New York: The Grolier Club, 1898)
—, *Two Reminiscences of Thomas Carlyle*, ed. John Clubbe (Durham, NC: Duke University Press, 1974)
Carr, David, *Time, Narrative, and History* (Bloomington: Indiana University Press, 1986)
Castanheira, Maria Zulmira, '"The best laid schemes sometimes turn out the worst": Robert Southey's Success and Failure', *Via Panorâmica*, 2 (2009), 89–100
Castellano, Katy, 'Burke's "Revolutionary Book": Conservative Politics and Revolutionary Aesthetics in the *Reflections*', *Romanticism on the Net*, 45 (2007), <https://www.erudit.org/en/journals/ron/1900-v1-n1-ron1728/015818ar/> (last accessed July 2019)
Censer, Jack R., *Debating Modern Revolution: The Evolution of Revolutionary Ideas* (London: Bloomsbury, 2016)
Certeau, Michel de, *The Writing of History*, trans. Tom Conley (Columbia: Columbia University Press, 1992)
Chakrabarty, Dipesh, *Provincializing Europe: Postcolonial Thought and Historical Difference*, rev. edn (Princeton: Princeton University Press, 2009)
Chandler, James, *An Archaeology of Sympathy: The Sentimental Mode in Literature and Cinema* (Chicago: University of Chicago Press, 2013)
Childers, Joseph W., 'Carlyle's *Past and Present*, History, and a Question of Hermeneutics', *Clio*, 13.3 (1984), 247–58
Christie, William, *The Edinburgh Review in the Literary Culture of Romantic Britain: Mammoth and Megalonyx* (London and Brookfield: Pickering & Chatto, 2009)
—, 'The Modern Athenians: The *Edinburgh Review* in the Knowledge Economy of the Early Nineteenth Century', *Studies in Scottish Literature*, 39.1 (2013), 115–18
Clemit, Pamela, *The Godwinian Novel: The Rational Fictions of Godwin, Brockden Brown, Mary Shelley* (Oxford: Clarendon Press, 1993)
Clive, John, *Not by Fact Alone: Essays on the Writing and Reading of History* (New York: Alfred Knopf, 1989)
—, *Thomas Babington Macaulay: The Shaping of the Historian* (London: Knopf, 1973)
Coleridge, Samuel Taylor, *Biographia Literaria*, 2 vols (London: Rest Fenner, 1817)
Colla, Marcus, 'The Spectre of the Present: Time, Presentism, and the Writing of Contemporary History', *Contemporary European History*, 30.1 (2021), 124–35
Colley, Linda, *Britons: Forging the Nation, 1707–1837* (New Haven, NC, and London: Yale University Press, 1992)
Collini, Stefan, *Public Moralists: Political Thought and Intellectual Life in Britain, 1850–1930* (Oxford: Oxford University Press, 1992)
Confino, Alon, Ute Frevert, Uffa Jensen, and Lyndal Roper, 'Forum: History of Emotions', *German History*, 28.1 (2010), 67–80

Connelly, James, 'Philosophising History: Distinguishing History as a Discipline', in *The Edinburgh Critical History of Nineteenth-Century Philosophy*, ed. Alison Stone (Edinburgh: Edinburgh University Press, 2011), pp. 145–67

Connolly, Claire, 'Reflections on the Act of Union', in *Edmund Burke's Reflections on the Revolution in France: New Interdisciplinary Essays*, ed. John Whale (Manchester: Manchester University Press, 2000), pp. 168–92

Connolly, William E., *Political Theory and Modernity* (Oxford: Basil Blackwell, 1989)

Costelloe, Timothy M., 'Hume on History', in *The Continuum Companion to Hume*, ed. Alan Bailey and Dan O'Brien (London and New York: Continuum, 2012), pp. 364–76

—, *The Imagination in Hume's Philosophy: The Canvas of the Mind* (Edinburgh: Edinburgh University Press, 2018)

Crafton, Lisa Plummer, *Transgressive Theatricality, Romanticism, and Mary Wollstonecraft* (Farnham: Ashgate, 2011)

Craig, David M., 'Burke and the Constitution', in *The Cambridge Companion to Edmund Burke*, ed. David Dwan and Christopher Insole (Cambridge: Cambridge University Press, 2012), pp. 104–16

—, *Robert Southey and Romantic Apostasy: Political Argument in Britain, 1780–1840* (Suffolk: Boydell Press, 2007)

Crawford, Robert, *Devolving English Literature* (Oxford: Clarendon Press, 1992)

Crimmins, Jonathan, *The Romantic Historicism to Come* (London: Bloomsbury Academic, 2018)

Crocco, Francesco, *Literature and the Growth of British Nationalism: The Influence of Romantic Poetry and Bardic Criticism* (Jefferson, NC: McFarland, 2014)

Croker, John Wilson, 'Mr Macaulay's *History of England*', *Quarterly Review*, 84 (Dec. 1848), 549–630

—, 'Secret History of the Court of England from the Accession of George III to the Death of George IV', *Quarterly Review*, 61 (April 1838), 425–7

—, and George Murray, 'History of the War in the Peninsula &c', *Quarterly Review*, 56 (June 1836), 437–89

Crosby, Christina, *The Ends of History: Victorians and the 'Woman Question'* (New York and London: Routledge, 1991)

Crossley, Ceri, 'History, Nature and National Identity in France, 1800–30', *Literature and History*, 10.1 (2001), 18–27

Crowley, Sharon, *The Methodical Memory: Invention in Current-Traditional Rhetoric* (Carbondale and Edwardsville: Southern Illinois University Press, 1990)

Crozier-De Rosa, Sharon, 'Anger, Resentment, and the Limits of Historical Narratives in Protest Politics: The Case of Early Twentieth-Century Irish Women's Intersectional Movements', *Emotions: History, Culture, Society*, 5 (2021), 68–86

Csengei, Ildiko, *Sympathy, Sensibility and the Literature of Feeling in the Eighteenth Century* (Basingstoke: Palgrave Macmillan, 2012)

Cumming, Mark (ed.), *The Carlyle Encyclopedia* (Cranbury, NJ: Associated University Presses, 2004)

—, *A Disimprisoned Epic: Form and Vision in Carlyle's "French Revolution"* (Philadelphia: Pennsylvania University Press, 1988)
Curran, Stuart, 'Women and the *Edinburgh Review*', in *British Romanticism and the Edinburgh Review: Bicentenary Essays*, ed. Massimiliano Demata and Duncan Wu (Basingstoke: Palgrave Macmillan, 2002), pp. 195–208
Daiches, David, 'Sir Walter Scott and History', *Études anglais*, 24 (1971), 458–77
Daly, Eoin, 'Alchemising Peoplehood: Rousseau's Lawgiver as a Model of Constituent Power', *History of European Ideas*, 47.1 (2021), 1278–91
Damasio, Antonio, *Looking for Spinoza: Joy, Sorrow and the Feeling Brain* (London: Heinemann, 2003)
Dames, Nicholas, 'On Not Close Reading: The Prolonged Excerpt as Victorian Critical Protocol', in *The Feeling of Reading: Affective Experience and Victorian Literature*, ed. Rachael Ablow (Ann Arbor: University of Michigan Press, 2010), pp. 11–26
Danhay, Peter, *The Feminization of the Novel* (Gainesville: University of Florida Press, 1991)
Darnton, Robert, *Mesmerism and the End of the Enlightenment in France* (New York: Schocken Books, 1968)
Dart, Gregory, *Rousseau, Robespierre, and English Romanticism* (Cambridge: Cambridge University Press, 1999)
Davidson, Jenny, 'Recent Studies in the Restoration and Eighteenth Century', *Studies in English Literature*, 56.3 (2016), 671–725
Davies, Damian Walford, 'Counterfactual Obstetrics: Mary Wollstonecraft's *Frankenstein*', in *Counterfactual Romanticism*, ed. Damian Walford Davies (Manchester: Manchester University Press, 2019), pp. 155–201
Davis, Kathleen, *Periodization and Sovereignty: How Ideas of Feudalism and Secularization Govern the Politics of Time* (Philadelphia: University of Pennsylvania Press, 2008)
Davis, Leith, 'Irish Bards and English Consumers: Thomas Moore's "Irish Melodies" and the Colonized Nation', *ariel*, 24.2 (1993), 7–25
Davis, Thomas Osbourne, *Thomas Davis: Selections from his Poetry and Prose* (1842; repr. New York: AMS Press, 1982)
Davis, William A., Jr, '"This is My Theory": Macaulay on Periodical Style', *Victorian Periodicals Review*, 20.1 (1987), 12–22
Deane, Seamus, *Celtic Revivals: Essays in Modern Irish Literature, 1880–1890* (London: Faber and Faber, 1985)
De Lauretis, Teresa, 'Eccentric Subjects: Feminist Theory and Historical Consciousness', *Feminist Studies*, 16.1 (1990), 115–50
De Quincey, Thomas, 'Style I', *Blackwood's Edinburgh Magazine*, 48 (July 1840), 1–17
De Sousa, Ronald, *The Rationality of Emotion* (Cambridge, MA: MIT Press, 1987)
Deigh, John, 'Concepts of Emotions in Modern Philosophy and Psychology', in *The Oxford Handbook of the Philosophy of Emotion*, ed. Peter Goldie (Oxford: Oxford University Press, 2010), pp. 17–40
Demata, Massimiliano, 'Prejudiced Knowledge: Travel Literature in the *Edinburgh Review*', in *British Romanticism and the Edinburgh Review: Bicentenary Essays*, ed. Massimiliano Demata and Duncan Wu (Basingstoke: Palgrave Macmillan, 2002), pp. 82–101

Desaulniers, Mary, *Carlyle and the Economics of Terror: A Study of Revisionary Gothicism in The French Revolution* (Kingston, Ontario: McGill-Queens University Press, 1995)

Dew, Ben, and Fiona Price, 'Introduction: Visions of History', in *Historical Writing in Britain, 1688–1830: Visions of History*, ed. Ben Drew and Fiona Price (Basingstoke: Palgrave Macmillan, 2014), pp. 1–17

De Waard, Marco, '"The Morality of Style": John Morley as Essayistic Liberal', *Nineteenth-Century Prose*, 43.1–2 (2016), 227–44

Dilthey, Wilhelm, *Ideas Concerning a Descriptive and Analytic Psychology* (1894), in *Descriptive Psychology and Historical Understanding*, trans. Kenneth Heiges and Richard Zaner (The Hague: Martinus Nijhoff, 1977)

Dinshaw, Carolyn, *Getting Medieval* (Durham, NC: Duke University Press, 1999)

Dinwiddy, J. R., 'Charles James Fox as Historian', *The Historical Journal*, 12.1 (1969), 23–34

Dixon, Thomas, *From Passions to Emotions: The Creation of a Secular Psychological Category* (Cambridge: Cambridge University Press, 2003)

—, *Weeping Britannia: Portrait of a Nation in Tears* (Oxford: Oxford University Press, 2015)

Dolan, Seán Patrick, '"They put to the torture all the ancient monuments": Glib Reflections on Making Eighteenth-Century Irish Legal History and the Proceedings of Some Writers on Ireland Relative to that Subject', in *Making Legal History: Approaches and Methodologies*, ed. Anthony Musson and Chantal Stebbings (Cambridge: Cambridge University Press, 2012), pp. 146–63

Domanska, Ewa, 'Frank Ankersmit: From Narrative to Experience', *Rethinking History*, 13.2 (2009), 175–95

Donoghue, Frank, *The Fame Machine: Book Reviewing and Eighteenth-Century Literary Careers* (Stanford: Stanford University Press, 1996)

Dowling, Linda, 'Roman Decadence and Victorian Historiography', *Victorian Studies*, 28.4 (1985), 579–607

Doyle, Laura, *Freedom's Empire: Race and the Rise of the Novel in Atlantic Modernity, 1640–1940* (Durham, NC: Duke University Press, 2008)

Duggett, Tom, 'Southey's "Colloquies" and Romantic History', *The Wordsworth Circle*, 44.2/3 (2013), 87–93

Duncan, Ian, 'Edinburgh and Lowland Scotland', in *The Cambridge History of English Romantic Literature*, ed. James Chandler (Cambridge: Cambridge University Press, 2009), pp. 159–81

—, *Scott's Shadow: The Novel in Romantic Edinburgh* (Princeton: Princeton University Press, 2007)

Dwan, David, 'Edmund Burke and the Emotions', *Journal of the History of Ideas*, 72.4 (2011), 571–93

—, 'Romantic Nationalism: History and Illusion in Ireland', *Modern Intellectual History*, 14.3 (2017), 717–45

Eagleton, Terry, 'Aesthetics and Politics in Edmund Burke', *History Workshop*, 28 (1989), 53–62

Easley, Alexis, *First-Person Anonymous: Women Writers and Victorian Print Media, 1830–1870* (London: Routledge, 2004)

—, Clare Gill, and Beth Rodgers (eds), *Women, Periodicals, and Print Culture, 1830s–1900s: The Victorian Period* (Edinburgh: Edinburgh University Press, 2019)

Eastwood, David, 'Robert Southey and the Meaning of Patriotism', *Journal of British Studies*, 31.3 (1992), 265–87

Edelstein, Dan, 'Future Perfect: Political and Emotional Economies of Revolutionary Time', in *Power and Time: Temporalities in Conflict and the Making of History*, ed. Dan Edelstein, Stefanos Geroulanos, and Natasha Wheatley (Chicago: University of Chicago Press, 2020), pp. 357–78

Edson, Michael, 'Godwin's Anti-Mass Politics Revisited: Sympathy, Retirement, and Epistemic Diversity', *Nineteenth-Century Prose*, 41.1/2 (2014), 161–94

Edwards, Owen Dudley, 'Carlyle Versus Macaulay? – A Study in History', *Carlyle Studies Annual*, 27 (2011), 177–206

Elfenbein, Andrew, *Romanticism and the Rise of English* (Stanford: Stanford University Press, 2008)

Elias, Norbert, *The Civilizing Process: Sociogenetic and Psychogenetic Investigations* (1939; repr. Oxford: Blackwell, 2000)

Ellegard, Alvar, *The Readership of the Periodical Press in Mid-Victorian Britain* (Gothenburg: Almqvist and Wiksell, 1957)

Ellenberger, Henri, *The Discovery of the Unconscious: The History and Evolution of Dramatic Psychiatry* (New York: Basic Books, 1970)

Ellis, Heather, 'Enlightened Networks in Anglo-German Collaboration in Classical Scholarship', in *Anglo-German Scholarly Networks in the Long Nineteenth Century*, ed. Heather Ellis and Ulrike Kirchberger (Leiden: Brill, 2014), pp. 23–8

Ellis, T. F., 'Palgrave's *Truths and Fictions*', *Edinburgh Review*, 66 (Jan. 1838), 464–76

Ellison, Julie, *Cato's Tears and the Making of Anglo-American Emotion* (Chicago: Chicago University Press, 1999)

Emerson, Ralph Waldo, *The Works of Ralph Waldo Emerson in 12 Volumes, Fireside Edition, Vol. 5 English Traits* (Boston and New York: n.pub., 1909)

Empson, William, 'Sismondi's *Italian Republics*', *Edinburgh Review*, 55 (July 1832), 362–97

—, 'Providential and Prophetical Histories', *Edinburgh Review*, 50 (Jan. 1830), 287–344

Esterhammer, Angela, 'Godwin's Suspicion of Speech Acts', *Studies in Romanticism*, 39.4 (2000), 553–78

Faflak, Joel, 'Speaking of Godwin's *Caleb Williams*: The Talking Cure and the Pyschopathology of Enlightenment', *English Studies in Canada*, 31.2–3 (2005), 99–122

Fairclough, Mary, *The Romantic Crowd: Sympathy, Controversy and Print Culture* (Cambridge: Cambridge University Press, 2013)

Farrell, Gerard, *The 'Mere' Irish and the Colonisation of Ulster, 1570–1641* (Basingstoke: Palgrave Macmillan, 2017)

Febvre, Lucien, 'Sensibility and History: How to Reconstitute the Emotional Life of the Past', in *A New Kind of History: From the Writings of Febvre*, ed. Peter Burke, trans. K. Folca (New York: Harper & Row, 1973), pp. 12–26

Ferguson, Frances, 'Envy Rising', *English Literary History*, 69.4 (2002), 889–905

Fermanis, Porscha, 'Countering the Counterfactual: Joanna Baillie's *Metrical Legends of Exalted Characters* (1821) and the Paratexts of History', *Women's Writing*, 19.3 (2012), 333–50

—, and John Regan, 'Introduction', in *Rethinking British Romantic History, 1770–1845*, ed. Porscha Fermanis and John Regan (Oxford: Oxford University Press, 2014), pp. 1–34

Ferris, Ina, '"Before Our Eyes": Romantic Historical Fiction and the Apparitions of Reading', *Representations*, 121.1 (2013), 60–84

—, *Book-Men, Book Clubs, and the Romantic Literary Sphere* (Basingstoke: Palgrave Macmillan, 2015)

—, 'The Debut of the *Edinburgh Review*, 1802', BRANCH: Britain, Representation and Nineteenth-Century History, ed. Dino Franco Felluga, n.p., <http://www.branchcollective.org/?ps_articles=ina-ferris-the-debut-of-the-edinburgh-review-1802> (last accessed 2 July 2019)

—, 'Printing the Past: Walter Scott's Bannatyne Club and the Antiquarian Document', *Romanticism*, 11.2 (2005), 143–60

—, 'Re-Positioning the Novel: "Waverley" and the Gender of Fiction', *Studies in Romanticism*, 28.2 (1989), 291–301

—, *The Romantic National Tale and the Question of Ireland* (Cambridge: Cambridge University Press, 2004)

—, 'Transformations of the Novel – II', in *The Cambridge History of English Romantic Literature*, ed. James K. Chandler (Cambridge: Cambridge University Press, 2009), pp. 473–89

—, 'Writing on the Border: The National Tale, Female Writing, and the Public Sphere', in *Romanticism, History, and the Possibilities of Genre: Re-forming Literature 1789–1837*, ed. Tilottama Rajan and Julia M. Wright (Cambridge: Cambridge University Press: 1998), pp. 86–109

Festa, Lynn, *Sentimental Figures of Empire in Eighteenth-Century Britain and France* (Baltimore: Johns Hopkins University Press, 2006)

Fetter, Frank Whitson, 'The Authorship of Economic Articles in the Edinburgh Review', *Journal of Political Economy*, 61 (1953), 232–59

Fielding, K. J., 'Carlyle and Cromwell: The Writing of History and "Dryasdust"', in *Lectures on Carlyle and his Era*, ed. Jerry D. James and Rita D. Bottoms (Santa Cruz: University Library, University of California, 1985), pp. 45–68

Findlay, L. M., '"Maternity must forth": The Poetics and Politics of Gender in Carlyle's *French Revolution*', *Dalhousie Review*, 66.1&2 (1986), 130–54

Firth, Charles, *A Commentary on Macaulay's History of England* (1938; repr. Abingdon: Frank Cass & Co., 1964)

Fleissner, Jennifer L., 'Is Feminism a Historicism?', *Tulsa Studies in Women's Literature*, 21.1 (2002), 45–66

Fong, David, 'Macaulay: The Essayist as Historian', *Dalhousie Review*, 51 (1971), 38–48

Forbes, Duncan, *Hume's Philosophical Politics* (Cambridge: Cambridge University Press, 1975)

—, *The Liberal Anglican Idea of History* (Cambridge: Cambridge University Press, 1952)

—, 'The Rationalism of Sir Walter Scott', *Cambridge Journal*, 7 (1953), 20–35

Foster, John, 'Nationality, Social Change and Class: Transformations of National Identity in Scotland', in *The Making of Scotland*, ed. D. McCrone,

S. Kendrick, and P. Strow (Edinburgh: Edinburgh University Press, 1989), pp. 31–52

Foster, Roy, 'History and the Irish Question', *Transactions of the Royal Historical Society*, 33 (1983), 169–92

Foucault, Michel, *Society Must Be Defended: Lectures at the Collège de France 1975–76*, ed. Mauro Bertani and Alexandro Fontana, trans. David Macey (New York: Picador, 2003)

—, 'What is Enlightenment?', in *The Foucault Reader*, ed. Paul Rabinow (New York: Pantheon Books, 1984), pp. 32–50

Fox, W. J., 'On the Study of History. No. 2', *People's Journal*, 1 (1846), 187–93

Frank, Jason, '"Delightful Horror": Edmund Burke and the Aesthetics of Democratic Revolution', in *The Aesthetic Turn in Political Thought*, ed. Nikolas Kompridis (New York and London: Bloomsbury, 2014), pp. 3–28

—, *The Democratic Sublime: On Aesthetics and Popular Assembly* (Oxford: Oxford University Press, 2021)

Fraser, G. S., 'Macaulay's Style as an Essayist', *Review of English Literature*, 1.4 (1960), 9–19

Frazer, Michael, *The Enlightenment of Sympathy: Justice and the Moral Sentiments in the Eighteenth Century and Today* (Oxford: Oxford University Press, 2012)

Frey, Anne, *British State Romanticism: Authorship, Agency, and Bureaucratic Nationalism* (Stanford: Stanford University Press, 2009)

Freyre, Gilberto, *New World in the Tropics: The Culture of Modern Brazil* (New York: Alfred A. Knopf, 1959)

Fritzsche, Peter, 'The Archive', *History and Memory*, 17.1/2 (2005), 15–44

Froeyman, Anton, 'Frank Ankersmit and Eelco Runia: The Presence and Otherness of the Past', *Rethinking History*, 15.3 (2012), 393–415

Frye, Lowell T., '"Leaving Blair's Lectures Quite Behind": Thomas Carlyle's Rhetorical Revolution', *Occasional Papers 26: The Carlyle Society* (Edinburgh: Carlyle Society, 2013), pp. 21–43, <https://www.ed.ac.uk/files/atoms/files/carlyle_papers_no._26.pdf> (last accessed 19 November 2020)

Fulford, Tim, 'Blessed Bane: Christianity and Colonial Disease in Southey's *Tale of Paraguay*', *Romanticism on the Net*, 24 (2001), n.p., <https://id.erudit.org/iderudit/005998ar> (last accessed 12 June 2019)

Furet, François, *Interpreting the French Revolution*, trans. Elborg Forster (Cambridge: Cambridge University Press, 1981)

Furniss, Tom, *Edmund Burke's Aesthetic Ideology: Language, Gender, and Political Economy in Revolution* (Cambridge: Cambridge University Press, 1993)

Gallagher, Catherine, 'The Rise of Fictionality', in *The Novel: History, Geography and Culture, Vol. 1*, ed. Franco Moretti (Princeton: Princeton University Press, 2006), pp. 336–63

Garafolo, Daniela, 'Communities in Mourning: Making Capital out of Loss in Carlyle's *Past and Present* and *Heroes*', *Texan Studies in Literature and Language*, 45.3 (2003), 293–314

Garritzen, Elise, 'Women Historians, Gender and Fashioning the Authoritative Self in Paratexts in Late-Victorian Britain', *Women's History Review*, 30.4 (2021), 650–68

Garside, Peter, 'Scott and the "Philosophical" Historians', *Journal of the History of Ideas*, 36 (1975), 497–512

Gay, Peter, *Style in History: Gibbon, Ranke, Macaulay, Burckhardt* (New York: Basic Books, 1974)

Gayangos, Pascual de, 'Prescott's *The History of the Reign of Ferdinand and Isabella*', *Edinburgh Review*, 68 (Jan. 1839), 376–405

Gearhart, Suzanne, *The Open Boundaries of History and Fiction* (Princeton: Princeton University Press, 1984)

George, Anne L., 'Grounds of Assent in Joseph Priestley's *A Course of Lectures on Oratory and Criticism*', *Rhetoric*, 16 (1998), 81–109

Gere, Cathy, *Pain, Pleasure, and the Greater Good: From the Panopticon to the Skinner Box and Beyond* (Chicago: University of Chicago Press, 2017)

Gibbons, Luke, *Edmund Burke and Ireland: Aesthetics, Politics, and the Colonial Sublime* (Cambridge: Cambridge University Press, 2003)

—, 'Romantic Ireland: 1750–1845', in *The Cambridge History of English Romantic Literature*, ed. James K. Chandler (Cambridge: Cambridge University Press, 2009), pp. 182–203

Gibbs, Luke, 'Great Britain and Latin America: The Romantics and Informal Empire' (PhD thesis, University of Missouri, 2013)

Gieryn, Thomas F., 'Boundary-Work and the Demarcation of Science from Non-Science: Strains and Interests in Professional Ideologies of Scientists', *American Sociological Review*, 48.6 (1983), 781–95

Gilmartin, Kevin, *Writing against the Revolution: Literary Conservatism in Britain, 1790–1832* (Cambridge: Cambridge University Press, 2007).

Gödde, Günter, 'The Unconscious in the German Philosophy and Psychology of the Nineteenth Century', trans. Ciaran Cronan, in *The Edinburgh Critical History of Nineteenth-Century Philosophy*, ed. Alison Stone (Edinburgh: Edinburgh University Press, 2011), pp. 204–22

Godwin, William, *An Account of the Seminary* (1783), in *Four Early Pamphlets (1783–1784)*, ed. Burton R. Pollin (Gainesville, FL: Scholars Facsimiles and Reprints, 1966), pp. 147–202

—, *Cloudesley, A Tale*, 3 vols (London: Henry Colburn and Richard Bentley, 1830)

—, *The Enquirer: Reflections on Education, Manners, and Literature in a Series of Essays* (London: G. G. and J. Robinson, 1797)

—, *An Enquiry Concerning Political Justice, and its Influence on Morals and Happiness*, 2 vols (London: G. G. and J. Robinson, 1798 [1793, 1796])

—, *History of the Commonwealth of England: From its Commencement to the Restoration of Charles the Second*, 4 vols (London: Henry Colburn, 1824–8)

—, *The History of the Life of William Pitt, Earl of Chatham* (London: G. Kearsley, 1783)

—, *Letters of Mucius*, in *The Political and Philosophical Writing of William Godwin: Volume 1*, ed. Martin Fitzpatrick (London: Pickering and Chatto, 1993)

—, *Life of Geoffrey Chaucer, The Early English Poet*, 4 vols (London: Richard Phillips, 1804)

—, *Memoirs of the Author of a Vindication of the Rights of Woman* (London: J. Johnson, 1798)

—, 'Of History and Romance' (wr. 1797), in *Caleb Williams, or Things as they Are*, ed. Maurice Hindle (1794; repr. Harmondsworth: Penguin, 1988), pp. 359–73
—, 'On the Composition of History: An Occasional Reflection', MS. Abinger c.29, undated, watermarked 1808
—, *Sketches of History in Six Sermons* (London: T. Cadell, 1784)
Goldberg, Michael K., '"Demigods and Philistines": Macaulay and Carlyle – A Study in Contrasts', *Studies in Scottish Literature*, 24.1 (1989), 116–28
—, 'Gigantic Philistines: Carlyle, Dickens, and the Visual Arts', in *Lectures on Carlyle and his Era*, ed. Jerry D. James and Charles S. Fineman (Santa Cruz: University Library, University of California, 1982), pp. 17–43
Goldhill, Simon, *Victorian Culture and Classical Antiquity* (Princeton: Princeton University Press, 2012)
Goldstein, Jan, *The Post-Revolutionary Self: Politics and Psyche in France, 1750–1850* (Cambridge, MA: Harvard University Press, 2005)
Goode, Mike, 'The Man of Feeling History: The Erotics of Historicism in *Reflections on the Revolution in France*', *English Literary History*, 74.4 (2007), 829–57
—, *Sentimental Masculinity and the Rise of History 1790–1890* (Cambridge: Cambridge University Press, 2009)
Goodman, Kevis, *Georgic Modernity and British Romanticism: Poetry and the Mediation of History* (Cambridge: Cambridge University Press, 2004)
Gossman, Lionel, *Between History and Literature* (Cambridge, MA: Harvard University Press, 1990)
—, 'History as Decipherment: Romantic Historiography and the Discovery of the Other', *New Literary History*, 18.1 (1986), 23–57
—, 'Towards a Rational Historiography', *Transactions of the American Philosophic Society*, 79.3 (1989), 1–68
Grafton, Anthony, *The Footnote: A Curious History* (Cambridge, MA: Harvard University Press, 1997)
—, 'The Footnote from De Thou to Ranke', *History and Theory*, 33.4 (1994), 53–76
Graham, Maria, *Journal of a Voyage to Brazil and Residence There During Part of the Years 1821, 1822, 1823* (London: Longman and John Murray, 1824)
Graham, Kenneth W., *William Godwin Reviewed: A Reception History, 1783–1834* (New York: AMS Press, 2001)
Green, Karen, 'The Passions and the Imagination in Wollstonecraft's Theory of Moral Judgement', *Utilitas*, 9.3 (1997), 271–90
—, 'Will the Real Enlightenment Historian Please Stand Up? Catherine Macaulay versus David Hume', in *Hume and the Enlightenment*, ed. Craig Taylor and Stephen Buckle (London: Pickering & Chatto, 2011), pp. 39–51
Greentree, Shane, 'The "Equal Eye" of Compassion: Reading Sympathy in Catherine Macaulay's *History of England*', *Eighteenth-Century Studies*, 52.3 (2019), 299–318
Griffiths, Devin, *The Age of Analogy: Science and Literature Between the Darwins* (Baltimore: Johns Hopkins University Press, 2016)
Gross, Daniel M., *The Secret History of Emotions: From Aristotle's Rhetoric to Modern Brain Science* (Chicago: University of Chicago Press, 2006)

Gross, John, *The Rise and Fall of the Man of Letters: Aspects of English Literary Life Since 1800* (London: Weidenfeld and Nicolson, 1969)

Gubar, Susan, 'Feminist Misogyny: Mary Wollstonecraft and the Paradox of "It Takes One to Know One"', *Feminist Studies*, 20 (1994), 452–73

Guest, Harriet, *Unbounded Attachment: Sentiment and Politics in the Age of the French Revolution* (Oxford: Oxford University Press, 2013)

Guillory, John, 'The Memo and Modernity', *Critical Inquiry*, 31.1 (2004), 108–32

Gunther-Canada, Wendy, 'The Politics of Sense and Sensibility: Mary Wollstonecraft and Catherine Macaulay Graham on Edmund Burke's *Reflections on the Revolution in France*', in *Women Writers and the Early Modern British Political Tradition*, ed. Hilda L. Smith (Cambridge: Cambridge University Press, 1998), pp. 126–47

Gust, Onni, 'Empire, Exile, Identity: Locating Sir James Mackintosh's Histories of England' (PhD thesis, University College London, 2010)

—, 'Remembering and Forgetting the Scottish Highlands: Sir James Mackintosh and the Forging of a British Imperial Identity', *Journal of British Studies*, 52.3 (2014), 615–37

—, *Unhomely Empire: Whiteness and Belonging, c. 1760–1830* (London: Bloomsbury, 2020)

Hall, Catherine, 'Macaulay's Nation', *Victorian Studies*, 51.3 (2009), 505–23

Hallam, Henry, *The Constitutional History of England, from the Accession of Henry VII, to the Death of George II*, 2 vols (London: John Murray, 1827)

—, 'Francis Palgrave's *Rise and Progress* and *History of England*', *Edinburgh Review*, 55 (Jan. 1832), 305–37

—, 'Lingard's *History of England*', *Edinburgh Review*, 53 (March 1831), 1–42

Hamilton, Paul, 'Inexhaustible Fertility: Contemporary Re-figurations of the French Revolution', *Comparative Critical Studies*, 15.2 (2018), 153–68

—, *Metaromanticism: Aesthetics, Literature, Theory* (Chicago: University of Chicago Press, 2003)

Handwerk, Gary, 'Of Caleb's Guilt and Godwin's Truth: Ideology and Ethics in *Caleb Williams*', *English Literary History*, 60.4 (1993), 939–60

Hansson, John-Erik, 'The Genre of Radical Thought and the Practices of Equality: The Trajectories of William Godwin and John Thelwall in the mid-1790s', *History of European Ideas*, 43.7 (2017), 776–90

Hargraves, Neil K., 'National History and "Philosophical" History: Character and Narrative in William Robertson's History of Scotland', *History of European Ideas*, 26.1 (2000), 19–33

Harootunian, Harry, 'Remembering the Historical Present', *Critical Inquiry*, 33.3 (2007), 471–94

—, 'Shadowing the Past: National History and the Persistence of the Everyday', *Cultural Studies*, 18.2/3 (2004), 181–200

Hartog, François, *Regimes of Historicity: Presentism and Experiences of Time*, trans. Saskia Brown (New York: Columbia University Press, 2016)

Haskell, Thomas, *Objectivity is not Neutrality: Explanatory Schemes in History* (Baltimore: Johns Hopkins University Press, 1998)

Healy, Róisín, *Poland and the Irish National Imagination, 1772–1922: Anti-Colonialism within Europe* (Basingstoke: Palgrave Macmillan, 2017)

Heaney, Jonathan G., 'Emotions and Nationalism: A Reappraisal', in *Emotions in Politics: The Affect Dimension in Political Tension*, ed. Nicolas Demertzis (New York: Palgrave Macmillan, 2013), pp. 243–63

Heinowitz, Rebecca Cole, *Spanish America and British Romanticism, 1777–1826: Rewriting Conquest* (Edinburgh: Edinburgh University Press, 2010)

Hemmings, Claire, 'Invoking Affect: Cultural Theory and the Ontological Turn', *Cultural Studies*, 19.5 (2005), 548–67

Henderson, Andrea, *Romantic Identities: Varieties of Subjectivity, 1774–1830* (Cambridge: Cambridge University Press, 1996)

Henderson, Heather, 'Carlyle and the Book Clubs: A New Approach to Publishing?', *Publishing History*, 6 (1979), 37–62

Herdt, Jennifer A., 'Artificial Lives, Providential History, and the Apparent Limits of Sympathetic Understanding', in *David Hume: Historical Thinker, Historical Writer*, ed. Mark G. Spencer (University Park, PA: Penn State University Press, 2013), pp. 37–61

Hesketh, Ian, 'Diagnosing Froude's Disease: Boundary Work and the Discipline of History in Late-Victorian Britain', *History and Theory*, 47.3 (2008), 373–95

—, *The Science of History in Victorian Britain: Making the Past Speak* (London: Pickering & Chatto, 2006)

—, *Victorian Jesus: J. R. Seeley, Religion, and the Cultural Significance of Anonymity* (Toronto: University of Toronto Press, 2017)

Heyck, T. W., 'From Men of Letters to Intellectuals: The Transformation of Intellectual Life in Nineteenth-Century England', *Journal of British Studies*, 20.1 (1980), 158–83

—, *The Transformation of Intellectual Life in Victorian England* (New York: St Martin's Press, 1982)

Heyrendt-Sherman, Catherine, 'Re-presenting the French Revolution: The Impact of Carlyle's Work on British Society and its Self-representation', *French Journal of British Studies*, 15.4 (2010), n.p., <https://doi.org/10.4000/rfcb.6118> (last accessed 2 June 2019)

Hill, Marylu, '"History is a Real Prophetic Manuscript": Reason and Revelation in Thomas Carlyle's Historical Essays', *Literature and Belief*, 25.1 (2005), 1–16

—, 'Of Bricklayers and Kings: Burke, Carlyle, and the Defense of Monarchy', in *Thomas Carlyle Resartus: Reappraising Carlyle's Contribution to the Philosophy of History, Political Theory, and Cultural Criticism*, ed. Paul E. Kerry and Marylu Hill (Madison, NJ: Fairleigh Dickinson University Press, 2010), pp. 18–105

Hobsbawm, Eric J., *Nations and Nationalism Since 1780: Programme, Myth, Reality* (Cambridge: Cambridge University Press, 1990)

Hodson, Jane, *Language and Revolution in Burke, Wollstonecraft, Paine, and Godwin* (Aldershot: Ashgate, 2007)

Hogan, J. Michael, 'Historiography and Ethics in Adam Smith's Lectures on Rhetoric, 1762–1763', *Rhetorica*, 2.1 (1984), 75–91

Hogg, Thomas Jefferson, '*The History of Rome* by B. G. Niebuhr', *Edinburgh Review*, 51 (July 1830), 358–96

Howell, Peter, 'Godwin, Contractarianism, and the Political Dead End of Empiricism', *Eighteenth-Century Life*, 28.2 (2004), 61–86

Howsam, Leslie, 'Academic Discipline or Literary Genre?: The Establishment of Boundaries in Historical Writing', *Victorian Literature and Culture*, 32.2 (2004), 525–45

—, 'Mediated Histories: How Did Victorian Periodicals Parse the Past', *Victorian Periodicals Review*, 50.4 (2017), 802–24

—, *Past into Print: The Publishing of History in Britain* (London and Toronto: British Library and the University of Toronto Press, 2009)

Hudson, Nicholas, 'From "Nation" to "Race": The Origin of Racial Classification in Eighteenth-Century Thought', *Eighteenth-Century Studies*, 29.3 (1996), 247–64

Hughes-Warrington, Marnie, *History as Wonder: Beginning with Historiography* (New York: Routledge, 2019)

Hultquist, Aleksondra, 'New Directions in History of Emotion and Affect Theory in Eighteenth-Century Studies', *Literature Compass*, 13.12 (2016), 762–70

Hume, David, *Enquiries Concerning Human Understanding and Concerning the Principles of Morals*, ed. L. A. Selby-Bigge, rev. P. H. Nidditch, 3rd edn (Oxford: Clarendon Press, 1975)

—, *Essays Moral, Political, and Literary*, ed. Eugene F. Miller (Indianapolis: Liberty Fund, 1994)

—, *The History of England by Hume and Smollett with a Continuation by the Rev. T. S. Hughes* (London: Valpy, 1834–6)

—, *A Treatise of Human Nature*, ed. L. A. Selby-Bigge, rev. P. H. Nidditch, 2nd edn (Oxford: Clarendon Press, 1978)

Humphreys, Robert Arthur, *Robert Southey and his History of Brazil* (London: Hispanic and Luso Brazilian Council, 1978)

Hunt, Lynn, *The Family Romance of the French Revolution* (Berkeley: University of California Press, 1992)

Hurley, Michael D., and Marcus Waithe, 'Introduction: Thinkers, Thinking, Style, Stylists', in *Thinking Through Style: Non-Fiction Prose of the Long Nineteenth Century*, ed. Michael D. Hurley and Marcus Waithe (Oxford: Oxford University Press, 2018), pp. 1–10

Hutchinson, John, 'Myth against Myth: The Nation as Ethnic Overlay', *Nations and Nationalism*, 10.1–2 (2004), 109–23

Huyssen, Andreas, *After the Great Divide: Modernism, Mass Culture, Postmodernism* (Bloomington: Indiana University Press, 1986)

Icke, Peter P., *Frank Ankersmit's Lost Historical Cause: A Journey from Language to Experience* (New York and London: Routledge, 2012)

Ingram, Malcolm, 'Carlylese', *Occasional Papers 26: The Carlyle Society* (Edinburgh: Carlyle Society, 2013), pp. 5–20, <https://www.ed.ac.uk/files/atoms/files/carlyle_papers_no._26.pdf> (last accessed 19 November 2020)

Ireland, Craig, *The Subaltern Appeal to Experience: Self-Identity, Late Modernity, and the Politics of Immediacy* (Montreal and Kingston: McGill-Queen's University Press, 2004)

Isaacson, Saul, 'Carlyle and Macaulay in the Journals: Towards a New Historiography', *Carlyle Annual*, 10 (1989), 21–30

Iseli, Markus, *Thomas De Quincey and the Cognitive Unconscious* (Basingstoke: Palgrave Macmillan, 2015)

Jacob, William, 'Travels in Brazil', *Quarterly Review*, 31 (April 1824), 1–26

Jaeger, Friedrich, and Jörn Rüsen, *Geschichte des Historismus* (Munich: Beck, 1992)
Jann, Rosemary, *The Art and Science of Victorian History* (Athens: Ohio State University Press, 1985)
—, 'Changing Styles in Victorian Military History', *Clio*, 11.2 (1982), 159–60
Jay, Martin, *Songs of Experience: Modern American and European Variations on a Universal Theme* (Berkeley: University of California Press, 2005)
Jeffrey, Francis, 'Brodie's *Constitutional History of the British Empire*', *Edinburgh Review*, 40 (March 1824), 92–146
—, 'The Ecclesiastical and Political History of the Popes of Rome, during the Sixteenth and Seventeenth Centuries', *Dublin Review*, 14 (May 1843), 321–79
—, '*Memoirs of Lady Fanshawe*', *Edinburgh Review*, 50 (Oct. 1829), 75–85
—, 'O'Driscol's *History of Ireland*', *Edinburgh Review*, 46 (Oct. 1827), 433–70
Jenkins, Keith, 'Cohen contra Ankersmit', *Rethinking History*, 12.4 (2008), 537–55
—, and Alun Munslow (eds), *The Nature of History Reader* (London and New York: Routledge, 2004)
Jessop, Ralph, *Carlyle and Scottish Thought* (Basingstoke: Palgrave Macmillan, 1997)
Jinzenji, Mônica Yumi and Maria de Oliveira Galvão, 'History of Brazil for the "fair sex": Appropriations of the Foreign Perspective for Nineteenth-Century Female Readers', *Revista Brasileira de Histórica*, 30 (2010), 119–36
Johnson, Claudia L., *Equivocal Beings: Politics, Gender, and Sentimentality in the 1790s, Wollstonecraft, Radcliffe, Burney, Austen* (Chicago and London: University of Chicago Press, 1995)
Johnson, Samuel, *A Dictionary of the English Language*, 4th edn (Dublin: Thomas Ewing, 1775)
Jones, Edwin, *John Lingard and the Pursuit of Historical Truth* (Brighton: Sussex Academic Press, 2001)
Jones, Emily, *Edmund Burke and the Invention of Modern Conservatism, 1830–1914: An Intellectual History* (Oxford: Oxford University Press, 2017)
Jones, Jason B., *Lost Causes: Historical Consciousness in Victorian Literature* (Columbus: Ohio State University Press, 2006)
Jones, Peter (ed.), *The Reception of David Hume in Europe* (London: Thoemmes Continuum, 2005)
Jones, Vivien, 'Women Writing Revolution: Narratives of History and Sexuality in Wollstonecraft and Williams', *History of European Ideas*, 16 (1991), 299–305
Kasmer, Lisa, *Novel Histories: British Women Writing History, 1760–1830* (Madison, NJ: Fairleigh Dickinson University Press, 2012)
Keane, Angela, 'The Importance of Elsewhere: Romantic Subjectivity and the Romance of History', *Wordsworth Circle*, 27.1 (1996), 16–21
—, 'Mary Wollstonecraft's Imperious Sympathies: Population, Maternity, and Romantic Individualism', in *Body Matters: Feminism, Textuality, Corporeality*, ed. Avril Horner and Angela Keane (Manchester: Manchester University Press, 2000), pp. 29–42
—, 'Reflections and Correspondences: The Familiarity of Burke's Unfamiliar Letter', in *Edmund Burke's Reflections on the Revolution in France:*

New Interdisciplinary Essays, ed. John Whale (Manchester: Manchester University Press, 2000), pp. 193–218

Kellner, Hans, 'However Imperceptibly: From the Historical to the Sublime', *PMLA*, 118.3 (2003), 591–6

—, *Language and Historical Representation: Getting the Story Crooked* (Madison: University of Wisconsin Press, 1989)

Kelly, Gary, *Revolutionary Feminism: The Mind and Career of Mary Wollstonecraft* (New York: St Martin's Press, 1992)

—, 'Romanticism and the Feminist Uses of History', in *Romanticism, History, Historicism: Essays on an Orthodoxy*, ed. Damian Walford Davies (New York and London: Routledge, 2009), pp. 163–81

Kelly, James, 'Dreaming the Future while Arguing the Past: Temperaments and Temporalities in Irish Writing', in *Dreams of the Future in Nineteenth-Century Ireland*, ed. Richard J. Butler (Liverpool: Liverpool University Press, 2021), pp. 19–36

Kelly, Ronan, *Bard of Erin: The Life of Thomas Moore* (Dublin: Penguin Ireland, 2008)

Kent, Christopher, 'Higher Journalism and the Mid-Victorian Clerisy', *Victorian Studies*, 13.2 (1969), 181–98

Khin Zaw, Susan, 'The Reasonable Heart: Mary Wollstonecraft's View of the Relation Between Reason and Feeling in Morality', *Hypatia*, 13.1 (1998), 78–117

Kidd, Colin, 'Gaelic Antiquity and National Identity in Enlightenment Ireland and Scotland', *English Historical Review*, 434 (1994), 1197–214

—, 'The Ideological Significance of Robertson's *History of Scotland*', in *William Robertson and the Expansion of Empire*, ed. S. J. Brown (Cambridge: Cambridge University Press, 1997), pp. 122–44

—, 'North Britishness and the Nature of Eighteenth-Century Patriotisms', *The Historical Journal*, 39.2 (1996), 361–82

—, '"The Strange Death of Scottish History" Revisited: Constructions of the Past, c. 1790–1914', *The Scottish Historical Review*, 76.201 (1997), 86–102

—, *Subverting Scotland's Past: Scottish Whig Historians and the Creation of an Anglo-British Identity 1689–c. 1830* (Cambridge: Cambridge University Press, 1993)

Kijinski, John L., 'John Morley's "English Men of Letters" Series and the Politics of Reading', *Victorian Studies*, 34.2 (1991), 205–25

Kirby, James, *Historians and the Church of England: Religion and Historical Scholarship, 1870–1920* (Oxford: Oxford University Press, 2016)

Klancher, Jon, 'Godwin and the Genre Reformers: On Necessity and Contingency in Romantic Narrative Theory', in *Romanticism, History, and the Possibilities of Genre: Re-forming Literature 1789–1837*, ed. Tilottama Rajan and Julia M. Wright (Cambridge: Cambridge University Press: 1998), pp. 21–38

—, 'Godwin and the Republican Romance: Genre, Politics, and Contingency in Cultural History', *Modern Language Quarterly*, 56.2 (1995), 145–65

—, 'The Vocation of Criticism and the Crisis of the Republic of Letters', in *The Cambridge History of Literary Criticism, Vol. 5: Romanticism*, ed. Marshall Brown (Cambridge: University of Cambridge Press, 2000), pp. 296–320

Kleinberg, Ethan, *Haunting History: For a Deconstructive Approach to the Past* (Stanford: Stanford University Press, 2017)
Knezevic, Borislav, *Figures of Finance Capitalism: Writing, Class and Capital in Mid-Victorian Narratives* (New York and London: Routledge, 2003)
Knott, Sarah, 'Narrating the Age of Revolution', *William and Mary Quarterly*, 73.1 (2016), 3–36
Koselleck, Reinhart, *Futures Past: On the Semantics of Historical Time*, trans. and introd. Keith Tribe (New York: Columbia University Press, 2004)
Koster, Henry, *Travels in Brazil* (London: Longman, Hurst, Rees, Orme, and Brown, 1816)
LaCapra, Dominick, *History and Criticism* (Ithaca, NY: Cornell University Press, 1984)
—, *Rethinking Intellectual History: Texts, Contexts, Language* (Ithaca, NY: Cornell University Press, 1983)
Lamb, John B., 'The Paper Age: Currency, Crisis, and Carlyle', *Prose Studies*, 30.1 (2008), 27–44
Larson, Magali Sarfatti, *The Rise of Professionalism: A Sociological Analysis* (Berkeley: University of California Press, 1979)
Laurence, Anne, 'Women Historians and Documentary Research: Lucy Aikin, Agnes Strickland, Mary Anne Everett Green and Lucy Toulmin Smith', in *Women, Scholarship and Criticism: Gender and Knowledge c. 1790–1900*, ed. Anne Laurence, Joan Bellamy, and Gillian Perry (Manchester: Manchester University Press, 2011), pp. 125–41
Lawrance, Hannah, 'Francis Palgrave's *A History of England*', *Athenaeum*, 21 (30 April 1831), 183
—, *Historical Memoirs of the Queens of England, from the Commencement of the Twelfth Century* (London: Edward Moxon, 1838)
—, 'Mackintosh's *History of England*', *Athenaeum*, 185 (14 May 1831), 308–10
Leask, Nigel, *British Romantic Writers and the East: Anxieties of Empire* (Cambridge: Cambridge University Press, 1992)
—, 'Southey's *Madoc*: Reimagining the Conquest of America', in *Robert Southey and the Contexts of English Romanticism*, ed. Lynda Pratt (Aldershot: Ashgate, 2006), pp. 133–50
Lecky, Elizabeth Van Dendem, *A Memoir of the Right Honourable William Edward Hartpole Lecky* (London: Longmans, Green and Co., 1909)
Lee, Yoon Sun, 'A Divided Inheritance: Scott's Antiquarian Novel and the British Nation', *English Literary History*, 64.2 (1997), 537–67
—, *Nationalism and Irony: Burke, Scott, Carlyle* (Oxford and New York: Oxford University Press, 2004)
Leerssen, Joep T., 'Englishness, Ethnicity and Matthew Arnold', *European Journal of English Studies*, 10.1 (2006), 63–79
—, 'Ethnography and Ethnicity: English', <https://ernie.uva.nl/viewer.p/21/56/object/122-160545> (last accessed 2 July 2020)
—, 'Literary Historicism: Romanticism, Philologists, and the Presence of the Past', *Modern Languages Quarterly*, 62 (2004), 221–43
—, *Mere Irish and Fíor-Ghael: Studies in the Idea of Irish Nationality, its Development and Literary Expression Prior to the Nineteenth Century* (Cork: Cork University Press, 1986)

—, *Remembrance and Imagination: Patterns in the Historical and Literary Representation of Ireland in the Nineteenth Century* (Cork: Cork University Press, 1996)

Levine, George, *The Boundaries of Fiction: Carlyle, Macaulay, Newman* (Princeton: Princeton University Press, 1968)

Levine, Philippa, *The Amateur and the Professional: Antiquarians, Historians and Archaeologists in Victorian England, 1838–1886* (Cambridge: Cambridge University Press, 2003)

Lika, Foteini, 'Fact and Fancy in Nineteenth-Century Historiography and Fiction: The Case of Macaulay and Roidis', in *The Making of the Humanities Volume II. From Early Modern to Modern Disciplines*, ed. Rens Bod, Jaap Maat, and Thijs Weststeijn (Amsterdam: Amsterdam University Press, 2012), pp. 149–66

Linton, Marisa, *The Politics of Virtue in Enlightenment France* (Basingstoke: Palgrave Macmillan, 2001)

Lister, Thomas Henry, 'Aiken's *Memoirs of the Court of Charles I*', *Edinburgh Review*, 58 (Jan. 1834), 398–442

Lloyd, David, 'Adulteration and the Nation: Monologic Nationalism and the Colonial Hybrid', in *An Other Tongue: Nation and Ethnicity in the Linguistic Borderlands*, ed. Alfred Artega (Durham, NC: Duke University Press, 1994), pp. 53–92

Locke, Don, *A Fantasy of Reason: The Life and Thought of William Godwin* (London: Routledge & Kegan Paul, 1980)

Locke, F., 'Rhetoric and Representation in Burke's *Reflections*', in *Edmund Burke's Reflections on the Revolution in France: New Interdisciplinary Essays*, ed. John Whale (Manchester: Manchester University Press, 2000), pp. 19–20

Long, Douglas, 'Hume's Historiographical Imagination', in *David Hume: Historical Thinker, Historical Writer*, ed. Mark G. Spencer (University Park, PA: Penn State University Press, 2013), pp. 201–24

Looser, Devoney, *British Women Writers and the Writing of History, 1670–1820* (Baltimore: Johns Hopkins University Press, 2000)

López, Rosario, 'John Stuart Mill's Idea of History: A Rhetoric of Progress', *Res Publica*, 27 (2012), 63–74

Lorenz, Chris, 'Can Histories be True? Narrativism, Positivism, and the "Metaphorical Turn"', *History and Theory*, 37.3 (1998), 309–29

Luhmann, Niklas, *The Differentiation of Society* (New York: Columbia University Press, 1982)

—, *Love as Passion: The Codification of Intimacy*, trans. Jeremy L. Gaines and Doris L. Jones (Cambridge, MA: Harvard University Press, 1987)

Lukács, Georg, *History and Class Consciousness: Studies in Marxist Dialectics*, trans. Rodney Livingstone (Cambridge, MA: MIT Press, 1971)

Lutz, Catherine A., 'The Language and Politics of Emotion', *Journal of Linguistic Anthropology*, 1.1 (1995), 115–17

Lydon, Jane, *Imperial Emotions: The Politics of Empathy Across the British Empire* (Oxford: Oxford University Press, 2019)

Lynch, Deidre Shauna, *The Economy of Character: Novels, Market Culture, and the Business of Inner Meaning* (Chicago: Chicago University Press, 1998)

—, *Loving Literature: A Cultural History* (Chicago: Chicago University Press, 2014)

—, 'Nationalizing Women and Domesticating Fiction: Edmund Burke and the Genres of Englishness', *The Wordsworth Circle*, 25.1 (1994), 45–9

Macaulay, Catherine, *The History of England, from the Accession of James I to that of the Brunswick Line*, 8 vols (London: J. Nourse, 1763–83)

—, *Observations on the Reflections of the Right Hon. Edmund Burke, on the Revolution in France, in a Letter to the Right Hon. Earl of Stanhope* (London: C. Dilly, 1790)

Macaulay, Thomas Babington, *Critical and Historical Essays Contributed to the Edinburgh Review*, 3 vols (London: Longman, Brown, Green and Longman, 1843)

—, 'Hallam's *Constitutional History*', *Edinburgh Review*, 48 (Sep. 1828), 96–169

—, *The History of England, from the Accession of James II*, 5 vols (Philadelphia: Porter & Coates, n.d.), Project Gutenberg EBook #1468, produced by Ken West and David Widger

—, '*A History of the Revolution in England in 1668* by James Mackintosh', *Edinburgh Review*, 61 (July 1835), 265–322

—, '*A History of the War of the Succession in Spain* by Lord Mahon', *Edinburgh Review*, 56 (Jan. 1833), 499–543

—, *The Journals of Thomas Babington Macaulay*, ed. William Thomas, 5 vols (London: Pickering & Chatto, 2008)

—, 'Leopold von Ranke's *History of the Popes*', *Edinburgh Review*, 72 (Oct. 1840), 227–58

—, *Letters of Thomas Babington Macaulay*, ed. Thomas Pinney, 6 vols (Cambridge: Cambridge University Press, 1981)

—, 'Mill's Essay on Government', *Edinburgh Review*, 49 (June 1829), 273–99

—, 'Mitford's History of Greece', *Knight's Quarterly Magazine*, 3 (Aug. 1824), 285–304

—, *Selections from the Edinburgh Review*, ed. Maurice Cross, 4 vols (London: Rees, Orme, Brown, Green, & Longman, 1833)

—, 'Southey's *Colloquies*', *Edinburgh Review*, 50 (Jan. 1830), 528–65

McAvoy, Jean, 'From Ideology to Feeling: Discourse, Emotion, and an Analytic Synthesis', *Sociology*, 12.1 (2015), 22–33

McBride, Ian, 'Burke and Ireland', in *The Cambridge Companion to Edmund Burke*, ed. David Dwan and Christopher Insole (Cambridge: Cambridge University Press, 2012), pp. 181–94

McCallum, Pamela, 'Misogyny, the Great Man, and Carlyle's *The French Revolution*: The Epic as Pastiche', *Cultural Critique*, 14 (1989–90), 153–78

MacDonagh, Oliver, *States of Mind: A Study of Anglo-Irish Conflict, 1780–1980* (Boston: Allen & Unwin, 1983)

McGeough, Jared, '"Imperfect, Confused, Interrupted": Biography, Nationalism, and Generic Hybridity in William Godwin's *Life of Chaucer*', *European Romantic Review*, 30.4 (2019), 367–82

MacIntyre, Alisdair, *After Virtue: A Study in Moral Theory*, 2nd edn (Notre Dame, IN: University of Notre Dame Press, 1984)

MacKenzie, John M., 'Empire and National Identities: The Case of Scotland', *Transactions of the Royal Historical Society*, 8 (1998), 215–31

McKeon, Michael, *The Origins of the English Novel, 1600–1740* (1987; repr. Baltimore and London: Johns Hopkins University Press, 2002)

—, 'Prose Fiction: Great Britain', in *The Cambridge History of Literary Criticism. Volume IV: The Eighteenth Century*, ed. H. B. Nisbet and Claude Rawson (Cambridge: Cambridge University Press, 1997), pp. 238–63

—, *The Secret History of Domesticity: Private, Public, and the Division of Knowledge* (Baltimore: Johns Hopkins University Press, 2005)

Mackintosh, James, 'Godwin's *Lives of Milton's Nephews*', *Edinburgh Review*, 25 (Oct. 1815), 435–501

—, *The History of England, Vol. I* (London: Longman, Rees, Orme, Brown & Green and J. Taylor, 1830)

—, *History of the Revolution in England in 1688* (London: Longman, Rees, Orme, Brown, Green, & Longman, 1834)

—, 'Sismondi's *History of France*', *Edinburgh Review*, 35 (July 1821), 488–509

McPhee, Peter, *Living the French Revolution, 1789–99* (Basingstoke: Palgrave Macmillan, 2006)

MacWhite, Eoin, 'Thomas Moore and Poland', *Proceedings of the Royal Irish Academy*, 72 (1972), 49–62

Madden, Lionel (ed.), *Robert Southey: The Critical Heritage* (London and Boston: Routledge & Kegan Paul, 1972)

Madden, William A., 'Macaulay's Style', in *The Art of Victorian Prose*, ed. George Levine and William A. Madden (New York: Oxford University Press, 1968), pp. 127–53

Maioli, Roger, 'David Hume, Literary Cognitivism, and the Truth of the Novel', *Studies in English Literature 1500–1900*, 54.3 (2014), 625–48

—, *Empiricism and the Early History of the Novel: Fielding to Austen* (Basingstoke: Palgrave Macmillan, 2016)

Maione, Angela, 'Over the Centuries: A History of Wollstonecraft Interpretation', *Journal of Gender Studies*, 28.7 (2019), 777–88

Maitzen, Rohan Amanda, *Gender, Genre, and Victorian Historical Writing* (New York and London: Garland Publishing, 1998)

—, '"This Feminine Preserve": Historical Biographies by Victorian Women', *Victorian Studies*, 38.3 (1995), 371–93

Majeed, Javed, *Ungoverned Imaginings: James Mill's "History of British India" and Orientalism* (Oxford: Clarendon Press, 1992)

Makdisi, Saree, *Romantic Imperialism: Universal Empire and the Culture of Modernity* (Cambridge: Cambridge University Press, 1998)

Malden, Henry, 'Niebuhr's *History of Rome* Volumes I and II', *Edinburgh Review*, 56 (Jan. 1833), 267–312

Malecka, Joanna, 'The Ethics, Aesthetics and Politics of Thomas Carlyle's "French Revolution"' (PhD thesis, University of Glasgow, 2017), <http://theses.gla.ac.uk/8182/1/2016MaleckaPhD.pdf> (last accessed 12 November 2020)

—, 'Thomas Carlyle's Calvinist Dialogue with the Nineteenth-Century Periodical Press', *History of European Ideas*, 45.1 (2019), 15–32

Mallory, Anne, 'Burke, Boredom, and the Theatre of Counterrevolution', *PMLA*, 118.2 (2003), 224–38

Mallory-Kani, Amy, '"A Healthy State": Mary Wollstonecraft's Medical Politics', *The Eighteenth Century*, 56.1 (2015), 21–40

Mandell, Laura, 'Virtue and Evidence: Catherine Macaulay's Historical Realism', *Journal for Early Modern Cultural Studies*, 4.1 (2004), 127–57

Manning, Peter J., 'Cleansing the Images: Wordsworth, Rome, and the Rise of Historicism', *Texas Studies in Languages and Literature*, 33.2 (1991), 271–326
—, 'The History of Cobbett's *A History of the Protestant "Reformation"*', *Huntington Library Quarterly*, 64.3/4 (2001), 429–43
Manning, Susan, 'Antiquarianism, Balladry, and the Rehabilitation of Romance', in *The Cambridge History of English Romantic Literature*, ed. James K. Chandler (Cambridge: Cambridge University Press, 2009), pp. 45–70
—, 'Walter Scott, Antiquarianism, and the Political Discourse of the *Edinburgh Review*, 1802–11', in *British Romanticism and the Edinburgh Review: Bicentenary Essays*, ed. Massimiliano Demata and Duncan Wu (Basingstoke: Palgrave Macmillan, 2002), pp. 10–23
Marsden, Richard, 'In Defiance of Discipline: Antiquarianism, Archaeology and History in Late Nineteenth-Century Scotland', *Journal of Scottish Historical Studies*, 40.2 (2020), 103–33
Marshall, Peter, *William Godwin* (New Haven, CT: Yale University Press, 1984)
Martin, Kelly, 'On the Origin of Hume's Philosophy in the Passions', pp. 1–33, <http://econfaculty.gmu.edu/klein/PdfPapers/SHLE_paper/Martin%20Kelly%20Hume8.pdf> (last accessed 3 March 2019)
Martineau, Harriet, 'Lord Macaulay', *Daily News* (31 Dec. 1859), p. 5
Mary, Jacobus, '"The science of herself": Scenes of Female Enlightenment', in *Romanticism, History, and the Possibilities of Genre: Re-forming Literature 1789–1837*, ed. Tilottama Rajan and Julia M. Wright (Cambridge: Cambridge University Press, 1998), pp. 240–69
Massumi, Brian, *Politics of Affect* (London: Polity Press, 2015)
Matthews, Sean, 'Change and Theory in Raymond Williams's Structure of Feeling', *Pretexts: Literary and Cultural Studies*, 10 (2001), 179–94
Maurer, Oscar, Jr, 'Anonymity vs. Signature in Victorian Reviewing', *University of Texas Studies in English*, 27.1 (1848), 1–27
Maxwell, Richard, *The Historical Novel in Europe, 1650–1950* (Cambridge: Cambridge University Press, 2009)
Mayer, Robert, *History and the Early English Novel* (Cambridge: Cambridge University Press, 1997)
—, 'The Illogical Status of Novelistic Discourse: Scott's Footnotes for the Waverley Novels', *English Literary History*, 66 (1999), 911–38
Mee, Jon, *Conversable Worlds: Literature, Contention, and Community 1762 to 1830* (Oxford: Oxford University Press, 2011)
Meinecke, Friedrich, *Die Entstehung des Historismus*, 2 vols (Berlin and Munich: R. Oldenbourg, 1965)
—, 'Kausalitäten und Werte in der Geschichte', *Historische Zeitschrift*, 137 (1928), 1–27
Meisel, Martin, *Realizations: Narrative, Pictorial, and Theatrical Arts in Nineteenth-Century England* (Princeton: Princeton University Press, 1984)
Melman, Billie, 'Gender, History and Memory: The Invention of Women's Past in the Nineteenth and Early Twentieth Centuries', *History and Memory*, 5.1 (1993), 5–41
Merivale, Herman, 'Carlyle, *The French Revolution*', *Edinburgh Review*, 71 (July 1840), 411–45

—, 'Thirlwall's *History of Greece*', *Edinburgh Review*, 62 (Oct. 1835), 83–108
Michael, Timothy, *British Romanticism and the Critique of Political Reason* (Baltimore: Johns Hopkins University Press, 2016)
Mill, James, *The History of British India*, 3 vols (London: Baldwin, Cradock and Joy, 1817)
—, 'State of Ireland', *Edinburgh Review*, 21 (July 1813), 340–64
Mill, John Stuart, 'Brodie's *History of the British Empire*', *Westminster Review*, 2 (Oct. 1824), 346–402
—, *Collected Works of J. S. Mill*, ed. J. A. Robson et al. 31 vols (Toronto: University of Toronto Press, 1963–1991)
—, 'French Revolution – Scott's *Life of Napoleon*', *London and Westminster Review*, 9 (April 1828), 313–28.
—, 'The French Revolution', *London and Westminster Review*, 27 (July 1837), 17–53
Miller, Elizabeth Carolyn, 'Reading in Review: The Victorian Book Review in the New Media Moment', *Victorian Periodicals Review*, 49.4 (2016), 626–42
Mills, Charles W., *The Racial Contract* (Ithaca, NY, and London: Cornell University Press, 1997)
Milnes, Timothy, 'Is it true? … What is the meaning of it?': Bentham, Romanticism, and the Fictions of Reason', in *Bentham and the Arts*, ed. Anthony Julius, Philip Schofield, and Malcom Quinn (London: UCL Press, 2020), pp. 140–59
—, *The Testimony of Sense: Empiricism and the Essay from Hume to Hazlitt* (Oxford: Oxford University Press, 2019)
Mitchell, Rosemary Ann, '"The busy daughters of Clio": Women Writers of History from 1820 to 1880', *Women's History Review*, 7.1 (1998), 107–34
—, *Picturing the Past: English History in Text and Image, 1830–1870* (Oxford: Oxford University Press, 2000)
Mitchell, Timothy, 'The Stage of Modernity', in *Questions of Modernity*, ed. Timothy Mitchell (Minneapolis: University of Minnesota Press, 2000), pp. 1–34
Mixon, Rex W., Jr, 'Bentham, Science and Utility', *Revue d'études benthamiennes*, 18 (2020), <https://journals.openedition.org/etudes-benthamiennes/8127> (last accessed 1 January 2021)
Momigliano, Arnaldo D., *Contributo alla storia degli studi classici* (Rome: Edizioni di storia e letteratura, 1955)
—, *Studies in Historiography* (New York and London: Weidenfeld & Nicolson, 1966)
Moncreiff, James, 'Macaulay's History of England', *Edinburgh Review*, 90 (July 1849), 249–92
Moore, Thomas, *The History of Ireland*, 4 vols (London: Longman, Brown, Green, and Longmans, 1835–46)
—, *The Journal of Thomas Moore*, ed. Wilfred S. Dowden, 6 vols (Newark: University of Delaware Press; London and Toronto: Associated University Presses, 1983–92)
—, *The Letters of Thomas Moore*, ed. Wilfred S. Dowden, 2 vols (Oxford: Clarendon Press, 1964)
—, 'Prefatory Letter on Music' to *Irish Melodies* (1807–28), in *The Poetical Works of Thomas Moore* (London: Frederick Warne, n.d.)

Morelli, Harriet M., '"An Incarnated Word": A Revisionary Reading of "The Insurrection of Women" in Thomas Carlyle's *The French Revolution*', *Women's Studies*, 34.7 (2005), 533–50

Morgan, Peter F., *Literary Critics and Reviewers in Early Nineteenth-Century Britain* (London: Croom Helm, 1983)

—, 'Macaulay on Periodical Style', *Victorian Periodicals Newsletter*, 1 (1968), 26–7

Morley, John, *Critical Miscellanies, Vol. 1* (London and New York: Macmillan, 1904)

Morrow, John, 'Heroes and Constitutionalists: The Ideological Significance of Thomas Carlyle's Treatment of the English Revolution', *History of Political Thought*, 14.2 (1993), 205–23

—, 'Republicanism and Public Virtue: William Godwin's *History of the Commonwealth of England*', *The Historical Journal*, 34.3 (1991), 645–64

—, *Thomas Carlyle* (London: Hambledon Continuum, 2006)

—, 'Thomas Carlyle, "Young Ireland", and the "Condition of Ireland Question"', *The Historical Journal*, 51.3 (2008), 643–67

Mourão, Manuela, 'Robert Southey on Portugal: Travel Narrative and the Writing of History', *Nineteenth-Century Contexts*, 37.1 (2015), 43–60

Mullan, John, *Anonymity: A Secret History of English Literature* (Princeton: Princeton University Press, 2007)

Mullen, Mary, 'How the Irish Became Settlers: Metaphors of Indigeneity and the Erasure of Indigenous People', *New Hibernia Review*, 20.3 (2016), 81–96

—, *Novel Institutions: Anachronism, Irish Novels and Nineteenth-Century Realism* (Edinburgh: Edinburgh University Press, 2019)

Munslow, Alan, 'Cohen contra Ankersmit', *Rethinking History*, 12.4 (2008), 537–55

—, *The New History* (Edinburgh: Pearson, 2003)

Murray, Oswyn, 'Neibuhr in Britain', in *Historiographie de l'antiquité et transferts culturels: Les histoires anciennes dans l'Europe des XVIIIe et XIXe siècles*, ed. Chyrssanthi Avlami, Jaime Alvar, and Mirella Romero Recio (Leiden: Brill/Rodopi, 2010), pp. 239–54

Myers, Mitzi, 'Godwin's *Memoirs* of Mary Wollstonecraft: The Shaping of Self and Subject', *Studies in Romanticism*, 20.3 (1981), 299–316

Myers, Victoria, 'William Godwin and the *Ars Rhetorica*', *Studies in Romanticism*, 41.3 (2002), 415–44

Nahaboo, Zaki, 'Subverting Orientalism: Political Subjectivity in Edmund Burke's India and Liberal Multiculturalism', *Citizenship Studies*, 15.5–6 (2012), 587–603

Nesvet, Rebecca, 'Robert Southey, Historian of El Dorado', *Keats–Shelley Journal*, 61 (2012), 116–21

Neumann, Erich, *Depth Psychology and a New Ethic*, trans. Eugene Rolfe (New York: Putnam, 1969)

Nienkamp, Jean, *Internal Rhetorics: Toward a History and Theory of Self-Persuasion* (Carbondale: Southern Illinois University Press, 2001)

Nolan, Emer, *Catholic Emancipations: Irish Fiction from Thomas Moore to James Joyce* (Syracuse, NY: Syracuse University Press, 2007)

Norbrook, David, 'The English Revolution and English Historiography', in *The Cambridge Companion to Writing of the English Revolution*, ed. N. H. Keeble (Cambridge: Cambridge University Press, 2001), pp. 233–50

North, Julian, 'Portraying Presence: Thomas Carlyle, Portraiture, and Biography', *Victorian Literature and Culture*, 43.3 (2015), 465–88

Novick, Peter, *That Noble Dream: The 'Objectivity' Question and the American Historical Profession* (Cambridge: Cambridge University Press, 1988)

O'Brien, Eliza, '"The most inconsistent of men": William Godwin and the "Apology" of Sir Thomas More', *Nineteenth-Century Prose*, 41.1/2 (2014), 79–110

O'Brien, Karen, 'History and Literature 1660–1780', in *The Cambridge History of English Literature, 1660–1780*, ed. John Richetti (Cambridge: Cambridge University Press, 2005), pp. 363–90

—, 'The History Market in Eighteenth-Century England', in *Books and their Readers in Eighteenth-Century England: New Essays*, ed. Isabel Rivers (London: Continuum, 2001), pp. 105–33

—, 'History and the Novel in Eighteenth-Century Britain', in *The Uses of History in Early Modern England*, ed. Paula Kewes (San Marino, CA: Huntington Library, 2006), pp. 389–406

—, *Narratives of Enlightenment: Cosmopolitan History from Voltaire to Gibbon* (Cambridge: Cambridge University Press, 1997)

—, 'Uneasy Settlement: Wordsworth and Emigration', in *Romanticism's Debatable Lands*, ed. Claire Lamont and Michael Rossington (Basingstoke: Palgrave Macmillan, 2007), pp. 121–35

Ó Ciosáin, Niall, *Print and Popular Culture in Ireland, 1750–1850* (Basingstoke: Palgrave Macmillan, 1997)

O'Donnell, Katherine, 'Effeminate Edmund Burke and the Masculine Voice of Mary Wollstonecraft', *Journal of Gender Studies*, 28.7 (2019), 789–801

O'Halloran, Clare, *Golden Ages and Barbarous Nations: Antiquarian Debate and Cultural Politics in Ireland, 1750–1800* (Cork: Cork University Press, 2004)

O'Malley, Patrick, *Liffey & Lethe: Paramnesiac History in Nineteenth-Century Anglo-Ireland* (Oxford: Oxford University Press, 2017)

O'Neill, Daniel I., *The Burke–Wollstonecraft Debate: Savagery, Civilization, and Democracy* (University Park, PA: Penn State University Press, 2007)

—, 'Edmund Burke, the "Science of Man," and Statesmanship', in *Scientific Statesmanship, Governance, and the History of Political Philosophy*, ed. Kyriakos N. Demetriou and Antis Loizides (New York and London: Routledge, 2015), pp. 174–92

—, 'Shifting the Scottish Paradigm: The Discourse of Morals and Manners in Mary Wollstonecraft's *French Revolution*', *History of Political Thought*, 23.1 (2002), 90–116

—, 'The Sublime, The Beautiful, and the Political in Burke's Work', in *The Science of Sensibility: Reading Burke's Philosophical Enquiry*, ed. Koen Vermeir and Michael Funk Deckard (Dordrecht: Springer, 2011), pp. 193–224

O'Shaughnessy, David, 'Godwin, Ireland, and Historical Tragedy', in *New Approaches to William Godwin: Forms, Fears, Futures*, ed. Eliza O'Brien, Helen Stark, and Beatrice Turner (Cham: Palgrave Macmillan, 2021), pp. 13–36

Ozouf, Mona, *Festivals and the French Revolution*, trans. Alan Sheridan (Cambridge, MA: Harvard University Press, 1988)
Paine, Thomas, *Rights of Man: Being an Answer to Mr. Burke's Attack on the French Revolution* (London: J. S. Jordan, 1791)
Palgrave, Francis Turner, 'Hume and his Influence upon History' ['Augustin Thierry *Histoire de la conquête de l'Angleterre par les normands*'], *Quarterly Review*, 73 (March 1844), 536–92
—, 'Memoirs of the Queen of France … By Mrs Forbes Bush', *Quarterly Review*, 71 (March 1843), 411–16
Park, Suzi Asha, '*Caleb Williams* and the Smithian Spectator: Reading the "Reasonable Demand"', *Nineteenth-Century Prose*, 41.1/2 (2014), 195–224
Parker, Mark, *Literary Magazines and British Romanticism* (Cambridge: Cambridge University Press, 2000)
Pasanek, Brad, *Metaphors of Mind: An Eighteenth-Century Dictionary* (Baltimore: Johns Hopkins University Press, 2015)
Paul, Herman, 'Scholarly Personae: What They Are and Why They Matter', in *How to Be a Historian: Scholarly Personae in Historical Studies, 1800–2000*, ed. Herman Paul (Manchester: Manchester University Press, 2019), pp. 1–14
—, 'The Virtues of a Good Historian in Early Imperial Germany: Georg Waitz's Contested Example', *Modern Intellectual History*, 15.3 (2018), 681–709
—, and Ethan Kleinberg, 'Are Historians Ontological Realists? An Exchange', *Rethinking History*, 22.4 (2018), 546–67
Paulson, Ronald, 'Burke's Sublime and the Representation of Revolution', in *Culture and Politics: From Puritanism to the Enlightenment*, ed. Perez Zargorin (Berkeley and Los Angeles: University of California Press, 1980), pp. 241–69
Peardon, T. P., *The Transition in English Historical Writing, 1760–1830* (New York: Columbia University Press, 1933)
Persak, Christine, 'Rhetoric in Praise of Silence: The Ideology of Carlyle's Paradox', *Rhetoric Society Quarterly*, 21.1 (1991), 38–52
Pettitt, Clare, *Serial Forms: The Unfinished Project of Modernity, 1815–1848* (Oxford: Oxford University Press, 2020)
Philp, Mark, *Godwin's Political Justice* (London: Gerald Duckworth & Co., 1986)
Phillips, Mark Salber, 'Adam Smith, Belletrist', in *The Cambridge Companion to Adam Smith*, ed. Knud Haakonssen (Cambridge: Cambridge University Press, 2006), pp. 57–78
—, *On Historical Distance* (New Haven, CT: Yale University Press, 2013)
—, 'Reconsiderations on History and Antiquarianism: Arnaldo Momigliano and the Historiography of Eighteenth-Century Britain', *Journal of the History of Ideas*, 57.2 (1996), 297–316
—, 'Relocating Inwardness: Historical Distance and the Transition from Enlightenment to Romantic Historiography', *PMLA*, 118.3 (2003), 436–49
—, *Society and Sentiment: Genres of Historical Writing in Britain, 1740–1820* (Princeton: Princeton University Press, 2000)
Phillipson, Nicholas, *David Hume: The Philosopher as Historian* (New Haven, CT: Yale University Press, 2012)
Phillipson, Robert, *Linguistic Imperialism* (Oxford: Oxford University Press, 1992)

Pinch, Adela, *Strange Fits of Passion: Epistemologies of Emotion, Hume to Austen* (Stanford: Stanford University Press, 1996)
Pittock, Murray, 'History and the Teleology of Civility in the Scottish Enlightenment', in *Enlightenment and Emancipation*, ed. Peter France and Susan Manning (Lewisburg, PA: Bucknell University Press, 2006), pp. 81–96
—, *The Invention of Scotland: The Stuart Myth and the Scottish Identity, 1638 to the Present* (London: Routledge, 1991)
—, *The Myth of the Jacobite Clans: The Jacobite Army in 1745* (Edinburgh: Edinburgh University Press, 2009)
—, *Scottish and Irish Romanticism* (Oxford: Oxford University Press, 2008)
Plotz, John, 'Crowd Power: Chartism, Carlyle, and the Victorian Public Sphere', *Representations*, 70 (2000), 87–114
Pocock, J. G. A., 'Adam Smith and History', in *The Cambridge Companion to Adam Smith*, ed. Knud Haakonssen (Cambridge: Cambridge University Press, 2006), pp. 270–87
—, 'Burke and the Ancient Constitution: A Problem in the History of Ideas', *The Historical Journal*, 3 (1960), 125–43
—, 'Catherine Macaulay: Patriot Historian', in *Women Writers and the Early Modern British Political Tradition*, ed. Hilda L. Smith (Cambridge: Cambridge University Press, 1998), pp. 243–58
—, 'The Political Economy of Burke's Analysis of the French Revolution', *Historical Journal*, 25.2 (1982), 331–49
—, *Virtue, Commerce, and History: Essays on Political Thought and History, Chiefly in the Eighteenth Century* (Cambridge: Cambridge University Press, 1985)
Pois, Robert A., 'Two Poles Within Historicism: Croce and Meinecke', *Journal of the History of Ideas*, 31.2 (1970), 253–72
Poovey, Mary, *Genres of the Credit Economy: Mediating Value in Eighteenth- and Nineteenth-Century Britain* (Chicago: University of Chicago Press, 2008)
—, *A History of the Modern Fact: Problems of Knowledge in the Sciences of Wealth and Society* (Chicago: University of Chicago Press, 1998)
—, *Making a Social Body: British Cultural Formation 1830–1864* (Chicago: University of Chicago Press, 1995)
—, *The Proper Lady and the Woman Writer: Ideology as Style in the Works of Mary Wollstonecraft, Mary Shelley, and Jane Austen* (Chicago and London: University of Chicago Press, 1984)
Pratt, Mary Louise, *Imperial Eyes: Travel Writing and Transculturation* (London and New York: Routledge, 1992)
Price, Fiona, '"Experiments Made by the Airpump": Jane West's *The Loyalists* (1812) and the Science of History', *Women's Writing*, 19 (2012), 315–32
—, *Reinventing Liberty: Nation, Commerce and the Historical Novel from Walpole to Scott* (Edinburgh: Edinburgh University Press, 2016)
—, 'Resisting "the Spirit of Innovation": The Other Historical Novel and Jane Porter', *Modern Language Review*, 101.3 (2006), 638–51
Price, Richard, 'Historiography, Narrative, and the Nineteenth Century', *Journal of British Studies*, 35.2 (1996), 220–56
Quinn, James, *Young Ireland and the Writing of Irish History* (Dublin: UCD Press, 2015)

Radcliffe, Elizabeth S., 'Hume on the Generation of Motives: Why Beliefs Alone Never Motivate', *Hume Studies*, 25.1-2 (1999), 101–22
Rajan, Tilottama, 'Between Individual and General History: Godwin's Seventeenth-Century Texts', *Nineteenth-Century Prose*, 41.1/2 (2014), 111–60
—, *Romantic Narrative: Shelley, Hays, Godwin, Wollstonecraft* (Baltimore: John Hopkins University Press, 2010)
—, 'Uncertain Futures: History and Genealogy in William Godwin's *The Lives of Edward and John Philips, Nephews and Pupils of Milton*', *Milton Quarterly*, 32.3 (1998), 75–86
—, and Julia M. Wright, 'Introduction', in *Romanticism, History, and the Possibilities of Genre: Re-forming Literature 1789–1837* (Cambridge: Cambridge University Press, 1998), pp. 1–21
Ramsden, Guendolen (ed.), *Correspondence of Two Brothers: Edward Adolphus, Eleventh Duke of Somerset, and his Brother, Lord Webb Seymour, 1800–1819 and After* (London: Longmans Green, 1906)
Rancière, Jacques, 'The Concept of Anachronism and the Historian's Truth', *InPrint*, 3.1 (2015), 13–48, <https://arrow.tudublin.ie/cgi/viewcontent.cgi?article=1020&context=inp> (last accessed 2 December 2020)
—, *The Names of History: On the Poetics of Knowledge*, trans. Hassan Melehy, foreword Hayden White (Minneapolis: University of Minnesota Press, 1994)
Ranke, Leopold von, *The Theory and Practice of History*, ed. Georg G. Iggers (London: Routledge, 2011)
Reddy, William M., 'Against Constructionism: The Historical Ethnography of Emotions', *Current Anthropology*, 38.3 (1997), 327–51.
—, *The Navigation of Feeling: A Framework for the History of Emotions* (Cambridge: Cambridge University Press, 2009)
Reeder, Jessie, *The Forms of Informal Empire: Britain, Latin America, and Nineteenth-Century Literature* (Baltimore: Johns Hopkins University Press, 2020)
Reill, Peter Hanns, *The German Enlightenment and the Rise of Historicism* (Berkeley: University of California Press, 1975)
Reisman, David A., *Adam Smith's Sociological Economics* (London: Croom Helm, 1976)
Renan, Ernst, *Qu'est-ce qu'une nation?*, trans. and annot. Martin Thom, in *Nation and Narration*, ed. Homi K. Bhabha (London and New York: Routledge, 1990), pp. 8–22
Rendell, Jane, '"The grand causes which combine to carry mankind forward": Wollstonecraft, History and Revolution', *Women's Writing*, 4.2 (1997), 155–72
—, 'Scottish Orientalism: From Robertson to James Mill', *The Historical Journal*, 25.1 (1983), 43–69
Reno, Seth, T., 'Introduction: Romanticism and Affect Studies', *Romantic Circles*, <https://romantic-circles.org/praxis/affect/praxis.2018.affect.introduction.html> (last accessed 5 January 2020)
Revel, Jacques, 'History and the Social Sciences', in *The Cambridge History of Science, Vol. 7: The Modern Social Sciences*, ed. Theodore M. Porter and Dorothy Ross (Cambridge: Cambridge University Press, 2008), pp. 391–404

Richardson, R. C., *The Debate on the English Revolution Revisited* (London and New York: Routledge, 1988)

Ricoeur, Paul, 'The Metaphorical Process as Cognition, Imagination, and Feeling', *Critical Inquiry*, 5.1 (1978), 143–59

—, *Time and Narrative, Volume 3*, trans. Katherine Blarney and David Pellauer (Chicago: Chicago University Press, 1988)

Rigney, Ann, *Imperfect Histories: The Elusive Past and the Legacy of Romantic Historicism* (Ithaca, NY: Cornell University Press, 2001)

—, 'Relevance, Revision, and the Fear of Long Books', in *A New Philosophy of History*, ed. Frank R. Ankersmit and Hans Kellner (Chicago: University of Chicago Press, 1995), pp. 127–47

—, *The Rhetoric of Historical Representation: Three Narrative Histories of the French Revolution* (Cambridge: Cambridge University Press, 1990)

—, 'Semantic Slides: History and the Concept of Fiction', in *History-Making: The Intellectual and Social Formation of a Discipline*, ed. Irmline Veit-Brause and Rolf Thorstendahl (Stockholm: Kungl. Vitterhets Historie och Antikvitets Akademien, 1996), pp. 31–46

—, 'The Untenanted Places of the Past: Thomas Carlyle and the Varieties of Historical Ignorance', *History and Theory*, 35.3 (1996), 338–57

Riskin, Jessica, *Science in the Age of Sensibility: The Sentimental Empiricists of the French Enlightenment* (Chicago: University of Chicago Press, 2002)

Ritchie, Leitch, '*Tales of a Grandfather*', *Athenaeum*, 167 (8 Jan. 1831), 18–20.

Robertson, William, *History of Scotland During the Reigns of Queen Mary and King James VI*, 3 vols (Edinburgh: A. Millar, 1759)

Roebuck, J. A., 'Military Education', *Edinburgh Review*, 49 (June 1829), 388–420.

Roellinger, Francis X., Jr, 'The Early Development of Carlyle's Style', *PMLA*, 72.5 (1957), 936–51

Romani, Roberto, 'British Views on Irish National Character, 1800–1846. An Intellectual History', *History of European Ideas*, 23.5–6 (1997), 193–219

Roney, John B., 'Negotiating the Middle Ground: Thomas Moore on Religion and Irish Nationalism', in *Representing Irish Religious Histories: Histories of the Sacred and Secular, 1700–2000*, ed. Jacqueline Hill and Mary Ann Lyons (Cham: Palgrave Macmillan, 2017), pp. 151–64

Roper, Derek, *Reviewing Before the Edinburgh, 1788–1832* (London: Methuen, 1978)

Rosaldo, Renato, *Culture and Truth: The Remaking of Social Analysis* (London: Beacon Press, 1993)

Rosenberg, John D., *Carlyle and the Burden of History* (Oxford: Clarendon Press, 1985)

Rosenfeld, Sophia, 'Thinking about Feeling, 1789–1799', *French Historical Studies*, 32.4 (2009), 697–706

Rosenwein, Barbara H., *Generations of Feeling: A History of Emotions, 800–1700* (Cambridge: Cambridge University Press, 2015)

—, 'Modernity: A Problematic Category in the History of Emotions', *History and Theory*, 53 (2014), 69–78

—, 'Problems and Methods in the History of Emotions', *Passions in Context: Journal of the History and Philosophy of the Emotions*, 1.1 (2010), <http://www.passionsincontext.de/%3e/> (last accessed 24 April 2017)

—, 'Worrying about Emotions in History', *The American Historical Review*, 107.3 (2002), 821–45
Rude, George, *The Crowd in the French Revolution* (Oxford: Oxford University Press, 1967)
Runia, Eelco, 'Presence', *History and Theory*, 45.1 (2006), 1–29
Ryan, Vanessa L., 'The Unreliable Editor: Carlyle's *Sartor Resartus* and the Art of Biography', *The Review of English Studies*, 54.215 (2003), 287–307
Ryley, John, 'Scott's Life of Napoleon', *Eclectic Review*, 28 (July 1827), 148–62
Saccamano, Neil, 'Parting with Prejudice: Hume, Identity, and Aesthetic Universality', in *Politics and the Passions, 1500–1850*, ed. Victoria Kahn, Neil Saccamano, and Daniela Coli (Princeton: Princeton University Press, 2006), pp. 217–30
Sachs, Jonathan, 'History Writing', in *Mary Wollstonecraft in Context*, ed. Nancy E. Johnson and Paul Keen (Cambridge: Cambridge University Press, 2020), pp. 305–13
—, *The Poetics of Decline in British Romanticism* (Cambridge: Cambridge University Press, 2018)
Saglia, Diego, '"O My Mother Spain!": The Peninsular War, Family Matters, and the Practice of Romantic Nation-Writing', *English Literary History*, 65.2 (1998), 363–93
—, 'Nationalist Texts and Counter-Texts: Southey's *Roderick* and the Dissensions of the Annotated Romance', *Nineteenth-Century Literature*, 53.4 (1991), 421–51
—, *Poetic Castles in Spain: British Romanticism and Figurations of Iberia* (Amsterdam and Atlanta: Rodopi, 2000), pp. 40–52
St Clair, William, 'Romantic Biography: Conveying Personality, Intimacy, and Authenticity in an Age of Ink on Paper', in *On Life-Writing*, ed. Zachary Leader (Oxford: Oxford University Press, 2015), pp. 48–71
Salmon, Richard, *The Formation of the Victorian Literary Profession* (Cambridge: Cambridge University Press, 2013)
Samet, Elizabeth D., 'Spectacular History and the Politics of Theatre: Sympathetic Arts in the Shadow of the Bastille', *PMLA*, 118.5 (2005), 1305–19
Sandford, Daniel Keyte, 'Edward Lytton Bulwer's *Athens*', *Edinburgh Review*, 65 (July 1837), 151–77
Sapiro, Virginia, *A Vindication of Political Virtue: The Political Theory of Mary Wollstonecraft* (Chicago: University of Chicago Press, 1992)
Sanders, Charles Richard, 'Carlyle and Wordsworth', *Browning Institute Studies*, 9 (1981), 115–22
Sarafianos, Aris, 'Pain, Labour, and the Sublime: Medical Gymnastics and Burke's Aesthetics', *Representations*, 91.1 (2005), 58–83
Satia, Priya, *Time's Monster: History, Conscience and Britain's Empire* (Cambridge, MA: Harvard University Press, 2020)
Sato, Sora, *Edmund Burke as Historian: War, Order and Civilisation* (Basingstoke: Palgrave Macmillan 2018)
Scheer, Monique, 'Are Emotions a Kind of Practice (and is That What Makes Them Have a History)? A Bourdieuian Approach to Understanding Emotion', *History and Theory*, 51.2 (2012), 193–220
Schmidt, Claudia M., 'David Hume as a Philosopher of History', in *David*

Hume: Historical Thinker, Historical Writer, ed. Mark G. Spencer (University Park, PA: Penn State University Press, 2013), pp. 163–180

Schnapp, Alain, *The Discovery of the Past: The Origins of Archaeology* (London: British Museum Press, 1996)

Schoenfield, Mark, *British Periodicals and Romantic Identity: The 'Literary Lower Empire'* (Basingstoke: Palgrave Macmillan, 2009)

Schulman, Alex, 'Gothic Piles and Endless Forests: Wollstonecraft Between Burke and Rousseau', *Eighteenth-Century Studies*, 41.1 (2007), 41–54

Schwarzmantel, John, *The Age of Ideology: Political Ideologies from the American Revolution to Postmodern Times* (New York: New York University Press, 1998)

Schwerin, Alan, *Hume's Labyrinth: A Search for the Self* (Newcastle upon Tyne: Cambridge Scholars Publishers, 2012)

Scott, Joan Wallach, 'After History?', *Common Knowledge*, 5.3 (1996), 8–26

—, 'The Evidence of Experience', *Critical Inquiry*, 17.4 (1991), 773–97

Scott, Walter, 'Ellis and Ritson', *Edinburgh Review*, 7 (Jan. 1806), 387–413

—, 'Essay on Romance', in *The Miscellaneous Prose Works of Sir Walter Scott*, 6 vols (Boston: Wells and Lilly, 1829), 6:100–63

—, 'Godwin's *Life of Chaucer*', *Edinburgh Review*, 3 (Jan. 1804), 437–52

—, *The History of Scotland*, 2 vols (London: Longman, Rees, Orme, Brown, and Green, 1829–30)

—, '*History of Scotland*. By Patrick Fraser Tytler', *Quarterly Review*, 41 (Nov. 1829), 328–59

Scurr, Ruth, '"The greatest irregular": Thomas Carlyle's Re-creative Purpose in *The French Revolution*', in *Thinking Through Style*, ed. Michael D. Hurley and Marcus Waithe (Oxford: Oxford University Press, 2018), pp. 87–105

Sebastini, Silvia, 'National Characters and Race: A Scottish Enlightenment Debate', in *Character, Self, and Sociability in the Scottish Enlightenment*, ed. Thomas Ahnert and Susan Manning (Basingstoke: Palgrave Macmillan, 2011), pp. 187–205

Seeley, J. R., *Expansion of England: Two Courses of Lectures* (London: Macmillan, 1883)

—, 'History and Politics I', *Macmillan's Magazine*, 40 (Aug. 1879), 289–99

—, *Lectures and Essays* (London: Macmillan, 1870)

Seigel, Jules Paul (ed.), *Thomas Carlyle: The Critical Heritage* (London: Routledge & Kegan Paul, 1971)

Selinger, William, 'Patronage and Revolution: Edmund Burke's "Reflections on the Revolution in France" and his Theory of Legislative Corruption', *The Review of Politics*, 76.1 (2014), 43–67

Seoane, Mateo, 'Napier's *History of the Peninsular War*', *Athenaeum*, 178 (26 March 1831), 193–5

—, 'Napier's *History of the Peninsular War*', *Athenaeum*, 181 (16 April 1831), 247–9

Sessler, Randall, 'Recasting the Revolution: The Media Debate between Edmund Burke, Mary Wollstonecraft, and Thomas Paine', *European Romantic Review*, 25.5 (2015), 611–26

Shapiro, James, 'Unravelling Shakespeare's Life', in *On Life-Writing*, ed. Zachary Leader (Oxford: Oxford University Press, 2015), pp. 7–24

Shattock, Joanne, 'Politics and Literature: Macaulay, Brougham, and the

Edinburgh Review under Napier', *The Yearbook of English Studies*, 16 (1986), 32–50
—, *Politics and Reviewers: The Edinburgh and the Quarterly in the Early Victorian Age* (London and New York: Leicester University Press, 1989)
Shovlin, John, *The Political Economy of Virtue: Luxury, Patriotism, and the Origins of the French Revolution* (Ithaca, NY: Cornell University Press, 2006)
Simon, Zoltán Boldizsár, *History in Times of Unprecedented Change: A Theory for the 21st Century* (London: Bloomsbury, 2019)
Simpson, David, 'Raymond Williams: Feeling for Structures, Voicing "History"', *Social Text*, 30 (1992), 9–26
—, 'Review: Locating Southey', *Eighteenth-Century Studies*, 41.4 (2008), 565–8
—, *Romanticism, Nationalism, and the Revolt against Theory* (Chicago: University of Chicago Press, 1993)
—, *Romanticism and the Question of the Stranger* (Chicago: University of Chicago Press, 2013)
Siskin, Clifford, *The Historicity of Romantic Discourse* (Oxford: Oxford University Press, 1988)
—, *The Work of Writing: Literature and Social Change in Britain, 1700–1830* (Baltimore: Johns Hopkins University Press, 1988)
—, and William Warner, 'If This is Enlightenment Then What is Romanticism?', *European Romantic Review*, 22.3 (2011), 281–91
Skidmore, Thomas E., *Black into White: Race and Nationality in Brazilian Thought* (New York: Oxford University Press, 1974)
Slater, Graeme, 'Hume's Revisions of the "History of England"', *Studies in Bibliography*, 45 (1992), 130–57
Slee, Peter, *Learning and a Liberal Education: The Study of Modern History in the Universities of Oxford, Cambridge and Manchester, 1880–1914* (Manchester: Manchester University Press, 1986)
Smith, Adam, *Lectures on Rhetoric and Belles Lettres*, ed. J. C. Bryce (Oxford: Oxford University Press, 1983)
Smith, Anthony D., 'A Europe of Nations – or a Nation of Europe?', *Journal of Peace Research*, 30.2 (1993), 129–35
Smith, Bonnie G., *The Gender of History: Men, Women, and Historical Practice* (Cambridge, MA: Harvard University Press, 1998)
Smith, Nadia Clare, *A "Manly Study"?: Irish Women Historians, 1868–1949* (New York: Palgrave Macmillan, 2006)
Smith, Olivia, *The Politics of Language* (Oxford: Clarendon Press, 1984)
Smith, R. J., *The Gothic Bequest: Medieval Institutions in British Political Thought, 1688–1863* (Cambridge: Cambridge University Press, 1987)
Smith, Vanessa, *Intimate Strangers: Friendship, Exchange and Pacific Encounters* (Cambridge: Cambridge University Press, 2010)
Soffer, Reba, *Discipline and Power: The University, History, and the Making of an English Elite* (Cambridge: Cambridge University Press, 1994)
Sorensen, David, 'Carlyle, Macaulay, and the "Dignity of History"', *Carlyle Studies Annual*, 11 (1990), 41–52
—, '"Natural Supernaturalism": Carlyle's Redemption of the Past in *The French Revolution*', *Revue LISA*, 7.3 (2009), <https://journals.openedition.org/lisa/132> (last accessed 3 July 2019)

Sorensen, Janet, *The Grammar of Empire in Eighteenth-Century British Writing* (Cambridge: Cambridge University Press, 2000)

Sortain, Joseph, 'Lathbury's *History of the English Episcopacy*', *Edinburgh Review*, 64 (Oct. 1836), 93–105

Southey, Robert, *The Expedition of Orsua; and the Crimes of Aguirre* (London: Longman, Hurst, Rees, Orme, and Brown, 1821)

—, 'Godwin's *Life of Geoffrey Chaucer*', *Annual Review, and History of Literature; for 1803*, ed. Arthur Aiken, 2 vols (London: Longman, 1804), 2:462–73

—, *History of Brazil*, 3 vols (London: Longman, Hurst, Rees, and Orme, 1810–19)

—, *History of the Peninsular War*, 3 vols (London: John Murray, 1823–32)

—, 'Inquiry into the Poor Laws, &c.', *Quarterly Review*, 8 (Dec. 1812), 319–56

—, *Journals of a Residence in Portugal 1800–1801 and a Visit to France 1838*, ed. Adolfo Cabral (Oxford: Clarendon Press, 1960)

—, 'Life of Cromwell', *Quarterly Review*, 25 (July 1821), 279–347

—, *Madoc*, 2 vols (London: Longman, Reese, and Orme, 1805)

—, 'The Roman Catholic Question', *Quarterly Review*, 38 (Oct. 1828), 535–96

—, *Selections from the Letters of Robert Southey*, ed. John Wood Warter, 4 vols (London: Longman, Brown, Green, and Longmans, 1856)

—, 'Transactions of the Missionary Society', *Annual Review, and History of Literature; for 1803*, ed. Arthur Aiken, 2 vols (London: Longman, 1804), 2:189–201

—, and Edward Edwards, 'Hallam's *Constitutional History of England*', *Quarterly Review*, 37 (Jan. 1828), 194–260

Southgate, Beverley, 'Macaulay 1828: History, Biography, and Portraiture', *Rethinking History*, 20.4 (2016), 544–55

Spongberg, Mary, *Women Writers and the Nation's Past 1790–1860: Empathetic Histories* (London: Bloomsbury Academic, 2020)

Stabler, Jane, *Burke to Byron, Barbauld to Baillie, 1790–1830* (Basingstoke: Palgrave Macmillan, 2002)

Staebler, Warren, *The Liberal Mind of John Morley* (Princeton: Princeton University Press, 1943)

Stafford, Fiona, 'The *Edinburgh Review* and the Representation of Scotland', in *British Romanticism and the Edinburgh Review: Bicentenary Essays*, ed. Massimiliano Demata and Duncan Wu (Basingstoke: Palgrave Macmillan, 2002), pp. 33–57

Stearns, Carol Z., and Peter N. Stearns (eds), *Emotional and Social Change: Towards a New Psychohistory* (New York: Holmes and Meier, 1988)

Stearns, Peter N., with Carol Z. Stearns, 'Emotionology: Clarifying the History of Emotions and Emotional Standards', *The American Historical Review*, 90.4 (1985), 813–36

Steinberg, Oded Y., '"Contesting Teutomania": Robert Gordon Latham, "Race", Ethnology and Historical Migrations', *Journal of European Ideas* (2021), 1–17, <https://doi.org/10.1080/01916599.2021.1894592> (last accessed 7 October 2021)

—, *Race, Nation, History: Anglo-German Thought in the Victorian Era* (Philadelphia: University of Pennsylvania Press, 2019)

Stephen, James, '*History of the Great Reformation of the Sixteenth Century*, in

Germany, Switzerland &c by J. H. Merle D'Aubigne', *Edinburgh Review*, 68 (Jan. 1839), 273–315

Stephen, Leslie, 'Thomas Carlyle', *Cornhill Magazine*, 43 (March 1881), 349–58

Stewart, David, *Romantic Magazines and Metropolitan Literary Culture* (Basingstoke: Palgrave Macmillan, 2011)

Stewart, Dugald, *Elements of the Philosophy of the Human Mind* (London and Edinburgh: Strahan, Cadell and Creech, 1792)

Stoler, Ann Laura, 'Affective States', in *A Companion to the Anthropology of Politics*, ed. David Nugent and Joan Vincent (Oxford: Blackwell, 2007), pp. 4–20

Storey, Mark, '"Bob Southey! – Poet Laureate": Public and Private in Southey's Poems of 1816', in *Robert Southey and the Contexts of English Romanticism*, ed. Lynda Pratt (Aldershot: Ashgate, 2006), pp. 87–100

Stout, Daniel M., *Corporate Romanticism: Liberalism, Justice, and the Novel* (New York: Fordham University Press, 2017)

Stuchtey, Benedikt, 'Literature, Liberty and Life of the Nation: British Historiography from Macaulay to Trevelyan', in *Writing National Histories: Western Europe since 1800*, ed. Stefan Berger, Mark Donovan, and Kevin Passmore (London and New York: Routledge, 1999), pp. 30–46

Stuckey, Michael, 'Francis Palgrave's Historico-Legal World of Science and Theology', *Legal Roots*, 3 (2015), 297–312

—, 'The Study of English National History by Sir Francis Palgrave: The Original Use of the National Records in an Imaginative Historical Narrative', *Law, Culture and Humanities*, 15.2 (2019), 421–47

Surkis, Judith, 'When was the Linguistic Turn? A Genealogy', *American Historical Review*, 117.3 (2012), 700–22

Swaim, Barton, '"Our own periodical pulpit": Thomas Carlyle's Sermons', *Christianity and Literature*, 52.2 (2003), 137–58

—, *Scottish Men of Letters and the New Public Sphere, 1802–1834* (Lewisburg, PA: Bucknell University Press, 2009)

Sweet, Rosemary, *Antiquaries: The Discovery of the Past in Eighteenth-Century Britain* (London: Bloomsbury Academic, 2004)

Swift, Roger, 'Thomas Carlyle, *Chartism* and the Irish in Early Victorian England', *Victorian Literature and Culture*, 29.1 (2001), 67–83

Szacki, Jerry, 'On the So-Called Historicism in the Social Sciences', *The Polish Sociological Bulletin*, 22 (1970), 36–46

Tamm, Marek, 'Truth, Objectivity and Evidence in History Writing', *Journal of the Philosophy of History*, 8 (2014), 265–90

Tauchert, Ashley, 'Maternity, Castration and Mary Wollstonecraft's *Historical and Moral View of the French Revolution*', *Women's Writing*, 4.2 (1997), 173–99

Taylor, Barbara, *Mary Wollstonecraft and the Feminist Imagination* (Cambridge: Cambridge University Press, 2003)

Thackeray, William Makepeace, 'Carlyle's *French Revolution*', *Times* (3 Aug. 1837), p. 6, repr. in *Thomas Carlyle: The Critical Heritage*, ed. Jules Paul Seigel (London and New York: Routledge, 1971), pp. 69–75

Thompson, Carl, 'Sentiment and Scholarship: Hybrid Historiography and Historical Authority in Maria Graham's South American Journals', *Women's Writing*, 24.2 (2017), 185–206

Thompson, E. P., 'History from Below', *TLS*, 3345 (7 April 1966), pp. 279–80

Thompson, Spurgeon 'Edmund Burke's *Reflections on the Revolution in France* and the Subject of Eurocentrism', *Irish University Review*, 33.2 (2003), 245–62

Tierney-Hynes, Rebecca, 'Shaftesbury's "Soliloquy": Authorship and the Psychology of Romance', *Eighteenth-Century Studies*, 38.4 (2005), 605–21

Todd, Janet, *Gender, Art and Death* (Cambridge: Polity Press, 1993)

Tongson, Karen, 'The Cultural Transnationalism of Thomas Moore's *Irish Melodies*', *Repercussions*, 9.1 (2001), 5–31

Torstendahl, Rolf, *The Rise and Propagation of Professional History* (New York: Routledge, 2015)

Townsend, Dale, *Gothic Antiquity: History, Romance, and the Architectural Imagination, 1760–1840* (Oxford: Oxford University Press, 2019)

Trela, D. J., *Cromwell in Context: The Conception, Writing and Reception of Carlyle's Second History* (Edinburgh: Carlyle Newsletter, 1986)

—, 'Dryasdust's Revenge: Carlyle, *Cromwell* and John Harland', *Bibliotheck*, 27.1–3 (1991), 45–56

—, *A History of Carlyle's 'Oliver Cromwell's Letters and Speeches'* (Lewiston, NY: Edwin Mellen Press, 1992)

—, 'The Writing of "An Election to the Long Parliament": Carlyle, Primary Research and the Book Clubs', *Carlyle Studies Annual*, 14 (1994), 71–82

Tremenheere, Hugh Seymour, '*Lectures on European Civilisation*. By M. Guizot. Translated by Priscilla Maria Beckwith', *Edinburgh Review*, 67 (April 1838), 357–83

Trumpner, Katie, *Bardic Nationalism: The Romantic Novel and the British Empire* (Princeton: Princeton University Press, 1997)

Tucker, Ericka L., 'The Subject of History: Historical Subjectivity and Historical Science', *Journal of the Philosophy of History*, 7.2 (2013), 205–29

Tuite, Clara, *Romantic Austen: Sexual Politics and the Literary Canon* (Cambridge: Cambridge University Press, 2002)

Ulrich, John M., *Signs of Their Times: History, Labor, and the Body in Cobbett, Carlyle, and Disraeli* (Athens: Ohio University Press, 2002)

Valenza, Robin, *Literature, Language, and the Rise of the Intellectual Disciplines in Britain, 1680–1820* (Cambridge: Cambridge University Press, 2009)

Vance, Norman, 'Celts, Carthaginians and Constitutions: Anglo-Irish Literary Relations, 1780–1830', *Irish Historical Studies*, 22.87 (1981), 216–38

Vanden Bossche, Chris R., *Carlyle and the Search for Authority* (Columbus: Ohio State University Press, 1991)

—, 'Chartism, Class Discourse, and the Captain of Industry: Social Agency in *Past and Present*', in *Thomas Carlyle Resartus: Reappraising Carlyle's Contribution to the Philosophy of History, Political Theory, and Cultural Criticism*, ed. Paul E. Kerry and Marylu Hill (Madison, NJ: Fairleigh Dickinson University Press, 2010), pp. 30–48

—, 'Fictive Text and Transcendental Self: Carlyle's Art of Biography', *Biography*, 10 (1987), 116–28

Varella, Flávia Florentino, 'Robert Southey, William Robertson e a teoria dos quatro estágios na construção da macronarrativa da história dos autóctones americanos', *Revista de História*, 175 (2016), 349–84

Vermeir, Koen, and Michael Funk Deckard, 'Preface', in *The Science of Sensibility: Reading Burke's Philosophical Enquiry*, ed. Koen Vermeir and Michael Funk Deckard (Dordrecht: Springer, 2011), pp. v–xx

Vidal, Fernando, *The Sciences of the Soul: The Early Modern Origins of Psychology* (Chicago: University of Chicago Press, 2011)
Vila, Anne C., *Enlightenment and Pathology: Sensibility in the Literature and Medicine of Eighteenth-Century France* (Baltimore: Johns Hopkins University Press, 1998)
Wahnich, Sophie, *In Defence of the Terror: Liberty or Death in the French Revolution*, trans. David Fernbach (New York and London: Verso, 2012)
Walker, David Blaine, 'Periodicals in Transition: Politics and Style in Victorian Higher Journalism' (PhD thesis, University of Arkansas, 2018)
Ward, Ian, 'The Perversions of History: Constitutionalism and Revolution in Burke's *Reflections*', *Liverpool Law Review*, 31.3 (2010), 207–32
Warhman, Dror, *The Making of the Modern Self: Identity and Culture in Eighteenth-Century England* (New Haven, CT: Yale University Press, 2004)
Watson, Alex, *Romantic Marginality: Nation and Empire on the Borders of the Page* (London: Routledge, 2012)
Watson, Nicola J., *Revolution and the Form of the British Novel, 1790–1825: Intercepted Letters, Interrupted Seductions* (Oxford: Oxford University Press, 1994)
Watt, James, 'Scott, the Scottish Enlightenment, and Romantic Orientalism', in *Scotland and the Borders of Romanticism*, ed. Leith Davis, Ian Duncan, and Janet Sorensen (Cambridge: Cambridge University Press, 2004), pp. 94–112
Webb, Timothy, 'A "great theatre of outrage and disorder": Figuring Ireland in the *Edinburgh Review*, 1802–29', in *British Romanticism and the Edinburgh Review: Bicentenary Essays*, ed. Massimiliano Demata and Duncan Wu (Basingstoke: Palgrave Macmillan, 2002), pp. 58–81
Weiss, Deborah, *The Female Philosopher and her Afterlives: Mary Wollstonecraft, the British Novel, and the Transformation of Feminism, 1796–1811* (Basingstoke: Palgrave Macmillan, 2017)
Welsh, David, 'George Waddington's *History of the Church from the Earlier Ages to the Reformation* (1833)', *Edinburgh Review*, 62 (Oct. 1835), 132–66
Wertz, S. K., 'Moral Judgments in History: Hume's Position', *Hume Studies*, 22.2 (1996), 339–67
Wesner, Samantha, 'Revolutionary Electricity in 1790: Shock, Consensus, and the Birth of a Political Metaphor', *The British Journal for the History of Science*, 54.3 (2021), 257–75
Weston, Rowland, 'History, Memory, Knowledge: William Godwin's *Essay on Sepulchres* (1809)', *The European Legacy*, 14.6 (2009), 651–65
—, 'Introduction: William Godwin and Political Justice', *Nineteenth-Century Prose*, 41.1/2 (2014), 1–26
White, Hayden, *Metahistory: The Historical Imagination in Nineteenth-Century Europe* (Baltimore: Johns Hopkins University Press, 1973)
White, Paul, 'Darwin Wept: Science and the Sentimental Subject', *Journal of Victorian Culture*, 16.2 (2011), 195–213
Wickberg, Daniel, 'What is the History of Sensibilities? On Cultural History, Old and New', *The American Historical Review*, 112.3 (2007), 661–84
Wilkes, Joanne, *Women Reviewing Women in Nineteenth-Century Britain: The Critical Reception of Jane Austen, Charlotte Brontë and George Eliot* (Farnham: Ashgate, 2010)

Williams, Raymond, *Culture and Society: 1780–1950* (Harmondsworth: Penguin, 1963)
—, *Keywords: A Vocabulary of Culture and Society* (1976; repr. New York: Oxford University Press, 1983)
—, *Marxism and Literature* (Oxford and New York: Oxford University Press, 1977)
Wollstonecraft, Mary, *A Historical and Moral View of the Origin and Progress of the French Revolution; and the Effect it has Produced in Europe* (London: J. Johnson, 1794)
—, *A Vindication of the Rights of Men*, 2nd edn (London: J. Johnson, 1790)
—, *A Vindication of the Rights of Woman: With Strictures on Political and Moral Subjects* (London: J. Johnson, 1792)
Wood, Dustin M. Frazier, *Anglo-Saxonism and the Idea of Englishness in Eighteenth-Century Britain* (Woodbridge: Boydell, 2020)
Wood, Marcus, *Slavery, Empathy, and Pornography* (Oxford: Oxford University Press, 2002)
Woolf, Daniel, 'Disciplinary History and Historical Discourse. A Critique of the History of History: The Case of Early Modern England', *Cromohs*, 2 (1997), 1–25
—, 'Getting Back to Normal: On Normativity in History and Historiography', *History and Theory*, 60.3 (2021), 469–512
Worden, Blair, 'Classical Republicanism and the Puritan Revolution', in *History & Imagination: Essays in Honor of H. R. Trevor-Roper*, ed. Hugh Lloyd-Jones, Valerie Pearl, and Blair Worden (London: Duckworth, 1981), pp. 196–8
—, 'Historians and Poets', in *The Uses of History in Early Modern England*, ed. Paula Kewes (San Marino, CA: Huntington Library, 2005), pp. 69–78
—, *Roundhead Reputations: The English Civil Wars and the Passions of Posterity* (London: Penguin, 2002)
Wordsworth, William, and Samuel Taylor Coleridge, *Lyrical Ballads, 1798 and 1802*, ed. Fiona Stafford (Oxford: Oxford University Press, 2013)
Wright, Julia M., *Ireland, India, and Nationalism in Nineteenth-Century Literature* (Cambridge: Cambridge University Press, 2007)
—, 'Irish Literary Theory: From Politeness to Politics', in *Irish Literature in Transition, 1780–1830*, ed. Claire Connolly (Cambridge: Cambridge University Press, 2020), pp. 69–84
Wylie, W. H., *Thomas Carlyle: The Man and his Books* (London: Marshall Japp, 1881)
Zagorin, Perez, 'Thomas Carlyle and Oliver Cromwell', in *Historians and Ideologues: Essays in Honour of Donald R. Kelley*, ed. Anthony Grafton and J. H. M. Salmon (Rochester, NY: University of Rochester Press, 2001), pp. 231–58
Zerilli, Linda, 'Text/Woman as Spectacle: Edmund Burke's "French Revolution"', *The Eighteenth Century*, 33.1 (1992), 47–72
Zimmerman, Everett, *The Boundaries of Fiction* (Ithaca, NY: Cornell University Press, 1996)
Zinn, Howard, *A People's History of the United States* (New York: HarperPerennial, 1980)

Index

Addison, Joseph, 119, 133
affects, 3, 8–11, 183
   affective attachment, 95, 96, 113
   affective immersion, 6, 159
   management of, 38–45
   public affections, 32–9, 40
   rational affections, 9, 32, 38
agency, 15, 21, 56, 57, 137–8, 182
Aiken, Lucy, 157, 158, 172
Alison, Archibald, 99, 129
Allen, John, 153, 158, 162, 163–4, 165, 167, 171
American Revolution, 34, 182
anachronism, 13, 98, 104–5, 187–9
Ankersmit, Frank R., 7, 29, 185–7
antiquarianism, 88–92, 158, 176
   neo-antiquarianism, 162–3
Aristotle, 53, 65, 123
Arnold, Matthew, 135, 165
Arnold, Thomas, 153
Athenaeum, 149, 150, 152, 157, 162, 163, 166, 168, 169, 172

Bacon, Francis, 16, 65–6, 123
Bagehot, Walter, 126, 127, 129–30
Baillie, Joanna, 19
Bain, Alexander, 21
ballad theory, 92
behaviouralism, 3, 4, 22
Bell, Charles, 79
belles lettres, 12, 26–7, 62
Bentham, Jeremy, 17, 18, 123
Bernard of Clairvaux, 105
Bildungsroman, 7, 16, 60
Blair, Hugh, 65, 119, 120 133, 134, 170
Blake, William, 13

Bolingbroke, Lord (Henry St John), 61
book clubs, 128, 144–5, 148, 153
Boswell, James, 77
Brazil, 173
   History of Brazil (Southey), 87–8, 108–15, 116
Brodie, George, 58, 166
Brooke, Charlotte, 90
Brougham, Henry, 158, 167
Browne, James, 162–3
Bruce, John, 159
Bulwer, Edward Lytton, 151, 171
Burke, Edmund, 3, 5–6, 10, 27, 50, 86, 126, 136
   emotions and political causes, 33
   explanation of the French Revolution, 34–5
   feeling, understanding of, 30–1, 37
   and historical progress, 55
   and national identity, 36
   A Philosophical Enquiry into the Origin of Our Ideas of the Sublime and Beautiful, 36, 41
   and political authority, 37
   Reflections on the Revolution in France, 30–1, 32–8, 39, 40, 41, 45, 46–7, 55, 95, 136, 186
   and rhetoric, 41
   and science of man, 33–4
   and sensibility, 32, 38
   sensus communis, 35–7, 50, 60
   style of, 41–2
   Wollstonecraft's criticism of, 38, 39, 40–2, 44, 46, 47–8
Burkhardt, Jacob, 188
Burnet, Gilbert (Bishop), 76
Burns, Robert, 134–5, 144–5
Burton, John Hill, 96

Capefigue, Jean-Baptiste, 163–4
Carlyle, Thomas, 6, 15, 17, 18, 20, 22, 23, 25, 26, 27, 91, 92–3, 127–8, 171, 181, 182, 188, 189
  and biographical portraiture, 78–9
  and Calvinism, 119, 133, 139, 140, 141
  Chartism, 135, 137
  criticism of, 132, 135, 139, 143–4
  'Essay on Burns', 134–5
  and fictionalisation, 79–81
  The French Revolution: A History, 51, 56–7, 118, 135–42, 145
  'Goethe's Works', 63
  On Heroes, Hero-Worship, and the Heroic in History, 74–5, 76, 135
  as a historian, 142–6
  Historical Sketches of Notable Persons and Events in the Reigns of James I and Charles I, 74
  and historical subjectivity, 74–82
  and national style, 132–42
  Oliver Cromwell's Letters and Speeches, 4, 59, 60, 66, 74–82, 83, 137, 145
  rejection of Anglo-British linguistic standards, 133–4, 138, 139–40
  and revolutionary crowds, 137–8
  Sartor Resartus, 140–1
  and sentimentalism, 79–80, 83–4
  'State of German Literature', 134
  style of, 118–20, 133, 145
  Two Reminiscences, 133
Carpenter, William, 21–2
Catholic Emancipation, 107, 108, 128, 131, 168
causality, 13–14
cause and effect, 45–55, 62–3
Celts, 88–90, 95, 97, 100, 103, 130–1
Celticism, 100, 101–2, 119, 135
character portrayals, 58–85, 127
  in Carlyle's *Cromwell*, 74–82
  eyewitness accounts, 64–5, 68, 71–2, 76, 77, 84–5
  fictitious speeches, 65, 66, 68, 71, 72
  in Godwin's *History of the Commonwealth*, 67–74
  internal rhetoric, 60–6
  orations, 64–5, 71–3, 82–3
Charles I, 3, 68, 70, 74
chivalry, 34, 41, 42–3, 47–8, 94
Clarendon, Lord (Edward Hyde), 58, 64, 166
Cobbett, William, 171

Coleridge, Samuel Taylor, 19, 175
comparativism, 13, 188
compassion, 41–2, 45, 89, 112, 113
Congregational Magazine, 69
Critical Review, 172
Croker, John Wilson, 169, 171
Cromwell, Oliver, 21, 133
  in Carlyle's *Cromwell*, 59–60, 66, 74–82, 83, 137, 145
  character portrayals of, 58–60, 71
  in Godwin's *History of the Commonwealth*, 58–60, 66, 68–72
  treatment of the Irish, 70–2, 81–2
custom, 72–3

Davies, John, 106, 107
Davis, Thomas, 101
Defoe, Daniel, 60, 76
democracy, 33, 37, 95, 113, 114, 140
De Quincey, Thomas, 118–19
determinism, 2, 15
Dilthey, Wilhelm, 23
Dissent (religious), 39, 67
documentary sources, 5, 64, 67–8, 75–6, 81, 84–5, 99–100, 103, 115–16, 138–9, 148
  and reviews, 158–9
  and source criticism, 159–65

Eclectic Review, 115, 168
Edinburgh Review, 28, 119, 122, 124, 129, 133, 139, 149, 151, 153, 160, 161, 162–4, 165, 166, 167, 168, 169, 170, 171, 172, 175, 176, 177
  and historical reviewing, 154–9
  selection of works for review, 155–6
  and women reviewers, 156–7
  women writers, lack of reviews of, 157–8
electricity, language of, 50–1
Ellis, Henry, 158
Emerson, Ralph Waldo, 132
emotions, 4, 8–11, 22, 44, 79–80, 179
  criticism of emotional style, 172
  emotional governance, 40
  emotionology, 11
  as historical subdiscipline, 182
  history of, 4, 10–11, 20, 179, 182–3
  and political causes, 33
  racialisation of, 89–90
  social and unsocial emotions, 30, 34–5, 47, 55, 89–90, 95
  and transmissibility, 182
  and value ethics, 48

empiricism, 21, 36, 65
English Civil Wars, 4, 39, 58, 68, 127, 166, 167
English Historical Review, 177
ethnogenesis, 86–117
  and affective attachment, 95
  and antiquarianism, 88–92
  and historiography, 88–9
  in Moore's *History of Ireland*, 99–108
  and methodological nationalism, 115–17
  and racial difference, 89–90
  in Scott's *History of Scotland*, 92–9
  in Southey's *History of Brazil*, 108–15, 116
  and *volkish* culture, 92
experience, 55–7, 182
  historicisation of, 184–7

Febvre, Lucien, 4, 8, 20, 23
feeling, 1–29, 183
  collective feeling, 28, 31, 36, 40, 46, 50–2, 56–7, 72–3, 86, 88, 137, 182
  emotions and affects, 8–11
  feelings as social mechanisms, 37
  fiction/history relationship, 24–7
  history and the novel, 16–20
  objectification of, 3–4, 5, 14, 20–1, 23, 179, 187, 189
  objects and subjects, 12–15
  periodising feeling, 181–4
  psychology and psychological processes, 20–4
  rhetorical representation of feelings, 11
  social and political value of, 39
  structures of feeling, 9–10, 187
feminism, 13, 42, 43
Ferrier, David, 22
fiction, 17–18
  relationship with history, 24–7
Firth, Charles, 127
Fitzmaurice, James, 101
Fox, Charles James, 155, 160, 170
Fox, W. J., 77–8
Freeman, E. A., 124
French National Assembly, 30, 35, 49, 52, 55, 140
French Revolution, 4, 10, 15, 39, 86, 126, 181–2, 183
  in Burke's *Reflections*, 30–1, 32–8, 39, 40, 41, 45, 46–7, 55, 136, 186
  in Carlyle's *French Revolution: A History*, 51, 56–7, 118, 135–42, 145
  and history of emotions, 181–2
  October Days, 30, 34, 53
  representation of revolutionary crowds, 51–3, 56, 137–8
  in Wollstonecraft's *Historical and Moral View*, 30, 31–2, 45–55, 57, 139

Gayangos, Pascual de, 168
Geddes, Jenny, 74, 75
gender issues, 6–7, 16, 31, 42–4, 50
  in reviewing, 156–8, 172–3
Gibbon, Edward, 115, 123, 132, 134, 164
Glorious Revolution (1688), 32–3, 34, 39, 128
Godwin, William, 1–2, 4, 6, 15, 23, 26, 27, 42, 82–3, 127, 173, 181, 189
  antipathy to mass protest, 73
  An Enquiry Concerning Political Justice, 1, 66, 72
  History of the Commonwealth of England, 1, 2–3, 4, 14, 58–9, 64, 66, 67–74, 171
  The History of the Life of William Pitt, 71
  and internal rhetoric, 67–74
  Letters of Mucius, 66
  Life of Geoffrey Chaucer, 59, 172
  Lives of Edward and John Philips, Nephews and Pupils of Milton, 59
  Mandeville, 19–20
  'Of History and Romance', 2, 19, 23, 58, 67, 69, 74, 80
Goethe, Johann Wolfgang von, 18, 60, 63, 83
Graham, Maria, 173
Green, J. R., 131
Guizot, François, 155, 164

Hallam, Henry, 58, 59, 122–3, 124, 151, 159–61, 166, 167–8, 170, 171
Hazlitt, William, 19
historical reviews *see* reviews and review essays
historicism, 11–12, 13–14, 19, 43, 92, 178, 181, 188
  and experience, 184–7

history writing, 3, 6–7
    changing trends, 147–8
    classical/neoclassical history, 6, 25, 61, 116, 120
    as a communicative process, 10
    constitutional history, 6, 122–4, 156, 170
    and contingency, 2, 56, 68, 130, 179
    and exemplarity, 61, 63–4, 78, 93, 96, 158
    and eyewitness accounts, 64–5, 68, 71–2, 76, 77, 84–5, 139
    and fictitious speeches, 65, 66, 68, 71, 72
    gendering of history as masculine, 6–7, 172–4
    and hermeneutic models, 7, 85, 92, 145, 178, 184, 188
    historical professionalisation and specialisation, 142–6, 147–8
    and indirect narration, 60–1, 62, 63
    inductive historical method, 123–6, 130, 131
    and internalising techniques, 60, 64–6, 67–74, 82–3
    linguistic turn, 12–13, 28–9
    narrative history, 6, 24, 62–3, 116, 163
    and the novel/fiction, 12–13, 16–20, 24–7, 143
    novelistic techniques, 25–6
    and objectivity, 29, 54, 67–8, 166, 170–1, 176, 180
    and particularity, 125
    philosophic history, 4, 5–6, 7, 11–12, 14, 31, 46, 52, 53–4, 63, 68–9, 84, 91–2, 93, 98, 115–6, 122, 131, 139, 164–5, 172, 187
    and predictive statements, 125–6
    and presence/distance, 68, 138, 180
    and reality effect, 125
    and rhetoric, 12–13, 32, 44, 60–7, 83–4, 170
    and the sublime, 36, 38, 109, 185–6
    vernacular history, 125
    see also documentary sources; reviews and review essays; stadial theory; style
Hobbes, Thomas, 19, 182
Hogg, Thomas Jefferson, 155–6, 164, 174
human nature, 15, 19, 36

Humboldt, Alexander von, 109
Hume, David, 3, 4, 5, 17, 18, 34, 38, 55, 86, 93, 100, 109, 115, 123, 132, 179, 190–1
    criticism of, 134, 166–7
    An Enquiry Concerning the Principles of Morals, 23
    The History of England, 2, 58, 59, 69, 166
    'Of National Characters', 134
    'Of the Original Contract', 55
    A Treatise of Human Nature, 2, 22, 61–2

identity, 39, 61, 66, 76; see also national identity
imaginative colouring, 5, 6
imperialism, 108–9, 110, 114
individuality, 14–15, 35, 39, 40, 182
institutions, 2, 20, 34
    and embodiment, 37
    and feeling, 38
    and human nature, 36
    and social structures, 10, 15, 16, 27
interiority, 24
Ireland, 87, 90, 168–9
    in Carlyle's *Cromwell*, 81–2
    in Godwin's *History of the Commonwealth*, 70–1
    in Macaulay's *History of England*, 130–1
    in Moore's *History of Ireland*, 99–108
Irving, Edward, 119, 132, 133, 140, 141

James, G. P. R., 152
James I, 101
James II, 98
James, William, 23
Jeffrey, Francis, 126, 153, 156–7, 158, 160, 165, 168, 175
John, King of England, 101
Johnson, Joseph, 39
Johnson, Samuel, 8
Jones, Edward, 90
journalism, 28, 120, 129, 156, 177

Kingsley, Charles, 131, 153
Knox, John, 119, 140
Koster, Henry, 114

Lamb, John, 140
Lardner, Dionysius, 87, 99

Lathbury, Thomas, 169
Lawrance, Hannah, 150–1, 152, 161, 163, 173, 174
Lecky, William, 127
Ledwich, Edward, 102
letters, 4, 59, 60, 66, 74–82, 83
Lingard, John, 100, 155, 159–60, 160–1, 165, 167–8, 171
Lister, Thomas Henry, 157
Livy, 61
Locke, John, 17, 19, 22, 23, 36, 39
Lynch, William, 100

Mably, Abbé, 39–40
Macaulay, Catherine, 39, 48, 58, 71, 172
Macaulay, Thomas Babington, 4, 17, 18, 25, 26, 59, 89, 120–32, 153, 160, 166, 167, 169–70, 170, 176, 181
  'Burleigh and his Times', 144
  Carlyle, review of, 132
  Critical and Historical Essays, 175
  criticism of, 126–32, 143, 171
  'double vision' technique, 128, 189
  Hallam, review of, 122–3
  as a historian, 142–3, 144, 145–6, 147
  The History of England, 118, 126–30, 135
  inductive technique, 120–32
  and Ireland, 130–1
  linguistic purification, 130–1
  Mackintosh and Mill, reviews of, 123, 124
  popularity of, 120–1
  preference for continuous narrative, 124–5, 128
  style, 118–20
MacCulloch, John, 131
Mackintosh, James, 89, 96, 123, 124 155, 163, 167, 170
  The History of England, 152, 163
  History of the Revolution in England of 1688, 123, 124
Macpherson, James (Ossian), 102–3, 133
Mahon, Lord (Philip Henry Stanhope), 160, 167
Malden, Henry, 164–5
Marie Antoinette, 3, 30, 33, 38, 43, 49–51, 53
Marsden, Richard, 92
Marsh, Anne, 173

Martineau, Harriet, 126, 173
Mary of Guise, 97
Mary, Queen of Scots, 3, 92, 97
Maxwell, William Hamilton, 169
Meinecke, Friedrich, 13–14
Merivale, Charles, 153
Merivale, Herman, 127–8, 139, 151
Michelet, Jules, 5, 51
Mill, James
  Essay on Government, 123
  The History of British India, 123, 131
Mill, John Stuart, 121, 126, 138, 166
Miller, George, 169
Milton, John, 64, 74, 116, 133
Mirabeau, Honoré Gabriel Riqueti (Comte de), 49, 136
misogyny, 42, 50
Mitford, William, 144, 160, 165, 167
modernity, 13, 18–19, 87, 98, 181–3, 188
Moncreiff, James, 129
Montesquieu, Charles-Louis de Secondat, 36
Moore, Thomas, 4, 27, 86, 89, 117, 189
  and Catholic Emancipation, 107–8
  characterisation of Ireland as a fated nation, 104–5
  English misrule in Ireland, 106–7
  The History of Ireland, 87, 99–108
  Irish civic advancement, 101–2
  Irish Melodies, 87, 100, 101, 102
  The Life and Death of Lord Edward Fitzgerald, 107
  Memoirs of Captain Rock, 87, 101
  portrayal of Irish rebels, 101
  scepticism towards Ireland's prehistoric past and legends, 101–4
moral sense, 65–6
Morley, John, 118, 120–1, 126–7, 129, 131–2, 143
motivation, 22
  motivational rationalism, 2, 38
Müller, Karl Otfried, 116
Murray, George, 169

Napier, William, 155, 169, 177
National Association for the Vindication of Scottish Rights (NAVSR), 96

national identity, 36, 86–117, 126
  and affective attachment, 95
  and antiquarianism, 90–2
  and ethnonationalism, 88–92
  and foundation myths, 90, 116
  and 'invented traditions', 87
  in Moore's *History of Ireland*, 99–108
  and methodological nationalism, 115–17
  in nineteenth-century historiography, 88–9
  and racial difference, 89–90
  in Scott's *History of Scotland*, 92–9
  in Southey's *History of Brazil*, 108–15, 116
  and *volkish* culture, 92
Necker, Jacques, 49
Neele, Henry, 124
Niebuhr, Barthold Georg, 12, 92, 116, 153, 155–6, 161, 164–5, 174
novels, 143
  and history, 16–20, 24–7
  novelistic style, 120–32
  realist novels, 16–17, 18, 39, 60, 76

O'Connor, Charles, 103
O'Driscol, John, 160, 168
O'Halloran, Sylvester, 90, 103
O'Kelly, Patrick, 169
ontology, 14, 15, 19, 61
Ossian, 102–3, 133

Palgrave, Francis, 124, 150, 151, 152, 158, 161–2, 166, 171–2
peoplehood, 35–8, 50–3, 55–7
Pinkerton, John, 89–90, 131
Pitt, William, 71
Plato, 65
Plutarch, 61
poetry, 17, 18–19
Pope, Alexander, 133
popular history, 151–2, 159, 163
positivism, 21, 181
Prescott, William H., 168
presence paradigm, 5, 124
Price, Richard, 39
psychology and psychological processes
  faculty psychology, 60–6
  as historical phenomena, 3, 20–1, 23–4
  psychological determinism, 72
  and physiology 21–2
Pugin, Augustus, 171

Quarterly Review, 96, 108, 156, 169, 171, 172, 173
Quin, Edward, 155

racial assimilation, 97, 111, 112–13, 114–15, 117, 130
racial contract, 89
Ranke, Leopold von, 12, 13, 84, 92, 169–70, 181
realism, 16–17, 18, 39, 60, 76, 84, 127
Reform Acts, 128, 156, 166
republicanism, 39–40, 52, 55, 58, 59, 67, 73, 112–3, 156
reviews and review essays, 28, 147–77
  in the *Edinburgh Review*, 154–9
  of French writers, 163–4
  gendering of history as masculine, 172–4
  and historical specialisation, 150–3
  of histories of Ireland, 168–9
  of histories of the Peninsular War, 169
  and objectivity, 166
  opinion and expertise, 174–7
  party politics and impartiality, 165–70
  and polemic, 170–4
  of religious works, 169–70
  selection of works for review, 155–6
  source criticism and neo-antiquarianism, 159–65
  women reviewers, 156–7
  women writers, lack of reviews of, 157–8
rhetoric, 41, 43–4, 46, 60
  internal rhetoric, 60–6
  in Godwin's *History of the Commonwealth*, 67–74, 83
  rhetorical self, 65
Ritchie, Leitch, 168
Robertson, William, 5, 34, 55, 86, 93, 94, 109, 115, 132, 166
Robespierre, Maximilien, 136–7
Roebuck, J. A., 155
Rousseau, Jean-Jacques, 14, 51, 53, 109, 144–5, 182
Ryley, John, 168

Saint-Simon, Henri de, 133, 136
Sandford, Daniel Keyte, 171
Sattelzeit, 14
Schiller, Johann Christoph Friedrich, 74

science of man, 33–4
Scotland, 87
  in Scott's *History of Scotland*, 87, 92–9
  Scottish enlightenment, 15, 33, 34, 44, 47, 89, 90, 91, 95, 111, 133, 139
Scott, Walter, 17, 18, 24, 27, 64, 84, 86, 100, 117, 122, 124–5, 128, 153, 172
  'Essay on Romance', 92
  Highlanders, depictions of, 95–6, 97
  The History of Scotland, 87, 92–9
  The Life of Napoleon Buonaparte, 138, 168
  on Scotland's union with England, 96–8
  Tales of a Grandfather series, 93, 151, 168
Seeley, J. R., 118, 127–8, 143, 152, 169
selfhood, 59, 63, 143, 182–3
  self-examination, 65
sensibility, cult of, 181–2, 183
sensory perceptions, 61–2, 127
sentiment and sentimentalism, 5–6, 14, 30–57, 79–80, 83–4, 110, 178, 179
  counter-sentimentalism in Wollstonecraft's *Vindications*, 38–45
  distinction from psychology, 20
  and experience, 55–7
  rhetorical sentimentality, 46, 70
  sensus communis in Burke's *Reflections*, 32–8
  in Wollstonecraft's *Historical and Moral View*, 45–55
Seoane, Mateo, 169
Shaftesbury, Lord (Anthony Ashley Cooper), 65
Shakespeare, William, 61, 63
Shelley, Mary, 17–18, 19
Sismondi, Jean Charles Léonard de, 155, 161, 163, 170
slavery, 110, 112–13
Smith, Adam, 44, 62, 63, 109, 119, 133, 179
  'Lectures on Rhetoric', 60–1, 62–3
social contract theory, 31, 39, 40
Sortain, Joseph, 169
Southey, Robert, 4, 15, 27, 59, 86, 169, 171, 172
  Brazilian nationalism, 112, 113–14
  criticism of, 115
  The Expedition of Orsua and the Crimes of Aguirre, 109
  and foundation myths, 116
  History of Brazil, 87–8, 108–15, 116
  History of the Peninsular War, 163, 169
  Indigenous peoples, representation of, 109, 110–11, 113
  and *marronage* culture, 112–13
  and mixing of races, 111, 112–13, 114–15
  and the Peninsular War, 108–9
  philosophic history, rejection of, 116
  'Poems on the Slave Trade', 110
  research into Portuguese history, 115–16
  settlers, representation of, 111–12, 113–14
  slavery, 110, 112–13
sovereignty, 34, 53, 89, 104, 107
speeches, 59, 60, 74–82
  fictitious speeches, 65, 66, 68, 71, 72, 83
  internal orations, 82–3
Spencer, Herbert, 22, 127
Spenser, Edmund, 106
stadial theory, 30, 31, 34, 41, 46–7, 52, 55, 86, 95, 105, 111, 130
Steele, Richard, 119
Stephen, Leslie, 145
Stewart, Dugald, 63, 93
Strafford, Lord (Thomas Wentworth), 74
style, 28–9, 41–2, 118–46
  common style, 170–1
  national style (Carlyle), 132–42
  novelistic style (Macaulay), 120–32
  organology (De Quincey), 118
  picturesque evocation, 171
  in reviews, 148–9, 152, 160
  and specialisation, 142–6, 147–8
subjectivity, 4, 15, 16, 182–3
  in Carlyle's *Cromwell*, 74–82
Sully, James, 21–2, 23
sympathy, 23, 45, 48, 50, 89, 110

Taaffe, Denis, 169
Tacitus, 88, 127
Taylor, W. C., 168–9
Thackeray, William Makepeace, 134, 143
Thierry, Augustin, 70, 131
Thirwall, Connop, 151

Thucydides, 12
truth, 17, 18
Tytler, Alexander Fraser, 93, 155
Tytler, Patrick Fraser, 96, 159

Union, Act of (1707; 1800), 94, 96–7, 105, 112, 134
　and disunion, 104
　repeal of, 81, 108, 156

Vallancey, Charles, 104
Vieira, João Fernandes, 112
virtue, 38–40, 206n
　virtue ethics, 31, 48, 55
　virtuous passions, 39–40
Voltaire (François-Marie Arouet), 109, 132

Ward, R. Plumer, 171
Welsh, David, 163
Westminster Review, 77, 157, 166
Whately, Richard, 65–6
Whitelocke, Bulstrode, 58
Wilkinson, John Gardner, 162–3
Williams, Helen Maria, 45–6
Williams, Raymond, 9–10, 140, 184–5, 187
Wollstonecraft, Mary, 4, 6, 10, 15, 20, 27, 67, 86, 136, 174, 181, 189
　and affect management, 38–45
　Burke, criticism of, 38, 39, 40–2, 44, 46, 47–8
　cause and effect, 45–55

consent, understanding of, 56
counter-sentimentalism, 44–5
criticism of, 172
first-person narrative, 54–5
A Historical and Moral View of the French Revolution, 30, 31–2, 45–55, 57, 139, 172
language of electricity, use of, 50–1
Marie Antoinette, discussion of, 49–51, 53
and novelty, 55–6
and peoplehood, 56–7
representation of revolutionary crowds, 51–3, 56, 137
and sentimentalism, 43
style of, 42
A Vindication of the Rights of Men, 9, 38–45
A Vindication of the Rights of Woman, 42–3
and virtue, 38–40
women, 6–7, 42–3
　gendering of history as masculine, 16–7, 172–4
　lack of reviews by, 156–8
　women writers, reviews of, 172–3
Wordsworth, William, 17–18, 19, 132–3

Young Ireland, 101, 102, 106, 108

Zumbi (Francisco Nzumbi), 112–13

EU representative:
Easy Access System Europe
Mustamäe tee 50, 10621 Tallinn, Estonia
Gpsr.requests@easproject.com

www.ingramcontent.com/pod-product-compliance
Lightning Source LLC
Chambersburg PA
CBHW051110230426
43667CB00014B/2517